The 1st Amendment in the Classroom Series, Number 4

ACADEMIC Freedom

EDITED BY HAIG A. BOSMAJIAN

NEAL-SCHUMAN PUBLISHERS, INC.
NEW YORK   LONDON

**THE FIRST AMENDMENT IN THE CLASSROOM
SERIES
Edited by Haig A. Bosmajian**

The Freedom to Read Books, Films and Plays. The First
Amendment in the Classroom Series, No. 1. Foreword by Ken
Donelson. ISBN 1-55570-001-2.

Freedom of Religion. The First Amendment in the Classroom
Series, No. 2. ISBN 1-55570-002-0.

Freedom of Expression. The First Amendment in the Classroom
Series, No. 3. ISBN 1-55570-003-9.

Academic Freedom. The First Amendment in the Classroom
Series, No. 4. ISBN 1-55570-004-7.

The Freedom to Publish. The First Amendment in the Classroom
Series, No. 5. ISBN 1-55570-005-5.

Published by Neal-Schuman Publishers, Inc.
23 Leonard Street
New York, NY 10013

Printed and bound in the United States of America.

Library of Congress Cataloging-in-Publication Data

Academic freedom.

  (The 1st Amendment in the classroom series; no. 4)
  Includes index.
  1. Teachers—Legal status, laws, etc.—United States
—Cases. 2. Freedom of speech—United States—Cases.
3. Academic freedom—United States—Cases.
I. Bosmajian, Haig A. II. Series.
KF4175.A52A26 1988   344.73′078   88-31265
ISBN 1-55570-004-7   347.30478

Contents

Preface

THE *First Amendment in the Classroom Series* responds to the need for teachers, students, parents, and school board members to become more aware of how First Amendment rights apply to the classrooms of a free society. Those cherished rights, if they have any meaning, are directly relevant and essential to our schools. What is especially needed is a wider familiarity with and understanding of the arguments and reasoning used to reach judgments regarding First Amendment issues, so often controversial and divisive, affecting what goes on in the classroom. To be unfamiliar with those arguments is to be unprepared to defend the First Amendment rights of students and teachers. Those arguments will be found in this series devoted to (1) the banning of books, plays, and films; (2) religion and prayer in the classroom; (3) symbolic speech; (4) teaching methods and teachers' classroom behavior; and (5) school publications and underground newspapers. My earlier volume, *Censorship, Libraries, and the Law,* covers cases of school library censorship.

When United States District Judge Hugh Bownes declared unconstitutional a Portsmouth, New Hampshire, Board of Education rule forbidding "distribution of non-school sponsored written materials within the Portsmouth schools and on school grounds for a distance of 200 feet from school entrances," he declared in the order of the court that "this opinion and Order is to be posted on the school bulletin board in a prominent place, and copies of this opinion and Order are to be made available to the students in the school library."[1]

This was a reminder to students, teachers, and school board members—but especially to the students—that First Amendment rights applied to them. As the United States Supreme Court had put it exactly thirty years earlier in *Barnette,* the First Amendment rights need to be practiced in our schools "if we are not to strangle the free mind at its source and teach youth to discount important principles of our government as mere platitudes."[2]

While the actual decisions in the cases involving the First Amendment rights of students and teachers in the classroom are crucial, the arguments and reasoning in the opinions are equally important. *Why* did the court decide that students could not be prohibited from distributing their literature? *Why* did the court decide that students could not be compelled to salute the flag? *Why* could the teacher not be dismissed for using books containing "offensive" language? *Why* could not the school board dismiss the teacher for using "unorthodox" teaching methods? *Why* could not parents have sex education banned from the school? *Why* did the court decide that prayer in the classroom was unconstitutional? Understanding the "whys" leads to an understanding of the workings of a democratic society.

In 1937, when throughout the world democratic institutions were being threatened and some were being destroyed, John Dewey observed that wherever political democracy has fallen, "it was too exclusively political in nature. It had not become part of the bone and blood of the people in daily conduct of life. Democratic forms were limited to Parliament, elections, and combats between parties. What is happening proves conclusively, I think, that unless democratic habits of thought and action are part of the fibre of a people, political democracy is insecure. It cannot stand in isolation. It must be buttressed by the presence of democratic methods in all social relationships."[3]

When the students, teachers, school boards, and parents involved in these cases insisted on exercising their First Amendment freedoms, they learned that the principles of our democracy are not "mere platitudes." For the students especially, the cases helped demonstrate that the Bill of Rights and "democratic habits of thought and action are part of the fibre of a people." These cases show political democracy "buttressed by the presence of democratic methods" in one realm of our society—the classroom.

It has been clearly established at several levels of our judicial system that protecting the First Amendment freedoms of teachers and students is crucial in a free society. In *Barnette,* the United States Supreme Court declared: "The Fourteenth Amendment, as now applied to the States, protects the citizen against the State itself and all of its creatures—Boards of Education not excepted. These have, of course, important, delicate, and highly discretionary functions, but none that they may not perform within the limits of the Bill of Rights. That they are educating the young for citizenship is reason for scrupulous protection of Constitutional freedoms of the individual, if we are not to strangle the free mind at its source and teach youth to discount important principles of our government as mere platitudes."

In giving First Amendment protection to junior and senior high school students who had worn black armbands to school to protest U.S. involvement in the Vietnam War, the United States Supreme Court spoke most clearly in *Tinker* on the issue of the First Amendment rights of teachers and students. Justice Abe Fortas, delivering the opinion of the Court, said in 1969: "First Amendment rights, applied in light of the special characteristics of the school environment, are available to teachers and students. It can hardly be argued that either students or teachers shed their constitutional rights to freedom of speech or expression at the schoolhouse gate. This has been the unmistakable holding of this Court for almost 50 years."[4]

When in 1978 United States District Court Judge Joseph Tauro ordered school authorities to return to the high school library a book which had been removed because it contained a "dirty, filthy" poem, he reiterated in his own words what had been declared in *Tinker:* " . . . the First Amendment is not merely a mantle which students and faculty doff when they take their places in the classroom."[5]

On these pages are the stories of students and teachers who risked much to fight for their First Amendment rights in the classroom, who did not "shed their constitutional rights to freedom of speech or expression at the schoolhouse gate" and did not see the First Amendment as "merely a mantle which students and teachers doff when they take their places in the classroom." What is encouraging is that in almost all the cases appearing in this series, students and teachers have been given First Amendment protection by the courts.

The reasons given in the opinions on these pages are applicable to many of those First Amendment controversies which may never reach the courts. Edward Jenkinson, who has done much research and writing on censorship in the schools and who chaired the National Council of Teachers of English Committee Against Censorship has reported: "During the early seventies, approximately one hundred censorship incidents were reported to the ALA [American Library Association]'s Office for Intellectual Freedom each year. By 1976, the number had risen to slightly less than two hundred and climbed to nearly three hundred in 1977." Shortly after the 1980 Presidential election, Judith Krug of the American Library Association estimation a threefold increase in reported censorship incidents, "which would mean roughly nine hundred reported incidents a year." But as Jenkinson points out, the reported incidents "are only a small part of the censorship attempts each year. . . . After talking with teachers, librarians and administrators in meetings in 33 states, I believe that for every reported incident of censorship at least fifty go unreported."[6]

The First Amendment in the Classroom makes available the many substantial arguments that can be used by students, teachers, and parents involved in First Amendment controversies surrounding teachers and students in the classroom. The reasons given by the judges on these pages are there for students, teachers, and parents to use in their efforts to persuade school boards and others that the First Amendment applies to the school environment and that the "Fourteenth Amendment, as now applied to the States, protects the citizen against the State itself and all of its creatures—Boards of Education not excepted."

In his discussion of the nature and function of the judicial court opinion, legal scholar Piero Calamandrei has observed that "the most important and most typical indication of the rationality of the judicial function is the reasoned opinion." Of the need for the judge to present the reasoned opinion, Calamandrei says that

> "ever since justice descended from heaven to earth and the idea gained ground that the judge is a human being and not a supernatural and infallible oracle to be adored, whose authority is beyond question, man has felt the need of a rational explanation to give validity to the word of the judge." [The major function of the reasoned opinion, explains Calamandrei,] "is an explanatory or, one might say, a pedagogical one. No longer content merely to command, to proclaim a *sic volo, sic iubeo* [So I wish, so I command] from his high bench, the judge descends to the level of the parties, and although still commanding, seeks to impress them with the reasonableness of the command. The reasoned opinion is above all the justification of the decision and as such it attempts to be as persuasive as it can."[7]

Like the judge, neither supernatural nor infallible, we are asked for rational explanations to justify our decisions. The judicial opinions on these pages provide useful and persuasive reasons.

I hope that readers of the books in this series—students, teachers, school board members, parents, and others—will develop their appreciation for and commitment to the First Amendment rights of students and teachers in the classroom and will recognize the variety of arguments available to counter those who would not have the First Amendment apply to teachers and students. The First Amendment freedoms were put into the Bill of Rights to be used; the court opinions in this series demonstrate that teachers and students usually get First Amendment protection from the courts. We must recognize, however, that freedoms not exercised by the citizenry lose their vitality. Teachers and students, said Chief Justice Earl Warren, "must always remain free to inquire, to study and to evaluate, to gain new maturity and understanding; otherwise our civilization will stagnate and die."[8]

NOTES

1. *Vail v. Bd. of Ed. of Portsmouth School Dist.*, 354 F. Supp. 592 (1973).
2. *West Virginia State Bd. of Ed.* v. *Barnette*, 319 U.S. 624 (1943).
3. John Dewey, "Democracy and Educational Administration," *School and Society,* 45(April 3, 1937), p. 462.
4. *Tinker v. Des Moines School Dist.*, 393 U.S. 503 (1969).
5. *Right to Read Defense Committee* v. *School Committee, Etc.*, 454 F. Supp. 703 (1978).
6. Edward Jenkinson, "Protecting Holden Caulfield and His Friends from the Censors," *English Journal*, 74(January 1985), p. 74.
7. Piero Calamandrei, *Procedure and Democracy*, trans. John C. Adams and Helen Adams (New York: New York University Press, 1956), p. 53.
8. *Sweezy* v. *New Hampshire*, 354 U.S. 234 (1957).

Constitutional Amendments

ARTICLE I

Congress shall make no law respecting an establishment of religion, or prohibiting the free exercise thereof; or abridging the freedom of speech, or of the press; or the right of the people peaceably to assemble, and to petition the government for a redress of grievances.

ARTICLE XIV

All persons born or naturalized in the United States, and subject to the jurisdiction thereof, are citizens of the United States and of the State wherein they reside. No State shall make or enforce any law which shall abridge the privileges or immunities of citizens of the United States; nor shall any state deprive any person of life, liberty or property, without due process of law; nor deny to any person within its jurisdiction the equal protection of the law.

Judicial Circuits

Circuits	*Composition*
District of Columbia	District of Columbia
First	Maine, Massachusetts, New Hampshire, Puerto Rico, Rhode Island
Second	Connecticut, New York, Vermont
Third	Delaware, New Jersey, Pennsylvania, Virgin Islands
Fourth	Maryland, North Carolina, South Carolina, Virginia, West Virginia
Fifth	Louisiana, Mississippi, Texas
Sixth	Kentucky, Michigan, Ohio, Tennessee
Seventh	Illinois, Indiana, Wisconsin
Eighth	Arkansas, Iowa, Minnesota, Missouri, Nebraska, North Dakota, South Dakota
Ninth	Alaska, Arizona, California, Idaho, Montana, Nevada, Oregon, Washington, Guam, Hawaii, Northern Marianna Islands
Tenth	Colorado, Kansas, New Mexico, Oklahoma, Utah, Wyoming
Eleventh	Alabama, Georgia, Florida

Foreword

by Donald Aguillard

EVERY science teacher vividly recalls his or her initiation to the classroom. After the completion of student teaching, an interview with the principal, several days of meetings with other teachers, and encouragement from peers, the neophyte begins the planning of the first lesson by examining the textbooks provided by the school system. It was at this point, as a beginning teacher, that I first perceived a major flaw in science education.

In most science classes the textbook is the curriculum, yet the text often fails to take into account the explosion of scientific knowledge and understanding over the past 20 years. As we hear today about super conductivity, fiber optics, genetic engineering, quarks, and super plastics, we can safely conclude that science has not finished changing our world. In fact, scientists state that we will see more technical innovations and high-tech products in the next 15 years than we did in the preceding 30 years. Yet the textbooks stacked in my first classroom were uninspiring, unimaginative, and profoundly boring to students.

How could the quality of our science textbooks have deteriorated while the body of scientific knowledge expanded like the mushroom cloud of a nuclear explosion? One answer is that many states have established excessively detailed textbook specifications. Adoption committees often overzealously attempt to find a textbook that matches an established curriculum. Publishers sacrifice depth and understanding to concentrate on coverage, however inadequate it may be, so that committees will select their textbooks.[1]

Can we change the current state of affairs in science education?

Presented with an inadequate textbook, I chose to broaden the curriculum of my classroom. I read widely from scientific journals and a variety of current science texts. I emulated the practices of a master teacher I had observed who never failed to have a story to share with his students. In his classes biology came to life through the experiences and bits of information he wove into his daily lessons. In time, I also began to rely less on the textbook as my primary teaching tool. I obtained my class notes from multiple sources, including college introductory biology texts, and I began the practice of enriching my lectures with information derived from my readings of current materials.

Based on my experiences in the science classroom, I have concluded that the major cause of our textbook problem today is the failure to entrust the classroom teacher with curriculum decisions. Teachers have not been asked to assume an active role in adopting new textbooks or revising the curriculum. The pressures of special-interest groups causes policymakers to alter the curriculum and publishers to sacrifice essential material to avoid criticism or loss of sales. Many teachers, unfortunately, view the textbook not as another source for student reading but as a guide to determine what should, or should not, be discussed in class.

And so, the more stringently we regulate the content of textbooks, the less useful they become for our students.

These practices have undoubtedly had a profound impact on our students. The National Science Teachers Association (NSTA) has documented a significant decline in the number of undergraduates entering science education. Additionally, a survey conducted by Aldridge and Johnston in 1984 estimated that 30 percent of the secondary teachers are either unqualified or severly underqualified to teach science.[2] Given these findings, it is imperative that we resist any attempt to further impair science instruction in this country.

Because of the threat it posed to science education, I chose to challenge a 1981 Louisiana statute which required teachers to give equal time to creation science and evolution science in the classroom. A similar statute had already failed in California and Arkansas. The Louisiana law and similar legislation pending in other states would have caused science textbook publishers to insert creation science into their textbooks in response to market pressures. Realizing the detrimental effects of this law on Louisiana students and on science teaching in general, I conferred with my principal and superintendent to determine my vulnerability in filing suit against the State of Louisiana. Both administrators gave me assurances and support and expressed the view that the constitutionality of the recently enacted legislation should be tested.

My colleagues' reaction further motivated me to become actively involved. Many biology teachers were prepared to forego teaching evolution rather than give equal time to religious ideas mislabeled as science. These capable science instructors, by their conviction that it would be preferable to strip evolution from the curriculum rather than teach creation science, were clearly signalling that creation science has no place in the public school science classroom.

I was heartened by the number of scientific organizations and individuals who also viewed creation science as a threat to science education. The National Academy of Sciences published *Science and Creationism* in 1984 in an attempt to examine the major issues of this debate openly and candidly. The Academy concluded that incorporating religious beliefs into our current science curriculum jeopardized the quality of public science education.

In addition, 72 Nobel laureates in science urged the U.S. Supreme Court to declare unconstitutional the Louisiana creation-science statute. Seventeen academies of science and seven scientific organizations also petitioned the court to reject the arguments for creation science.

Popular reaction to the court challenge was often critical. Each time the local newspaper or television station publicized the case, letters and calls, mostly anonymous, indicated that supporters of creation science viewed my position as a threat to their religious beliefs. The creation science lobby had successfully packaged a religious fundamentalist belief as science, shielding the truth from our elected legislators.

The State Attorney General was unrelenting in his defense of the Louisiana statute. Each time a court declared the Louisiana Balanced Treatment Act unconstitutional, he filed an appeal. The U.S. Supreme Court ultimately heard oral arguments for *Edwards* v. *Aguillard* in December 1986.

Following the court's decision on creation science, I addressed a group of science teachers at the NSTA convention in St. Louis, Missouri. I was not surprised to hear from those in attendance that creation science is far from dead in this country. Many teachers could recount at least one confrontation with a school board member, religious leader, or concerned parent who demanded inclusion of creation science in the curriculum. Rather than attempting to gain statewide support, advocates of creation science now approach local boards and individual classroom teachers. Since the threat to science education will continue, educators must encourage publishers to resist the pressures of special-interest groups.

The Louisiana Creationism Act was ruled unconstitutional by the Supreme

Court because the statute violated the Establishment Clause, which forbids a state to intend to or to achieve approval or disapproval of a particular religious belief, or excessively to entangle government and religion. Supreme Court Justice William J. Brennan, writing for the majority, said that the "purpose of the Creationism Act was to restructure the science curriculum to conform with a particular religious viewpoint."[3]

Whether beginning or experienced, the science teacher can contribute to the field not only through inspired teaching but also through insistence on sound educational practices. In designing curricula, selecting materials, and determining teaching methods, school system officials must not disregard the judgments of the classroom teachers. The cases collected in this volume demonstrate that the courts tend to support teacher's efforts—even when unorthodox—to create an environment of academic inquiry. That should encourage educators to hold firm their principles, assuring that vocal minorities do not overpower less vocal majorities in maintaining the integrity of education.

NOTES

1. Tyson-Bernstein, Harriet. "America's Textbook Fiasco," *American Educator*. Summer 1988. pp. 20–27 and 39.
2. Aldridge, B.G. and Johnston, K.L. "The Crisis in Science Education—What Is It?—How Can We Respond?" *Journal of College Science Teaching*. September/October. 1984. pp. 20–28.
3. *Edwards* v. *Aguillard* 107 S. Ct. 2573, 2582 (1987).

Introduction

A MICHIGAN junior high school Biology teacher is suspended for allegedly "behaving improperly and teaching 'sex education' in an extremely insensitive manner." An Ohio high school Spanish teacher is reprimanded by the principal because of her use of classroom time to denounce the local police department. An Illinois kindergarten teacher is discharged for refusing "to teach any subjects having to do with love of country, the flag or other patriotic matters in the prescribed curriculum." A Missouri high school Math teacher is dismissed for denouncing in his Algebra class the military personnel recruiting on the campus and for suggesting to his students they take action against the recruiters. A North Carolina student teacher is discharged "because he gave unorthodox answers to student questions (derived from the day's text) about creation, evolution, immortality, and the nature and existence of God." A Texas high school Civics teacher is dismissed after parents' complaints concerning his "truthful response to a student's classroom question that he was not opposed to interracial marriages" and after he had been instructed to teach his current events course "within the text and not discuss controversial issues" in his civics class.

The teachers' classroom behavior, speech and teaching methods have raised constitutional questions which the courts have had to answer. While the courts have been willing to give First Amendment protection to teachers who use "controversial" books, films and plays (see Volume One of this Series), they have not been so consistently ready to give as much protection to teachers whose classroom speech and behavior might be irrelevant to the subject-matter of the class. As the cases in this volume demonstrate, there are some types of classroom behavior and teaching methods the courts have argued do not warrant constitutional protection. There are, however, cases in which the courts have given protection to the teachers who have used "unorthodox" teaching methods or expressed in class views which parents and school officials found "offensive."

The judges have generally been careful to point out that in a free society teachers must not be forced into teaching only orthodox ideas through orthodox teaching methods. As a United States District Court in North Carolina stated in *Moore*: "Although academic freedom is not one of the enumerated rights of the First Amendment, the Supreme Court has on numerous occasions emphasized that the right to teach, to inquire, to evaluate and to study is fundamental to a democratic society. . . . [T]he safeguards of the First Amendment will quickly be brought into play to protect the right of academic freedom because any unwarranted invasion of this right will tend to have a chilling effect on the exercise of the right by other teachers."

In 1964, the United States Supreme Court declared unconstitutional in *Baggett* v. *Bullitt* a Washington State loyalty oath which required that teachers "by precept and example will promote respect for the flag and the institutions of the United States of America and the State of Washington, reverence for law and order and undivided allegiance to the government of the United States." The Court found some parts of the oath too vague with terms of uncertain meaning; teachers, said the Court, might avoid presenting controversial lectures and materials since it was not clear what precisely was prohibited by the statute.

When a United States District Court in Texas gave constitutional protection in *Sterzing* to a high school Civics teacher who had been dismissed for, among other things, remarks he made and teaching methods he used in class when dealing with issues related to race, prejudice and protest, the court while noting that "a teacher's methods are not without limits," went on to say: "[A] teacher must not be manacled with rigid regulations, which preclude full adaptation of the course to the times in which we live. It would be ill-advised to presume that a teacher would be limited, in essence to a single textbook in teaching a course today in civics and social studies." "The freedom of speech of a teacher and a citizen of the United States," said the court, "must not be so lightly regarded that he stands in jeopardy of dismissal for raising controversial issues in an eager but disciplined classroom."

In deciding to give constitutional protection to a teacher's controversial expression outside the classroom, the United States Supreme Court in *Pickering* took into account the possible effects of such speech on what went on in the teacher's classroom. In deciding for Pickering, a high school teacher who had been dismissed for sending to a local newspaper a letter critical of the District Superintendent and the school board, the Supreme Court noted that "this case does not present a situation in which a teacher's public statements are so without foundation as to call into question his fitness to perform his duties in the classroom. In such a case, of course, the statements would merely be evidence of the teacher's general competence, or lack thereof, and not an independent basis for dismissal." Justice Marshall, delivering the opinion of the Court, referred to the fact that Pickering's public criticism had not interfered with his classroom teaching:

> What we do have before us is a case in which a teacher has made erroneous public statements upon issues then currently the subject of public attention, which are critical of his ultimate employer but which are neither shown nor can be presumed to have in any way either impeded the teacher's proper performance of his daily duties in the classroom or to have interfered with the regular operation of the schools generally. In these circumstances we conclude that the interest of the school administration in limiting teachers' opportunities to contribute to public debate is not significantly greater than its interest in limiting a similar contribution by any member of the general public.

Pickering became a landmark case and Justice Marshall's arguments subsequently were used by various lower courts in deciding cases involving the First Amendment rights of teachers.

In giving constitutional protection to a Texas high school teacher, a United States District Court in Texas declared in *Lusk* that "*Pickering* made it clear that a teacher's employment may not be conditioned upon the surrender of his constitutional rights. A citizen's right to engage in protected expression is substantially unaffected by the fact that he is also a teacher and, as a general rule, he cannot be deprived of his teaching position merely because he exercises these rights." School authorities, said the court, "must nurture and protect, not extinguish and inhibit, the teacher's right to express his ideas. Only if the exercise of these rights by the teacher materially and substantially impedes the teacher's proper performance of his daily duties in the classroom or disrupts the regular operation of the school will a restriction of his rights be tolerated."

In 1979, the United States Court of Appeals, Seventh Circuit, decided for an Illinois elementary school teacher who had been transferred because "she had complained about school procedures on a number of occasions, and that she was 'stirring up trouble' in the teachers' lounge." In so deciding, the court referred to *Pickering* which it said "can be read as establishing that two limits on a teacher's right to speak out may be permissible. First, speech that is so disruptive as to impede the teacher's performance or to interfere with the operation of the school may be proper grounds for discipline. Second, if the speech does not involve matters of public interest it may not be entitled to constitutional protection." In this case, said the court, the school officials had "not shown that plaintiff's statements impeded her classroom duties or interfered with the regular operation of the schools generally." Since the teacher had "established that her speech was not unduly disruptive, *Pickering* does not support the school board's position."

The humorous anti-superintendent remarks expressed by another teacher in the classroom, however, did not receive constitutional protection from a California court. Among other things, the teacher had "advised his philosophy class that the district superintendent could be a good superintendent 'but he spends too much time * * * (at this point in the statement he [the teacher] stepped over to the wall and simulated licking the wall with his tongue in an up and down manner and then continued speaking) * * * licking up the board.'" While the court agreed in *Hensey* that a teacher has a right to differ with and to criticize the superintendent, the means of expression is crucial in deciding whether the speech warranted First Amendment protection. The court went on to say that "while humor is an important part of a stimulating and entertaining presentation, a co-educational classroom does not appear to be the place for the barracks type of language used by this defendant."

Another teacher who did not get First Amendment protection had been dismissed for using the classroom "as a forum for expression of disagreement with her administrators on internal affairs." As with the California court, the United States District Court in Nebraska said in *Ahern* that a teacher has a right to express opinions and concerns, as does any other citizen, on matters of public concern, but the District Court "doubted" that she "has a right to express them *during class* in deliberate violation of a superior's admonition not to do so, when the subject of her opinions and concerns is directly related to student and teacher discipline." The court argued that while the teacher could express disagreement with views of the school administration, "a teacher is not constitutionally entitled to use the classroom as a forum for expression of disagreement with her administrators on internal affairs."

The same year (1971) the District Court decided against the teacher in *Ahern*, a United States District Court in Arkansas decided in *Downs* for a teacher who had been dismissed because she had her students "criticize" through cartoons, shown to the principal, an unsafe incinerator on school grounds and a broken-down water fountain. In deciding for Mildred Downs who had taught in the Arkansas Public School System for twenty five years, the District Court in Arkansas declared: "A citizen, be he teacher or layman, has the legal right to seek redress be it judicial or administrative for substantial dangers and/or threats to his health and/or safety and a court cannot sanction attempts to so intimidate a citizen, that they forego such fundamental rights. . . . .When a School Board acts, as it did here, to punish a teacher who seeks to protect the health and safety of herself and her pupils, the resulting intimidation can only cause a severe chilling, if not freezing, effect on the free discussion of more controversial subjects."

While the United States District Courts have given First Amendment protection to teachers' in-class "controversial" comments, as in *Moore* and *Sterzing*, the United States Court of Appeals, Eighth Circuit, decided in 1974 in *Birdwell* against a teacher who upon hearing that Army personnel would be speaking to the students said, among other things to the students in his Algebra class, that the pupils were "4,000 strong" and could get the military off the high school campus. The court argued that the dismissal of the probationary teacher was warranted inasmuch as he used his Algebra class to encourage young and immature minds to "employ measures of violence as a demonstrative device." The Court of Appeals rejected Birdwell's argument and his reliance on *Tinker*, Birdwell arguing that "there was no material or substantial disruption of the school." The court responded: "In a situation of potential disruption there is no requirement in the law that the proper authorities must wait for the blow to fall before taking remedial measures. Moreover, even should violence not have occurred, we do not take it that such is a *sine qua non* of disruptive conduct. The trial court found that the appellant's actions, both in the classroom and in the hallway, were 'disruptions of the orderly and disciplined operation of the school in and of themselves.' It is clear upon this record that appellant's termination did not result from the exercise of a constitutionally protected right of free speech."

In 1979, a Michigan jury awarded a high school Biology teacher $275,000 in compensatory damages and $46,000 in punitive damages after school officials removed him from the classroom when a few parents alleged that he was "behaving improperly in the classroom and teaching 'sex education' in an extremely insensitive manner. These allegations were made public at a school board meeting held on April 23, 1979." Stachura, the teacher, argued that his First Amendment freedoms had been infringed. The jury was instructed that Stachura's academic freedom "is limited by the right of the school board to inculcate community values through control of the substantive content of the curriculum. However, the jury was also instructed that an instructor's teaching methods are entitled to first amendment protection as long as the substantive values the school board seeks to inculcate are not subverted by those methods." As Judge Harvey indicated in his 1983 *Stachura* opinion, "Evidence was presented that the biology text used by Stachura was approved by the board of education, as was the film used to supplement the text discussion of reproduction. Stachura testified concerning the instruction techniques he used in teaching reproduction. This testimony was at odds with the allegations of the parents and the claims of the defendants. Moreover, plaintiff was suspended only after a vehement protest by certain parents; evidence which certainly raises the inference that Stachura was suspended in retaliation for his allegedly improper teaching methods. This evidence would permit a reasonable jury to find for plaintiff Stachura."

Judge Harvey also contended that the circumstances of the case gave rise to a due process right. Stachura, said the judge, "was removed from the classroom under circumstances which invited stigmatization. Given the humiliating nature of the publicity surrounding the removal, Stachura had a right to a forum which would permit an opportunity for swift public vindication. Plaintiff's liberty interest claim was properly submitted to the jury."

In affirming the District Court's judgment, the United States Court of Appeals, Sixth Circuit, declared in 1985: "Turning directly to the appellate issues in Stachura's suit against the School District defendants, we hold, as indicated above, that plaintiff Stachura's First Amendment rights were infringed and that his exercise of 'academic freedom' had followed rather than violated his superior's instructions." The Court of Appeals agreed with the District Court and the jury that "Stachura's property interests were invaded by his being effectively discharged" and that "the actions of the School Board 'imposed a stigma on Stachura and foreclosed a definite range of employment opportunities' which plaintiff would otherwise have available." Further, said the court, the facts "also indicate clearly that Stachura was never given a fair opportunity to present his defense to the School Board nor do we believe that the Board's action can be held as a matter of law to have been taken in good faith."

Among the cases in this volume are decisions concerned with a teacher who, for religious reasons, refused to teach subjects dealing with patriotism, love of country, patriotic holidays and songs; an elementary school teacher who had his students write letters to his fiancee to practice their penmanship, the students later receiving from the fiancee letters affirming her being a communist along with her husband [the teacher] and their son Chris who she said was learning to be a communist; a history teacher who used "role playing" as a teaching method during a unit on the post-Civil War Reconstruction period.

What the court opinions in this volume appear to be saying, among other things, is that teachers whose classroom teaching methods and comments are appropriate for the age-level of the students and relevant to the subject-matter being taught will get constitutional protection, even if the comments and teaching methods are "unorthodox." While "a teacher's methods are not without limits," a teacher "must not be manacled with rigid regulations, which preclude full adaptation of the course to the times in which we live." A teacher's teaching methods "are entitled to first amendment protection as long as the substantive values the school board seeks to inculcate are not subverted by those methods." Due process must be observed and teachers who have been reprimanded or suspended must be given a "fair opportunity to present" their defenses to the School Board and the Boards must "act in good faith." If the teachers did not have the right to be warned before they were discharged, they "might be more timid than it is in the public interest" that they should be and they "might steer away from reasonable methods with which it is in the public interest to experiment." On the other hand, teachers who use the classroom, the captive audience of students, to proselytize religious and political views and to criticize school officials are not likely to receive constitutional protection.

The court opinions in this volume reflect, for the most part, what has been declared by various professional organizations such as the National Council for the Social Studies, the American Association of University Professors and many others. In its "Statement on Academic Freedom and Tenure" the AAUP, along with scores of other organizations such as the Modern Language Association, Speech Communication Association, American Library Association, and American Association of Schools and Departments of Journalism which endorsed the AAUP Statement, declared in part that "the teacher is entitled to freedom in the classroom in discussing his subject, but he should be careful not to introduce into his teaching controversial matter which has no relation to his subject." The intent of this part of the Statement "is not to discourage what is 'controversial.' Controversy is at the heart of the free academic inquiry which the entire Statement is designed to foster. The passage serves to underscore the need for the teacher to avoid persistently intruding material which has no relation to his subject."

The National Council for Social Studies declared in the Preface to its "Statement on Academic Freedom and the Social Studies Teacher": "Democracy is a way of life that prizes alternatives. Alternatives mean that people must make choices. Wisdom with which to make choices can come only if there are freedom of speech, of press, assembly, and of teaching. They protect the people in their right to hear, to read, to discuss, and reach judgments according to individual conscience. Without the possession and the exercise of these rights, self-government is impossible."

As to the selection of educational materials used in the schools, the Statement on Academic Freedom and the Social Studies Teacher stated: "The availability of adequate and diversified materials is essential to academic freedom. Selection, exclusion, or alteration of materials may infringe upon academic freedom. Official lists of supplementary 'materials approved' for classroom use, school library purchases, or school book shops may also restrict academic freedom. Actively involving teachers in selection procedures based on written criteria to which all interested persons have access is an essential safeguard."

When in 1972 a United States District Court in Texas decided for high school Civics teacher Henry K. Sterzing who had been dismissed because of his "controversial" teaching methods and comments in class, Judge Carl Bue, Jr. persuasively argued: "A responsible teacher must have freedom to use the tools of his profession as he sees fit. If the teacher cannot be trusted to use them fairly, then the teacher should never have been engaged in the first place. The Court finds Mr. Sterzing's objectives in his teaching to be proper to stimulate critical thinking, to create an awareness of our present political and social community and to enliven the educational process. These are desirable goals. . . . This discharge of Mr. Sterzing and failure to rehire him, for the reasons stated by the school board, constituted a denial of due process and a violation of rights granted and protected by the First and Fourteenth Amendments of the Constitution."

In ordering the reinstatement of a high school English teacher who had been dismissed for assigning her eleventh grade class Kurt Vonnegut's *Welcome to the Monkeyhouse*, a United States District Court in Alabama concluded in *Parducci* v. *Rutland* that the school officials had "failed to show either that the assignment was inappropriate reading for high school juniors, or that it created a significant disruption to the educational processes of this school"; hence, the teacher's dismissal "constituted an unwarranted invasion of her First Amendment right to academic freedom." In arriving at its decision the court recognized the crucial role of academic freedom in our nation: "Although academic freedom is not one of the enumerated rights of the First Amendment, the Supreme Court has on numerous occasions emphasized that the right to teach, to inquire, to evaluate and to study is fundamental to a democratic society." The court then relied on the often quoted and now classic lines from *Keyishian* v. *Board of Education* (1967) in which the United States Supreme Court declared a New York loyalty oath statute unconstitutional: "Our nation is deeply committed to safeguarding academic freedom, which is of transcendant value to all of us and not merely to the teachers concerned. That freedom is therefore a special concern of the First Amendment, which does not tolerate laws that cast a pall of orthodoxy over the classroom."

The United States Supreme Court, in a 7-2 decision, declares unconstitutional two Washington State statutes requiring oaths to be taken by all state employees, including teachers, one of which requires teachers to swear that they will "support the Constitution and laws of the United States of America and of the State of Washington, and will by precept and example promote respect for the flag and the institutions of the United States of America and the State of Washington, reverence for law and order and undivided allegiance to the government of the United States." This oath, said the Court, "offends due process because of vagueness. The oath exacts a promise that the affiant will, by precept and example, promote respect for the flag and the institutions of the United States and the State of Washington. The range of activities which are or might be deemed inconsistent with the required promise is very wide indeed. The teacher who refused to salute the flag or advocated refusal because of religious beliefs might well be accused of breaching this promise. . . . Even criticism of the design or color scheme of the state flag or unfavorable comparison of it with that of a sister state or foreign country could be deemed disrespectful and therefore violative of the oath. And what are 'institutions' for the purposes of this oath? It is likewise difficult," continued the Court, "to ascertain what might be done without transgressing the promise to 'promote . . . undivided allegiance to the government of the United States.' It would not be unreasonable for the serious-minded oathtaker to conclude that he should dispense with lectures voicing far-reaching criticism of any old or new policy followed by the Government of the United States. He could find it questionable under this language to ally himself with any interest group dedicated to opposing any current public policy or law of the federal government, for if he did, he might well be accused of placing loyalty to the group above allegiance to the United States. . . . We are dealing with indefinite statutes whose terms, even narrowly construed, abut upon sensitive areas of basic First Amendment freedoms. The uncertain meanings of the oaths require the oath-taker—teachers and public servants—to 'steer far wider of the unlawful zone,' . . . than if the boundaries of the forbidden areas were clearly marked. Those with a conscientious regard for what they solemnly swear or affirm, sensitive to the perils posed by the oath's indefinite language, avoid the risk of loss of employment, and perhaps profession, only by restricting their conduct to that which is unquestionably safe. Free speech may not be so inhibited."

Baggett v. *Bullitt*, 377 U.S. 360 (1964)

Mr. Justice WHITE delivered the opinion of the Court.

Appellants, approximately 64 in number, are members of the faculty, staff and student body of the University of Washington who brought this class action asking for a judgment declaring unconstitutional two Washington statutes requiring the execution of two different oaths by state employees and for an injunction against the enforcement of these statutes by appellees, the President of the University, members of the Washington State Board of Regents and the State Attorney General.

The statutes under attack are Chapter 377, Laws of 1955, and Chapter 103, Laws of 1931, both of which require employees of the State of Washington to take the oaths prescribed in the statutes as a condition of their employment. The 1931 legislation applies only to teachers, who, upon applying for a license to teach or renewing an existing contract, are required to subscribe to the following:

"I solemnly swear (or affirm) that I will support the constitution and laws of the United States of America and of the State of Washington, and will by precept and example promote respect for the flag and the institutions of the United States of America and the State of Washington, reverence for law and order and undivided allegiance to the government of the United States." Wash. Laws 1931, c. 103.

The oath requirements of the 1955 Act, Wash. Laws 1955, c. 377, applicable to all state employees, incorporate various provisions of the Washington Subversive Activities Act of 1951, which provides generally that "[n]o subversive person, as defined in this act, shall be eligible for employment in, or appointment to any office, or any position of trust or profit in the government, or in the administration of the business, of this state, or of any county, municipality, or other political subdivision of this state." Wash. Rev. Code § 9.81.060. The term "subversive person" is defined as follows:

"'Subversive person' means any person who commits, attempts to commit, or aids in the commission, or advocates, abets, advises or teaches by any means any person to commit, attempt to commit or aid in the commission of any act intended to overthrow, destroy or alter, or to assist in the overthrow, destruction or alteration of, the constitutional form of the government of the United States, or of the state of Washington, or any political subdivision of either of them by revolution, force, or violence; or who with knowledge that the organization is an organization as described in subsections (2) and (3) hereof, becomes or remains a member of a subversive organization or a foreign subversive organization." Wash. Rev. Code § 9.81.010 (5).

The act goes on to define at similar length and in similar terms "subversive organization" and "foreign subversive organization" and to declare the Communist Party a subversive organization and membership therein a subversive activity.[1]

On May 28, 1962, some four months after this Court's dismissal of the appeal in *Nostrand* v. *Little*, 368 U.S. 436, also a challenge to the 1955 oath,[2] the University President, acting pursuant to directions of the Board of Regents, issued a memorandum to all University employees notifying them that they would be required to take an oath. Oath Form A[3] requires all teaching personnel to swear to the oath of allegiance set out above, to aver that they have read, are familiar with and understand the provisions defining "subversive person" in the Subversive Activities Act of 1951 and to disclaim being a subversive person and membership in the Communist Party or any other subversive or foreign subversive organization. Oath Form B[4] requires other state employees to subscribe to all of the above provisions except the 1931 oath. Both forms pro-

vide that the oath and statements pertinent thereto are made subject to the penalties of perjury.

Pursuant to 28 U.S.C. §§ 2281, 2284, a three-judge District Court was convened and a trial was had. That court determined that the 1955 oath and underlying statutory provisions did not infringe upon any First and Fourteenth Amendment freedoms and were not unduly vague. In respect to the claim that the 1931 oath was unconstitutionally vague on its face, the court held that although the challenge raised a substantial constitutional issue, adjudication was not proper in the absence of proceedings in the state courts which might resolve or avoid the constitutional issue. The action was dismissed. 215 F. Supp. 439. We noted probable jurisdiction because of the public importance of this type of legislation and the recurring serious constitutional questions which it presents. 375 U.S. 808. We reverse.

I.

Appellants contend in this Court that the oath requirements and the statutory provisions on which they are based are invalid on their face because their language is unduly vague, uncertain and broad. We agree with this contention and therefore, without reaching the numerous other contentions pressed upon us, confine our considerations to that particular question.[5]

In *Cramp* v. *Board of Public Instruction*, 368 U.S. 278, the Court invalidated an oath requiring teachers and other employees of the State to swear that they had never lent their "aid, support, advice, counsel or influence to the Communist Party" because the oath was lacking in "terms susceptible of objective measurement" and failed to inform as to what the State commanded or forbade. The statute therefore fell within the compass of those decisions of the court holding that a law forbidding or requiring conduct in terms so vague that men of common intelligence must necessarily guess at its meaning and differ as to its application violates due process of law. *Connally* v. *General Construction Co.*, 269 U.S. 385; *Lanzetta* v. *New Jersey*, 306 U.S. 451; *Joseph Burstyn, Inc.*, v. *Wilson*, 343 U.S. 495; *United States* v. *Cardiff*, 344 U.S. 174; *Champlin Refining Co.* v. *Corporation Comm'n of Oklahoma*, 286 U.S. 210.

The oath required by the 1955 statute suffers from similar infirmities. A teacher must swear that he is not a subversive person: that he is not one who commits an act or who advises, teaches, abets or advocates by any means another person to commit or aid in the commission of any act intended to overthrow or alter, or to assist the overthrow or alteration, of the constitutional form of government by revolution, force or violence. A subversive organization is defined as one which engages in or assists activities intended to alter or overthrow the Government by force or violence or which has as a purpose the commission of such acts. The Communist Party is declared in the statute to be a subversive organization, that is, it is presumed that the Party does and will engage in activities intended to overthrow the Government.[6] Persons required to swear they understand this oath may quite reasonably conclude that any person who aids the Communist Party or teaches or advises known members of the Party is a subversive person because such teaching or advice may now or at some future date aid the activities of the Party. Teaching and advising are clearly acts, and one cannot confidently assert that his counsel, aid, influence or support which adds to the resources, rights and knowledge of the Communist Party or its members does not aid the Party in its activities, activities which the statute tells us are all in furtherance of the stated purpose of overthrowing the Government by revolution, force, or violence. The questions put by the Court in *Cramp* may with equal force be asked here. Does the statute reach endorsement or support for Communist candidates for office? Does it reach a lawyer who represents the Communist Party or its members or a journalist who defends constitutional rights of the Communist Party or its members or anyone who supports any cause which is likewise supported by Communists or the Communist Party? The susceptibility of the statutory language to require forswearing of an undefined variety of "guiltless knowing behavior" is what the Court condemned in *Cramp*. This statute, like the one at issue in *Cramp*, is unconstitutionally vague.[7]

The Washington statute suffers from additional difficulties on vagueness grounds. A person is subversive not only if he himself commits the specified acts but if he abets or advises another in aiding a third person to commit an act which will assist yet a fourth person in the overthrow or alteration of constitutional government. The Washington Supreme Court has said that knowledge is to be read into every provision and we accept this construction. *Nostrand* v. *Balmer*, 53 Wash. 2d 460, 483-484, 335 P. 2d 10, 24; *Nostrand* v. *Little*, 58 Wash. 2d 111, 123-124, 361 P. 2d 551, 559. But what is it that the Washington professor must "know?" Must he know that his aid or teaching will be used by another and that the person aided has the requisite guilty intent or is it sufficient that he know that his aid or teaching would or might be useful to others in the commission of acts intended to overthrow the Government? Is it subversive activity, for example, to attend and participate in international conventions of mathematicians and exchange views with scholars from Communist countries? What about the editor of a scholarly journal who analyzes and criticizes the manuscripts of Communist scholars submitted for publica-

tion? Is selecting outstanding scholars from Communist countries as visiting professors and advising, teaching, or consulting with them at the University of Washington a subversive activity if such scholars are known to be Communists, or regardless of their affiliations, regularly teach students who are members of the Communist Party, which by statutory definition is subversive and dedicated to the overthrow of the Government?

The Washington oath goes beyond overthrow or alteration by force or violence. It extends to alteration by "revolution" which, unless wholly redundant and its ordinary meaning distorted, includes any rapid or fundamental change. Would, therefore, any organization or any person supporting, advocating or teaching peaceful but far-reaching constitutional amendments be engaged in subversive activity? Could one support the repeal of the Twenty-second Amendment or participation by this country in a world government?[8]

II.

We also conclude that the 1931 oath offends due process because of vagueness. The oath exacts a promise that the affiant will, by precept and example, promote respect for the flag and the institutions of the United States and the State of Washington. The range of activities which are or might be deemed inconsistent with the required promise is very wide indeed. The teacher who refused to salute the flag or advocated refusal because of religious beliefs might well be accused of breaching his promise. Cf. *West Virginia State Board of Education* v. *Barnette*, 319 U.S. 624. Even criticism of the design or color scheme of the state flag or unfavorable comparison of it with that of a sister State or foreign country could be deemed disrespectful and therefore violative of the oath. And what are "institutions" for the purposes of this oath? Is it every "practice, law, custom, etc., which is a material and persistent element in the life or culture of an organized social group" or every "established society or corporation," every "establishment, esp[ecially] one of a public character"?[9] The oath may prevent a professor from criticizing his state judicial system or the Supreme Court or the institution of judicial review. Or it might be deemed to proscribe advocating the abolition, for example, of the Civil Rights Commission, the House Committee on Un-American Activities, or foreign aid.

It is likewise difficult to ascertain what might be done without transgressing the promise to "promote . . . undivided allegiance to the government of the United States." It would not be unreasonable for the serious-minded oathtaker to conclude that he should dispense with lectures voicing far-reaching criticism of any old or new policy followed by the Government of the United States. He could find it questionable under this language to ally himself with any interest group dedicated to opposing any current public policy or law of the Federal Government, for if he did, he might well be accused of placing loyalty to the group above allegiance to the United States.

Indulging every presumption of a narrow construction of the provisions of the 1931 oath, consistent, however, with a proper respect for the English language, we cannot say that this oath provides an ascertainable standard of conduct or that it does not require more than a State may command under the guarantees of the First and Fourteenth Amendments.

As in *Cramp* v. *Board of Public Instruction*, "[t]he vice of unconstitutional vagueness is further aggravated where, as here, the statute in question operates to inhibit the exercise of individual freedoms affirmatively protected by the Constitution." 368 U.S. 278, 287. We are dealing with indefinite statutes whose terms, even narrowly construed, abut upon sensitive areas of basic First Amendment freedoms. The uncertain meanings of the oaths require the oath-taker—teachers and public servants—to "steer far wider of the unlawful zone," *Speiser* v. *Randall*, 357 U.S. 513, 526, than if the boundaries of the forbidden areas were clearly marked. Those with a conscientious regard for what they solemnly swear or affirm, sensitive to the perils posed by the oath's indefinite language, avoid the risk of loss of employment, and perhaps profession, only by restricting their conduct to that which is unquestionably safe. Free speech may not be so inhibited.[10]

Smith v. *California*, 361 U.S. 147; *Stromberg* v. *California*, 283 U.S. 359, 369. See also *Herndon* v. *Lowry*, 301 U.S. 242; *Thornhill* v. *Alabama*, 310 U.S. 88; and *Winters* v. *New York*, 333 U.S. 507.

III.

The State labels as wholly fanciful the suggested possible coverage of the two oaths. It may well be correct, but the contention only emphasizes the difficulties with the two statutes; for if the oaths do not reach some or any of the behavior suggested, what specific conduct do the oaths cover? Where does fanciful possibility end and intended coverage begin?

It will not do to say that a prosecutor's sense of fairness and the Constitution would prevent a successful perjury prosecution for some of the activities seemingly embraced within the sweeping statutory definitions. The hazard of being prosecuted for knowing but guiltless behavior nevertheless remains. "It would be blinking reality not to acknowledge that there are some among us always ready to affix a Communist label upon those whose ideas they violently oppose. And experience teaches us that prosecutors too are human."

Cramp, supra, at 286-287. Well-intentioned prosecutors and judicial safeguards do not neutralize the vice of a vague law. Nor should we encourage the casual taking of oaths by upholding the discharge or exclusion from public employment of those with a conscientious and scrupulous regard for such undertakings.

It is further argued, however, that, notwithstanding the uncertainties of the 1931 oath and the statute on which it is based, the oath does not offend due process because the vagaries are contained in a promise of future conduct, the breach of which would not support a conviction for perjury. Without the criminal sanctions, it is said, one need not fear taking this oath, regardless of whether he understands it and can comply with its mandate, however understood. This contention ignores not only the effect of the oath on those who will not solemnly swear unless they can do so honestly and without prevarication and reservation, but also its effect on those who believe the written law means what it says. Oath Form A contains both oaths, and expressly requires that the signer "understand that this statement and oath are made subject to the penalties of perjury." Moreover, Wash. Rev. Code § 9.72.030 provides that "[e]very person who, whether orally or in writing . . . shall knowingly swear falsely concerning any matter whatsoever" commits perjury in the second degree. Even if it can be said that a conviction for falsely taking this oath would not be sustained, the possibility of a prosecution cannot be gainsaid. The State may not require one to choose between subscribing to an unduly vague and broad oath, thereby incurring the likelihood of prosecution, and conscientiously refusing to take the oath with the consequent loss of employment, and perhaps profession, particularly where "the free dissemination of ideas may be the loser." *Smith* v. *California*, 361 U.S. 147, 151. "It is not the penalty itself that is invalid but the exaction of obedience to a rule or standard that is so vague and indefinite as to be really no rule or standard at all. *Champlin Refg. Co.* v. *Corporation Comm'n of Oklahoma*, 286 U.S. 210, 243; cf. *Small Co.* v. *American Refg. Co.*, 267 U.S. 233.

IV.

We are asked not to examine the 1931 oath statute because, although on the books for over three decades, it has never been interpreted by the Washington courts. The argument is that ever since *Railroad Comm'n* v. *Pullman Co.*, 312 U.S. 496, the Court on many occasions has ordered abstention where state tribunals were thought to be more appropriate for resolution of complex or unsettled questions of local law. *A. F. L.* v. *Watson*, 327 U.S. 582; *Spector Motor*

Service v. *McLaughlin,* 323 U.S. 101; *Harrison* v. *NAACP,* 360 U.S. 167. Because this Court ordinarily accepts the construction given a state statute in the local courts and also presumes that the statute will be construed in such a way as to avoid the constitutional question presented, *Fox* v. *Washington,* 236 U.S. 273; *Poulos* v. *New Hampshire,* 345 U.S. 395, an interpretation of the 1931 oath in the Washington courts in light of the vagueness attack may eliminate the necessity of deciding this issue.

We are not persuaded. The abstention doctrine is not an automatic rule applied whenever a federal court is faced with a doubtful issue of state law; it rather involves a discretionary exercise of a court's equity powers. Ascertainment of whether there exist the "special circumstances," *Propper* v. *Clark,* 337 U.S. 472, prerequisite to its application must be made on a case-by-case basis. *Railroad Comm'n* v. *Pullman Co,* 312 U.S. 496, 500; *NAACP* v. *Bennett,* 360 U.S. 471.[11] Those special circumstances are not present here. We doubt, in the first place, that a construction of the oath provisions, in light of the vagueness challenge, would avoid or fundamentally alter the constitutional issue raised in this litigation. See *Chicago* v. *Atchison, T. & S. F. R. Co.,* 357 U.S. 77. In the bulk of abstention cases in this Court,[12] including those few cases where vagueness was at issue,[13] the unsettled issue of state law principally concerned the applicability of the challenged statute to a certain person or a defined course of conduct, whose resolution in a particular manner would eliminate the constitutional issue and terminate the litigation. Here the uncertain issue of state law does not turn upon a choice between one or several alternative meanings of a state statute. The challenged oath is not open to one or a few interpretations, but to an indefinite number. There is no uncertainty that the oath applies to the appellants and the issue they raise is not whether the oath permits them to engage in certain definable activities. Rather their complaint is that they, about 64 in number, cannot understand the required promise, cannot define the range of activities in which they might engage in the future, and do not want to forswear doing all that is literally or arguably within the purview of the vague terms. In these circumstances it is difficult to see how an abstract construction of the challenged terms, such as precept, example, allegiance, institutions, and the like, in a declaratory judgment action could eliminate the vagueness from these terms. It is fictional to believe that anything less than extensive adjudications, under the impact of a variety of factual situations, would bring the oath within the bounds of permissible constitutional certainty. Abstention does not require this.

Other considerations also militate against abstention here. Construction of this oath in the state court,

abstractly and without reference to concrete, particularized situations so necessary to bring into focus the impact of the terms on constitutionally protected rights of speech and association, *Ashwander* v. *Tennessee Valley Authority,* 297 U.S. 288, 341 (Brandeis, J., concurring), would not only hold little hope of eliminating the issue of vagueness but also would very likely pose other constitutional issues for decision, a result not serving the abstention-justifying end of avoiding constitutional adjudication.

We also cannot ignore that abstention operates to require piecemeal adjudication in many courts, *England* v. *Louisiana State Board of Medical Examiners,* 375 U.S. 411, thereby delaying ultimate adjudication on the merits for an undue length of time, *England, supra; Spector, supra; Government & Civic Employees Organizing Committee* v. *Windsor,* 353 U.S. 364,[14] a result quite costly where the vagueness of a state statute may inhibit the exercise of First Amendment freedoms. Indeed the 1955 subversive person oath has been under continuous constitutional attack since at least 1957, *Nostrand* v. *Balmer,* 53 Wash. 2d 460, 463, 335 P. 2d 10, 12, and is now before this Court for the third time. Remitting these litigants to the state courts for a construction of the 1931 oath would further protract these proceedings, already pending for almost two years, with only the likelihood that the case, perhaps years later, will return to the three-judge District Court and perhaps this Court for a decision on the identical issue herein decided. See *Chicago* v. *Atchison, T. & S. F. R. Co.,* 357 U.S. 77, 84; *Public Utilities Comm'n of Ohio* v. *United Fuel Co.,* 317 U.S. 456.[15] Meanwhile, where the vagueness of the statute deters constitutionally protected conduct, "the free dissemination of ideas may be the loser." *Smith* v. *California,* 361 U.S. 147, 151.

V.

As in *Cramp* v. *Board of Public Instruction, supra,* we do not question the power of a State to take proper measures safeguarding the public service from disloyal conduct. But measures which purport to define disloyalty must allow public servants to know what is and is not disloyal. "The fact . . . that a person is not compelled to hold public office cannot possibly be an excuse for barring him from office by state-imposed criteria forbidden by the Constitution." *Torcaso* v. *Watkins,* 367 U.S. 488, 495-496.

Reversed.

NOTES

1. " 'Subversive organization' means any organization which engages in or advocates, abets, advises, or teaches, or a purpose of which is to engage in or advo-

cate, abet, advise, or teach activities intended to overthrow, destroy or alter, or to assist in the overthrow, destruction or alteration of, the constitutional form of the government of the United States, or of the state of Washington, or of any political subdivision of either of them, by revolution, force or violence." Wash. Rev. Code § 9.81.010 (2).

"'Foreign subversive organization' means any organization directed, dominated or controlled directly or indirectly by a foreign government which engages in or advocates, abets, advises, or teaches, or a purpose of which is to engage in or to advocate, abet, advise, or teach, activities intended to overthrow, destroy or alter, or to assist in the overthrow, destruction or alteration of the constitutional form of the government of the United States, or of the state of Washington, or of any political subdivision of either of them, and to establish in place thereof any form of government the direction and control of which is to be vested in, or exercised by or under, the domination or control of any foreign government, organization, or individual." Wash. Rev. Code § 9.81.010 (3).

"COMMUNIST PARTY DECLARED A SUBVERSIVE ORGANIZATION.

"The communist party is a subversive organization within the purview of chapter 9.81 and membership in the communist party is a subversive activity thereunder." Wash. Rev. Code § 9.81.083.

2. Although the 1931 Act has not been the subject of previous challenge, an attack upon the 1955 loyalty statute was instituted by two of the appellants in the present case, Professors Howard Nostrand and Max Savelle, who brought a declaratory judgment action in the Superior Court of the State of Washington asking that Chapter 377, Laws of 1955, be declared unconstitutional and that its enforcement be enjoined. The Washington Supreme Court held that one section was unconstitutional but severable from the rest of the Act, whose validity was upheld. *Nostrand* v. *Balmer,* 53 Wash. 2d 460, 335 P. 2d 10. On appeal to this Court the decision of the Washington court was vacated and the case remanded for a determination of whether employees who refused to sign the oath would be afforded a hearing at which they could explain or defend the reasons for their refusal. *Nostrand* v. *Little,* 362 U.S. 474. The Washington Supreme Court held upon remand that since Professors Nostrand and Savelle were tenured professors the terms of their contracts and rules promulgated by the Board of Regents entitled them to a hearing. *Nostrand* v. *Little,* 58 Wash. 2d 111, 361 P. 2d 551. This Court dismissed a further appeal, *Nostrand* v. *Little,* 368 U.S. 436. The issue we find dispositive of the case at bar was not presented to this Court in the above proceedings.

3.   "Oath Form A
STATE OF WASHINGTON
"Statement and Oath for Teaching Faculty of the University of Washington

"I, the undersigned, do solemnly swear (or affirm) that I will support the constitution and laws of the United States of America and of the state of Washington, and will by precept and example promote respect for the flag and the institutions of the United States of America and the state of Washington, reverence for law and order, and undivided allegiance to the government of the United States;

"I further certify that I have read the provisions of RCW 9.81.010 (2), (3), and (5); RCW 9.81.060; RCW 9.81.070; and RCW 9.81.083, which are printed on the reverse hereof; that I understand and am familiar with the contents thereof; that I am not a subversive person as therein defined; and

"I do solemnly swear (or affirm) that I am not a member of the Communist party or knowingly of any other subversive organization.

"I understand that this statement and oath are made subject to the penalties of perjury.

....
(SIGNATURE)

....
(TITLE AND DEPARTMENT)
"Subscribed and sworn (or affirmed) to before me this..
day of ...., 19.....

....
NOTARY PUBLIC IN AND FOR THE STATE OF WASHINGTON, RESIDING AT ....
"(To be executed in duplicate, one copy to be retained by individual.)
"NOTE: Those desiring to affirm may strike the words 'swear' and 'sworn to' and substitute 'affirm' and 'affirmed,' respectively."

4.   Oath Form B
"STATE OF WASHINGTON
"Statement and Oath for Staff of the University of Washington Other Than Teaching Faculty

"I certify that I have read the provisions of RCW 9.81.010 (2), (3), and (5); RCW 9.81.060; RCW 9.81.070; and RCW 9.81.083 which are printed on the reverse hereof; that I understand and am familiar with the contents thereof; that I am not a subversive person as therein defined; and

"I do solemnly swear (or affirm) that I am not a member of the Communist party or knowingly of any other subversive organization.

"I understand that this statement and oath are made subject to the penalties of perjury.

....
(SIGNATURE)

....
(TITLE AND DEPARTMENT OR OFFICE)
"Subscribed and sworn (or affirmed) to before me this..
day of ...., 19.....

....
NOTARY PUBLIC IN AND FOR THE STATE OF WASHINGTON, RESIDING AT ....
"(To be executed in duplicate, one copy to be retained by individual.)
"NOTE: Those desiring to affirm may strike the words 'swear' and 'sworn to' and substitute 'affirm' and 'affirmed,' respectively."

5. Since the ground we find dispositive immediately affects the professors and other state employees required to take the oath, and the interests of the students at the University in academic freedom are fully protected by a judgment in favor of the teaching personnel, we have no occasion to pass on the standing of the students to bring this suit.

6. The drafters of the 1951 Subversive Activities Act stated to the Washington Legislature that "[t]he [Communist Party] dovetailed, nation-wide program is designed to . . . create unrest and civil strife, and im-

pede the normal processes of state and national government, all to the end of weakening and ultimately destroying the United States as a constitutional republic and thereby facilitating the avowed Soviet purpose of substituting here a totalitarian dictatorship." First Report of the Joint Legislative Fact-Finding Committee on Un-American Activities in Washington State, 1948, p. iv.

7. The contention that the Court found no constitutional difficulties with identical definitions of subversive person and subversive organizations in *Gerende* v. *Board of Supervisors*. 341 U.S. 56, is without merit. It was forcefully argued in *Gerende* that candidates for state office in Maryland were required to take an oath incorporating a section of the Maryland statutes defining subversive person and organization in the identical terms challenged herein. But the Court rejected this interpretation of Maryland law and did not pass upon or approve the definitions of subversive person and organization contained in the Maryland statutes. Instead it made very clear that the judgment below was affirmed solely on the basis that the actual oath to be imposed under Maryland law requires one to swear that he is not a person who is engaged " 'in the attempt to overthrow the government by *force or violence*,' and that he is not knowingly a member of an organization engaged in such an attempt." *Id.*, at 56-57 (emphasis in original). The Court said: "At the bar of this Court the Attorney General of the State of Maryland declared that he would advise the proper authorities to accept an affidavit in these terms as satisfying in full the statutory requirement. Under these circumstances and with this understanding, the judgment of the Maryland Court of Appeals is *Affirmed*." *Id.*, at 57.

8. It is also argued that §2 of the Smith Act, 18 U.S.C. §2385, upheld over a vagueness challenge in *Dennis* v. *United States*, 341 U.S. 494, proscribes the same activity in the same language as the Washington statute. This argument is founded on a misreading of § 2 and *Dennis* v. *United States, supra.*

That section provides:

"Whoever knowingly or willfully advocates, abets, advises, or teaches the duty, necessity, desirability, or propriety of overthrowing or destroying the government of the United States or the government of any State . . . by force or violence. . . . "

The convictions under this provision were sustained in *Dennis, supra*, on the construction that the statute means "teaching and advocacy of action for the accomplishment of [overthrowing or destroying organized government] by language reasonably and ordinarily calculated to incite persons to such action . . . as speedily as circumstances would permit." *Id.*, at 511-512. In connection with the vagueness attack, it was noted that "[t]his is a federal statute which we must interpret as well as judge. Herein lies the fallacy of reliance upon the manner in which this Court has treated judgments of state courts. . . . " *Id.*, at 502.

In reversing convictions under this section in *Yates* v. *United States*, 354 U.S. 298, the Court made quite clear exactly what all the above terms do and do not proscribe: "[T]he Smith Act reaches only advocacy of action for the overthrow of government by force and violence." *Id.*, at 324.

9. Webster's New Int. Dictionary (2d ed.), at 1288.

10. "The maintenance of the opportunity for free political discussion to the end that government may be responsive to the will of the people and that changes may be obtained by lawful means, an opportunity essential to the security of the Republic, is a fundamental principle of our constitutional system. A statute which upon its face . . . is so vague and indefinite as to permit the punishment of the fair use of this opportunity is repugnant to the guaranty of liberty contained in the Fourteenth Amendment." *Stromberg* v. *California*, 283 U.S. 359, 369. "[S]tatutes restrictive of or purporting to place limits to those [First Amendment] freedoms must be narrowly drawn to meet the precise evil the legislature seeks to curb . . . and . . . the conduct proscribed must be defined specifically so that the person or persons affected remain secure and unrestrained in their rights to engage in activities not encompassed by the legislation." *United States* v. *Congress of Industrial Organizations*, 335 U.S. 106, 141-142 (Rutledge, J., concurring).

11. "When the validity of a state statute, challenged under the United States Constitution, is properly for adjudication before a United States District Court, reference to the state courts for construction of the statute should not automatically be made." *NAACP* v. *Bennett*, 360 U.S. 471. See also *United States* v. *Livingston*, 179 F. Supp. 9, 12-13 (D.C.E.D.S.C.), aff'd, *Livingston* v. *United States*, 364 U.S. 281: "Though never interpreted by a state court, if a state statute is not fairly subject to an interpretation which will avoid or modify the federal constitutional question, it is the duty of a federal court to decide the federal question when presented to it." *Shelton* v. *McKinley*, 174 F. Supp. 351 (D.C.E.D. Ark.) (abstention inappropriate where there are no substantial problems of statutory construction and delay would prejudice constitutional rights); *All American Airways* v. *Village of Cedarhurst*, 201 F. 2d 273 (C.A. 2d Cir.); *Sterling Drug* v. *Anderson*, 127 F. Supp. 511, 513 (D.C.E.D. Tenn.).

12. See, *e.g.*, *Railroad Comm'n of Texas* v. *Pullman Co.*, 312 U.S. 496; *Chicago* v. *Fieldcrest Dairies, Inc.*, 316 U.S. 168; *Spector Motor Service, Inc.*, v. *McLaughlin*, 323 U.S. 101; *Alabama State Federation of Labor* v. *McAdory*, 325 U.S. 450; *American Federation of Labor* v. *Watson*, 327 U.S. 582; *Stainback* v. *Mo Hock Ke Lok Po*, 336 U.S. 368; *Shipman* v. *DuPre*, 339 U.S. 321; *Albertson* v. *Millard*, 345 U.S. 242; *Leiter Minerals, Inc.*, v. *United States*, 352 U.S. 220; *Government & Civic Employees Organizing Committee, C.I.O.*, v. *Windsor*, 353 U.S. 364; *City of Meridian* v. *Southern Bell Tel. & Tel. Co.*, 358 U.S. 639.

13. In *Musser* v. *Utah*, 333 U.S. 95, the appellants were convicted of committing "acts injurious to public morals." The vagueness challenge to the statute, either as applied or on its face, was raised for the first time in oral argument before this Court, and the Court vacated the conviction and remanded for a determination of whether the conviction for urging persons to commit polygamy rested solely on this broad-challenged provision. In *Albertson* v. *Millard*, U.S. 242, the Communist Party of the State of Michigan and its secretary sought to enjoin on several constitutional grounds the application to them of a state statute, five days after its passage, requiring registration, under pain of criminal penalties, of "any organization which is substantially directed, dominated or controlled by the Union of Soviet Socialist Republics or its satellites, or which . . . acts to further, the world communist movement" and of members of such an organization. They argued that

the definitions were vague and failed to inform them if a local Communist organization and its members were required to register. The lower court took judicial notice of the fact that the Communist Party of the United States, with whom the local party was associated, was a part of the world Communist movement dominated by the Soviet Union, and held the statute constitutional in all other respects. This Court vacated the judgment and declined to pass on the appellants' constitutional claims until the Michigan courts, in a suit already pending, construed the statutory terms and determined if they required the local Party and its secretary, without more, to register. The approach was that the constitutional claims, including the one founded on vagueness, would be wholly eliminated if the statute, as construed by the state court, did not require all local Communist organizations without substantial ties to a foreign country and their members to register. Stated differently, the question was whether this statute applied to these plaintiffs, a question to be authoritatively answered in the state courts.

In *Harrison* v. *NAACP,* 360 U.S. 167, the NAACP and the NAACP Legal Defense and Education Fund sought a declaratory judgment and injunction on several constitutional grounds in respect to numerous recently enacted state statutes. The lower court enjoined the implementation of three statutes, including one provision on vagueness grounds, and ordered abstention as to two others, finding them ambiguous. This Court ordered abstention as to all the statutes, finding that they were all susceptible of constructions that would limit or eliminate their effect on the litigative and legal activities of the NAACP and construction might thereby eliminate the necessity for passing on the many constitutional questions raised. The vagueness issue, for example, would not require adjudication if the state courts found that the challenged provisions did not restrict the activities of the NAACP or require the NAACP to register. Unlike the instant case, the necessity for deciding the federal constitutional issues in the above and other abstention cases turned on whether the restrictions or requirements of an uncertain or unclear state statute were imposed on the persons bringing the action or on their activities as defined in the complaint.

14. See Clark, Federal Procedural Reform and States' Rights, 40 Tex. L. Rev. 211 (1961); Note, 73 Harv. L. Rev. 1358, 1363 (1960).

15. "Where the disposition of a doubtful question of local law might terminate the entire controversy and thus make it unnecessary to decide a substantial constitutional question, considerations of equity justify a rule of abstention. But where, as here, no state court ruling on local law could settle the federal questions that necessarily remain, and where, as here, the litigation has already been in the federal courts an inordinately long time, considerations of equity require that the litigation be brought to an end as quickly as possible." 317 U.S. 456, at 463.

T HE United States Supreme Court decides for a teacher who had been dismissed from his position as a high school teacher in Will County, Illinois, "for sending a letter to a local newspaper in connection with a recently proposed tax increase that was critical of the way in which the board and the district superintendent of schools had handled past proposals to raise new revenue for the schools." In deciding for the teacher, the Court stated: "What we do have before us is a case in which a teacher has made erroneous public statements upon issues then currently the subject of public attention, which are critical of his ultimate employer but which are neither shown nor can be presumed to have in any way either impeded the teacher's proper performance of his daily duties in the classroom[5]or to have interfered with the regular operation of the schools generally. In these circumstances we conclude that the interest of the school administration in limiting teachers' opportunities to contribute to public debate is not significantly greater than its interest in limiting a similar contribution by any member of the general public." In footnote 5, the Court said: "We also note that this case does not present a situation in which a teacher's public statements are so without foundation as to call into question his fitness to perform his duties in the classroom. In such a case, of course, the statements would merely be evidence of the teacher's general competence, or lack thereof, and not an independent basis for dismissal."

Pickering v. *Board of Education,* 391 U.S. 563 (1968)

Mr. Justice MARSHALL delivered the opinion of the Court.

Appellant Marvin L. Pickering, a teacher in Township High School District 205, Will County, Illinois, was dismissed from his position by the appellee Board of Education for sending a letter to a local newspaper in connection with a recently proposed tax increase that was critical of the way in which the Board and the district superintendent of schools had handled past proposals to raise new revenue for the schools. Appellant's dismissal resulted from a determination by the Board, after a full hearing, that the publication of the letter was "detrimental to the efficient operation and administration of the schools of the district" and hence, under the relevant Illinois statute, Ill. Rev. Stat., c. 122, § 10-22.4 (1963), that "interests of the school require[d] [his dismissal]."

Appellant's claim that his writing of the letter was protected by the First and Fourteenth Amendments was rejected. Appellant then sought review of the Board's action in the Circuit Court of Will County, which affirmed his dismissal on the ground that the determination that appellant's letter was detrimental to the interests of the school system was supported by substantial evidence and that the interests of the schools overrode appellant's First Amendment rights. On appeal, the Supreme Court of Illinois, two Justices

dissenting, affirmed the judgment of the Circuit Court. 36 Ill. 2d 568, 225 N.E. 2d 1 (1967). We noted probable jurisdiction of appellant's claim that the Illinois statute permitting his dismissal on the facts of this case was unconstitutional as applied under the First and Fourteenth Amendments.[1] 389 U.S. 925 (1967). For the reasons detailed below we agree that appellant's rights to freedom of speech were violated and we reverse.

I.

In February of 1961 the appellee Board of Education asked the voters of the school district to approve a bond issue to raise $4,875,000 to erect two new schools. The proposal was defeated. Then, in December of 1961, the Board submitted another bond proposal to the voters which called for the raising of $5,500,000 to build two new schools. This second proposal passed and the schools were built with the money raised by the bond sales. In May of 1964 a proposed increase in the tax rate to be used for educational purposes was submitted to the voters by the Board and was defeated. Finally, on September 19, 1964, a second proposal to increase the tax rate was submitted by the Board and was likewise defeated. It was in connection with this last proposal of the School Board that appellant wrote the letter to the editor (which we reproduce in an Appendix to this opinion) that resulted in his dismissal.

Prior to the vote on the second tax increase proposal a variety of articles attributed to the District 205 Teachers' Organization appeared in the local paper. These articles urged passage of the tax increase and stated that failure to pass the increase would result in a decline in the quality of education afforded children in the district's schools. A letter from the superintendent of schools making the same point was published in the paper two days before the election and submitted to the voters in mimeographed form the following day. It was in response to the foregoing material, together with the failure of the tax increase to pass, that appellant submitted the letter in question to the editor of the local paper.

The letter constituted, basically, an attack on the School Board's handling of the 1961 bond issue proposals and its subsequent allocation of financial resources between the schools' educational and athletic programs. It also charged the superintendent of schools with attempting to prevent teachers in the district from opposing or criticizing the proposed bond issue.

The Board dismissed Pickering for writing and publishing the letter. Pursuant to Illinois law, the Board was then required to hold a hearing on the dismissal. At the hearing the Board charged that numrous statements in the letter were false and that the publication of the statements unjustifiably impugned the "motives, honesty, integrity, truthfulness, responsibility and competence" of both the Board and the school administration. The Board also charged that the false statements damaged the professional reputations of its members and of the school administrators, would be disruptive of faculty discipline, and would tend to foment "controversy, conflict and dissension" among teachers, administrators, the Board of Education, and the residents of the district. Testimony was introduced from a variety of witnesses on the truth or falsity of the particular statements in the letter with which the Board took issue. The Board found the statements to be false as charged. No evidence was introduced at any point in the proceedings as to the effect of the publication of the letter on the community as a whole or on the administration of the school system in particular, and no specific findings along these lines were made.

The Illinois courts reviewed the proceedings solely to determine whether the Board's findings were supported by substantial evidence and whether, on the facts as found, the Board could reasonably conclude that appellant's publication of the letter was "detrimental to the best interests of the schools." Pickering's claim that his letter was protected by the First Amendment was rejected on the ground that his acceptance of a teaching position in the public schools obliged him to refrain from making statements about the operation of the schools "which in the absence of such position he would have an undoubted right to engage in." It is not altogether clear whether the Illinois Supreme Court held that the First Amendment had no applicability to appellant's dismissal for writing the letter in question or whether it determined that the particular statements made in the letter were not entitled to First Amendment protection. In any event, it clearly rejected Pickering's claim that, on the facts of this case, he could not constitutionally be dismissed from his teaching position.

II.

To the extent that the Illinois Supreme Court's opinion may be read to suggest that teachers may constitutionally be compelled to relinquish the First Amendment rights they would otherwise enjoy as citizens to comment on matters of public interest in connection with the operation of the public schools in which they work, it proceeds on a premise that has been unequivocally rejected in numerous prior decisions of this Court. *E.g., Wieman* v. *Updegraff,* 344 U.S. 183 (1952); *Shelton* v. *Tucker,* 364 U.S. 479 (1960); *Keyishian* v. *Board of Regents,* 385 U.S. 589 (1967). "[T]he theory that public employment which may be denied altogether may be subjected to any conditions, regardless of how unreasonable, has been uniformly rejected." *Keyishian* v. *Board of Regents, supra,* at 605-606. At the same time it cannot be gainsaid that the State has interests as an employer in regulating the speech of its employees that differ significantly from those it possesses in connection with regulation of the speech of the citizenry in general. The problem in any case is to arrive at a balance between the interests of the teacher, as a citizen, in commenting upon matters of public concern and the interest of the State, as an employer, in promoting the efficiency of the public services it performs through its employees.

III.

The Board contends that "the teacher by virtue of his public employment has a duty of loyalty to support his superiors in attaining the generally accepted goals of education and that, if he must speak out publicly, he should do so factually and accurately, commensurate with his education and experience." Appellant, on the other hand, argues that the test applicable to defamatory statements directed against public officials by persons having no occupational relationship with them, namely, that statements to be legally actionable must be made "with knowledge that [they were] . . . false or with reckless disregard of whether [they were] . . . false or not," *New York Times Co.* v. *Sullivan,* 376 U.S. 254, 280 (1964), should also be applied to public statements made by teachers. Because of the enormous variety of fact situations in which critical statements by teachers and other public employees may be thought by their superiors, against whom the statements are directed, to furnish grounds for dismissal, we do not deem it either appropriate or feasible to attempt to lay down a general standard against which all such statements may be judged. However, in the course of evaluating the conflicting claims of First Amendment protection and the need for orderly school administration in the context of this case, we shall indicate some of the general lines along which an analysis of the controlling interests should run.

An examination of the statements in appellant's letter objected to by the Board[2] reveals that they, like the letter as a whole, consist essentially of criticism of the Board's allocation of school funds between educational and athletic programs, and of both the Board's and the superintendent's methods of informing, or preventing the informing of, the district's taxpayers of the real reasons why additional tax revenues were being sought for the schools. The statements are in no way directed towards any person with whom appellant would normally be in contact in the course of his daily work as a teacher. Thus no question of maintaining either discipline by immediate superiors or harmony among coworkers is presented here. Appellant's employment relationships with the Board and, to a somewhat lesser extent, with the superintendent are not the kind of close working relationships for which it can persuasively be claimed that personal loyalty and confidence are necessary to their proper functioning. Accordingly, to the extent that the Board's position here can be taken to suggest that even comments on matters of public concern that are substantially correct, such as statements (1)-(4) of appellant's letter, see Appendix, *infra*, may furnish grounds for dismissal if they are sufficiently critical in tone, we unequivocally reject it.[3]

We next consider the statements in appellant's letter which we agree to be false. The Board's original charges included allegations that the publication of the letter damaged the professional reputations of the Board and the superintendent and would foment controversy and conflict among the Board, teachers, administrators, and the residents of the district. However, no evidence to support these allegations was introduced at the hearing. So far as the record reveals, Pickering's letter was greeted by everyone but its main target, the Board, with massive apathy and total disbelief. The Board must, therefore, have decided, perhaps by analogy with the law of libel, that the statements were *per se* harmful to the operation of the schools.

However, the only way in which the Board could conclude, absent any evidence of the actual effect of the letter, that the statements contained therein were *per se* detrimental to the interest of the schools was to equate the Board members' own interests with that of the schools. Certainly an accusation that too much money is being spent on athletics by the administrators of the school system (which is precisely the import of that portion of appellant's letter containing the statements that we have found to be false, see Appendix, *infra*) cannot reasonably be regarded as *per se* detrimental to the district's schools. Such an accusation reflects rather a difference of opinion between Pickering and the Board as to the preferable manner of operating the school system, a difference of opinion that clearly concerns an issue of general public interest.

In addition, the fact that particular illustrations of the Board's claimed undesirable emphasis on athletic programs are false would not normally have any necessary impact on the actual operation of the schools, beyond its tendency to anger the Board. For example, Pickering's letter was written after the defeat at the polls of the second proposed tax increase. It could, therefore, have had no effect on the ability of the school district to raise necessary revenue, since there was no showing that there was any proposal to increase taxes pending when the letter was written.

More importantly, the question whether a school system requires additional funds is a matter of legitimate public concern on which the judgment of the school administration, including the School Board, cannot, in a society that leaves such questions to popular vote, be taken as conclusive. On such a question free and open debate is vital to informed decision-making by the electorate. Teachers are, as a class, the members of a community most likely to have informed and definite opinions as to how funds allotted to the operation of the schools should be spent. Accordingly, it is essential that they be able to speak out freely on such questions without fear of retaliatory dismissal.

In addition, the amounts expended on athletics which Pickering reported erroneously were matters of public record on which his position as a teacher in the district did not qualify him to speak with any greater authority than any other taxpayer. The Board could easily have rebutted appellant's errors by publishing the accurate figures itself, either via a letter to the same newspaper or otherwise. We are thus not presented with a situation in which a teacher has carelessly made false statements about matters so closely related to the day-to-day operations of the schools that any harmful impact on the public would be difficult to counter because of the teacher's presumed greater access to the real facts. Accordingly, we have no occasion to consider at this time whether under such circumstances a school board could reasonably require that a teacher make substantial efforts to verify the accuracy of his charges before publishing them.[4]

What we do have before us is a case in which a teacher has made erroneous public statements upon issues then currently the subject of public attention, which are critical of his ultimate employer but which are neither shown nor can be presumed to have in any way either impeded the teacher's proper performance of his daily duties in the classroom[5] or to have interfered with the regular operation of the schools generally. In these circumstances we conclude that the interest of the school administration in limiting teachers' opportunities to contribute to public debate is not significantly greater than its interest in limiting a similar contribution by any member of the general public.

IV.

The public interest in having free and unhindered debate on matters of public importance—the core value of the Free Speech Clause of the First Amendment—is so great that it has been held that a State cannot authorize the recovery of damages by a public official for defamatory statements directed at him except when such statements are shown to have been made either with knowledge of their falsity or with reckless disregard for their truth or falsity. *New York Times Co.* v. *Sullivan*, 376 U.S. 254 (1964); *St. Amant* v. *Thompson*, 390 U.S. 727 (1968). Compare *Linn* v. *United Plant Guard Workers*, 383 U.S. 53 (1966). The same test has been applied to suits for invasion of privacy based on false statements where a "matter of public interest" is involved. *Time, Inc.* v. *Hill*, 385 U.S. 374 (1967). It is therefore perfectly clear that, were appellant a member of the general public, the State's power to afford the appellee Board of Education or its members any legal right to sue him for writing the letter at issue here would be limited by the requirement that the letter be judged by the standard laid down in *New York Times*.

This court has also indicated, in more general terms, that statements by public officials on matters of public concern must be accorded First Amendment protection despite the fact that the statements are directed at their nominal superiors. *Garrison* v. *Louisiana*, 379 U.S. 64 (1964); *Wood* v. *Georgia*, 370 U.S. 375 (1962). In *Garrison*, the *New York Times* test was specifically applied to a case involving a criminal defamation conviction stemming from statements made by a district attorney about the judges before whom he regularly appeared.

While criminal sanctions and damage awards have a somewhat different impact on the exercise of the right to freedom of speech from dismissal from employment, it is apparent that the threat of dismissal from public employment is nonetheless a potent means of inhibiting speech. We have already noted our disinclination to make an across-the-board equation of dismissal from public employment for remarks critical of superiors with awarding damages in a libel suit by a public official for similar criticism. However, in a case such as the present one, in which the fact of employment is only tangentially and insubstantially involved in the subject matter of the public communication made by a teacher, we conclude that it is necessary to regard the teacher as the member of the general public he seeks to be.

In sum, we hold that, in a case such as this, absent proof of false statements knowingly or recklessly made by him,[6] a teacher's exercise of his right to speak on issues of public importance may not furnish the basis for his dismissal from public employment. Since no such showing has been made in this case regarding appellant's letter, see Appendix *infra*, his dismissal for writing it cannot be upheld and the judgment of the Illinois Supreme Court must, accordingly, be reversed and the case remanded for further proceedings not inconsistent with this opinion.

It is so ordered.

NOTES

1. Appellant also challenged the statutory standard on which the Board based his dismissal as vague and overbroad. See *Keyishian* v. *Board of Regents*, 385 U.S. 589 (1967); *NAACP* v. *Button*, 371 U.S. 415 (1963); *Shelton* v. *Tucker*, 364 U.S. 479 (1960). Because of our disposition of this case we do not reach appellant's challenge to the statute on its face.

2. We have set out in the Appendix our detailed analysis of the specific statements in appellant's letter which the Board found to be false, together with our reasons for concluding that several of the statements were, contrary to the findings of the Board, substantially correct.

3. It is possible to conceive of some positions in public employment in which the need for confidentiality is so great that even completely correct public statements might furnish a permissible ground for dismissal. Likewise, positions in public employment in which the relationship between superior and subordinate is of such a personal and intimate nature that certain forms of public criticism of the superior by the subordinate would seriously undermine the effectiveness of the working relationship between them can also be imagined. We intimate no views as to how we would resolve any specific instances of such situations, but merely note that significantly different considerations would be involved in such cases.

4. There is likewise no occasion furnished by this case for consideration of the extent to which teachers can be required by narrowly drawn grievance procedures to submit complaints about the operation of the schools to their superiors for action thereon prior to bringing the complaints before the public.

5. We also note that this case does not present a situation in which a teacher's public statements are so without foundation as to call into question his fitness to perform his duties in the classroom. In such a case, of course, the statements would merely be evidence of the teacher's general competence, or lack thereof, and not an independent basis for dismissal.

6. Because we conclude that appellant's statements were not knowingly or recklessly false, we have no occasion to pass upon the additional question whether a statement that was knowingly or recklessly false would, if it were neither shown nor could reasonably be presumed to have had any harmful effects, still be protected by the First Amendment. See also n. 5, *supra*.

T HE United States Court of Appeals, District of Columbia Circuit, concludes that the dismissal of an instructor in the Air Force Language School at Lackland Air Force Base, Texas, who had been warned against discussing controversial subjects in his basic English class for foreign military officers and who subsequently made statements in his classes about the Viet Nam War and discrimination against Jews in the United States, did not violate his First Amendment rights. In deciding against the instructor the Court compared the facts of *Pickering* [in which the U.S. Supreme Court gave constitutional protection to teacher's speech] and the facts of this case: "[W]e note that the public school teacher in *Pickering* was not fired for what he said *in* class, but for writing a letter to a newspaper critical of the policies espoused by the school board and school superintendent in the allocation of school funds as between different educational programs. The efficiency with which Pickering taught Geography or Algebra to the pupils immediately in front of him was not affected by his extracurricular expressions. The Air Force's case against appellant largely rests, however, upon the fact that he was supposed to be giving foreign officers a quick training in basic English, and that efficient utilization of the short time involved was of critical importance. . . . On the record before us, we must assume that appellant was fired for what he said *within* the classroom to foreign officers who were supposed to be learning how to cope with an English-speaking dentist or garage repairman, and not for airing his views outside the classroom to anyone who would listen."

Goldwasser v. *Brown*, 417 F. 2d 1169 (1969)

McGOWAN, Circuit Judge:

This federal employee discharge case was heard by the District Court on cross-motions for summary judgment, and this appeal is from a decision adverse to the employee. The evidentiary record before the court was the administrative record compiled in the proceedings before the Civil Service Commission following upon the appeal to that agency of appellant's discharge by the Air Force.[1] A number of procedural errors are asserted as rendering the Commission's action defective. In addition, it is said that to terminate appellant's employment for the reason given is to trench upon rights protected by the Constitution, especially the First Amendment. We find none of these contentions to be compelling, and we affirm the District Court.

I.

Appellant was a civilian employee of the Air Force who served as a language instructor in the Air Force Language School at Lackland Air Force Base, Texas. His job was to teach basic English to foreign military officers in this country as guests of the U.S. Government. The charge against him was that, in the face of prior warnings that discussion of controversial subjects (*i.e.*, religion, politics, race) during the class hours was contrary to Air Force policy, he made such forbidden statements on two separate occasions to his classes. One was to the effect that those who burn themselves to death as a protest against the Viet Nam War are the true heroes, and he wished he had the courage to do it himself. The other was that Jews are discriminated against in America, and that he had felt such discrimination throughout his life, including his service at the Language School.

The chief of the Language School regarded this conduct on the part of appellant, after having been repeatedly warned not to engage in it, as prejudicial to the interests of the United States Government, and this was the stated ground in the notice of discharge given to appellant. The ultimate issue resides in the statutory formulation that "[N]o person in the classified civil service of the United States shall be removed or suspended * * * except for such cause as will promote the efficiency of such service * * *." 5 U.S.C. §652 (a) (now 5 U.S.C.§ 7501, recodified with minor variations in wording).

A hearing on appellant's appeal to the Civil Service Commission was held by an Appeals Examiner of the Dallas Regional Office. The position taken by appellant was that he had not made the two statements attributed to him and that he was, therefore, innocent of the charges against him. He represented, according to the Appeals Examiner, that he could not have made the statements because (1) his personal views on Viet Nam did not differ from those of the U.S. Government, (2) he had not experienced racial discrimination, and (3) the alleged statements were alien to any possible discussion of the lesson plan for the days in question.[2]

The record before the Appeals Examiner included affidavits from Air Force personnel, a report by a Civil Service Commission investigator, and oral testimony by appellant and other witnesses on his behalf. The Appeals Examiner concluded that the evidence supported the charges against appellant and that he had in fact made the statements in question after having been warned to refrain from such conduct.

The Commission's Board of Appeals and Review sustained this finding as against a challenge that it was contrary to the weight of the evidence, and it went on to find that the Air Force had not been "arbitrary, capricious, or unreasonable, and that [appellant's discharge] was for such cause as will promote the efficiency of the service." The Commission adopted the decision of its Board of Appeals and Review and denied appellant's request for reopening and reconsideration.

II.

We turn first to appellant's claims of procedural inadequacies in the Commission proceedings. The principal one of these is that a fair hearing was denied appellant because the Air Force failed to produce certain witnesses pursuant to appellant's request. These witnesses were said to be under the Air Force's control and direction, and that the failure to produce them at the hearing was a conscious effort to impede appellant's presentation of his defense.

The witnesses in question were the foreign officers in the classes to which appellant allegedly made the offending statements. The record shows that on January 14, 1966, just after the Language School gave appellant preliminary written notice of its proposed dismissal action and of his opportunity to answer the charges upon which such dismissal would be based,

appellant's retained counsel responded in a letter denying the charges and purporting to give notice that, if the Air Force persisted in appellant's removal, appellant would require the personal presence of the foreign students at the Commission hearing and that he looked to the Air Force to assure that presence. After the final notice of dismissal was forthcoming a few days later, appellant's counsel wrote again, identifying some additional foreign students and stating the same expectation as to their presence. The concern of these letters, however, was that the students might finish their visits and depart before the hearing, and it appeared to be counsel's purpose that he be notified of such departure in time for him to arrange to take depositions at appellant's expense.

The Air Force, on February 7, 1966, wrote appellant's counsel that the foreign students were in the country on invitational travel orders. As such, they were said to be in effect "guests of the United States Government" and not under its military jurisdiction; accordingly, the Air Force was "in no position to take any action on your request" that the students be produced at the hearing. The letter went on as follows:

The students will be here until May and it is entirely discretionary with them as to whether they would make statements, appear as witnesses or take any part in the matter in question. You are at liberty, however, to communicate with them directly should you so desire. The appropriate method would be to address your communication to the Liaison Officer or Senior Officer of the respective national group. For the Iranian students the Liaison Officer is Captain Mehdi Mirhosseini, 118 Surfrider, San Antonio, Texas; for the Greek students, the Senior Officer is Captain John Triantfillos, Greece - AF, CHR # 2, Lackland AFB Tex; and the Senior Officer for the Japanese students is Major Junkichi Imata, Japan - AF, CMR # 2, Lackland AFB Tex. They will in turn relay your request to the students in question and will, I am sure, advise you of what action you may expect from them.

Instead of approaching the students directly, however, appellant's counsel appeared to conclude that, with the appeal to the Commission filed, he would prefer to have the Commission do so. On March 4, 1966, he wrote the Appeals Examiner requesting that the Commission's investigator interview the students. The investigator was instructed to do so, and the result of his efforts in this regard is described in the portion of his report set forth in the margin.[3]

At the hearing, appellant objected to the failure of the Air Force to have the students present as witnesses. The Appeals Examiner pointed out that appellant had been notified that the Commission had no subpoena power and that it was appellant's responsibility to arrange for the appearance of witnesses. He directed that the hearing proceed. Appellant himself testified as to conversations he had had with some of the students in which they stated that they did not remember his having made the remarks in question. On cross-examination, appellant said he had not asked any of the students for written statements "since he believed they would appear to testify on his behalf at the time of the hearing, but that he had not personally asked the students to appear at the time of the Commission's hearing since he understood from his Attorney that he did not have access to these individuals." The Air Force representative at the hearing stated that the Air Force had not at any time interviewed the students on this subject, and had no information as to their recollections.

The Appeals Examiner saw no procedural error in all this. He found as a fact that the students were not Air Force employees; that the Air Force had offered appellant full access to them; that appellant had talked to some of the students but he had not asked them to give statements or testify; and that the Air Force had not interviewed the students itself. To the Commission's Board of Appeals and Review, appellant asserted that there had been a deliberate concealment of evidence obtained by the Air Force in interviews with the students. The Board concluded that the record supported the Examiner's findings of fact to the contrary; and that there was, on this record and taking due account of the peculiar status of the foreign officer students, no failure by the Air Force to produce witnesses within its control amounting to a deprivation of due process of law.

We cannot say that the Commission erred in this view of the matter. The Commission regulations in being at the time of the hearing provided that, the Commission being without subpoena power, each side would arrange for the appearance of its witnesses. 5 C.F.R. § 772.305 (c). It is true, of course, that there can be circumstances where the employing agency is so uncooperative and indeed aggressively hostile in responding to efforts to secure testimony from persons under its control as to make the proceeding unacceptably unfair. *See* Williams v. Zuckert, 371 U.S. 531, 83 S. Ct. 403, 9 L. Ed. 2d 486, rehearing granted and case remanded for further proceedings, 372 U.S. 765, 83 S. Ct. 1102, 10 L. Ed. 2d 136 (1963). But this record is far from showing such conduct as this. The Examiner found, rather, that the Air Force left the foreign students free to do as they wished about testifying at the hearing, and gave appellant full and complete access to them. Appellant failed to pursue that access systematically or effectively, and is in no position, whatever the precise relationship of the foreign students to the Air Force may have been, to claim unfairness amounting to a breach of the Constitution. *Cf.*

Bishop v. McKee, 400 F. 2d 87 (10th Cir. 1968); Brown v. Zuckert, 349 F. 2d 461 (7th Cir. 1965), cert. denied, 382 U.S. 998, 86 S. Ct. 588, 15 L. Ed. 2d 486 (1966); and McTiernan v. Gronouski, 337 F. 2d 31 (2d Cir. 1964).

As a second procedural defect, appellant now urges that it was improper for the Air Force to present its testimony at the hearing entirely by affidavit. The Commission's regulations, however, expressly provided for this manner of proceeding, 5 C.F.R. § 772.304 (b), and these do not appear to have been beyond the contemplation of the underlying statute. 5 U.S.C. § 7501. In any event, any concern appellant might have entertained on this score could have been dissipated by his own request that the affiants be produced for cross-examination—a privilege clearly available to him as a matter of law. 5 C.F.R. § 772.305 (c). Having failed to manifest that concern at the hearing, we are not disposed to make its present assertion the occasion for overturning the Commission proceeding. Appellant was not denied a procedural right to which he was entitled. He rather must be taken to have decided, in the light of the nature of the affidavits and their compatibility with the report of the investigator, that it was not necessary to exercise it.

A third claim—made for the first time on this appeal—is that the Commission failed to afford appellant due process of law in that the Appeals Examiner had to reach his decision without the benefit of any clearly articulated standard for weighing the proof. We think that this contention comes far too late to warrant its being made the occasion for *judicial* invalidation of *administrative* proceedings. The issue is one peculiarly appropriate for bringing to the attention of the administrative tribunal in the first instance in order that it may have the opportunity to consider, and to dispel if necessary, any infirmities which cause litigants before it to doubt the essential fairness of the hearing.

In any event, we are not convinced that appellant suffered any deprivation of constitutional proportions in this particular. The Appeals Examiner appears to have treated the case as one involving evidence looking in different directions, and that his job was to decide which side had made the more persuasive showing on the question of whether appellant had made the remarks in issue or whether he had not. The Board of Appeals and Review regarded this as the essential task placed upon the Examiner, and it thought the record amply supported the result he reached. Whatever the words used, or which might be used, in describing this process, appellant here received essentially what he was entitled to, namely, a chance to put his version of the facts before the Commission in competition with that supplied by the Air Force and to have the Commission decide whether the Air Force could fairly be taken to have supported its charges.[4]

Appellant's final claim of procedural injury is derived from an Air Force regulation which provided that any charges more than three years old should not be considered in connection with any removal of an employee from service. Appellant points out that the letter first informing him of the proposed removal referred to earlier warnings,[5] two of which fell outside the three year limit. Despite that, says appellant, the Appeals Examiner referred to these two outlawed incidents, and must, therefore, have had them in mind, to appellant's prejudice, in making his decision.

Whatever weight the Appeals Examiner may have given these items, however, the Board of Appeals and Review was explicit in its statement that, in order to avoid any question under the regulation, it "had dismissed them from consideration in arriving at its decision;" and we think this is adequate to preclude the nullification of the Commission proceedings for any fear of prejudicial error on this score. Moreover, we share the Board's expressed doubt that there was any error on the part of the Appeals Examiner, prejudicial or otherwise. The reference to the earlier warnings was not to make them occasions for dismissal, but to show that appellant was not unaware of the Air Force's policy against the injection into classroom teaching of unrelated controversial subjects. The purpose of the regulation is to prevent present discharge for past conduct of a proscribed vintage. Appellant's discharge was not for what he had done more than three years back, but because he was still doing the same thing despite the prior history of notice and warning.

III.

In his judicial challenge to the propriety of his dismissal, appellant invokes substantive protections of the Constitution as well. He asserts that, even if it be assumed that he made the classroom statements attributed to him and under the circumstances alleged, he cannot be dismissed for that reason without infringement of his First Amendment right of free speech, and his Fifth Amendment right not to be subjected to a code of conduct which is unacceptably vague.

The latter contention is not one meriting detailed treatment in view of the concessions made by appellant at the administrative level. He did not there suggest that he was surprised by the view taken of his alleged conduct, or that he was confused as to what the Air Force standards of appropriate classroom conduct were. His denials that he said the things charged were repeatedly coupled with volunteered opinions that such conduct would, if it had occurred, have been improper. We are, thus, not impressed with his current claim of a constitutional deprivation which is rooted in the concept of the impenetrable mistiness of a governmental policy or prohibition.

The First Amendment issue deserves more sustained examination. Appellant and appellees join in identifying Pickering v. Board of Education, 391 U.S. 563, 88 S. Ct. 1731, 20 L. Ed. 2d 811 (1968), as the most relevant authority. Appellant urges that the view taken there by the Supreme Court of the right of a teacher to speak his mind without forfeiting his job has full and complete application here. The Government distinguishes Pickering on its facts, but recognizes the significance for this case of the principle there stated. That principle is stated in essence to be that the public employer's interest in the efficient despatch of its business by no means invariably overrides the employee's interest in saying what he thinks. Where there is tension between the two, accommodation must be sought in the balancing process which not infrequently characterizes the task of constitutional interpretation.

The parties are, thus, in agreement upon the test to be applied but not upon its result. In Pickering the Supreme Court defined the clashing interests with some particularity. It recognized that public employment may properly encompass limitations upon speech that would not survive constitutional scrutiny if directed against a private citizen, although there is certainly no easy leap from this to the proposition that a public employee necessarily assumes monastic vows of silence when he looks to the taxpayer for his salary. The Government's interest as an employer is in heightening the level of the public services it renders by assuring the efficiency of its employees in the performance of their tasks; and efficiency comprehends the maintenance of discipline, the prevalence of harmony among co-workers, and the elimination of conduct which may reasonably be thought to have "impeded" the proper performance by a teacher of "his daily duties in the classroom." Conversely, the free speech interest of the teacher is to have his say on any and every thing about which he has feelings, provided there is no significant likelihood of impairment of his efficiency.

What are the weights to be placed in the scale in the case at hand? Preliminarily we note that the public school teacher in Pickering was not fired for what he said in class, but for writing a letter to a newspaper critical of the policies espoused by the School Board and School Superintendent in the allocation of school funds as between different educational programs. The efficiency with which Pickering taught geography or algebra to the pupils immediately in front of him was not affected by his extracurricular expressions.

The Air Force's case against appellant largely rests, however, upon the fact that he was supposed to be giving foreign officers a quick training in basic English, and that efficient utilization of the short time involved was of critical importance. Furthermore, appellant was not teaching the foreign officers current events, political science, sociology, or international relations. This is plainly evident from the record's disclosure that the Lesson Plan appellant was supposed to follow at the times in question called for language instruction on the subjects "At the Dentist" and "How to Test a Used Car." Appellant's observations on Viet Nam and anti-Semitism would appear to have, at best, minimal relevance to the immediate classroom objectives.

We would also be blinking reality if we did not recognize that a class of foreign military officers at an Air Force installation on invitational orders presents special problems affecting the national interest in harmonious international relations. We are certainly not equipped to second-guess the agency judgment that the instructional goals of the Air Force program would be jeopardized by the teacher's volunteering his views on subjects of potential explosiveness in a multicultural group.

On the record before us, we must assume that appellant was fired for what he said *within* the classroom to foreign officers who were supposed to be learning how to cope with an English-speaking dentist or garage repairman, and not for airing his views outside the classroom to anyone who would listen. There is nothing to suggest that appellant was required to keep his opinions to himself at all times or under all circumstances, but only in the immediate context of his highly specialized teaching assignment—and we stress the uniqueness of appellant's teaching function in our disposition of this point. In view of that uniqueness, we cannot say that any of the interests underlying the First Amendment were served by appellant's insistence upon intruding his personal views into the classroom, or that his employer was disabled by those interests from imposing and enforcing the very limited restriction emerging from this record. Much greater limitations upon the civil freedoms of public employees generally have heretofore been sustained. *See* United Public Workers v. Mitchell, 330 U.S. 75, 67 S.Ct. 556, 91 L.Ed. 754 (1947).

Affirmed.

NOTES

1. We have adverted before to the need for legislative reexamination of the situation which presently obtains with respect to judicial review of Civil Service Commission determinations. There appears to be no reason why two courts should be required to review, by reference solely to the administrative record, the Commission's determinations. *See* Connelly v. Nitze, 130 U.S. App. D.C. 351, 401 F.2d 416, 417 n. 1 (1968).

2. In the written argument submitted on appellant's behalf to the Appeals Examiner, this statement appeared: We will have to concede, initially that, just as a matter of good common horse sense, instructors in his position teaching foreign students should do their utmost to avoid controversial subjects, and there is no question but that he had been counseled to avoid controversial subjects. For instance, it is simply a matter of good common horse sense for Mr. Goldwasser, with his Yiddish background, to avoid engaging in head-on arguments with Arab students over the Arab-Israel problem.

Appellant's essential position throughout the Commission proceedings was that the Air Force was out to get him because he had resisted an overseas assignment—an assignment which was cancelled after appellant's Congressman had intervened on his behalf. Thus, appellant attacked the charges against him as fabrications masking the true reason for discharge, and not as improper grounds for discharge if true.

3. Briefing instructions indicated the Investigator should obtain affidavits from ten former students of the Appellant. Five of these students were from Iran, four from Greece and one from Japan. Foreign students at the Air Force Language School, Lackland Air Force Base, are guests of the U.S. Government and are not under the military jurisdiction of the U.S. Air Force. Each national group is represented by a Liaison Officer or a Senior Officer. A meeting was held with the Liaison Officer from Iran and the Senior Officers from Greece and Japan. The purpose of this investigation was explained to them and they were told that the only persons available to substantiate the contentions of the Appellant were the students under their jurisdiction, and that this information could be vital in making a decision on this case. They were told that any testimony volunteered would be appreciated, whether it be favorable or unfavorable to the Appellant, and that their respective students would not ever be subject to subpoena to be a witness in a court.

The Liaison Officer from Iran and the Senior Officer from Greece indicated they were definitely not in favor of the proposal. They indicated that they had been instructed not to get involved in United States' matters. They said they felt that this was a local matter which should be handled by the Language School. They did agree that they would contact the students, whose names were furnished by the Appellant, explain the matter to them and see if any of them desired to testify. They both reported back that each of their students, whose names were furnished, were contacted and that none of these desired to give * * * testimony or an affidavit.

Major Junkichi Imata, the Senior Officer from Japan, was one of the Appellant's former students, whose name was listed as having joined the class on December 2, 1965. Major Imata declined to take an oath or execute an affidavit. He merely stated that while he was in Appellant's class he had no recollection of the Appellant making any remarks concerning discrimination against Jews or any discussion concerning people who commit suicide by burning themselves. He stated that he was not familiar with the word "immolation."

4. Appellant argues in this court that, even if the requisite degree of procedural due process be deemed to have obtained in the conduct of the Commission proceeding, the finding that appellant made the statements in question

does not justify any conclusion that his removal will, in the statutory phrase, "promote the efficiency" of the classified civil service. 5 U.S.C. § 7501. He asserts that the record is deficient in showing any adverse impact of appellant's conduct upon the interests of his employer. It is perhaps the case that neither the Appeals Examiner nor the Board of Appeals and Review addressed themselves in detail to this matter, but this appears to be due to the fact that appellant did not regard this as an issue at the hearing. His attorney's first letter in response to the proposed dismissal said that appellant emphatically claimed to be innocent of having made the alleged remarks which were characterized "as completely incongruous to any discussion" of the "lesson plans in both of these classes." Appellant made the same characterization in his testimony at the hearing. *See* Note 2 *supra*. His defense was that he had not said the things charged, not that they were harmless or that he was not on adequate notice of a policy against such remarks.

To the extent appellant urges upon us that we, in the exercise of judicial review, should set aside the Commission's action for want of sufficient proof, we look only to see "whether there is evidence of substance in [the] record which supports the Commission's view of the matter." Dabney v. Freeman, 123 U.S. App. D.C. 166, 358 F. 2d 533 (1965). We find such evidence here.

5. "You had been warned on numerous occasions, specifically on or about 6 December 1960, 14 March 1961, 17 November 1963 and 20 September 1964 that controversial subjects must not be discussed with foreign students in the classroom. Despite this you made the following statements to foreign students."

A California Court of Appeals decides against a junior college teacher who had been dismissed for evident unfitness for service and immoral conduct after he had, among other things, torn from the classroom wall the defective loud speaker and told his students that the bell system sounded like a worn out "phonograph in a whorehouse" and the walls of the school looked as though someone had "peed on them and then smeared them with baby crap." In deciding against the teacher, who had also "advised his philosophy class that the district superintendent could be a good superintendent 'but he spends too much time * * * (at this point in the statement he stepped over to the wall and simulated licking the wall with his tongue in an up and down manner and then continued speaking) * * * licking up the Board,'" the Court said: "Defendant [the teacher] . . . wraps himself in the mantle of free speech and the right to dissent and to differ with and criticize the superintendent of schools. . . . It cannot be questioned that the defendant had a right as a teacher and a citizen to differ with, to dissent from, and to criticize the superintendent. However, the means of expression used puts him far outside the protection of the First Amendment." "While humor is an important part of a stimulating and entertaining presentation," said the Court, "a coeducational classroom does not appear to be the place for the barracks type of language used by this defendant."

Palo Verde Unified Sch. Dist. of Riverside Co. v. *Hensey,* 88 Cal. Rptr. 570 (1970)

GARDNER, Presiding Justice.

This is an appeal from a judgment permitting plaintiff to dismiss defendant and to terminate his employment as a permanent teacher in the Palo Verde Unified School District where he taught on a junior college level. The action was brought pursuant to sections 13412 and 13403 of the Education Code charging evident unfitness for service and immoral conduct.

Under well established rules of appellate review, there was substantial evidence to sustain the following findings by the trial court:

(1) That during a class session in the presence of students, defendant removed from its fixture a loud speaker which was an integral part of the fire alarm and bell system and stated to the president of the college that he would remove it again if it were replaced as well as stating to him that he had removed a similar facility from another of the classrooms.

(2) That the defendant stated the bell system of the college "sounded like a worn out phonograph in a whorehouse" and made numerous references during the semester to "whore" and "whorehouses" and, following a reprimand for this conduct, submitted to the president of the college a thesis on the justification of his use of these terms in his class.

(3) That he directed himself to several Mexican-American students seated in the rear of the classroom and stated, "I understand you have been to San Luis; I understand they have super-syphilis there, and you know that they don't have drugs to cure that. Be careful when you're there." This statement was made in a tone loud enough to be heard by all of the students in the class, both male and female.

(4) That the defendant advised his philosophy class that the district superintendent could be a good superintendent "but he spends too much time * * * (at this point in the statement he stepped over to the wall and simulated licking the wall with his tongue in an up and down manner and then continued speaking) * * * licking up the Board."

(5) That the defendant derogatorily referred to the walls of the high school and on one occasion he referred to them as looking as though "someone had peed on them and then smeared them with baby crap."

(6) The trial court further found that the sounds emanating from the fire alarm and bell system were annoying to some of the students and some of the teachers during the period of time the system was being adjusted and utilized as signifying commencement and termination of classes throughout the junior college classroom building which was new. However, the trial court found that it was not true that said sounds emanating from the fire alarm and bell system were such as to justify the defendant's actions in tearing the loud speaker out.

From these facts the trial court determined that the charges of evident unfitness for service and immoral conduct were true and constituted sufficient grounds for dismissal.

As there is substantial evidence to support the trial court's findings of these facts, we are bound to accept them in this review. (Board of Trustees v. Porini, 263 Cal. App. 2d 784, 70 Cal. Rptr. 73.)

However, the defendant contends that, conceding the validity of the finding of the trial court as to the above probative facts, nevertheless, its finding that the charges of evident unfitness for service and immoral conduct were true is erroneous as a matter of law.

As a general background, we recognize the guidelines as to the role of the teacher as established by the Supreme Court in the case of Board of Education of City of Los Angeles v. Swan, 41 Cal. 2d 546, 261 P. 2d 261, cert. den. 347 U.S. 937, 74 S. Ct. 627, 98 L. Ed. 1087, wherein at pp. 552-554, 261 P. 2d at p. 265, the court stated:

"A teacher * * * in the public school system is regarded by the public and pupils in the light of an exemplar, whose words and actions are likely to be followed by the children coming under her care and protection. (Citation.) In this connection the following language used in Johnson v. Taft School Dist., 19 Cal. App. 2d 405, at page 408, 65 P. 2d 912, is pertinent: 'A board of education is entrusted with the conduct of the schools under its jurisdiction, their standards of education, and the moral, mental, and physical welfare of the pupils during school hours. An important part of the education of any child is the instilling of a proper respect for authority and obedience to necessary discipline. Lessons are learned from example as well as from precept. The example of a teacher who is continually insubordinate and who refuses to recognize constituted authority may seriously affect the discipline in a school, impair its efficiency, and teach children lessons they should not learn. Such conduct may unfit a teacher for service in a school even though her other qualifications may be sufficient. "Book learning" is only a phase of the important lessons a child should learn in a school.'

"In Goldsmith v. Board of Education, supra, 66 Cal. App. 157, 225 P. 783, it was held that a teacher advocating before his class the election of a particular candidate for the office of county superintendent of schools was guilty of 'unprofessional conduct.' The fact that the term 'unprofessional conduct' is not defined by statute authorizing the dismissal of a teacher (Ed. Code, § 13521) does not render it void for uncertainty. As was said in the Goldsmith case at page 168, 225 P. 783: '* * * the calling [of a teacher] is so intimate, its duties so delicate, the things in which a teacher might prove unworthy or would fail are so numerous that they are incapable of enumeration in any legislative enactment * * * the teacher is entrusted with the custody of children and their high preparation for useful life. His habits, his speech, his good name, his cleanliness, the wisdom and propriety of his unofficial utterances, his associations, all are involved. His ability to inspire children and to govern them, his power as a teacher, and the character for which he stands are matters of major concern in a teacher's selection and retention. How can all of these things be provided for and offenses against them be particularly specified in a single statute?'"

Turning to the phrases "immoral conduct" and "evident unfitness for service," these terms as used in the Education Code are to be construed according to their common and approved usage having regard for the context in which the Legislature used them. (Education Code, § 10; 23 Cal. Jur., § 122, p. 745; see Board of Education of City of Los Angeles v. Swan, supra, 41 Cal. 2d 546, 553, 261 P. 2d 261.)

Of assistance in the interpretation of the phrase "immoral conduct" is the case of Board of Education of San Francisco Unified School District v. Weiland, 179 Cal. App. 2d 808, at p. 811, 4 Cal. Rptr. 286, which cited with approval Orloff v. Los Angeles Turf Club, 36 Cal. 2d 734, at p. 740, 227 P. 2d 449, at p. 453, wherein the Supreme Court quoted with approval the following from Words and Phrases, permanent edition, vol. 20, pps. 159-160:

"'The term "immoral" has been defined generally as that which is hostile to the welfare of the general public and contrary to good morals. Immorality has not been confined to sexual matters, but includes conduct inconsistent with rectitude, or indicative of corruption, indecency, depravity, dissoluteness; or as wilful, flagrant, or shameless conduct showing moral indifference to the opinions of respectable members of the community, and as an inconsiderate attitude toward good order and the public welfare.'" (Board of Education of San Francisco Unified School District v. Weiland, supra, p. 811, 227 P. 2d p. 453.)

In Morrison v. State Board of Education, 1 Cal. 3d

214, 82 Cal. Rptr. 175, 461 P. 2d 375, the Supreme Court adopted the *Orloff* standard of immorality for a teacher and held that immoral conduct cannot be the basis for removal of a teacher unless that conduct indicates the teacher is unfit to teach.

Insofar as the phrase "evident unfitness" is concerned, the parties refer us to dictionary definitions in which "evident" is defined in Webster's Collegiate Dictionary as "Clear to the vision and understanding," (Webster's Collegiate Dictionary, Seventh Ed. p. 288), and "unfit" as defined in the same tome at p. 968, as "not fit; not adapted to a purpose, unsuitable; incapable; incompetent; and physically or mentally unsound." The parties further refer us to a definition of the word "unfit" in California Words, Phrases and Maxims, p. 440, as in general "unfit" means "unsuitable, incompetent and not adapted for a particular use or service."

Applying the above rules, we proceed to a discussion of the various charges.

I.

THE TEARING OUT OF THE LOUD SPEAKER.

The public address system served three purposes, (1) as the announcement system for the college, (2) as a fire alarm, and (3) as a method of signalling the commencement and cessation of each class period by broadcasting an electrical tone.

The system was defective, troublesome and was eventually removed.

Whatever might be said of the defendant's conduct in this incident, we do not find it to be immoral.

The incident does, however, have a direct bearing on the issue of "evident unfitness."

While most business and professional men have had the frustrating experience of breaking in a new building or facility, and some sympathy may be engendered for the defendant's annoyance with the faulty system, this cannot excuse his removal of the loud speaker. The bell system, faulty though it was, was an integral part of the communication system of the school. In addition, it was a vital part of the fire alarm system. It served an essential purpose. Its removal by the defendant was highly improper—regardless of his annoyance. While we do not find fault with expression of displeasure with this apparatus *per se*, and are sensitive to defendant's desire to maintain the academic atmosphere of his classroom, we cannot condone the method used to express his dissatisfaction. His actions in this regard posed a potential danger to the safety of his students. Thus, we hold that this incident may be considered evidence of "evident unfitness for service."

II.

HIS REFERENCE TO THE BELL SYSTEM AS SOUNDING LIKE A WORN OUT PHONOGRAPH IN A WHOREHOUSE AND THE NUMEROUS REFERENCES TO WHORE AND WHOREHOUSES THROUGHOUT THE YEAR.

Were this an elementary school, these charges might bear more careful scrutiny. However, the defendant was teaching at a junior college level and while the use of the words may have shown bad taste and vulgarity,[1] we cannot find that these charges constitute or are evidence of immorality. Standing by themselves, they do not constitute "evident unfitness." However, the incidents could be considered by the trial judge with all of the other charges in his finding of "evident unfitness." Eventually, vulgarity, while not rising to the standards of immorality, can have a bearing on the fitness of a teacher to teach—even on a junior college level.

III.

THE INCIDENT OF THE DEFENDANT ADDRESSING HIMSELF TO THE MEXICAN-AMERICAN STUDENTS IN THE PRESENCE OF THE REST OF THE CLASS AND WARNING THEM OF SUPER-SYPHILIS IN SAN LUIS.[2]

Again, while we find this incident to be in bad taste, we can find in it no evidence of immorality.

However, again, it does bear on the trial court's finding of "evident unfitness." While there is no direct evidence of embarrassment felt by the Mexican-American students at being singled out by a charge that venereal disease was rampant in their culture, such a finding can be inferred from the record. While we do not contend that the subject matter of defendant's remarks is necessarily inappropriate in a classroom at the junior college level, so long as he chose to discuss the subject, we would hope that as a professional man he would approach it from a more mature and professional manner. Blurting it out in the class was not only humiliating and embarrassing to the Mexican-Americans, it again showed a lack of restraint and a tendency to vulgarity and bad taste which the trial court could validly consider on the subject of "evident unfitness."

IV.

THE INCIDENT OF THE GESTURE OF LICKING THE WALL WITH HIS TONGUE IN AN UP AND DOWN MANNER.

Here, we have passed the limits of bad taste and vulgarity. The defendant's contention that he was imitating a deaf mute ordering an ice cream cone was an insult to the intelligence of the trial judge. Rather, it is obviously a gesture which was intended to describe a person who would rather curry favor with his superiors than to do his duty and was specifically directed to the County Superintendent of Schools. The defendant's explanation that, in this context, he meant "face licking" was obviously not accepted by the trial court nor do we so accept it. Quite to the contrary, this expression means in common parlance licking an entirely different portion of the anatomy. It was obviously so intended by the defendant and so understood by his college age students. This obscene incident indicates both "immorality" and "evident unfitness."

Defendant attempts to bring himself within the doctrine of Los Angeles Teachers' Union v. Los Angeles City Board of Education, 71 A.C. 572, 78 Cal. Rptr. 723, 455 P. 2d 827, and Board of Trustees of Lassen Union High School Dist. v. Owens, 206 Cal. App. 2d 147, 23 Cal. Rptr. 710, and in so doing wraps himself in the mantle of free speech and the right to dissent and to differ with and criticize the superintendent of schools. Without the benefit of these cases it cannot be questioned that the defendant had a right as a teacher and a citizen to differ with, to dissent from, and to criticize the superintendent. However, the means of expression used puts him far outside the protection of the First Amendment or the above cases. In *Owens*, the teacher had written letters to a newspaper criticizing the school administration. In *Los Angeles Teachers' Union*, the teachers were trying to circulate a petition among themselves during their lunch hours. In each case the court held that the teachers' actions were constitutionally protected so long as they did not result in any disruption or impairment of discipline or the teaching process or substantially disrupt or materially interfere with school activities. In this case the activities of appellant in the presence of his students were disruptive, an impairment of the teaching process, and not an example of the responsible dissent which should be fostered in the classroom.

This incident is evidence of both "immorality" and "evident unfitness."

V.

REFERRING TO THE WALLS OF THE SCHOOL AS LOOKING AS THOUGH SOMEONE HAD PEED ON THEM AND THEN SMEARED THEM WITH BABY CRAP.

The record indicates that this was a class made up of both males and females. We assume that each of them

at that age was familiar with the words used. Again, we do not deny the defendant's right to criticize. Nevertheless, a teacher has a responsibility to respect the feelings and sensitivities of the members of his class and to conduct himself with a certain degree of rectitude. His behavior in this incident is inexcusable in the presence of his students.

His explanation that he had heard remarks made by the students describing the walls in other four letter words by which we infer that he refers to four letter words of ancient origin which describe body waste, both solid and liquid, and that he cleaned up their use of these words by his use of the words pee and crap, falls rather flat. We have no desire to become involved in the controversy between the Puritan Ethic and the Age of the Four Letter Word. We merely observe that while there may be a time and a place for everything, a classroom, even on a junior college level, is not the time or the place for the use of this language. While we do not consider the language used to be immoral, its obvious vulgarity was evidence of "evident unfitness."

The defendant points out that the students' reaction to this statement was that they thought it was funny. Of this, we have no doubt. To borrow from the language of show business, we may well assume that the tearing out of the public address system "laid them in the aisles" and the wall licking incident "brought down the house." However, while humor is an important part of a stimulating and entertaining presentation, a coeducational classroom does not appear to be the place for the barracks type of language used by this defendant.

The plaintiff was quite within its rights in its determination that the type of instructional process displayed by the defendant was improper and that it should not be forced to continue with this type of an educational process or with this teacher.

All of the incidents taken in the aggregate serve as a substantial basis for the trial court's determination that the charges of "immoral conduct" and "evident unfitness for service" were true and constituted cause for dismissal.

Judgment affirmed.

KERRIGAN and GABBERT, JJ., concur.

NOTES

1. On one occasion he referred to the public address system as sounding like a constipated elephant.
2. San Luis is a hamlet on the Mexican border.

A District Court of Appeal of Florida decides against a high school band instructor who had been dismissed for, among other things, "incompetency" and "immorality." According to the Florida Court, "There are many factors which may have a material bearing upon the competency of the instructor, among which could be his attitude toward the students, his manner of speaking to them and his general lack of proper personality conducive to a mutual understanding. The instructor's attitude and expression on moral conduct, sex questions and such, could also affect his competency. In addition, as to the immorality charge, there was evidence of unbecoming and unnecessary risqué remarks made by the petitioner in a class of mixed teenage boys and girls which we agree with the school board were of an immoral nature." The Court rather injudiciously then argued: "It may be that topless waitresses and entertainers are in vogue in certain areas of our Country and our Federal Courts may try to enjoin our State Courts from stopping the sale of lewd and obscene literature and the showing of obscene films, but we are still of the opinion that instructors in our schools should not be permitted to so risquely discuss sex problems in our teenage mixed classes as to cause embarrassment to the children or to invoke in them other feelings not incident to the courses of study being pursued."

Pyle v. *Washington County School Bd.*, 238 So. 2d 121 (1970)

JOHNSON, Chief Judge.

This matter is before this court on petition for a writ of certiorari to the Washington County School Board, Washington County, Florida.

The petition seeks to have reviewed a decision of the Washington County School Board dismissing the petitioner as an instructor in the Washington County School System.

The material allegations contained in the petition are that petitioner was employed for the 1969-70 school year as a band instructor in the Chipley High School; that complaints against petitioner began coming to the principal of the school as early as October of 1969 from parents about lack of discipline and that several students requested that they be allowed to drop band. The principal discussed these matters with petitioner and suggested changes he should make in his attitudes. Then, further complaints came to the school superintendent including remarks made by petitioner in the classroom of mixed boys and girls, relating to sex and virginity and premarital sex relations.

On February 24, 1970, the Superintendent wrote Mr. Pyle a letter, setting out in considerable detail the complaints he had heard and investigated, specifically stating in the letter that the five enumerated statements of complaint were not exclusive but indicated the current status of the overall situation.

On February 26, 1970, the Superintendent wrote a further letter to the petitioner in which he advised the petitioner of his suspension, and again asserted his reasons therefor, including some specifics of matters considered involved. This letter pointed out that in the letter of February 24, the Superintendent had given the petitioner 30 days to show significant improvement in his classroom administration but that the School Board deemed the immorality charges extremely serious circumstances (warranting the suspension). The petitioner was advised that he was entitled to a public hearing if he wanted one. Pursuant thereto, a public hearing was had on March 20, 1970, approximately 30 days after the suspension, at which the petitioner was present and represented by counsel of his own choice.

Since an official court reporter was not available, it was mutually agreed that the secretary for the Superintendent would make a transcript of the proceedings, admitting that it would not be verbatim, but would correctly state the main facts. [At this point, we point out that counsel for petitioner in his brief raises as an objection the fact that an official reporter did not transcribe the proceedings. We dispose of this point in petitioner's claim by saying that such procedure was not jurisdictional and was waived by petitioner and his counsel at the trial.]

Petitioner has raised five points on appeal as follows:

1. Whether petitioner's constitutional rights, both state and federal, were violated?

2. Whether or not petitioner's right to due process and orderly procedure was violated?

3. Whether petitioner's rights, as accorded to him by the rules of professional practices committee council were violated?

4. Whether the evidence, as presented, does as a matter of law, substantiate the allegations of the School Board?

5. Whether petitioner's rights as accorded to him under Florida Statutes 120.20 through 120.31, Part II of administrative adjudication procedure (new) were violated?

We quickly dispose of the first three points supra, by saying that we do not find any violation of petitioner's constitutional rights, nor of due process or his rights under the rules of professional practices. He was acquainted with his charges and given ample time to prepare his defense. If the charges were too vague or uncertain to acquaint him thereof, he had an adequate remedy at his disposal. The same holds true as to his other rights.

As to the fourth point, we think and so hold that there was sufficient competent evidence before the School Board, sitting as the trier of the facts, to support the conclusion reached by the Board both as to the incompetency of petitioner as well as to the charge of immorality. There are many factors which may have a material bearing upon the competency of the instructor, among which could be his attitude toward the students, his manner of speaking to them and his general lack of proper personality conducive to a mutual understanding. The instructor's attitude and expression on moral conduct, sex questions and such, could also affect his competency. In addition, as to the immorality charge, there was evidence of unbecoming and unnecessary risqué remarks made by the petitioner in a class of mixed teenage boys and girls which we agree with the School Board were of an immoral nature. It may be that topless waitresses and entertainers are in vogue in certain areas of our country and our federal courts may try to enjoin our state courts from stopping the sale of lewd and obscene literature and the showing of obscene films, but we are still of the opinion that instructors in our schools should not be permitted to so risquely discuss sex problems in our teenage mixed classes as to cause embarrassment to the children or to invoke in them other feelings not incident to the courses of study being pursued.

As to the fifth point raised, it appears that the only deviation from the cited statute, F.S. section 120.20, etc. part II, F.S.A. was the question of stenographic reporting of the hearing. This was effectively waived by the parties at the commencement of the hearing. This case did not involve a continuing contract held by the petitioner-teacher, and therefore his administrative review terminated with the School Board and his recourse to further review was properly by resort to this court by petition for writ of certiorari.[1]

For the reasons stated supra, however, the petition for writ of certiorari is denied.

WIGGINTON and SPECTOR, JJ., concur.

NOTE

1. Adams v. Board of Public Instruction of Okaloosa County, 225 So. 2d 423 (Fla. App. 1st 1969).

A United States District Court in Massachusetts decides for an eleventh grade English teacher who had been dismissed for using the word "fuck" in the classroom during a lesson on taboo words. In deciding for the teacher, the Court declared: "In support of a qualified right of a teacher, even at the secondary level, to use a teaching method which is relevant and in the opinion of experts of significant standing has a serious educational purpose is the central rationale of academic freedom. The Constitution recognizes that freedom in order to foster open minds, creative imaginations, and adventurous spirits. Our national belief is that the heterodox as well as the orthodox are a source of individual and of social growth. We do not confine academic freedom to conventional teachers or to those who can get a majority vote from their colleagues. . . . In the instant case it is not claimed that any regulation warned plaintiff not to follow the methods he chose. Nor can it be said that plaintiff should have known that his teaching methods were not permitted. There is no substantial evidence that his methods were contrary to an informal rule, to an understanding among school teachers of his school or teachers generally, to a body of disciplinary precedents, to precise canons of ethics, or to specific opinions expressed in professional journals or other publications."

Mailloux v. *Kiley,* 323 F. Supp. 1387 (1971)

WYZANSKI, Chief Judge.

This case involves an action by a public high school teacher against the City of Lawrence, the members of its school committee, the superintendent of its schools, and the principal of its high school. Plaintiff claims that in discharging him for his classroom conduct in connection with a taboo word the school committee deprived him of his rights under the First and Fourteenth Amendments to the United States Constitution, and that, therefore, he has a cause of action[1] under 42 U.S.C. § 1983 within this court's jurisdiction under 28 U.S.C. § 1343 (3).

These are the facts as found by this court after a full hearing.

Defendant members of the school committee employed plaintiff to teach in the Lawrence High School for the academic year 1970-71 at a salary of $8100. Defendant principal assigned plaintiff to teach basic English to a class of about 25 students, boys and girls 16 and 17 years of age, all in the junior class of 11th grade.

Plaintiff assigned to the class for outside reading chapters in a novel, The Thread That Runs So True, by Jesse Stuart. The novel describes an incident based on the experiences of the author as a young country school teacher in rural Kentucky. He had taken over a one-room school in which the class had been seated with boys on one side, and girls on the other side, of the room. He intermingled the sexes for seating. Some parents objected on the ground the new teacher was running a "courting school." Nowhere in the novel is there the word "fuck."

October 1, 1970, during a discussion of the book in class, some students thought the protest against changing the seating in the Kentucky classroom was ridiculous. Plaintiff said that other things today are just as ridiculous. He then introduced the subject of society and its ways, as illustrated by taboo words. He wrote the word "goo" on the board and asked the class for a definition. No one being able to define it, plaintiff said that this word did not exist in English but in another culture it might be a taboo word. He then wrote on the blackboard the word "fuck," and, in accordance with his customary teaching methods of calling for volunteers to respond to a question, asked the class in general for a definition. After a couple of minutes a boy volunteered that the word meant "sexual intercourse." Plaintiff, without using the word orally, said: "we have two words, sexual intercourse, and this word on the board * * * one * * * is acceptable by society * * * the other is not accepted. It is a taboo word." After a few minutes of discussion of other aspects of taboos, plaintiff went on to other matters.

At all times in the discussion plaintiff was in good

faith pursuing what he regarded as an educational goal. He was not attempting to probe the private feelings, or attitudes, or experiences of his students, or to embarrass them.

October 2, 1970, the parent of a girl in the class, being erroneously informed that plaintiff had called upon a particular girl in the class to define the taboo word, complained to the principal. He asked Miss Horner the head of the English department to investigate the incident. Plaintiff did admit that he had written on the board the taboo word. He also said he had "probably" called upon a specific girl to define the word. But this court is persuaded by all the testimony that he did not in fact call on any girl individually and that his statement to Miss Horner, repeated later to the union, of what he "probably" did is not an accurate statement of what he actually did. At his meeting with Miss Horner, plaintiff did not refer to the novel which the class had been discussing.

After plaintiff had been interviewed by Miss Horner, defendant superintendent on October 13, 1970 suspended him for seven days with pay.

Plaintiff engaged counsel who requested a hearing before the school committee, and a bill of particulars. The committee furnished particulars alleging that: "* * * Mr. Mailloux did write a list of words on the chalkboard. One of the words was 'fuck'."

"A female student was asked to define the word 'fuck'."

"When confronted with the incident by the head of the department, Mr. Mailloux admitted that the incident was true." [This is a reference to the confrontation in Miss Horner's office.]

The committee gave plaintiff and his counsel a hearing on October 20, 1970 .

October 21, 1970 the committee dismissed plaintiff on the general charge of "conduct unbecoming a teacher." It made no finding as to any specific particular.[2]

Following his discharge, plaintiff brought this action seeking temporary and permanent relief. After a two day hearing this court, regarding itself as bound by Keefe v. Geanakos 418 F. 2d 359 (1st Cir.), issued on December 21, 1970 a temporary injunction ordering the defendant members of the school committee to restore plaintiff to his employment.

The total amount of salary which, but for his dismissal, plaintiff would have been paid by the City of Lawrence for his services as a teacher at the Lawrence High School from the date of his discharge to the date of his reinstatement by this court is $2,279.20. During that period plaintiff's only earnings were $311.70.

Defendants appealed and asked for a stay pending appeal. For reasons stated in Mailloux v. Kiley, 1st Cir., 436 F. 2d 565 (1971), the Court of Appeals denied

the stay and dismissed the appeal. This court thereafter conducted a further hearing. Upon the basis of both hearings this court makes the following additional findings.

1. The topic of taboo words had a limited relevance to the Stuart novel which plaintiff's class was discussing, but it had a high degree of relevance to the proper teaching of eleventh grade basic English even to students not expecting to go to college and therefore placed in a "low track."

2. The word "fuck" is relevant to a discussion of taboo words. Its impact effectively illustrates how taboo words function.

3. Boys and girls in an eleventh grade have a sophistication sufficient to treat the word from a serious educational viewpoint. While at first they may be surprised and self-conscious to have the word discussed, they are not likely to be embarrassed or offended.

4. Plaintiffs' writing the word did not have a disturbing effect. A class might be less disturbed by having the word written than if it had been spoken. Most students had seen the word even if they had not used it.

5. Plaintiff's calling upon the class for a volunteer to define the word was a technique that was reasonable and was in accordance with customs in plaintiff's class. It avoided implicating anyone who did not wish to participate.

6. The word "fuck" is in books in the school library.

7. In the opinion of experts of significant standing, such as members of the faculties of the Harvard University School of Education and of Massachusetts Institute of Technology, the discussion of taboo words in the eleventh grade, the way plaintiff used the word "fuck," his writing of it on the blackboard, and the inquiry he addressed to the class, were appropriate and reasonable under the circumstances and served a serious educational purpose. In the opinion of other qualified persons plaintiff's use of the word was not under the circumstances reasonable, or appropriate, or conducive to a serious educational purpose. It has not been shown what is the preponderant opinion in the teaching profession, or in that part of the profession which teaches English.

The parties have not relied upon any express regulation of the Lawrence School Committee or the Lawrence High School. The regulations set forth in an attachment to the complaint have no general or specific provisions relevant to this case.

We now turn to questions of ultimate fact and of law.

Defendant members of the school committee acted for the state when they discharged plaintiff and were therefore subject to the Fourteenth Amendment's command. Pickering v. Board of Education, 391 U.S. 563, 88 S. Ct. 1731, 20 L. Ed. 2d 811; Keefe v. Geanakos, 418 F. 2d 359, 1st Cir.

The Fourteenth Amendment recognizes that a public school teacher has not only a civic right to freedom of speech both outside (Pickering v. Board of Education, *supra*) and inside (See Tinker v. Des Moines Independent Community School Dist., 393 U.S. 503, 506, 89 S. Ct. 733, 21 L. Ed. 2d 731) the schoolhouse, but also some measure of academic freedom as to his in-classroom teaching. Keefe v. Geanakos, *supra*; Parducci v. Rutland, 316 F. Supp. 352, M.D. Ala.

The last two cases cited upheld two kinds of academic freedom: the substantive right of a teacher to choose a teaching method which in the court's view served a demonstrated educational purpose; and the procedural right of a teacher not to be discharged for the use of a teaching method which was not proscribed by a regulation, and as to which it was not proven that he should have had notice that its use was prohibited.

Relying on those cases, plaintiff argues that both his substantive and procedural academic freedom rights, protected by the Fourteenth and First Amendments, were violated by defendant school committee when they discharged him.

The teaching methods plaintiff used were obviously not "necessary" to the proper teaching of the subject and students assigned to him, in the sense that a reference to Darwinian evolution might be thought necessary to the teaching of biology. See the concurrence of Mr. Justice Stewart in Epperson v. Arkansas, 393 U.S. 97, 116, 89 S. Ct. 266, 21 L. Ed. 2d 228.

Here we have the use of teaching methods which divide professional opinion. There is substantial support from expert witnesses of undoubted competence that the discussion of taboo words was relevant to an assigned book, and, whether or not so relevant, was at least relevant to the subject of eleventh grade English, that "fuck" was an appropriate choice of an illustrative taboo word, and that writing it on the board and calling upon the class to define it were appropriate techniques. Yet there was also substantial evidence, chiefly from persons with experience as principals but also from the head of the English department at plaintiff's school, that it was inappropriate to use the particular word under the circumstances of this case. The weight of the testimony offered leads this court to make an ultimate finding that plaintiff's methods served an educational purpose, in the sense that they were relevant and had professional endorsement from experts of significant standing. But this court has not implied that the weight of opinion in the teaching profession as a whole, or the weight of opinon among English teachers as a whole, would be that plaintiff's

methods were within limits that, even if they would not themselves use them, they would regard as permissible for others. To make a finding on that point would have required a more thorough sampling, especially of younger teachers, than the record offers.

Nor is this case, like *Keefe* or *Parducci*, one where the court, from its own evaluation of the teaching method used, may conclude that, even if the court would not use the method, it is plainly permissible for others to use it, at least in the absence of an express proscription.[3] *Keefe* indicated that the use in the classroom of the word "fuck" is not impermissible under all circumstances—as, for example when it appears in a book properly assigned for student reading. But a teacher who uses a taboo sexual word must take care not to transcend his legitimate professional purpose. When a male teacher asks a class of adolescent boys and girls to define a taboo sexual word the question must not go beyond asking for verbal knowledge and become a titillating probe of privacy. He must not sacrifice his dignity to join his pupils as "frére et cochon." Here, it should be stated unequivocally, there is no evidence that this plaintiff transcended legitimate professional purposes. Indeed, the court has specifically found he acted in good faith. But the risk of abuse involved in the technique of questioning students precludes this court from concluding that the method was *plainly* permissible. Too much depends on the context and the teacher's good faith.

Where, as here, a secondary school teacher chooses a teaching method that is not necessary for the proper instruction of his class, that is not shown to be regarded by the weight of opinion in his profession as permissible, that is not so transparently proper that a court can without expert testimony evaluate it as proper, but that is relevant to his subject and students and, in the opinion of experts of significant standing, serves a serious educational purpose, it is a heretofore undecided question whether the Constitution gives him any right to use the method or leaves the issue to the school authorities. Note, Developments in the Law of Academic Freedom, 81 Harv. L. Rev. 1050, Van Alstyne, The Constitutional Rights of Teachers and Professors, 1970 Duke Law Journal, p. 841.

In support of a qualified[4] right of a teacher, even at the secondary level, to use a teaching method which is relevant and in the opinion of experts of significant standing has a serious educational purpose is the central rationale of academic freedom. The Constitution recognizes that freedom in order to foster open minds, creative imaginations, and adventurous spirits. Our national belief is that the heterodox as well as the orthodox are a source of individual and of social growth. We do not confine academic freedom to conventional teachers or to those who can get a majority vote from their colleagues. Our faith is that the teacher's freedom to choose among options for which there is any substantial support will increase his intellectual vitality and his moral strength. The teacher whose responsibility has been nourished by independence, enterprise, and free choice becomes for his student a better model of the democratic citizen. His examples of applying and adapting the values of the old order to the demands and opportunities of a constantly changing world are among the most important lessons he gives to youth.

Yet the secondary school situation is distinguishable from higher levels of education. See Note, Developments in the Law of Academic Freedom, 81 Harv. L. Rev. 1045, 1050, 1098. There are constitutional considerations of magnitude which, predictably, might warrant a legal conclusion that the secondary school teacher's constitutional right in his classroom is only to be free from discriminatory religious, racial, political and like measures. Epperson v. Arkansas, *supra*, and from state action which is unreasonable, or perhaps has not even a plausible rational basis. See the concluding words in the penultimate paragraph in Mailloux v. Kiley, 1st Cir., 436 F. 2d 565 (1971).

The secondary school more clearly than the college or university acts *in loco parentis* with respect to minors. It is closely governed by a school board selected by a local community. The faculty does not have the independent traditions, the broad discretion as to teaching methods, not usually the intellectual qualifications, of university professors. Among secondary school teachers there are often many persons with little experience. Some teachers and most students have limited intellectual and emotional maturity. Most parents, students, school boards, and members of the community usually expect the secondary school to concentrate on transmitting basic information, teaching "the best that is known and thought in the world," training by established techniques, and, to some extent at least, indoctrinating in the *mores* of the surrounding society. While secondary schools are not rigid disciplinary institutions, neither are they open forums in which mature adults, already habituated to social restraints, exchange ideas on a level of parity. Moreover, it cannot be accepted as a premise that the student is voluntarily in the classroom and willing to be exposed to a teaching method which, though reasonable, is not approved by the school authorities or by the weight of professional opinion. A secondary school student, unlike most college students, is usually required to attend school classes, and may have no choice as to his teacher.

Bearing in mind these competing considerations, this court rules that when a secondary school teacher uses a teaching method which he does not prove has the support of the preponderant opinion of the teaching profession or of the part of it to which he belongs, but which he merely proves is relevant to his subject and students, is regarded by experts of significant standing as serving a serious educational purpose, and was used by him in good faith the state may suspend or discharge a teacher for using that method but it may not resort to such drastic sanctions unless the state proves he was put on notice either by a regulation or otherwise that he should not use that method. This exclusively procedural protection is afforded to a teacher not because he is a state employee, or because he is a citizen, but because in his teaching capacity he is engaged in the exercise of what may plausibly be considered "vital First Amendment rights." Keyishian v. Board of Regents, 385 U.S. 489, 604, 87 S. Ct. 675, 684, 17 L. Ed. 2d 629. In his teaching capacity he is not required to "guess what conduct or utterance may lose him his position," (*Ibid*). If he did not have the right to be warned before he was discharged, he might be more timid than it is in the public interest that he should be, and he might steer away from reasonable methods with which it is in the public interest to experiment. *Ibid.*

In the instant case it is not claimed that any regulation warned plaintiff not to follow the methods he chose. Nor can it be said that plaintiff should have known that his teaching methods were not permitted. There is no substantial evidence that his methods were contrary to an informal rule, to an understanding among school teachers of his school or teachers generally, to a body of disciplinary precendents, to precise canons of ethics, or to specific opinions expressed in professional journals or other publications. This was not the kind of unforeseeable outrageous conduct which all men of good will would, once their attention is called to it, immediately perceive to be forbidden. On this last point it is sufficient to refer to the testimony given by faculty members of Harvard University and M.I.T. who had prepared their students for secondary school teaching careers.

Finally, in the face of the record of judicial uncertainty in this case it cannot be held that it was self-evident that a teacher should not have used the methods followed by plaintiff. This Court, perhaps misreading the *Keefe* case, issued an injunction on the ground that plaintiff's conduct was, more probably than not, legally permissible. The Court of Appeals, which had before it this court's findings on the temporary injunction (which are not materially different from those now made) concluded that the temporary injunction was not such an abuse of discretion as to justify its dissolution. Mailloux v. Kiley, 1st Cir., 436 F. 2d 565 (1971). We can hardly say that plaintiff should have known what was not evident to judges after taking evidence, hearing argument, and reflecting in chambers.

Inasmuch as at the time he acted plaintiff did not know, and there was no reason that he should have known, that his conduct was proscribed, it was a violation of due process for the defendants to suspend or discharge him on that account. Cf. Keyishian v. Board of Regents, Keefe v. Geanakos and Parducci v. Rutland, all *supra*.

Plaintiff, in accordance with Parducci v. Rutland, is entitled to a judgment directing:

1. All defendants to continue plaintiff in employment until the end of the academic year 1970-1971, except for good cause.

2. All defendants to expunge from their employment records and transcripts all references to plaintiff's suspension and discharge.

3. The City of Lawrence, as his employer, and the school committee members, as the persons who discharged him, to compensate him for the salary loss he suffered, $2,279.20, less his earnings, $311.70, or $1,967.50, with 6% interest from the date of the complaint December 14, 1970.

4. The City of Lawrence and the school committee members to pay costs.

The court is not unmindful that both the opinion and the judgment cover not only plaintiff's discharge without compensation but also his suspension with pay. The reason that the suspension is covered is because in the circumstances of this case the superintendent and all others treated it as a penalty. Nothing herein suggests that school authorities are not free after they have learned that the teacher is using a teaching method of which they disapprove, and which is not appropriate to the proper teaching of the subject, to suspend him until he agrees to cease using the method. See the last of Mailloux v. Kiley, 1st Cir., 436 F. 2d 565 (1971).

NOTES

1. Plaintiff abandoned his contract claim.
2. Inasmuch as the committee made no finding as to whether plaintiff called upon a specific girl, this court has no need to consider whether it had substantial evidence which would have supported such a finding.
3. Perhaps, though *Keefe* and *Parducci* do not say so, the school authorities there involved were constitutionally free by express proscription to forbid the assignment of outside reading of magazine articles and novels of undoubted merit and propriety for which the teacher had not secured advance approval.
4. The so-called constitutional right is not absolute. It is akin to, and may indeed be a species of, the right to freedom of speech which is embraced by the concept of the "liberty" protected by the Fourteenth Amendment. Analytically, as distinguished from rhetorically, it is less a right than a constitutionally-recognized interest. Clearly, the teacher's right must yield to compelling public interests of greater constitutional significance. It may be that it will be held by the Supreme Court that the teacher's academic right to liberty in teaching methods in the classroom (unlike his civic right to freedom of speech) is subject to state regulatory control which is not actuated by compelling public interests but which, in the judiciary's opinion is merely "reasonable". See Epperson v. Arkansas, 393 U.S. 97, 89 S. Ct. 266, 21 L. Ed. 2d 228 and Tinker v. Des Moines School Dist., 393 U.S. 503, 89 S. Ct. 733, 21 L. Ed. 2d 731. Indeed it has been suggested that state regulatory control of the classroom is entitled to prevail unless the teacher bears the heavy burden of proving that it has no rational justification, (See Mr. Justice Black dissenting in Tinker v. Des Moines School Dist., 393 U.S. 503, 519-521, 89 S. Ct. 733,), or is discriminatory on religious, racial, political, or like grounds. See Epperson v. Arkansas, 393 U.S. 97, 89 S. Ct. 266.

A United States District Court in Nebraska decides against a teacher who had been dismissed for, among other things, criticizing in class a fellow teacher and using her economics class to consider student rights, after she had been warned by her principal to stop using class time for discussions of student rights and behavior of fellow employees. The District Court Judge asserts: "I am persuaded that the exercising of a constitutional right was not the reason for the discharge. Although a teacher has a right to express opinions and concerns, as does any other citizen, on matters of public concern, by virtue of the First and Fourteenth Amendments . . . , I doubt that she has a right to express them *during class* in deliberate violation of a superior's admonition not to do so, when the subject of her opinions and concerns is directly related to student and teacher discipline. . . . This is not to say that disagreement cannot be expressed with views of the administration, but it does mean that when reasonable alternatives for expression of dissent are available, as they were in the present case, a teacher is not constitutionally entitled to use the classroom as a forum for expression of disagreement with her administrators on internal affairs."

Ahern v. *Board of Education*, 327 F. Supp. 1391 (1971)

URBOM, District Judge.

The plaintiff was a non-tenured instructor at a public school and was discharged before expiration of her contract period. Seeking pecuniary damages and injunctive relief, she filed in this court a complaint framed within the Civil Rights Act, 42 U.S.C. §§ 1983 and 1985, naming as defendants the Board of Education, the individual board members, the superintendent of schools, the assistant superintendent of schools, who was also secretary of the board, and the principal of the high school. Trial has been concluded and extensive briefs have been submitted.

Issues raised by the complaint relate to deprivation of the plaintiff's rights of free speech, due process, and right to teach under the First, Fifth and Ninth Amendments to the Constitution of the United States.

FINDINGS OF FACT

Frances Ahern was employed as a public school-teacher by the School District of Grand Island, Nebraska, from September, 1966, until her discharge on March 31, 1969. The contract of employment for the year 1968-1969 was identical to the contract executed March 15, 1969, for the year 1969-1970,[1] except that Miss Ahern was to receive an increase in salary for the 1969-1970 term.

In the summer of 1968 Miss Ahern attended the N.D.E.A. Civic Institute, titled "American Liberties and Social Change," at the Center for Research and Education in American Liberties, Teachers College, Columbia University. The institute challenged the efficacy of the traditional authoritarian teaching approach in teaching about American liberties. The institute sought to provide the participants with a new approach to teaching, the inquiry method, which shifted to the students many decisions previously made unilaterally by the teacher, including the specific subject for daily discussion, the course material to be used, and rules of in-class behavior.

During the second semester of the 1968-1969 school year Miss Ahern was assigned to teach two classes of Economics and two classes of Consumer Economics and she was responsible for a study hall. There is some dispute as to whether the course in Consumer Economics was more properly denominated by Miss Ahern Consumer Politics and as to what the content of the course was supposed to be. The course was designed to accommodate high school seniors who ranked in the lower 20 per cent of their class. It is clear that the content of the course was expanded by Miss Ahern from merely economic analysis to politics and social change.

Miss Ahern's increased sensitivity to student rights

was manifested during her first semester course of Contemporary Government. Permission was requested and obtained from Dr. Eugene Miller, the principal, to use the school system as the government to be studied as a model. As a part of the Contemporary Government course, Miss Ahern's students under her guidance developed a statement of "student rights and responsibilities."

The first sign that the school administrators seriously questioned Miss Ahern's teaching method was on February 14, 1969, at a meeting with the principal and assistant principal. However, it was the week of March 10, 1969, and the ensuing events which culminated in the decision by the principal on March 21, 1969, to suspend Miss Ahern and the decision by the school board on March 31, 1969, to terminate her contracts.

During the week of March 10 Miss Ahern with the permission of the high school authorities attended a special seminar in Atlantic City, New Jersey. A substitute teacher was assigned to conduct Miss Ahern's classes. On March 17 Miss Ahern returned from the seminar and at the second and third period classes, which were both Consumer Economics or Consumer Politics classes, the students related to Miss Ahern that the substitute teacher had not permitted them to discuss in small groups, required them to sit in straight rows, changed the study plans, told them that the classroom was no longer a playroom, gave one student a low grade because she could not read his writing, and conducted the classes generally in a manner not in keeping with Miss Ahern's usual method. The students, at least in the third period Consumer Politics class, said that by the end of the substitute teacher's week of teaching the students were antagonistic and refused to give the substitute their names and that at the third period Consumer Politics class on Friday, March 14, the substitute had seized a boy by the hair and had slapped him three times across the face, knocking off his glasses, whereupon the boy left the room. On hearing this report Miss Ahern in the classroom said with reference to the substitute teacher, "That bitch," because she was terribly angry, and also said, "I hope that if this happens again * * * all of you will walk out."

At the sixth period Economics class, consisting of students not present at the slapping incident, on Monday, March 17, Miss Ahern had the slapping incident role-played and discussed. Using the incident as a current issue to which the students could relate in the experiencing of involvement in the study of democratic processes, Miss Ahern encouraged the focusing of all her classes' attention on the matter of devising a proposal for a school regulation regarding corporal punishment. She assisted her students in drafting a resolution, which stated:

"We think teachers should have authority.

"But the student has a right as a person not to be threatened with or to be subjected to physical coercion. The student has a right as a person to be free from verbal abuse intended to humiliate him, to cut him down.

"Teachers have the right as persons not to be threatened with or to be subjected to physical coercion. They have the right to be free from verbal abuse intended to humiliate them."

The plan developed by Miss Ahern and her students was to present the statement to the high school student council which was scheduled to meet on Wednesday, March 19. A prior commitment by the council caused its Wednesday meeting to be cancelled and no further attempt was made by Miss Ahern or her students to submit the statement to the council before her suspension. On March 19 Miss Ahern was called to Dr. Miller's office for a meeting, which was attended by Dr. Miller; the assistant principal, James Shehein; the department chairman, Jack Richards; and Miss Ahern. At the meeting Dr. Miller, among other things upbraided her for calling a substitute teacher a "bitch" in front of her class, read to her portions of her teaching contract[2], advised her not to sign a contract for the next year because her philosophy did not "fit in this school," told her to change her philosophy or he would see that she was removed from the classroom, told her that disciplinary action on a substitute or regular teacher was an administration function and not that of a teacher or students; told her that her main function was to teach economics during class time and not the discussing of teachers, and directed her to return to her class, to teach as she had during the first two years, not to discuss with any of her classes the slapping incident or any teacher, and to get her classes and her study hall under control by March 24 or she would be relieved of her classroom duties for the balance of the year.

The principal's admonitions were deliberately ignored by the plaintiff because she thought that adhering to them would have threatened her rapport with her students and because she believed that the principal could not dictate to her the philosophy or method of teaching to be used in the classroom. The day following, which was Thursday, March 20, at least one entire class session—the sixth period class in Economics—was consumed in a discussion of the slapping incident, the proposed resolution or statement, the refusal of Dr. Miller to meet with the students, and the advisability of the students' gathering in a substantial number at 8:10 the next morning before the 8:15 classes.[3] Lee Perkins, an assistant principal, attended the class session and thereafter reported to Dr. Miller that Miss Ahern's class was discussing the subjects noted above and was not discussing economics. Although Miss Ahern's classes in Consumer Politics or

Consumer Economics had previously taken the posture, with the knowledge of Jack Richards, the head of the department, of a course of study of democratic methods of problem-solving, the Economics classes were framed by Miss Ahern and approved by the administration as a course in "the development, operation, and problems of a market economy. * * * Economics is concerned with the way societies go about allocating scarce resources among competing wants."[4]

Also on March 20 Miss Ahern sent from her third period Consumer Politics class a copy of the resolution prepared by her and her students and a note saying:

"Dr. Miller, Third Period Consumer Politics class would like to discuss with you the subject raised in this statement today in class. Frances Ahern."[5]

Dr. Miller ignored the request. Miss Ahern then invited the principal by calling him from the classroom on the classroom telephone to speak to the class about the resolution on corporal punishment. Dr. Miller through his secretary again declined to meet with Miss Ahern and her students in the classroom, but offered to meet with students at his office.

On Friday morning, March 21, at 8:00, Miss Ahern appeared by request at the principal's office and was told by Dr. Miller:

"Miss Ahern, I have some statements to make. I ask you to listen and then you will be given an opportunity to speak. Since our meeting on Wednesday morning, you have failed to return to your classes and teach economics as directed. Instead, you have continued to discuss with students, students' rights and teachers' rights and non-rights of the students, and in addition have aided students in preparing slips of papers advocating a protest movement in the Senior Lounge this morning. For these reasons and the reasons that we gave you Wednesday morning, I am suspending you from all teaching duties here at Senior High, effective immediately, until at which time you will be given an opportunity for a hearing before the Board of Education.

* * * * * *

"Yes, your suspension will be with pay, your status will be determined at the Board of Education hearing."

Her reply was:

"I don't know what I should do. I question the second statement because the statement drafted by the students in my class expressed their feelings, and mine, too, but I did not push them and I was very careful to make sure that they felt strongly about this and that they wanted to make this kind of statement. The statement is very moderate and the purpose of having it drafted and submitted to the Student Council first is that it is the proper way to effect change. The Council refused to consider it or they were not permitted to consider it. The second step,

as far as they were concerned, was to ask you to come down to talk about it. You were asked once on the phone and once by letter. You did not come. The only purpose in this meeting, and you could stop it so easily, is to go out simply and sit down and talk about the statement or arrange for a time when you can talk about the statement. That's the only purpose of this. I feel that they want to make this statement, they want you to consider it with them and that is all. The meeting will disappear."[6]

The pre-class meeting of the students was orderly and involved 150 to 200 students. They were asked to disperse and to meet their 8:15 classes and were told that, if they have grievances, spokesmen should be selected and a meeting would be scheduled at the end of the day. The first bell for convening classes sounded at 8:10; the tardy bell sounded at 8:15. Twenty or twenty-five students remained long enough to be ten or fifteen minutes late to class. At the end of the day a meeting was held between seventeen or eighteen students and three administrators for forty-five minutes.

On March 25 the superintendent, Dr. Lundstrom, informed Miss Ahern by telephone that the school board would conduct a hearing into the matter of her suspension on March 27, 1969. There is no indication that she made any objection to the time of the hearing or requested any postponement. The hearing was held on March 27 and was attended by members of the board, Miss Ahern, Dr. Miller, and Miss Ahern's attorney. The meeting lasted approximately three hours and a transcript of the proceedings covers 66 double-spaced elite typewritten pages.[7] Miss Ahern testified at length at the hearing, under questioning by her counsel and by various board members, as to her philosophy of education, her characterization of the substitute teacher as a "bitch," the student petition drive to establish rules for discipline within the school, and the plans for the Friday morning pre-class meeting of students. Dr. Miller testified regarding the striking of the student, Miss Ahern's discussing that subject with her classes, his directing her to teach economics, her manner of maintaining or failing to maintain discipline in her classes and study hall, his philosophy of education, and his role in the suspension of Miss Ahern. Dr. Miller was cross-examined by Miss Ahern's counsel.

On March 31 the board of education held a final meeting, attended by Miss Ahern's counsel, into the Ahern[8] matter. The superintendent, Dr. Lundstrom, recommended that Miss Ahern's position be declared vacant by reason of a willful neglect of Article V of the policies and regulations of the school district.[9] By unanimous vote the position was declared vacant and Miss Ahern's contract for the 1968-1969 year was terminated as of March 31, 1969, and the 1969-1970 contract was declared void.

Miss Ahern's suspension, the declaration of the vacancy, the termination of her 1968-1969 contract, and the voiding of the 1969-1970 contract were solely for insubordination in the willful violation of Dr. Miller's directions to Miss Ahern related to her at the meeting of March 19, 1969, as specified in Dr. Miller's statement of March 21, 1969.

DUE PROCESS OF LAW

Persons, including teachers, who are employed by a state are entitled, because of the relationship with the state, to be free from discharge during the course of a contract of employment within the confines of due process of law. Slochower v. Board of Higher Education, 350 U.S. 551, 76 S. Ct. 637, 100 L. Ed. 692 (1956). Due process is a flexible concept, but means, at least, that there must be (1) a rational connection between the reason for the discharge and a rightful interest of the state, (2) a basis in fact for the reason for the discharge, Wieman v. Updegraff, 344 U.S. 183, 73 S. Ct. 215, 97 L. Ed. 216 (1952) and Slochower v. Board of Education, *supra,* and (3) a reason for discharge other than the exercise by the employee of a constitutional right, Pickering v. Board of Education, 391 U.S. 563, 88 S. Ct. 1731, 20 L. Ed. 2d 811 (1968). These elements, for convenience, may be referred to as substantive due process.

I have no difficulty in concluding that substantive due process was accorded the plaintiff. The discharge was bottomed, by the clear import of the evidence, upon insubordination arising from directives stemming from Miss Ahern's criticism in class of a fellow teacher who slapped a student and steps taken by Miss Ahern during classroom hours in seeking consideration of a declaration of student rights. The rightful interest of the state was that of maintaining harmony among members of the faculty, the students, and the administrators, as well as an interest in ascertaining that economics be taught in a course in economics. A rational, as well as factual, connection between the reason for discharge and a legitimate interest of the state is beyond question.

A basis in fact existed for the reason for discharge. Miss Ahern admittedly violated deliberately the principal's order to stop discussing in the classroom the slapping incident and the proposal for student rights, as well as his directive to teach economics. Her acts in these respects may have been honest and even laudable, but there remains no doubt of the factual basis for a finding of insubordination.

I am persuaded that the exercising of a constitutional right was not the reason for the discharge. Although a teacher has a right to express opinions and concerns, as does any other citizen, on matters of public concern, by virtue of the First and Fourteenth

Amendments, Pickering v. Board of Education, *supra,* I doubt that she has a right to express them *during class* in deliberate violation of a superior's admonition not to do so, when the subject of her opinions and concerns is directly related to student and teacher discipline. *Pickering* distinguishes the situation in the present case, as follows:

"* * * (I)t cannot be gainsaid that the State has interests as an employer in regulating the speech of its employees that differ significantly from those it possesses in connection with regulation of the speech of the citizenry in general. The problem in any case is to arrive at a balance between the interests of the teacher, as a citizen, in commenting upon matters of public concern and the interest of the State, as an employer, in promoting the efficiency of the public services it performed through its employees.

"* * * The statements are in no way directed towards any person with whom appellant would normally be in contact in the course of his daily work as a teacher. Thus no question of maintaining either discipline by immediate superiors or harmony among coworkers is presented here. Appellant's employment relationships with the Board and, to a somewhat lesser extent, with the superintendent are not the kind of close working relationships for which it can persuasively be claimed that personal loyalty and confidence are necessary to their proper functioning. * * *"

Miss Ahern, on the other hand, chose a subject for discussion and action which did involve "maintaining either discipline by immediate superiors or harmony among coworkers" and employment relations which were "the kind of close working relationships for which it can persuasively be claimed that personal loyalty and confidence are necessary to their proper functioning." The same observations are relevant to any claim that Miss Ahern's right to teach, to the extent that the Ninth Amendment protects such a right, was denied. Additionally, I doubt that she had a constitutional right to teach politics in a course in economics. The sixth period class—the one reported to Dr. Miller by Mr. Perkins as including no teaching of economics on March 20 and which clearly precipitated the suspension—was a class designed by Miss Ahern and approved by the administrators as a course in economics, which in no sense included by definition a study of methods of developing student rights or teacher rights on corporal punishment. With respect to whether the reason for discharge was that Miss Ahern was exercising a constitutional right it must also be noted that what ordinarily would be a right protected by the constitution may not be so protected if the exercise of that right constitutes a direct violation of an order by a superior on a subject rationally connected with legitimate interest of the state-employer. Thus in Nelson v. Los Angeles County, 362 U.S. 1, 80 S.Ct. 527, 4 L.Ed. 2d 494 (1960) the refusal of an employee to answer questions on Fifth Amendment grounds in violation of an order of the state-employer to testify was held to be a constitutionally permitted reason for the employee's discharge, where the subject of the questions which the employee refused to answer related to whether the employee was a security risk, a legitimate subject for inquiry by the employer. Insubordination, therefore, becomes a proper ground for discharge, even when it becomes enmeshed with the reliance upon constitutional rights. This is not to say that disagreement cannot be expressed with views of the administration, but it does mean that when reasonable alternatives for expression of dissent are available, as they were in the present case, a teacher is not constitutionally entitled to use the classroom as a forum for expression of disagreement with her administrators on internal affairs.

The matter of what may be called, for convenience, procedural due process—the right to a hearing and its concomitants—is more troublesome. The great majority of recently reported civil rights cases by public schoolteachers have involved non-renewal of the teaching contract, rather than discharge during the existing contract. See Freeman v. Gould Special School District of Lincoln County, Ark., 405 F.2d 1153 (C.A. 8th Cir. 1969); Harkless v. Sweeny Independent School District, 427 F.2d 319 (C.A. 5th Cir. 1970); Orr v. Trinter, 318 F.Supp. 1041 (U.S.D.C.S.D. Ohio 1970); Worthington v. Joint School District No. 16, 316 F. Supp. 808, 809 (U.S.D.C.E.D. Wis. 1970); Knarr v. Board of School Trustees of Griffith, Indiana, 317 F. Supp. 832 (U.S.D.C.N.D. Ind. 1970); Jones v. Hopper, 410 F.2d 1323 (C.A. 10th Cir. 1969); Thaw v. Board of Public Instruction of Dade Co., Fla., 432 F.2d 98 (C.A. 5th Cir. 1970); Schultz v. Palmberg, 317 F. Supp. 659 (U.S.D.C. Wyo. 1970); Roth v. Board of Regents of State Colleges, 310 F.Supp. 972 (U.S.D.C.W.D. Wis. 1970); Gouge v. Joint School District No. 1, 310 F. Supp. 984 (U.S.D.C.W.D. Wis. 1970); Lucas v. Chapman, 430 F.2d 945 (C.A. 5th Cir. 1970); Drown v. Portsmouth School District, 435 F.2d 1182 (C.A. 1st Cir. 1970). The Supreme Court of the United States has not declared that the steps of procedural due process are applicable to the termination of rights arising solely from contract. It reasonably may be argued that Goldberg v. Kelly, 397 U.S. 254, 90 S.Ct. 1011, 25 L. Ed.2d 287 (1970), establishes a standard which will be applicable to schoolteachers' contractual relationships. The plaintiff there was a welfare recipient who summarily had been removed from the welfare rolls without a hearing. No contention was made on behalf of the governmental officials that the plaintiff was not entitled to a hearing after the termination and the issue

was whether she was entitled to a pre-termination hearing. In holding that a pre-termination hearing was required by procedural due process the court balanced the interests of the state against the interests of the welfare recipient whose very livelihood depended upon the welfare fund. Such statutory rights in the recipient, when weighed with the monetary interests of the state, demanded the granting of a hearing prior to the termination. It may be said that contractual rights of a schoolteacher should be granted similar consideration, at least to the extent of the insistence upon a hearing at some time. On the other hand, it must be recognized that the interests of a schoolteacher in retaining a specific position of employment weigh less heavily than the interests of a person who in all probability cannot otherwise than by welfare obtain the essentials of existence. The court in *Goldberg* recognized the substantial interests of a welfare recipient by saying:

"* * * For qualified recipients, welfare provides the means to obtain essential food, clothing, housing, and medical care. * * * Thus the crucial factor in this context—a factor not present in the case of a blacklisted government contractor, the discharged government employee, the taxpayer denied a tax exemption, or virtually anyone else whose governmental entitlements are ended—is that termination of aid pending resolution of a controversy over eligibility may deprive an *eligible* recipient of the very means by which to live while he waits. * *"

The interest of the state in *Goldberg* was monetary only and commanded less consideration than the interest of the state in maintaining an orderly and harmonious educational faculty in a public high school.

A similar balancing was used in Cafeteria and Restaurant Workers Union Local 473, A.F.L.-C.I.O. v. McElroy, 367 U.S. 886, 81 S.Ct. 1743, 6 L.Ed.2d 1230 (1961), wherein it was held that a cook could be discharged without being accorded a hearing or being informed of the specific grounds for her exclusion. The interest of the government was substantial—"to manage the internal operation of an important federal military establishment," 367 U.S. at 896, 81 S.Ct. at 1749, and the interest of the cook was lighter by comparison—"the opportunity to work at one isolated and specific military installation," 367 U.S. at 896, 81 S.Ct. at 1749. It is not unreasonable to suggest that in the present case Miss Ahern was denied only the opportunity to work at one isolated and specific high school, as contrasted with denial of opportunity to be employed in any teaching institution, such as would be involved by denial of a lawyer's right to practice law, as in Schware v. Board of Bar Examiners, 353 U.S. 232, 77 S.Ct. 752, 1 L.Ed.2d 796 (1957) or perhaps the denial to a teacher of a teaching certificate.

The present case does not materially differ from

Cafeteria Workers insofar as the reason for discharge is concerned. In the *Cafeteria Workers* case the court said:

"We may assume that Rachel Brawner could not constitutionally have been excluded from the Gun Factory if the announced grounds for her exclusion had been patently arbitrary or discriminatory—that she could not have been kept out because she was a Democrat or a Methodist. It does not follow, however, that she was entitled to notice and a hearing when the reason advanced for her exclusion was, as here [failure to meet security requirements] entirely rational and in accordance with the contract with M & M." 367 U.S. at 898, 81 S.Ct. at 1750.

Similarly, in the present case the announced reason, insubordination, was entirely rational and in accordance with the contract between the school district and the teacher.

Nevertheless, the interest of a schoolteacher in specific employment may be of greater weight than a similar interest of a cook and the interest of the government in security on a military base may be more urgent than a state's interest in maintaining an orderly and harmonious faculty in a public high school.

I confess that the uncertainties which remain from a comparative analysis of *Cafeteria Workers* and *Goldberg* leave no clear answer for the present case. Were it not for Freeman v. Gould Special School District of Lincoln County, Ark., 405 F.2d 1153 (C.A. 8th Cir. 1969), my inclination would be to hold that the plaintiff was entitled to procedural due process, including at least the elements of a notice of the reasons advanced for proposed discharge, a hearing at which the factual bases for those reasons could be refuted, if she were able to refute them, and a right to cross-examine the person or persons primarily aware of the charges being leveled.[10] However, until the Supreme Court of the United States[11] or the Court of Appeals for this circuit makes a declaration that the principles of *Goldberg*, rather than those of *Cafeteria Workers*, are applicable to the discharge of a public schoolteacher for the reason of insubordination, I must respect the declaration of the Court of Appeals for the Eighth Circuit in *Freeman*:

"Absent statutory or contractual requirements, persons discharged for inefficiency, incompetency, or insubordination have no constitutional right to a hearing with rights of cross-examination and confrontation of witnesses."

In the present case there is no contractual requirement for a hearing. A statutory right to a hearing before the board of education exists upon the filing of a written request by the teacher whose contract is terminated,[12] but no such request was made by Miss Ahern.

Accordingly, judgment will be entered for the defendants and costs will be taxed to the plaintiff.

NOTES

1. For purposes of this decision the relative portions of the contracts were:

   "3. Said teacher hereby agrees to be governed by the rules and regulations of the Board of Education of said School District.

   "4. Said teacher agrees to accept such assignment of grades or classes as may be determined upon by the Superintendent of Schools, with the approval of the Board of Education, and to teach said grades or classes in an efficient manner. It is further agreed that the right to transfer said teacher to another position during the school year is reserved by the Board of Education."

   Published regulations of the school district included the following as Article V, at page 40:

   "1. The acceptance of a position in the Grand Island public schools will be regarded as a contract and pledge to follow all the directions and regulations of the board, superintendent and principal. When any willful neglect of such rules shall be manifested by any teacher, it shall be considered sufficient cause for the superintendent to declare that teacher's position vacant, subject to the approval of the board.

   * * * * *

   "4. *Teamwork* Teachers should, at all times, bear in mind the supreme importance of loyalty to the school and its constituted authorities. If there is just cause for criticism or complaint, the teacher may go directly to the principal or the superintendent, where the grievance will receive due consideration. Children profit when the entire staff works together in sympathy and hearty co-operation.

   "Employees who feel that they have just grievances which cannot be settled through normal channels are encouraged to state their grievances in writing within ninety days of the time they feel the injustice has occurred. Such grievances may be presented to the superintendent directly or through a regular grievance committee. The board of education will consider grievances promptly and will give a decision in writing through the superintendent of schools."

2. The portions read were those set out in footnote 1, not including the quotations from the published regulations of the school district.

3. Exhibit 26 is a transcript of the taped session of that class.

4. "Senior High School Course Outlines for Social-Studies," Exhibit 27, "A" ECONOMICS.

5. Exhibit 8.

6. Exhibit 23.

7. Exhibit 24.

8. Exhibit 42 is a transcript of the meeting.

9. The specific provision is paragraph 1 of Article V, quoted in footnote 1.

10. I do not reach the question of whether these elements were present in the proceedings by the board.

11. Guidance in this regard ultimately may come from cases presently pending in the Supreme Court of the United States. In DeCanio v. School Comm. of Boston, 260 N.E.2d 676 (1970) the Supreme Judicial Court of Massachusetts held that the summary dismissal of six

public school teachers who were non-tenured did not deprive the plaintiffs of due process. The dismissal was based on constitutionally permissible grounds, conduct unbecoming teachers, but it could be argued that the teachers' participation in a demonstration which resulted in their dismissal was protected activity under the First Amendment. The case is now in the Supreme Court as Fenton v. Boston School Committee, 401 U.S. 929, 91 S.Ct. 925, 28 L.Ed.2d 209. Also, in Perry v. Sindermann, No. 952, 39 U.S. L.W. 3303, certiorari was filed on November 9, 1970, from a Fifth Circuit ruling, the question being presented as "Does teacher without tenure and with no expectancy of having his contract renewed have any constitutionally protected right to continued employment?"

12.   Section 79-1254 Nebraska R.R.S. 1943.

A United States District Court in Arkansas decides for an elementary school teacher who had been dismissed because she had allowed her student to write a letter to the cafeteria supervisor requesting raw carrots and because she had shown to her principal some cartoons drawn by her students picturing wilted flowers, students lying down asking for water, etc., after a water fountain had broken. Further, the teacher had voiced concern to other teachers about an open incinerator in the playground, fearing that students might get hurt playing near the incinerator. In its decision ordering the teacher reinstated, the Court said: "It is patently clear from the evidence presented in this case . . . that association with the Conway School District, whether as a teacher or pupil, constitutes a waiver of the First Amendment rights of free speech and freedom to peaceably petition for the redress of grievances. This waiver has been effectuated by the superintendent through the unreasonable interpretation of school policy. . . . When a school board acts, as it did here, to punish a teacher who seeks to protect the health and safety of herself and her pupils, the resulting intimidation can only cause a severe chilling, if not freezing, effect on the free discussion of more controversial subjects."

Downs v. *Conway School District*, 328 F. Supp. 338 (1971)

OPINION

CLARY, Senior District Judge (Sitting by Special Designation).

Plaintiff here seeks a declaratory judgment, injunctive relief, and damages due to the alleged deprivation, under color of state law, of her rights, privileges, and immunities guaranteed by the 1st and 14th amendments of the United States Constitution. Jurisdiction is invoked pursuant to 28 U.S.C. § 1343(3) (4), 28 U.S.C. §§ 2201-2, and 42 U.S.C. § 1983, as well as under the Constitution of the United States.

The trial of the case having been held, and briefs submitted on the relevant issues of law, it is now ready for disposition.

THE FACTS

1. The plaintiff, Mildred S. Downs, is a qualified professional teacher, having a total experience of 25½ years in the Arkansas Public School System.

2. On or about December 1, 1966, plaintiff entered into a contract with the Conway School Board and was assigned to teach the second grade in the Ellen Smith School.

3. For the years 1967-8 and 1968-9 she was again of-

fered and signed a contract with the School Board to teach in the Ellen Smith Elementary School.

4. During the period encompassed by the 1967-68 school year a water fountain in her room became broken. She reported it to the principal who reported it to Carl White, superintendent of the maintenance department.

5. As the superintendent of maintenance, Carl White found that the fountain, which he thought was a Westinghouse fountain, was under a warranty and that the necessary parts could not be obtained under 10 days to 2 weeks, and so informed Mrs. Downs.

6. Some two to three weeks later, at a time when the temporary water supply (consisting of a plastic bucket and cups) provided by the plaintiff at her own expense for her pupils was exhausted and in need of refilling, and an art class was beginning, the teacher asked the pupils to draw pictures of their neighbors (other pupils) and express in the rough drawings the way that each one of the children of the class felt. The children drew the pictures as requested, and at least some of the pupils drew pictures of pupils lying down asking for water, wilted flowers, etc.

7. Plaintiff testified, without contradiction, that she exhibited some of these drawings to the principal and made no further dissemination thereof. The then prin-

cipal, James Stone, has no recollection of this episode. I find as a fact that these "cartoons" were actually delivered to the principal. The distribution thereof is uncertain, but Carl White did receive, through the mail, several of the cartoons. He immediately threw the pictures away and none of the so-called "cartoons" were ever seen by Carl Stuart, the superintendent of schools, and the first he heard about the drawings was in October of 1969.

8. Over the period of her employment with the Conway School District the plaintiff had on numerous occasions complained to the principal that the smoke from the open burning incinerator in the center of the playground was seeping into her classroom, particularly when the wind emanated from the north or northeast which blew the smoke and debris from the open incinerator directly at and into her room. The presence of the smoke resulted in bronchial and sinus disturbances to her personally and caused obvious physical discomfort to the members of her class. Complaints about this situation were made both by the plaintiff and her husband directly to the superintendent of schools. Unfortunately the then superintendent of schools was ill and no action was taken by the school superintendent or board to remedy the condition. In addition to the smoke hazard, the plaintiff testified, without contradiction, and the Court finds as a fact, that the burning of the trash in an open incinerator during school hours and recess hours constituted an open and imminent danger to the students of the plaintiff as well as other students in the school. It was testified, without contradiction, that one handicapped child made a habit of trying to ignite branches or sticks with which, after being ignited, he would run after and threaten other pupils in the immediate vicinity. Again it was testified, without contradiction, that the plaintiff herein, pursuant to her feeling of obligation, telephoned the mother of the pupil, who thereafter accompanied her child to school and at all times supervised him personally while he was playing in the school yard for the balance of the year. In addition to the smoke and flying debris, the testimony showed beyond peradventure of doubt that the overflow from the incinerator (burned and rusted tin cans, broken bottles, etc.) fell from the incinerator and constituted an obvious hazard to the children playing either basketball or baseball (See EX TT's EX 12 a b c). The testimony also showed that the children were attracted to the burning incinerator, climbed in and around the wall of the incinerator, and that it was only the extended and diligent supervision of the area afforded by the school teachers that prevented any substantial accident to any of the pupils. The evidence is also uncontradicted and shows that both plaintiff and her husband, in an effort to eliminate the whole hazard from the school, offered on several occasions to pay out of their own pockets the cost of trash removal to eliminate the hazard. The then superintendent of schools made no reply to this offer.

9. At the beginning of the 1968-9 session there was furnished, in addition to the open incinerator a barrel-type incinerator with a small smoke stack extruding from the top. The barrel-type incinerator was of limited capacity, and overflowed regularly, making necessary the additional use of the open incinerator which compounded instead of alleviating the problem. Again, in the fall of 1968 this problem was called to the attention of the present superintendent, Carl Stuart, who informed plaintiff and her husband that due to the lack of funds for the purpose he could not arrange to have the trash carried away and that because the district was unable to furnish trash disposal to all of the schools (5 in number) in Conway he could not accept the offer of the Downs to defray the cost and thereby prefer one school over another.

10. There was a committee of mothers of the second grade, comprised of 3 mothers, of which Mrs. William Saunders was Chairman. Her daughter was a pupil in Mrs. Downs' class. On 2 or 3 days a week, Mrs. Saunders visited the class, observed its operation and noticed the smoke nuisance and the hazards involved. Without the knowledge of the plaintiff she and the other 2 members of the committee visited the principal and complained of the situation. Thereafter on 3 occasions they called upon the school superintendent and registered their complaints. The only explanation ever given by the superintendent to either the plaintiff, her husband, or the committee of class mothers was that he was working on the problem with the School Board, but that there was nothing he could do about it.

11. Superintendent of Schools, Carl Stuart, at the time of these complaints knew that the incinerator posed a danger to both health and the physical well-being of the students, but took absolutely no steps to eliminate the hazards.

12. In the last week of January of 1970, in the course of and pursuant to a school outline of teaching, a situation arose as follows: The authorized text and materials discussed the relative nutritional value of many foods; included in this material was the information that the nutritional properties of raw carrots exceeded those of cooked carrots. Soon after this a pupil asked whether she might write a letter to the supervisor of the lunch program of the school asking that raw carrots be served at times in place of cooked carrots. A letter of this type asking someone to help or do something to help the writer was an integral part of the suggested teaching of the students at that particular time: Plaintiff's exhibit #9 showed that the workbook (Think and Do) which accompanied their text instructed the writing of this type of letter. The idea of such a letter

originated solely in the mind of one second-grade pupil (this will be discussed more fully later). Since it originated solely with the student and fit particularly well into the curriculum, the plaintiff readily acquiesced in the child's request and several letters were drafted, two of which were exhibits 10 and 10-A of plaintiff's exhibits. The plaintiff herself signed the letter upon the request of the students who had also signed the same. A student teacher who was then observing the class as part of her education to become an elementary teacher was present and also signed the letter. The letter, plaintiff's exhibit 10-A, read "Dear Mr. Glenn, The people in my room do not like cooked carrots so will you please serve the school raw carrots? Mrs. Downs Second Grade." The principal of the school, Mr. Parris, testified that he received the letter, or at least a copy thereof, but did not sign it. It was then sent in the mail to Mr. Glenn.

13. The matter came to the attention of the Superintendent of Schools, Carl Stuart and he thereupon brought it to the attention of the plaintiff, charged her with going over his head, violating school policies and for the first time brought to her attention that he took umbrage at the drawings or cartoons of the children which they had drawn during the episode of the broken water fountain. The plaintiff assured him that she had no intention of doing other than following school policies and felt that she had not violated any school policy and certainly had no intention of criticizing Carl White, the superintendent of maintenance with reference to the drawings and that she had considered the drawings to be rather creative on the part of the children and to be part of her duty to awaken interest in children to current events. The superintendent charged her with violating school policy in connection with the drawings and in connection with the letter stating that going over his head was a reflection upon him which could not be tolerated. Despite plaintiff's protest of any intention to go over his head, her warned her not to repeat the "offense".

14. In April of 1970, the incinerator nuisance became aggravated and again the plaintiff protested and was told by the superintendent that he had had no complaints from any other teacher in this regard. He failed to inform her of the fact that the class mother's committee had vigorously protested to him of this unhealthy situation.

15. Because of the fact that the plaintiff felt that she may have been wrong in her protest, she directed personal notes to all of the teachers and asked them whether the effusions were objectionable to them. The principal on that day, April 28, 1970, had also indicated to her he would recommend her for a contract renewal. The plaintiff did write notes to each of the teachers, submitted them to the teachers and received replies from most of the teachers. One of the teachers,

Geneva Bowlin, a first-grade teacher who had been out ill for some time and had returned to school did not have time or the inclination to answer whether or not the incinerator was objectionable to her. Upon the plaintiff's requesting and reminding her on one or two occasions that she had not answered it, she made a complaint to the superintendent. The superintendent testified that this occurred on April 29, 1970, and in addition stated that he had met an unknown 7 or 8 year old boy in the school yard who had stated to him that an unspecified teacher had become ill from the smoke of the incinerator and had asked the child to ask the superintendent to have the incinerator moved. As a result of the combination of circumstances, the letters (alleged by the superintendent to be petitions) and the request by the child, he determined that day not to recommend her for renewal of contract.

16. The Court finds as a fact that the statement as to the unknown boy specifying an unknown teacher is absolutely without foundation and has been used by the superintendent to justify an illegal failure of renewal of plaintiff's contract. A meeting or "hearing" was held before the School Board at Mrs. Downs request on May 5, 1970, at which the complaints of the superintendent against the plaintiff were supposed to be aired. The plaintiff offered to submit herself to questioning by the Board but no questions were asked of her. No written charges up to that time had been preferred against her but it was clear to all in attendance that the three factors and incidents above set forth in some detail were to be and actually were the sole and exclusive basis of the action of the School Board in refusing to renew the contract.

17. The plaintiff herein has had a record of 25½ years of outstanding service to the public school system of Arkansas. In fact the principal of her school under oath labeled her a "master teacher". There is not the slightest evidence that in all the 25½ years of devoted service to the children of Arkansas she ever had any other complaint registered against her, except the three by Carl Stuart.

18. At a meeting of the Ellen Smith School Parent-Teachers Association, held on April 27, 1970, the Association went on record requesting the School Board to abate the nuisance created by the incinerator and incinerators. The letter of May 25, 1970, notifying the plaintiff that her contract would not be renewed for cause contained the following three charges: This was the first written statement of charges of any kind ever furnished the plaintiff. The reasons are as follows: "(1) insubordination (2) lack of cooperation with the administration (3) teaching second graders to protest."

19. The evidence discloses as a fact that the plaintiff was never guilty of insubordination.

20. The evidence discloses as a fact that not only did the plaintiff not fail to cooperate with the administra-

tion, but that she used every reasonable means to fulfill her duties as a teacher and to comply with and follow the policies of the Board.

21. The Court finds as a fact that the plaintiff did not teach her second-grade pupils to protest the authority either of the teacher, the principal, the superintendent or the school board.

22. The Court finds as a fact that the superintendent demanded blind obedience to any directive he gave whether illegal, unconstitutional, arbitrary or capricious.

23. The Court finds that the interpretation given to the policy principles by the Superintendent Stuart went far and beyond the meaning intended by its drafters. The evidence was uncontradicted that the policy drafters intended that the policies be interpreted so as to maintain order and discipline within the classroom.

24. The Court finds that the superintendent of schools, intending to disregard every legal right of the plaintiff, and the pupils in her care, lumped three individual, unrelated, and innocent incidents into charges for the single and sole purpose of depriving the plaintiff of her legal rights under the contract of her employment and under the Constitution of the United States.

25. That the charges singly or in a group afforded no justification for failure to renew the plaintiff's contract with the School Board.

26. The Court also finds that at all times relevant Mrs. Downs stood ready, able, and willing to resume her teaching duties at the Ellen Smith School, and that she also made a sincere and diligent attempt to find like work for the 1970-71 school year and was unsuccessful in doing so.

27. That the Board's refusal to renew plaintiff's contract effectively acted as a barring of her in the Arkansas Public School System.

28. That the plaintiff, unless reinstated, will suffer irreparable damage.

DISCUSSION AND THE LAW

This Court finds, as a matter of law, that the plaintiff, having exhausted the administrative remedies available to her, is properly in the Federal Courts. That the plaintiff having requested a hearing before the School Board, and having appeared before the same has availed herself of the entire appellate process allowed by the Arkansas educational system. In fact, she was not "entitled" to even that under the law of this Circuit, see Freeman v. Gould Special Sch. Dist. of Lincoln Co., Ark., 405 F.2d 1153, 1160 (8th C.A. 1969), cert. denied, 396 U.S. 843, 90 S.Ct. 61, 24 L.Ed. 2d 93.

The *Freeman, supra* opinion is also dispositive of the issue of whether the plaintiff is afforded constitutional procedural due process. (Plaintiff's procedural rights

arising from her contract will be discussed later.) Plaintiff alleges that the hearing provided for her was unconstitutional in that she was not properly informed of the scope of the charges against her, and that the hearing, as conducted, failed to adequately air the issues. However, the 8th Circuit's holding in *Freeman, supra* which was based on an opinion of the Arkansas Attorney General dated May 10, 1967, specifically ruled that the Board is under no obligation to furnish any hearing for a teacher. Therefore, since a teacher does not have the right to require a hearing, it appears that there is also no right to demand that a hearing conform to any particular standards. This appears to be the law of the Circuit and this Court is bound by it, contra see Lucas v. Chapman, 430 F.2d 945 (5th C.A. 1970).

While *Freeman* defeats plaintiff's claimed denial of procedural due process, it does lend vitality to her allegation of denial of substantive due process and violation of constitutional rights. The Court there ruled:

"While the school boards in Arkansas have the right to decide whom they are going to employ or reemploy, the basis for failing to re-employ must not be on impermissible constitutional grounds. Smith v. Board of Education of Morrilton School District No. 32, 365 F.2d 770 (8 Cir. 1966) (racial discrimination); Johnson v. Branch, 364 F.2d 177 (4 Cir. 1966), cert. denied 385 U.S. 1003, 87 S.Ct. 706, 17 L.Ed.2d 542 (racial discrimination); Shelton v. Tucker, *supra* [364 U.S. 479, 81 S.Ct. 247, 5 L.Ed.2d 231] (a disclosure statute violative of the right of associational freedom, closely allied to freedom of speech)". 405 F.2d at 1158.

In Smith v. Board of Ed. of Morrilton Sch. Dist. #32, 365 F.2d 770 (8th C.A. 1966), the Court in discussing the near absolute freedom of school boards to hire and fire teachers, placed only one limitation on that freedom. They stated,

"Nothing contained in this opinion is intended to be restrictive of a school board's freedom to make full inquiry and to give due consideration to any applicant's qualifications and the district's needs in filling vacancies so long as the board does not act unreasonably, arbitrarily, capriciously, or unlawfully." 365 F.2d at 782.

Chief Judge Henley, of this district, in Norton v. Blaylock 285 F.Supp. 659 (E.D. Ark. 1968), aff'd 409 F.2d 772 (8th C.A. 1969), ruled:

"A complaint by an individual that he has been wrongfully barred or discharged from public employment can no longer be dismissed summarily by reference to Justice Holmes's familiar statement to the effect that no man has '[a] constitutional right to be a policeman,' McAuliffe v. City of New Bedford, 155 Mass. 216, 29 N.E. 517, quoted in Birnbaum v. Trussell, 2 Cir., 371 F.2d 672, 677. It is established by now that a State may not constitutionally impose arbitrary or discriminatory employment criteria and may not in general condition public employment upon the willingness of an employee or would-be employee to forego the exercise of right protected by some of the first ten amendments to the Constitution as brought forward into the 14th Amendment. See e.g.: Torcaso v. Watkins, 367 U.S. 488, 81 S.Ct. 1680, 6 L.Ed.2d 982; Shelton v. Tucker, 364 U.S. 479, 81 S.Ct. 247, 5 L.Ed. 2d 231; Slochower v. Board of Higher Education, 350 U.S. 551, 76 S.Ct. 637, 100 L.Ed. 692; Wieman v. Updegraff, 344 U.S. 183, 73 S.Ct. 215, 97 L.Ed. 216, * * *" 285 F.Supp. at 662.

The determination of what constitutes impermissible, unconstitutional, unreasonable, arbitrary, capricious, or unlawful grounds has been well litigated, and the law which has developed is especially protective of the first amendment rights of both teachers and students.

The 4th Circuit in Johnson v. Branch, 364 F.2d 177 (4th C.A. 1966) arises out of a similar situation in North Carolina, a jurisdiction whose laws regarding teacher tenure (or lack of it) and school board powers, are substantially identical to those of Arkansas. They found:

"The Supreme Court has recently had occasion to consider the law in this and analogous areas. It has pointed out on numerous occasions the importance of the teaching profession in our democratic society and the necessity of protecting its personal, associational and academic liberty. 'Scholarship cannot flourish in an atmosphere of suspicion and distrust. Teachers and students must always be free to inquire, to study, and to evaluate * * *.' Sweezy v. State of New Hampshire, 345 U.S. 234, 250, 77 S.Ct. 1203, 1212, 1 L.Ed.2d 1311 (1957); Barenblatt v. United States, 360 U.S. 109, 79 S.Ct. 1081, 3 L.Ed.2d 1115 (1959); Wieman v. Updegraff, 344 U.S. 183, 73 S.Ct. 215, 97 L.Ed. 216 (1952); Adler v. Board of Education, 342 U.S. 485, 72 S.Ct. 380, 96 L.Ed. 517 (1952)."

They continued:

We take it to be beyond cavil that the state may not force the plaintiff to choose between exercising her legitimate constitutional rights and her right of equality of opportunity to hold public employment. In Alston v. School Board of City of Norfolk, 112 F.2d 992 (4 Cir., 1940), cert. denied, 311 U.S. 693, 61 S.Ct. 75, 85 L.Ed. 448 (1940), this court struck down a practice of paying lesser salaries to Negro school teachers. In that case Chief Judge Parker said:

"It is no answer to this today that hiring of any teacher is a matter resting in the discretion of the school authorities. Plaintiffs, as teachers qualified and subject to employment by the state, are entitled to apply for the positions and to have the discretion of the authorities exercised lawfully and without unconstitutional discrimination as to the rate of pay to be awarded them, if their applications are accepted. "* * * If a state may compel the surrender of one constitutional right as a condition of its favor, it may, in like manner, compel a surrender of all. It is inconceivable that guarantees imbedded in the Constitution of the United States may thus be manipulated out of existence." [Citing and quoting Frost Trucking Co. v. Railroad Comm., 271 U.S. 583, 594, 46 S.Ct. 605, 70 L.Ed. 1101 (1926)] (112 F.2d at 996-997)." 364 F.2d at 180.

The leading case in this area is Tinker v. Des Moines Independent Community Sch. Dist., 393 U.S. 503, 506, 89 S.Ct. 733, 736, 21 L.Ed.2d 731 (1969). There the Court concluded that:

"First Amendment rights, applied in light of the special characteristics of the school environment, are available to teachers and students. It can hardly be argued that either students or teachers shed their constitutional rights to freedom of speech or expression at the schoolhouse gate. This has been the unmistakable holding of this Court for almost 50 years * * * In West Virginia State Board of Education v. Barnette, supra, [319 U.S. 624, 63 S.Ct. 1178, 87 L.Ed. 1628] this Court held that under the First Amendment, the student in public school may not be compelled to salute the flag. Speaking through Mr. Justice Jackson, the Court said:

'The Fourteenth Amendment, as now applied to the States, protects the citizen against the State itself and all of its creatures—Boards of Education not excepted. These have, of course important delicate, and highly discretionary functions, but none that they may not perform within the limits of the Bill of Rights. That they are educating the young for citizenship is reason for scrupulous protection of Constitutional freedoms of the individual, if we are not to strangle the free mind at its source and teach youth to discount important principles of our government as mere platitudes.' 319 U.S., at 637 [63 S.Ct. at 1185].

The Court further determined that:

The District Court concluded that the action of the school authorities was reasonable because it was based upon their fear of a disturbance from the wearing of the armbands. But, in our system, undifferentiated fear or apprehension of disturbance is not enough to overcome the right to freedom of expression. Any departure from absolute regimentation may cause trouble. Any variation from the majority's opinion may inspire fear. Any word spoken, in class, in the lunchroom, or on the campus, that deviates from the views of another person may start an argument or cause a disturbance. But our Constitution says we must take this risk, Terminiello v. Chicago, 337 U.S. 1 [69 S.Ct. 894, 93 L.Ed. 1131] (1949); and our history says that it is this sort of hazardous freedom—this kind of openness—that is the basis of our national strength and of the independence and vigor of Americans who grow up and live in this relatively permissive, often disputatious, society.

In order for the State in the person of school officials to justify prohibition of a particular expression of opinion, it must be able to show that its action was caused by something more than a mere desire to avoid the discomfort and unpleasantness that always accompany an unpopular viewpoint. Certainly where there is finding and no showing that engaging in the forbidden conduct would 'materially and substantially interfere with the requirements of appropriate discipline in the operation of the school,' the prohibition cannot be sustained. Burnside v. Byars, *supra*, [363 F.2d] at 749." 393 U.S. at 508, 509, 89 S.Ct. at 737, 738.

It is patently clear from the evidence presented in this case, especially the testimony of the Superintendent of Schools, that association with the Conway School District, whether as teacher or pupil, constitutes a waiver of the 1st amendment, rights of free speech and freedom to peaceably petition for the redress of grievances. This waiver has been effectuated by the Superintendent through the unreasonable interpretation of School policy. The policies of the school district are printed in a looseleaf publication entitled "Policies, Rules, and Regulations of the Conway Brd. of Education" (plaintiff's exhibit #3). In chapter VI B, Specific Operational Policies, number 10 (plaintiff's exhibit #7) reads:

"10. *Petitions:* No petition for any purpose may be circulated in any building without the approval of the Superintendent of Schools."

The testimony of Mr. Robbins of the Arkansas Education Association, who had been with the Conway Schools for 15 years and was chairman of the School Policies Committee, that created the Policies in question, was that it was the clear and public intention of the aforementioned policy to prevent the disruption of in class studies by the circulation of petitions. This interpretation of that policy would be wholly in keeping with the law as laid down in *Tinker, supra.* Mr. Stuart, however, interprets that section so as to preclude any and all correspondence, requests, and petitions unless blessed by himself prior to its circulation. This amounts to total censorship. This point was specifically covered in Friedman v. Union Free School Dist. No. 1, Town of Islip, 314 F.Supp. 223 (E.D. N.Y. 1970). The court pointed out that:

"* * * The Board's specious suggestion that 11F-21 (a policy similar to VI B 10) prevents all distribution in order to prevent the Board from becoming a censor is easily answered—it can accomplish the same objective by permitting all distribution, to the extent that such distribution does not materially and substantially interfere with the school's operation." 314 F.Supp. at 228 (parenthesis added). See also *Tinker, supra,* and Wolin v. Port of New York Authority, 392 F.2d 83, 90 (2nd Cir. 1968) cert. denied, 393 U.S. 940, 89 S.Ct. 290, 21 L.Ed.2d 275.

In the case at bar, the superintendent used his interpretation of VI B 10 to conclude that the plaintiff violated that policy when:

(1) she allowed her student to write a letter to the cafeteria supervisor requesting raw carrots, and (2) when she showed the children's cartoons to the principal (the Court would like to reiterate at this point its finding that both the letter and cartoons were completely reasonable and in keeping with the curriculum as prescribed in the authorized texts and materials provided for the second grade by the Conway School District) and, (3) when she wrote the other teachers concerning the incinerator (this incident will be discussed in greater depth later, as the Court finds that this is the real cause of friction and that the other incidents were brought in ex post facto, to strengthen a position that the superintendent must have recognized as being extremely weak). At no time has the defense averred that any of Mrs. Downs' conduct did or even could be reasonably expected to "materially and substantially interfere with the requirements of appropriate discipline in the operation of the school." *Tinker, supra,* 393 U.S. at p. 509, 89 S.Ct. at p. 738.

The Supreme Court of Arkansas in defining "cause" has stated in Williams v. Dent, 207 Ark. 440, 181 S.W.2d 29 (1944) that:

"'"Cause", or "sufficient cause," means "legal cause," and not any cause which the Council may think sufficient. The cause must be one which specifically relates to and affects the administration of the office, and must be restricted to something of a substantial nature directly affecting the rights and interests of the public.' And in Corpus Juris, vol. 43, § 1085, p. 658, the term 'for cause,' is said to mean *just* cause: 'And the cause assigned for removal must not be a mere whim or subterfuge, but must be of substance relating to the character, neglect of duty, or fitness of the person removed.'" 207 Ark. at 450, 181 S.W.2d at 39. See also Martin v. Cogbill, Commissioner, 214 Ark. 818, 218 S.W.2d 94 (1949).

Mr. Stuart, in his testimony took the rather paradoxical position that while he believes that freedom to discuss controversial subjects is essential to a democratic education he personally will not tolerate such. This same rationale was met in Los Angeles Teachers

Union v. Los Angeles City Board of Ed., 71 Cal.2d 551, 78 Cal.Rptr. 723, 455 P.2d 827 (1969). There the Court pointed out that:

"Harmony among public employees is undoubtedly a legitimate governmental objective as a general proposition (see Pickering v. Board of Education, 391 U.S. 563, 569-570, 88 S.Ct. 1731, 20 L.Ed.2d 811); however, as we have seen, government has no interest in preventing the sort of disharmony which inevitably results from the mere expression of controversial ideas. (Tinker v. Des Moines Independent Community Sch. Dist., 393 U.S. 503, 509, 89 S.Ct. 733, 21 L.Ed. 2d 731; Terminiello v. City of Chicago, 337 U.S. 1, 4, 69 S.Ct. 894, 93 L.Ed. 1131; Wirta v. Alameda-Contra Costa Transit Dist., 68 Cal.2d 51, 61-62, 64 Cal.Rptr. 430, 434 P.2d 982.) It cannot seriously be argued that school officials may demand a teaching faculty composed either of unthinking 'yes men' who will uniformly adhere to a designated side of any controversial issue or of thinking individuals sworn never to share their ideas with one another for fear they may disagree and, like children, extend their disagreement to the level of general hostility and uncooperativeness. Yet it is precisely the inevitable disharmony resulting from the clash of opposing viewpoints that defendants admittedly seek to avoid in the present case." 78 Cal.Rptr. at 729, 455 P.2d at 833.

It is the creation of this type of uniformity, by suppression, that has been attempted here.

Here we have uncontradicted testimony revealing several facts concerning the key dispute between Mrs. Downs and Mr. Stuart:

1. An open unfenced incinerator, consisting of 3 brick walls in a ⊔ shape was located nearly in the center of an elementary school playground. (see defendant 1).

2. Trash was burned in this incinerator throughout the school day including the times that the children were in the yard.

3. The fire was an attractive nuisance which drew children to it, and was so located as to cause children playing ball to come into inadvertent contact with it.

4. Not only was there a serious danger of a child getting burned, but there was additional danger from the refuse (broken bottles and burned tin cans) which were left around the incinerator.

5. Lastly and certainly not least, the smoke and ash created from burning such things as waxen milk cartons caused several rooms, (depending on wind conditions) to fill with enough smoke so as to cause drowsiness and illness in some children as well as for Mrs. Downs.

Confronted with the above facts, and coupled with the Superintendent's apparent inability or refusal to remedy the situation, the plaintiff was expected to either live with the incinerator or resign.

While some state statutes provide legal immunity for negligent acts by teachers and school supervisory personnel, this Court can not locate any jurisdiction that does not subscribe to the proposition that:

"It is the duty of a teacher in the public schools to exercise proper supervision over pupils in his charge and to exercise reasonable care to prevent injury to them." 78 C.J.S. Schools and School Districts §237 b.

Both alternatives left to plaintiff by Mr. Stuart would be violative of her moral, if not legal, duty to protect the health and safety of her students.

"At least in a limited sense the relation of a teacher to a pupil is that of one in loco parentis. We are not here concerned with the law applicable to punishment of a pupil by a teacher; but rather with the law applicable to the duties of a teacher in the care and custody of a pupil. In the faithful discharge of such duties the teacher is bound to use reasonable care, tested in the light of the existing relationship." Gaincott v. Davis, 281 Mich. 515, 275 N.W. 229, 231 (1937). See also Segerman v. Jones, 256 Md. 109, 259 A.2d 794, 801 (1969).

Nonfeasance is as much of a breach of a teacher's duty as misfeasance. Eastman v. Williams, 124 Vt. 445, 207 A.2d 146 (1965).

Aside from the moral and legal aspects of the plaintiff's duty she also was contractually bound to do the same. VII F 3 of the "Policies, Rules, and Regulations of the Conway Board of Education" (plaintiff's exhibit #3) states that:

"The total school curriculum, including the instructional program, all school facilities, and the general schedule of activities shall at all times be conducive to good health practices."

III F 4a (Major Duties and Responsibilities of a Teacher) reads:

"He shall be responsible for carrying out to the best of his ability the policies, rules and regulations established by the Board of Education and for maintaining at all times a classroom which actively demonstrates the current philosophy of the Conway Public Schools."

These rules were part of the teachers contract and plaintiff acted reasonably and responsibly under them (the legal contract considerations will be discussed later).

Confronted with a clear duty Mrs. Downs proceeded in strict accordance with the rules notwithstanding the unconstitutionally broad rule as to petitions. At all times she complied with the Board Rule requiring that:

"Teachers should work through proper channels. If it is at all possible, all problems should be solved by those immediately concerned. If this is not possible, the teacher will then ask help from the principal, the superintendent, the Board of Ed. in this order and only as it becomes necessary to embat [sic] the aid of a successively higher authority" (see plaintiff's exhibit #5 or plaintiff's exhibit #3, p. 5).

In the incident concerning the carrots, Mrs. Downs discussed the matter only with the cafeteria supervisor as he was the party most immediately concerned. With respect to the water fountain, again only the maintenance supervisor and later the principal were involved as it was unnecessary to enlist the aid of a successively higher authority re: the superintendent. Lastly regarding the incinerator Mrs. Downs again only went through the hierarchy as the need became evident.

At this point it should be pointed out that these events occurred over a period of 3 school years. Also, Mrs. Downs was not the only teacher to voice concern with the incinerator problems; another teacher testified that she had complained to the principal, and was informed that it would be useless for her to go higher as the superintendent had made up his mind to do nothing.

This Court realizes that the incidents complained of here do not, at first blush, seem to raise any real threat to democracy or the constitution, but upon further examination more ominous repercussions are revealed.

A citizen, be he teacher or layman, has the legal right to seek redress be it judicial or administrative for substantial dangers and/or threats to his health and/or safety and a court cannot sanction attempts to so intimidate a citizen, that they forego such fundamental rights Edwards v. Habib, 130 U.S.App. D.C. 126, 397 F.2d 687 (1968), cert. denied, 393 U.S. 1016, 89 S.Ct. 618, 21 L.Ed.2d 560.

When a School Board acts, as it did here, to punish a teacher who seeks to protect the health and safety of herself and her pupils, the resulting intimidation can only cause a severe chilling, if not freezing, effect on the free discussion of more controversial subjects.

"The vigilant protection of constitutional freedoms is nowhere more vital than in the community of American schools. 'By limiting the power of the States to interfere with freedom of speech and freedom of inquiry and freedom of association, the Fourteenth Amendment protects all persons, no matter what their calling. But, in view of the nature of the teacher's relation to the effective exercise of the rights which are safeguarded by the Bill of Rights and by the Fourteenth Amendment, inhibition of freedom of thought, and of action upon thought, in the case of teachers brings the safeguards of those amendments vividly into operation. Such unwarranted inhibition upon the free spirit of teachers * * * has an unmistakable tendency to chill

that free play of the spirit which all teachers ought especially to cultivate and practice; it makes for caution and timidity in their associations by potential teachers.' Wieman v. Updegraff, 344 U.S. 183, 195 [73 S.Ct. 215, 221, 97 L.Ed. 216] (concurring opinion). 'Scholarship cannot flourish in an atmosphere of suspicion and distrust. Teachers and students must always remain free to inquire, to study and to evaluate * *.' Sweezy v. New Hampshire, 354 U.S. 234, 250, 77 S.Ct. 1203, 1212, 1 L.Ed.2d 1311.'' Shelton v. Tucker, 364 U.S. 479, 487, 81 S.Ct. 247, 251, 5 L.Ed.2d 231 (1960) see also Parducci v. Rutland, 316 F.Supp. 352, 355 (M.D.Ala. 1970).

At this juncture the Court would like to specifically state that the infamous allegation of "licentious conduct" on the part of the plaintiff (defendant's ans. p. 4) is totally unfounded and its use is highly defamatory; illustrative of the highly malevolent attitude of the defendants.

On the question of whether the "Policies, Rules and Regulations of the Conway Board of Education" are in fact incorporated into a teacher's contract we must look at all of the facts surrounding the contract. The contract itself (plaintiff's exhibit #1) consists of one side of paper containing the bare minimum as to salary, how it is to be paid and the school to which the teacher is assigned. No mention is made of teacher, duties, responsibility, subject or grade to be taught or administrative practices. Therefore, looking only to the face of the document the contract is clearly not indicative of the entire agreement between the parties. The further information necessary to establish a clear relationship is contained in the aforementioned Policies. In fact III F 4a, *supra*, indicates that the Board clearly intends to hold each teacher to the conditions set forth therein. This situation falls clearly within the facts and findings in Greene v. Howard Univ., 134 U.S.App. D.C. 81, 412 F.2d 1128 (1969) which held that the duties and obligations set forth in the teachers handbook were to be incorporated into the contract. See also Ferguson v. Thomas, 430 F.2d 852 (5th Cir. 1970).

While the plaintiff here assigns error to the alleged failure of the Board of Education to give her sufficient notice and hearing, under the provisions of dismissal spelled out in the Policies, Rules and Regulations (III F 12), the Court need not rule whether these contract provisions were procedurally met, as it has already been found that substantively the action taken by defendant was plainly unconstitutional.

In conclusion this Court hopes that the defendants herein will adopt a reasonable attitude which will allow its teachers to comply with Policy III F 4e which provides, as to teachers that:

"He shall demonstrate the principles of democracy at all times in the operation of his classroom thereby providing each child with the opportunity to develop from actual experience a real understanding of the democratic way of life."

The Board should not allow naive and chimerical fears to disrupt the above objective as was done in this case.

The caveat of Justice Peters of California in Los Angeles Teacher Union v. Los Angeles City Board of Ed., *supra*, 78 Cal.Rptr. 723, 732, 455 P.2d 827, 836 that:

"* * * Education is in a state of ferment, if not turmoil. When controversies arising from or contributing to this turbulence are brought before the courts, it is imperative that the courts carefully differentiate in treatment those who are violent and heedless of the rights of others as they assert their cause and those whose concerns are no less burning but who seek to express themselves through peaceful, orderly means. In order to discourage persons from engaging in the former type of activity, the courts must take pains to assure that the channels of peaceful communication remain open and that peaceful activity is fully protected."

must be and will be heeded by this Court.

The opinion set forth above shall constitute the complete findings of act and conclusions of law of this court as required pursuant to Rule 52 of the F.R. Civ.P.

ORDER

And now, to wit, this 23rd day of June, 1971, it is ordered, adjudged and decreed, that:

1. the plaintiff, Mrs. Mildred Downs be reinstated to her teaching position at the Ellen Smith School, for the 1971-72 school year, and thereafter for so long as her conduct and competency comports with the standards of her profession, and the legal and reasonable policies of the Conway School System, and

2. the defendant is to compensate the plaintiff for her lost wages for the 1970-71 school year and she is to be restored to her position with the full rights, emoluments, and seniority that she would have been entitled to had her course of service not been interrupted, and

3. the defendant is assessed the full court costs and attorneys fees that have accrued as a result of this action the costs to be taxed by the Clerk and the attorney's fees to be fixed by the court upon written application.

A United States District Court in Texas decides for a high school civics teacher who had been dismissed for, among other things, remarks he had made and teaching methods he had used in class when dealing with issues related to race, prejudice, and protest. In deciding for the teacher, the Court stated: "The court finds that Mr. Sterzing's classroom methods were formulated and conducted within the ambit of accepted professional standards. . . . A responsible teacher must have freedom to use the tools of his profession as he sees fit. If the teacher cannot be trusted to use them fairly, then the teacher should never have been engaged in the first place. The Court finds Mr. Sterzing's objectives in his teaching to be proper to stimulate critical thinking, to create awareness of our present political and social community and to enliven the educational process. These are desirable goals. . . . This discharge of Mr. Sterzing and failure to rehire him, for the reasons stated by the school board, constituted a denial of due process and a violation of the First and Fourteenth Amendments of the Constitution."

Sterzing v. *Fort Bend Independent School Dist.*, 376 F.Supp. 657 (1972)

Carl O. BUE, Jr., District Judge.

FINDINGS AND CONCLUSIONS
THE COURT:

From September 1966 until February 26, 1968, Henry Keith Sterzing, plaintiff herein, was employed as a civics instructor at the John Foster Dulles High School, in Stafford, Texas, which is a part of the Ft. Bend Independent School District, a defendant herein.

At the end of the 1966-67 school year Mr. Sterzing was re-employed by the Board of Trustees for an additional year.

In September 1967, shortly after the start of the 1967-68 school year, Mr. H. L. Jenkins, principal of the John Foster Dulles High School, advised Mr. Sterzing that there had been some complaints by parents about the manner in which Mr. Sterzing was teaching his civics classes; specifically, complaints concerning plaintiff's truthful response to a student's classroom question that he was not opposed to interracial marriages.

Principal Jenkins at about the same time instructed Jane Schneider, chairwoman of Mr. Sterzing's social studies department, to instruct plaintiff to teach his current events course within the text and not discuss controversial issues. Thereafter Mr. Sterzing was ad-

vised by Mrs. Jane Schneider, his department head, that the school board, or school administration, wanted him to confine his teaching to the text. The problem was discussed by Mrs. Schneider and Mr. Sterzing and they both agreed that it was extremely difficult to avoid controversial issues, especially in the teaching of senior political science and civics. The agreed course of action between the department head and Mr. Sterzing was to use the textual material as a basis for the course and to build and supplement with other pertinent material, and further to use care in presenting controversial issues.

Shortly after this conversation with Mrs. Schneider, and still in September 1967, Mr. Sterzing was advised by Mr. James N. Ratcliff, director of secondary education for the Fort Bend Independent School District, that a group of parents planned to attend the school board meeting scheduled for September 27, 1967 in order to protest the manner in which Mr. Sterzing was teaching his classes.

In recognition of what was about to be put in issue, Mr. Sterzing wrote on the blackboard for each of his classes on September 27, 1968, the following:

"Academic freedom in the classroom. Watch local government in action tonight at 7:30, in the School Administration Building. Question of public policy, shall a teacher in local school be discharged or retained at his teaching position."

A group of parents did not materialize at the September 27, 1967 board meeting, but at that board meeting Mr. Sterzing and Mr. Jenkins suggested that the board go into executive session to discuss Mr. Sterzing's teaching.

Mr. Sterzing was not on the board's agenda and it had not planned to discuss any matter concerning him at that meeting. In executive session Mr. Jenkins advised the board of several complaints he had received from parents of children in Mr. Sterzing's classes, concerning comments made by Mr. Sterzing during class. These comments were diverse, but in each instance reflected Mr. Sterzing's opinion on a sensitive social or political issue.

After hearing these complaints and Mr. Sterzing's account with respect to each, the board suggested to Mr. Sterzing that he might be wise to confine his teaching to the text and to avoid controversial issues, to the extent possible.

Mr. Sterzing replied that he could not teach in this manner.

It was further suggested that Mr. Sterzing should take a more positive approach to teaching, although that term was never defined by the board. Mr. Sterzing explained that it was impossible to teach a high school senior class current events and avoid discussion of controversial issues. There was no actual resolution of the issues presented and no definite instructions issued.

Between September 1967 and February 1968 the plaintiff distributed an article to his classes written by Eric Schnapper denouncing the repression of anti-war dissent in the armed forces. Also, between September 1967 and February 1968 Mr. Sterzing distributed to his classes the fund solicitation letter from students at the University of Texas who had been arrested at Fort Hood in Killeen, Texas in connection with their anti-war protest during a speech by President Johnson. The presentation of the letter was accompanied by Mr. Sterzing's statement that this was not an appeal for funds from his students, but was for use as an original source document to aid their understanding of the manner in which interest groups arouse public support.

Early in February 1968 Mr. Sterzing taught in each of his classes a six day unit on race relations. In connection with this unit he distributed to his classes three articles and showed three films on the subject of race relations. The films were properly cleared by Mr. Sterzing through school channels and were, in fact, ordered through and paid for by the school authorities. The course curriculum and some of the actual reading materials were made available to Mr. Sterzing's new department head, Mrs. Ann Taylor.

At the conclusion of the six day unit on race re-

lations Mr. Sterzing gave each of his classes a true-false and multiple choice test over the textual material, class lectures and audio-visual materials. Before administering the test Mr. Sterzing showed such test to Mr. Elkins, assistant superintendent.

Parents of several of Mr. Sterzing's students, including Mr. Roy Kelly and Mrs. Manford, objected to several statements made in class by Mr. Sterzing regarding race and prejudice and with regard to the examinations. They communicated their objections to school officials and school board.

With the understanding of school officials, who indicated that he should not discuss the material in question, Mr. Sterzing made personal visits to two of these parents and explained his position to clarify the misunderstanding. The results did nothing to alleviate the problems.

On February 15, 1968, at such visit, Mr. Kelly told Mr. Sterzing he would do his best to get him fired as soon as possible, because plaintiff was teaching Mr. Kelly's daughter items inconsistent with what Mr. Kelly thought she should believe.

After these tests were given by Mr. Sterzing to his classes, and on February 28, 1968, Mr. Kelly, a defendant herein, appeared at the school board meeting. He reviewed the written materials described above and also reviewed the tests given by Mr. Sterzing over the unit on race relations.

Mr. Kelly took the position that the materials were of a propagandistic nature and were given to a captive audience without the opportunity to express opposing viewpoints being given to the students.

On February 27, 1968, without affording Mr. Sterzing notice or opportunity to be heard in his own defense, the board voted to discharge Mr. Sterzing, effective immediately. The dismissal was asserted to be based upon insubordination.

On February 28th, 1968, Mr. Sterzing was informed of the board's action and forbidden to enter the school grounds thereafter, except at a set and supervised occasion to remove his personal belongings.

Subsequently, the board affirmed the termination of Mr. Sterzing's employment and voted to pay him through the remainder of his contract term, ending June 1, 1968. Such payment was thereafter received by Mr. Sterzing.

Plaintiff appealed to the Texas Commissioner of Education. After a hearing the Commissioner rendered official findings and conclusions, including:

A. Plaintiff's dismissal was purportedly based upon insubordination;

B. The dismissal was without justifiable cause;

C. The Commissioner of Education had no jurisdiction to order reinstatement of plaintiff.

The Texas Board of Education thereafter affirmed the Commissioner's determination.

Mr. Sterzing attempted to secure a teaching position at numerous schools in Texas, but, at least in large part, as a result of defendant's dismissal of him he was unable to secure a teaching job thereafter. He eventually obtained a civilian job with the Air Force, which required overseas service. He is presently serving on Taiwan, with his present contract expiring in 1974. His salary in the Air Force since 1968 up to the present time has been in the range of $15,000. Thus, at all such times Mr. Sterzing has been earning in excess of what he would have earned as a teacher, had he remained in the Fort Bend School System. However, Mr. Sterzing at all times desired, and still desires, to remain in the teaching profession.

Viewing all of the evidence in this case it becomes apparent to this Court that much of what has precipitated this lawsuit need never have occurred, had all parties been fully informed of the true circumstances under which events took place.

Between September 1967 and February 1968 there was a serious lack of communication through channels from the individual teachers such as Mr. Sterzing, to the principal, Mr. Jenkins, the assistant superintendent, Mr. Elkins, and the curriculum chairman, Mr. Ratcliff.

For example, it seems strange, indeed, to this Court that the principal had never visited the classroom of Mr. Sterzing and was wholly unfamiliar with his teaching methods. Yet it is this pattern of unfamiliarity which seems to permeate the so called chain of command, culminating with the board, which then proceeded to act and reach decisions without the benefit of firsthand knowledge as to what was going on in Mr. Sterzing's classroom.

This Court is obliged to reach a decision based on the record in this case. It cannot engage in surmise and conjecture. The Court has read the articles and reviewed the disputed tests. Inasmuch as there is only minimal proof apart from that of Mr. Sterzing's testimony concerning the nature of his class discussions it can only be concluded that, viewed overall, something approaching fair treatment of the various viewpoints on controversial issues was approached when all aspects of the course are considered. If it wasn't, Mr. Sterzing was wrong. And this Court stresses to him now that he should bear it in mind in his teaching in the future.

A teacher's methods are not without limits. Teachers occupy a unique position of trust in our society, and they must handle such trust and the instruction of young people with great care. On the other hand, a teacher must not be manacled with rigid regulations, which preclude full adaptation of the course to the times in which we live. It would be ill-advised to presume that a teacher would be limited, in essence, to a single textbook in teaching a course today in civics and

social studies. What is so anomalous about this case is that there is considerable agreement that, if Mr. Sterzing's methods were as he said they were, there would be little, if any, objection to his techniques. Yet no one criticizing Mr. Sterzing took the trouble to find out firsthand what these techniques were, either prior to September 1967, or thereafter, when the complaints began to surface.

From the proof in this case the testimony of the two immediate department supervisors must be viewed as generally approving the teaching procedures and conduct of the plaintiff.

The Court therefore feels compelled at this juncture to issue several caveats:

1. The freedom of speech of a teacher and a citizen of the United States must not be so lightly regarded that he stands in jeopardy of dismissal for raising controversial issues in an eager but disciplined classroom.[1]

2. However, it must also be that teacher's duty to be exceptionally fair and objective in presenting his personally held opinions, to actively and persuasively present different views, in addition to open discussion.[2] It is the duty of the teacher to be cognizant of and sensitive to the feelings of his students, their parents, and their community.

Further, it is the binding duty of an administrative body to act with full information, with reason and deliberation, and with full benefit of the views of supervisors, principals and others familiar with the curriculum and teaching techniques in the schools, before denying a teacher his livelihood and professional status. It is entirely unfitting that such a board should be swayed by the hearsay remarks of persons not in possession of the facts, without specifically warning the accused of the contemplated action and allowing him a fair and impartial hearing before they act.

Accordingly, from the record in this case, the Court finds that Mr. Sterzing's classroom methods were formulated and conducted within the ambit of accepted professional standards. At least there is clearly insufficient probative evidence to the contrary in this case.

While the best method might have been to take care to present written materials to support each viewpoint in controversy, the various class discussions which this Court finds did occur adequately fulfill the need for expression of dissident views. While the best method of testing over a unit on race and prejudice might have been a test in essay form, the objective true and false and multiple choice tests given, in light of the written material, were adequate. A responsible teacher must have freedom to use the tools of his profession as he sees fit. If the teacher cannot be trusted to use them fairly, then the teacher should never have been engaged in the first place. The Court finds Mr. Sterzing's objectives in his teaching to be proper to stimulate critical thinking, to create an awareness of our present political and social community and to enliven the educational process. These are desirable goals.

The Court further finds that, while Mr. Sterzing was undoubtedly zealous in his duties, perhaps at times overly so, perhaps due to inexperience as a teacher, at no time were Mr. Sterzing's actions such that they could be characterized as insubordinate to the defendants with respect to any duty owed to any of them, nor was there any basis in fact or law justifying dismissal of the plaintiff. Even assuming that the board action was taken specifically because of the statements of Mr. Sterzing in class rather than for insubordination, as stated in the resolution of the board, the Court finds that such statements neither, one, materially and substantially interfered with appropriate discipline, nor two, subjected students unfairly to indoctrination and influence.

The Court finds these rights to be evident, the substantive rights of a teacher to choose a teaching method, which, in the Court's view, on the basis of expert opinion, served a demonstrated educational purpose, and the procedural right of a teacher not to be discharged for the use of a teaching method which was not proscribed by a regulation or definitive administrative action, and as to which it was not proven that he had notice that its use was prohibited.[3]

This discharge of Mr. Sterzing and failure to rehire him, for the reasons stated by the school board, constituted a denial of due process and a violation of rights granted and protected by the First and Fourteenth Amendments of the Constitution.

As to Mr. Kelly, the Court does believe that Mr. Kelly acted improvidently, and without due deliberation, but finds such actions to have been made in good faith as a parent's concern for the well-being of his child. This is a normal, genuine and healthy concern of a parent and one that a teacher must recognize and diplomatically deal with.

The Court further finds that the defendant Roy Kelly did not unlawfully conspire with other persons to cause plaintiff to lose his job and be prevented from securing future employment, or to deprive the plaintiff of his rights under the Constitution and the Civil Rights Act.

The action taken by the school board as to Mr. Sterzing, and sanctioned by the school administration, constituted a denial of procedural and substantive due process to the plaintiff. Although the Court finds a denial of procedural due process, the Court further finds that this case is unsuitable for remand, and that plaintiff was accorded a full and fair procedural hearing on all issues on appeal to the State Commissioner of Education and the State Board of Education.

This Court accords great weight to the decisions of those bodies, both in comity and in agreement with the decisions there rendered. However, this Court does not feel bound by their findings or conclusions. Rather, it views this action, under 42 U.S. Code § 1983, as entirely a de novo hearing. Accordingly, the resolution of substantive issues is properly made by this Court.

The Court finds, as stated above, that the plaintiff has been denied the proper exercise of his right of free speech, and that this denial was a consequence of the arbitrary actions of the named defendants herein, except defendant Kelly, and that plaintiff has been damaged thereby. Because of such actions of defendant, the plaintiff has suffered monetary damages of lost compensation, loss of opportunity to remain in and advance in his career as a teacher, mental suffering, loss of professional status and reputation, and the incurring of legal fees and expenses.

The Court has considered the right of the plaintiff to reinstatement. Since the plaintiff was hired on a yearly contract, which contract was fully paid by the school administration, and since reinstatement at this late date would only serve to revive antagonisms, the Court believes the proper exercise of discretion to be denial of the requested reinstatement. This the Court does in realization of the fact that plaintiff had an expectancy of re-employment, taking into consideration the value of reinstatement in monetary damages. Such a holding was rendered in Smith versus Losee,[4] an opinion by Judge Ritter, where reinstatement was not awarded, even though a finding of denial of substantive due process was entered.

Accordingly, plaintiff is entitled to judgment:

1. Directing the defendants to expunge from their employment records and transcripts all references to plaintiff's discharge.[5]

2. A judgment against all defendants, except Roy Kelly, jointly and severally in the amount of $20,000 as general damages, together with costs.[6]

3. A judgment against all defendants, except Roy Kelly, jointly and severally, in the amount of $5,000 as attorney's fees.[7]

Counsel will submit within 20 days a proposed judgment agreed upon as to form, in accordance with these findings of fact and conclusions of law.

FINAL JUDGMENT AND DECREE

This Action came on for trial before the Court, Honorable Carl O. Bue, Jr., United States District Judge, presiding, in the regular order of the Docket on the fourth day of April, 1972, whereupon all parties appeared and announced ready for trial. No Jury having been demanded, all matters of fact and law were submitted to the Court. The case having been fully submitted and due consideration given to the pleadings, proof and arguments, and the Court made and entered, Findings of Facts and Conclusions of Law herein;

It is hereby ordered, adjudged and decreed by the Court as follows:

I.

That the plaintiff, Henry Keith Sterzing, (hereinafter called plaintiff), shall have his relief as sought by the complaint against the Fort Bend Independent School District, Fort Bend County, Texas, a public body corporate; and Kenneth A. Landin, President of the Board of Trustees of Fort Bend Independent School District, Fort Bend County, Texas; Tony Langelosi, Herbert R. Shelton, Jr., Bruce Edwards, William A. Little, Antonio Arriga and Don A. Whatley, members of the Board of Trustees of Fort Bend Independent School District, Fort Bend County, Texas (hereinafter called defendants) jointly and severally in the following particulars:

a. The defendant, its officers, agents, employees and privies, are ordered to expunge from their employment records, business records, and transcripts, all reference to plaintiff's discharge in any manner whatsoever;

b. The plaintiff is hereby awarded and shall have and recover of and from the defendants as compensation for lost monetary compensation, loss of opportunity to remain in and advance in his professional career as a classroom teacher, mental suffering, loss of professional status and reputation, and general damages to the sum of Twenty Thousand and No/100 ($20,000.00) Dollars, together with interest from time of judgment at the rate of six per cent (6%) per annum until same is paid;

c. The plaintiff is further hereby awarded and shall have and recover of and from the defendant as compensation for Attorney's fees incurred by the plaintiff herein the sum of Five Thousand and No/100 ($5,000.00) Dollars together with interest from time of judgment at the rate of six per cent (6%) per annum until the claim is paid.

d. The plaintiff is hereby awarded judgment against defendants for all costs and disbursements incurred in this action for which the Clerk shall forthwith tax and for which execution shall issue.

II.

That the defendant, Roy Kelly, is in all respects, discharged and the relief sought by the plaintiff against the defendant, Roy Kelly, is in all respects denied.

III.

That the plaintiff's request for reinstatement as a teacher in the Fort Bend Independent School District, Fort Bend County, Texas, is denied.

NOTES

1. Keefe v. Geanakos, 418 F.2d 359 (1st Cir. 1969); Mailloux v. Kiley, 323 F.Supp. 1387 (D.Mass.), aff'd, 448 F.2d 1242 (1st Cir. 1971); Parducci v. Rutland, 316 F.Supp. 352 (M.D.Ala.1970).
2. Cases cited n. 1, *supra*.
3. Mailloux v. Kiley, 323 F.Supp. 1387 (D.Mass.), aff'd, 448 F.2d 1242 (1st Cir. 1971).
4. Smith v. Losee, et al., C.A. No. C283-69 (D.Utah 1972).
5. Mailloux v. Kiley, 323 F.Supp. 1387 (D.Mass.), aff'd, 448 F.2d 1242 (1st Cir. 1971).
6. Ramsey v. Hopkins, 447 F.2d 128 (5th Cir. 1971); Harkless v. Sweeney Ind. School Dist., 427 F.2d 319 (5th Cir. 1970), cert. denied, 400 U.S. 991, 91 S.Ct. 451, 27 L.Ed.2d 459 (1971).
7. Karstetter v. Evans, 350 F.Supp. 209 (N.D.Tex.1972, opinion by Judge Hughes); Bates v. Hinds, 334 F.Supp. 528 (N.D.Tex. 1971); Moore v. Knowles, 333 F.Supp. 53 (N.D.Tex. 1971).

T HE Court of Appeal of Louisiana, Third Circuit, decides for a school board that had dismissed a fifth grade teacher who had required two of his female students to write a thousand times the "vulgar 'F' word" because they had used the "bad word" during lunch period. In deciding against the teacher, the court stated: "We do not believe that the right of academic freedom entitles a public school teacher to require his students, particularly very young people, to use and be exposed to vulgar words, particularly when no academic or educational purpose can possibly be served. In the instant case, we agree with the school board and the trial court that plaintiff did not have the right, under the principle of academic freedom or any other theory, to require an eleven year old girl to write the very vulgar word which was involved here even once, when no valid purpose conceivably could be served by the use of that word. He certainly had no right to require her to write such a word many times in the presence of her classmates."

Celestine v. *LaFayette Parish School Bd.*, 284 So.2d 650 (1973)

HOOD, Judge.

Allen Celestine instituted this action for judgment ordering that he be re-instated as a classroom teacher in the Lafayette Parish School System as of March 17, 1970 the date he was dismissed, with all of the emoluments and benefits of that employment. The defendant is the Lafayette Parish School Board. The trial judge rendered judgment in favor of the defendant School Board, dismissing plaintiff's suit. Plaintiff has appealed.

The issues are whether the evidence is sufficient to support the School Board's finding that plaintiff is incompetent, whether defendant acted arbitrarily or unreasonably in dismissing plaintiff, and whether plaintiff has been denied due process of law.

On March 16, 1970, plaintiff Celestine was serving as a fifth grade teacher in the N. P. Moss Elementary School in Lafayette Parish, pursuant to a contract of employment previously entered into between him and the Lafayette Parish School Board. He had been working as a classroom teacher for defendant for eleven years prior to that date, and he thus was a "permanent teacher," within the meaning of LSA-R.S. 17:442.

Shortly after his class reconvened following the noon lunch period on the above mentioned date, plaintiff was confronted by several students who told him that two of his girl students had been using "bad words." Plaintiff thereupon asked the two girls in the presence of other members of the class whether they had been using vulgar language, and when they responded that

they had, he instructed each of them to write the vulgar word 1,000 times and to turn that work in to the principal for his signature, and to their parents for their signatures. One of the two girls to whom this assignment was given was eleven years of age at that time.

Pursuant to the instructions given to them by plaintiff, each of these girls began writing a four letter word, beginning with the letter "F," being an extremely vulgar word meaning sexual intercourse. They spent the rest of that day carrying out the assignment of writing that word 1,000 times. One of them, the above mentioned eleven year old girl, finished about the time the rest of the class was dismissed for the day, and she turned in her paper to the plaintiff. Celestine then ordered her to take the paper to the principal, Robert Landry, for his signature, and she complied with that order. The other student who had been given the same type punishment did not finish her assignment that afternoon and the record indicates that she has never been required to complete it.

On the following day, March 17, the principal of the school met with plaintiff Celestine, the Parish Superintendent of Schools, the Parish Director of Elementary Schools, and two School Board members to discuss the incident. Plaintiff also conferred privately with the Parish Superintendent of Schools later that afternoon.

On that day, March 17, the Superintendent of Schools for Lafayette Parish wrote a letter to plaintiff informing him that he was being suspended indefinitely from duty, without pay, effective March 17, 1970. In that letter the Superintendent also offered plaintiff the option of resigning or of facing a recommendation of the Superintendent that he be dismissed for incompetency. Plaintiff refused to resign, and the Superintendent thereupon formally charged plaintiff with incompetency, and he recommended to the School Board that plaintiff be dismissed on the basis of that charge. The Superintendent specified in his recommendation that his charge of incompetency was based on the above mentioned incident.

A copy of the written charge was furnished to plaintiff, and he was formally notified by registered mail of the date and place scheduled for a hearing before the School Board and of his right to a public or private hearing. A full public hearing was held by the School Board at the time scheduled for it, and at the conclusion of that hearing the School Board, by unanimous vote, formally dismissed plaintiff as a teacher in the Lafayette Parish School System. Plaintiff then instituted this suit.

Plaintiff contends, first, that he did not assign the "word" which was written by the two girl students. He testified that after his students informed him that the two girls had been using bad words, he asked the girls shortly after the class reconvened if they had used vulgar language again, and when they admitted that they had he instructed each of them to write the vulgar word they had used 500 times. The one who completed the assignment testified that she was instructed to write the word 1,000 times, and the record shows that she did write it that many times. Celestine maintains that he did not ask and did not know what the word was until after the assignment had been completed by one student and her paper on which the word had been written many times had been handed to him.

The girl who finished the assignment testified that immediately before the punishment was imposed the word which she wrote 1000 times was spelled out to the plaintiff by another student in the classroom, and that although it was spelled in a low voice, she could hear it easily while sitting on the second or third row of seats in that class. Plaintiff does not deny that a student spelled the word for him before he gave the assignment, but he stated that if the student spelled it he didn't hear it. He concedes that he used poor judgment in giving that type punishment to a pupil, and that he would not require his own child to write the word which these two young girls wrote.

The evidence shows that the two students who were subjected to this punishment spent the rest of the day writing this vulgar word in the classroom in the presence of the other students, while classes were being conducted in the same room. At least some of the other students knew the word which was being written, because one of them testified that another student had told her what it was while the assignment was being carried out.

We do not feel that plaintiff's unawareness of the exact word which he required the girls to write relieves him of the responsibility of having assigned that specific word to them. According to his own testimony, he knew that he was requiring them to write a vulgar word. If he did not know or bother to inquire as to what the word was, then the assignment by chance could have involved a word which was even more vulgar than the one actually used in this instance, if such a word exists.

We can understand how upsetting the type of punishment administered by plaintiff in this instance may have been to the parents of all of the children in that school. We will not speculate as to the effect which such a punishment may have on the children who were given this assignment, or on the pupils in the class, but it at least is conceivable that the effect would be harmful to them and to the school.

When there is a rational basis for an administrative board's discretionary determinations which are supported by substantial evidence insofar as factually required, the Court has no right to substitute its judgment for the administrative board's or to interfere with the latter's bona fide exercise of its discretion. Chantlin v. Acadia Parish School Board, 100 So.2d 908 (La. App. 1 Cir. 1958); Lewing v. DeSoto Parish School Board, 238 La. 43, 113 So.2d 462 (1959); State ex rel. Rathe v. Jefferson Parish School Board, 206 La. 317, 19 So.2d 153 (1943); Frank v. St. Landry Parish School Board, 225 So.2d 62 (La.App. 3 Cir. 1969); Granderson v. Orleans Parish School Board, 216 So.2d 643 (La. App. 4 Cir. 1968).

Our Supreme Court said in Rathe v. Jefferson Parish School Board, *supra*, that:

"There is nothing more firmly established in law than the principle that, within the limits of their authority, the power and discretion of legally created governing boards is supreme. Their wisdom or good judgment cannot be questioned by the courts. Members of these boards are appointed or elected because of their peculiar fitness for the post. Judges are elected because of their legal knowledge and ability. They are not experienced in the business affairs of Parishes and municipalities, * * * or the conduct of a public school system. A presumption of legality and regularity attaches to the action of all government boards. It is only when it is clearly shown that the action of such a board is beyond its authority or is arbitrary, unreasonable, or fraudulent that a court is justified in interfering."

In Stewart v. East Baton Rouge Parish School Board, 251 So.2d 487 (La.App. 1 Cir. 1971), the Court said:

"Our courts have consistently held that the hearing body is the trier of fact, and the courts will not review the evidence before such agency, except to determine whether the action of the agency was; (1) in accordance with the authority and formalities of the statute; (2) supported by substantial evidence; and (3) arbitrary or an abuse of discretion, and, except for those purposes, court will not review wisdom, reasoning or judgment of administrative agencies."

In the instant suit, all of the formalities required by law have been observed, and the charges of incompetency made by the Parish Superintendent of Schools are supported by substantial evidence. We agree with the trial court that the defendant School Board was not arbitrary or unreasonable, and that it did not abuse its discretion in dismissing plaintiff.

Plaintiff contends, however, that the action of the School Board should be set aside because it deprives him of his rights under the due process of law clauses of the State and Federal Constitutions. He assigns two grounds which he feels support that contention.

He pointed out, first, that the School Board have never forbidden teachers from requiring students to write words as a method of disciplining them, and that the School Superintendent had "accepted in principle" this form of discipline. He argues that the School Board has "violated our concept of fair play which is embodied in the due process clauses" by dismissing plaintiff on the grounds that he used a form of discipline which had been accepted and had not been forbidden.

It is true that neither the School Board nor the Superintendent had ever forbidden teachers from using the form of punishment described by plaintiff. Celestine, however, was not dismissed because of the *form* or *method* of disciplining students which he used. He was dismissed because of his extremely poor judgment in requiring an eleven year old girl to write a very vulgar word many times, particularly in the presence of the other members of the class. It was the bad judgment, or the incompetency, of the teacher in requiring that a vulgar word be used which brought about his dismissal. It was not merely his selection of a form or method of punishment. We thus find no merit to plaintiff's argument that he has been denied due process because of the form of punishment which he used.

The second ground urged by plaintiff to support his argument that he has been deprived of due process of law, is that the School Board considered evidence as to other acts of misconduct allegedly committed by plaintiff, which acts were not included in the charges of incompetency made against him and were not specified in the notice which was given to him of the charges.

At the hearing the child who was required to write

the vulgar word testified that plaintiff told her at the time this punishment was imposed that he was going to mark her absent for that day. Plaintiff denied that he made any such statement or marked her absent, and he testified that if his records show her to be absent on that day then someone else had made entries to that effect on them. In connection with that testimony, plaintiff admitted that he had kept his classroom key and his records for three or four weeks after he had been suspended, and that he did not return them to the School Board until after the Board had threatened legal action to get them. Plaintiff contends that these acts were considered by the School Board in its determination that he should be dismissed, although they were not specified in the charges or in the notice which was given to him.

There is nothing in the record which indicates that either the School Board or the Trial Court considered these circumstances in determining that plaintiff was incompetent. Even if they should have considered them, we find them to be so inconsequential that they could have had no effect on the decision which was rendered.

The testimony of the above mentioned student that Celestine had told her that he was going to mark her absent for the day on which the punishment was given was incidental to the giving of the assignment which is in question here, and we think it was proper for all of the evidence relating to that punishment to be produced and considered. Plaintiff denied that he made any such statement to her or that he marked her absent, and the evidence apparently supports his statement because the evidence does not show that the class records were ever marked to show her absent. That evidence thus could not have prejudiced plaintiff's right in this proceeding.

The incident relating to the return of the classroom key and the class records occurred after the dismissal had been recommended. The evidence as to that incident was elicited from plaintiff on cross-examination merely to explain his earlier statement that a school official had threatened him with legal proceedings. We think the School Board was entitled to ask for that explanation under the circumstances, and that there was nothing improper or prejudicial to plaintiff in the admission of that evidence.

The case of Johns v. Jefferson Davis Parish School Board, 154 So.2d 581 (La.App. 3 Cir. 1963), relied on by plaintiff, does not support plaintiff's position here. In that case the dismissed teacher was found guilty of willful neglect of duty and incompetence in several particulars not included in the formal notice which had been sent to him. In the instant suit plaintiff has been found to be incompetent solely on the charge which was specifically set out in the notice which he received.

Plaintiff contends, finally, that his right to academic freedom as a teacher is protected by the First Amendment to the Federal Constitution, and that this right entitles him to administer the punishment which was administered to the two young girls in his class. He relies on Keefe v. Geanakos, 418 F.2d 359 (1 Cir. 1969), which involved the use of a much less offensive word in teaching high school students. The court held, in effect, that the use of the word involved there, under those circumstances, would not justify dismissal of the teacher. The court also stated, however, that:

"We of course agree with defendants that what is to be said or read to students is not to be determined by obscenity standards for adult consumption. . . . Furthermore, as in all other instances, the offensiveness of language and the particular propriety or impropriety is dependent on the circumstances of the utterance.

"We accept the conclusion of the court below that 'some measure of public regulation of classroom speech is inherent in every provision of public education.' "

We do not believe that the right of academic freedom entitles a public school teacher to require his students, particularly very young people, to use and be exposed to vulgar words, particularly when no academic or educational purpose can possibly be served. In the instant suit, we agree with the School Board and the trial court that plaintiff did not have the right, under the principle of academic freedom or any other theory, to require an eleven year old girl to write the very vulgar word which was involved here even once, when no valid purpose conceivably could be served by the use of that word. He certainly had no right to require her to write such a word many times in the presence of her classmates. His very poor judgment in imposing such a requirement is sufficient to support the action of the School Board in dismissing him.

For the reasons assigned, the judgment appealed from is affirmed. The costs of this appeal are assessed to plaintiff-appellant.

Affirmed.

AUnited States District Court in North Carolina decides for a student teacher who had been discharged from his teaching position because "he gave unorthodox answers to student questions (derived from the day's lesson text) about creation, evolution, immortality, and the nature and existence of God." In deciding against the school board, the Court asserted: "To discharge a teacher without warning because his answers to scientific and theological questions do not fit the notions of the local parents and teachers is a violation of the Establishment clause of the First Amendment. It is 'an establishment of religion,' the official approval of local orthodoxy, and a violation of the Constitution. . . . If a teacher has to answer searching, honest questions only in terms of the lowest common denominator of the professed beliefs of those parents who complain the loudest, this means that the state through the public schools is impressing the particular religious orthodoxy of those parents upon the religious and scientific education of the children by force of law. The prohibition against the establishment of religion must not be thus distorted and thwarted."

Moore v. *Gaston County Bd. of Education,* 357 F.Supp. 1037 (1973)

McMILLAN, District Judge.

George Ivey Moore III, plaintiff, brought this suit for injunctive and other relief, based upon his discharge from his position as a student teacher in the Gaston County, North Carolina, schools, because he gave unorthodox answers to student questions (derived from the day's lesson text) about creation, evolution, immortality, and the nature and existence of God,

Plaintiff is a 1970 graduate of the University of North Carolina at Chapel Hill. He enrolled at the University of North Carolina at Charlotte, seeking a master's degree and an "A" teaching certificate. For his "A" certificate he was required to do several months of practice teaching. This practice teaching, beginning in September 1971, was arranged for him by the University and the Gaston County school authorities, under the supervision of William T. Mauney, a teacher at the Highland Junior High School in Gaston County, North Carolina.

Up until November 10, 1971, his performance had been unremarkable; he maintained good control over his classes; he had done a lot of "practice" teaching, which was usually, in fact, substitute teaching, operating completely on his own.

On November 10, 1971, Moore was asked by the school principal, Mr. Wells, to substitute for a seventh grade teacher named Biggers. Moore conducted all of

Biggers' classes without incident until the 1:05 P.M. class in the history of Africa, Asia and the Middle East.

No one had told Moore what the lesson assignment was for the day. When the class opened Moore asked the students, and after several minutes learned that the lesson assignment was pages 77 through 84 of the prescribed text. The title of the text was "The Middle East—A Flowering of Religion." After several minutes of preliminary questioning it became apparent that the members of the class were not ready to recite. Moore thereupon directed the students to take fifteen minutes to read the seven-page lesson. After the reading period had passed, Moore attempted to get a discussion going on the subject of the lesson text, but with small success. His request for recitals on Judaism, Mohammedanism and the Hebrews produced little results. Some members of the class did give definitions of polytheism and monotheism. They were unable to say, as the text indicated, that Christianity and Judaism are both monotheistic religions.

On page 78 of the text appear the sentences:
"The Hebrews gave to all mankind a written record of how the belief in special tribal gods changed gradually to the belief in one God. We know this record as the Old Testament."

Moore, pursuing the lesson text, referred to the

evolution of Hebraic beliefs from polytheism (belief in many gods) to monotheism (belief in one God).

The word "evolution" apparently struck a nerve. A student asked if Moore believed that man descended from monkeys; Moore responded that Darwin's theory of the origin of the species and the evolution of life from one form to another is a valid theory. He was asked if he believed Adam and Eve were the first people; he responded that as he saw it they were generic or symbolic rather than literally the first people. A discussion ensued whether the Bible in whole or in part was to be taken literally; Moore thought some of it should not be taken literally. In response to questions from the class Moore, apparently an agnostic, responded with answers that he did not attend church; did not know what a soul was; did not believe in life after death, nor in heaven nor hell. In the discussion of the Gospels (Matthew, Mark, Luke and John) and their divine inspiration he appears to have suggested that a fifth gospel might yet be written by one divinely inspired, for example, by George Ivey Moore. In response to questions about the Bible, Moore referred to the Bible as a series of inspired writings which record the history, traditions, beliefs and practices of the ancient Hebrews.

None of these statements, according to Moore and the children who testified, was made by Moore except in answer to specific questions from the members of the class. He was responding to an extended cross-examination which started when, in following the lesson text, he undertook to discuss how the belief in numerous tribal gods evolved ("changed gradually") into belief in one God.

Some members of the class got excited. One or two members near the end of the period got up to leave, and were instructed by Moore to sit down. There was no physical disruption. Various students were displeased. The class was dismissed three or four minutes before the customary time for the class to end. They trooped back to the home room and talked to Mr. Mauney, their home room teacher, about the experience.

That evening the superintendent of schools, Mr. William H. Brown, received some telephone calls from irate parents—at his dinner time!

The next morning Mr. Brown talked with Mr. Wells, the principal, with Lee Phoenix, assistant superintendent for secondary education in the county schools, and with Robert Falls of the personnel office. Phoenix and Falls then talked with Moore. They apparently did not seek any understanding of what had happened, but simply asked Moore whether in fact he had or had not made the unorthodox statements that he did not believe in God nor in life after death. His response, in the traditional Christian funeral phrases, was "Ashes to ashes, dust to dust." Moore also told Phoenix that he could neither prove nor disprove the existence of a Supreme Being.

The following day, November 12, Mr. Brown, the school superintendent; Mr. Falls, the director of personnel; and Mr. Phoenix, the assistant superintendent, met early and decided that Moore had to go. They did not, before reaching this decision, talk with anybody who had been in the classroom other than Moore, and their conversation with Moore seems to have been confined simply to finding out whether he had, in fact, made the statements about which they had specifically inquired!

When the case was heard in this court, certain additional reasons were advanced for Moore's discharge, including "giving his own religion rather than reading the text"; talking Darwin to a "captive audience"; failing to observe a minimum "standard of rapport" with the students, which was inferred from the fact that the students were offended; attacking the fundamental Christian beliefs of the students. It was said that the class's reaction of wanting to leave because they thought he had ridiculed their religion showed that he should be discharged. (Moore was not asked in fact whether he had ridiculed their religion.)

Phoenix's criterion appears to have been that discussion of such matters was taboo because it was done in such an unaccustomed manner that it upset the class; the inference fairly arises that if his responses had conformed to locally accepted dogma, he would not have been discharged.

Moore, over the objections of the principal of the school, was relieved of his practice and substitute teaching duties. The University of North Carolina at Charlotte was requested to place him elsewhere. He did not, in fact, complete his practice teaching. Apparently, however, he was given full credit for his practice teaching towards his graduate degree because of his satisfactory work up to November 10, and because there were only a few weeks of practice teaching left to do.

North Carolina General Statutes § 115-160.6 provides that:

"A student teacher under the supervision of a certified teacher or principal shall have the protection of the laws accorded the certified teacher."

On the day in question Moore was a student teacher and as such student teacher was serving, without pay, as a substitute for Mr. Biggers and was under the supervision of Mr. Wells, the principal.

No instructions, specific or general, had been given to the plaintiff with regard to how he should teach the particular lesson nor as to whether he should answer or evade honest questions from the children.

Some of the constitutional principles which apply in this situation were set out by the court in Parducci v. Rutland, 316 F.Supp. 352 (N.D.Ala. 1970):

That teachers are entitled to First Amendment freedoms is an issue no longer in dispute. "It can hardly be argued that either students or teachers shed their constitutional rights to freedom of speech or expression at the schoolhouse gate." Tinker v. Des Moines Independent Community School District, 393 U.S. 503, 506, 89 S.Ct. 733, 736, 21 L.Ed.2d 731 (1969); see Pickering v. Board of Education, etc., 391 U.S. 563, 568, 88 S.Ct. 1731, 20 L.Ed.2d 811 (1968); Pred v. Board of Public Instruction, etc., 415 F.2d 851, 855 (5th Cir. 1969). These constitutional protections are unaffected by the presence or absence of tenure under state law. McLaughlin v. Tilendis, 398 F.2d 287 (7th Cir. 1968); Johnson v. Branch, 364 F.2d 177 (4th Cir. 1966), cert. denied, 385 U.S. 1003, 87 S.Ct. 706, 17 L.Ed.2d 542 (1967).

Although academic freedom is not one of the enumerated rights of the First Amendment, the Supreme Court has on numerous occasions emphasized that the right to teach, to inquire, to evaluate and to study is fundamental to a democratic society.[1] In holding a New York loyalty oath statute unconstitutionally vague, the Court stressed the need to expose students to a robust exchange of ideas in the classroom:

Our nation is deeply committed to safeguarding academic freedom, which is of transcendant value to all of us and not merely to the teachers concerned. That freedom is therefore a special concern of the First Amendment, which does not tolerate laws that cast a pall of orthodoxy over the classroom. * * * The classroom is peculiarly the "marketplace of ideas."[2]

Furthermore, the safeguards of the First Amendment will quickly be brought into play to protect the right of academic freedom because any unwarranted invasion of this right will tend to have a chilling effect on the exercise of the right by other teachers. Cf. Wieman v. Updegraff, 344 U.S. at 194, 195, 73 S.Ct. 215 (Frankfurter, J., concurring); Pickering v. Board of Education, etc., *supra* 391 U.S. at 574, 88 S.Ct. 1731.

The right to academic freedom, however, like all other constitutional rights, is not absolute and must be balanced against the competing interests of society. This Court is keenly aware of the state's vital interest in protecting the impressionable minds of its young people from *any* form of extreme propagandism in the classroom.

A teacher works in a sensitive area in a schoolroom. There he shapes the attitudes of young minds towards the society in which they live. In this, the state has a vital concern.[3]

While the balancing of these interests will necessarily depend on the particular facts before the Court, certain guidelines in this area were provided by the Supreme Court in Tinker v. Des Moines Independent Community School District, *supra.* The Court there observed that in order for the state to restrict the First Amendment right of a student, it must first demonstrate that:

[T]he forbidden conduct would "*materially* and *substantially* interfere with the requirements of appropriate discipline in the operation of the school". [Emphasis added.][4]

The Court was, however, quick to caution the student that:

[Any] conduct * * * in class or out of it, which for any reason—whether it stems from time, place or type of behavior—materially disrupts classwork or involves substantial disorder or invasion of the rights of others is, of course, not immunized by the constitutional guarantee of freedom of speech.[5]

Our laws in this country have long recognized that no person should be punished for conduct unless such conduct has been proscribed in clear and precise terms. See Connally v. General Constr. Co., 269 U.S. 385, 391, 46 S.Ct. 126, 70 L.Ed. 322 (1926). When the conduct being punished involves First Amendment rights, as is the case here, the standards for judging permissible vagueness will be even more strictly applied.[6]

In the case now before the Court, we are concerned not merely with vague standards, but with the total absence of standards. When a teacher is forced to speculate as to what conduct is permissible and what conduct is proscribed, he is apt to be overly cautious and reserved in the classroom.[7] Such a reluctance on the part of the teacher to investigate and experiment with new and different ideas is anathema to the entire concept of academic freedom.

This Court is well aware of the fact that "school officials should be given wide discretion in administering their schools" and that "courts should be reluctant to interfere with or place limits on that discretion." Such legal platitudes should not, however, be allowed to become euphemisms for "infringement upon" and "deprivations of" constitutional rights. However wide the discretion of school officials, such discretion cannot be exercised so as to arbitrarily deprive teachers of their First Amendment rights. See Johnson v. Branch, *supra,* 364 F.2d at 180. This Court cannot, on the facts of this case, find any substantial interest of the schools to be served by giving defendants unfettered discretion to decide how the First Amendment rights of teachers are to be exercised. Cf. Niemotko v. Maryland, 340 U.S. 268, 71 S.Ct. 325, 328, 95 L.Ed. 267, 280 (1951).

In Mailloux v. Kiley, 323 F.Supp. 1387 (D.Mass. 1971) (teacher discharged for writing taboo sex word on the blackboard and asking students to define it), Judge Wyzanski ruled that although a state had the power to suspend or discharge a teacher for using a teaching method not generally accepted in the profession, nevertheless:

" *. . . it may not resort to such drastic sanctions un-*

less the state proves he was put on notice either by a regulation or otherwise that he should not use that method. This exclusively procedural protection is afforded to a teacher not because he is a state employee, or because he is a citizen, but because *in his teaching capacity he is engaged in the exercise of what may plausibly be considered 'vital First Amendment rights.'* Keyishian v. Board of Regents, 385 U.S. 489, 604, 87 S.Ct. 675, 684, 17 L.Ed.2d 629. *In his teaching capacity he is not required to 'guess what conduct or utterance may lose him his position.' (Ibid).* If he did not have the right to be warned before he was discharged, he might be more timid than it is in the public interest that he should be, and he might steer away from reasonable methods with which it is in the public interest to experiment. *Ibid.*" *Mailloux,* at 1392. (Emphasis added.)

Plaintiff was entitled under North Carolina General Statutes § 115-160.6 (cited above) to the same "protection of the laws" as a certified teacher. The University and the Gaston school authorities had duly agreed that he have a term of practice teaching at the school in question. He had the reasonable expectation that this opportunity for practice teaching would continue until the end of the fall term as required by his University curriculum. The fact that he was not being paid is neither material nor controlling. Even if he had no right to compensation nor to permanent tenure he nevertheless had the right *not to be relieved of his teaching opportunity for unconstitutional reasons,* and he had the right to a fair hearing under due process safeguards, before being discharged. A hearing with just twenty minutes' notice before a hostile *ad hoc* committee without eyewitness testimony where the factual inquiry was confined to brief questioning concerning a few "unorthodox" statements can hardly pretend to comport with due process. See Board of Regents v. Roth, 408 U.S. 564, 92 S.Ct. 2701, 33 L.Ed. 548 (1972); Connell v. Higginbotham, 403 U.S. 207, 91 S.Ct. 1772, 29 L.Ed.2d 418 (1971); Shapiro v. Thompson, 394 U.S. 618, 89 S.Ct. 1322, 22 L.Ed.2d 600 (1969); Ferguson v. Thomas 430 F.2d 852 (5th Cir. 1970); Johnson v. Fraley, et.al., 470 F.2d 179 (4th Cir., 1972). Both the equal protection and the due process guarantees of the Fourteenth Amendment were violated by the action of the defendants.

As to the teaching of Darwin, it had once been thought that the "monkey trial" in Dayton, Tennessee, might have marked the last effort to suppress discussion of evolution; but as late as 1968 the Supreme Court in Epperson v. Arkansas, 393 U.S. 97, 89 S.Ct. 266, 21 L.Ed.2d 228 (1968), was called upon to invalidate a state statute forbidding the teaching of evolution in the public schools, and upheld the lower court who restrained the school authorities from discharging the teacher. In the opinion the Court said:

"There is and can be no doubt that the First Amendment does not permit the State to require that teaching and learning must be tailored to the principles or prohibitions of any religious sect or dogma." *Epperson,* at 106, 89 S.Ct. at 271.

"Arkansas' law cannot be defended as an act of religious neutrality. Arkansas did not seek to excise from the curricula of its schools and universities all discussion of the origin of man. The law's effort was confined to an attempt to blot out a particular theory because of its supposed conflict with the Biblical account, literally read. Plainly, the law is contrary to the mandate of the First, and in violation of the Fourteenth Amendment to the Constitution." *Epperson,* at 109, 89 S.Ct. at 273.

In Keyishian v. Board of Regents, 385 U.S. 589, 87 S.Ct. 675, 17 L.Ed.2d 629 (1967), the Supreme Court observed (at p. 603, 87 S.Ct. at p. 683):

"Our nation is deeply committed to safeguarding academic freedom, which is of transcendent value to all of us and not merely to the teachers concerned. That freedom is therefore a special concern of the First Amendment, which does not tolerate laws that cast a pall of orthodoxy over the classroom."

The First Amendment, which protects free speech, also provides for religious freedom:

"Congress shall make no law respecting establishment of religion, or prohibiting the free exercise thereof; or abridging the freedom of speech, or of the press. . . . "

Religious or scientific dogma supported by the power of the state has historically brought threat to liberty, and often death to the unorthodox. Jesus Christ himself was such a victim. History is filled with the names of individuals who were punished or burned, not for atheism nor for lack of religion, but because their particular form of Christianity did not accord with the precise convolutions and procrustean conventions of the reigning spiritual powers. The Inquisitions, especially in Italy and Spain, are longstanding illustrations of this bloody and arbitrary tendency of mankind. At the height of the Italian Renaissance a respectable scientist named Bruno sought to defend and advance the observations of Copernicus that the universe is broad beyond human measurement; that it has many worlds; and that the sun rather than the earth is the physical center of our corner of infinity. Bruno proclaimed the universe as the creation of God, but did not agree with the "right" or earth-centered view of the universe which since Aristotle had been proclaimed by the orthodox. Because he refused to repudiate Copernicus and reaffirm Aristotle's views that the sun and the stars revolve around the earth, he was imprisoned for seven years and then in 1600 (shortly before the first permanent English settlement at Jamestown in America) he was burned at the stake for his heresy. Galileo, his brilliant contemporary, was notified by the church that he faced the same fate if he kept on peddling Copernican notions; Galileo formally recanted and proclaimed the truth to be a lie and was allowed to spend his declining years looking through his telescope, through which he made further useful observations. Johannes Kepler, from another corner of Christendom, faced lesser pressures of the same sort and, with equal pragmatism, postponed the publication of his own most significant endorsement and advancement of the works of Copernicus. Kepler, however, in wry humor, reportedly observed in substance that since the sun-centered theory of the solar system was not acceptable to the church, and since the church's theory that the sun and the stars revolve around the earth was no longer acceptable to reason, it appeared that the heavenly bodies would have to arrange themselves according to some third order yet to be determined! Even the stars are not beyond reach of "orthodoxy."

The effect that this stifling of scientific inquiry, under the theory of "heresy," had upon the technological and scientific development of Italy and Spain is well known; it was through Newton and others in Britain and Northern Europe that the ensuing advancements of systematic scientific learning took place.

The United States Constitution was drafted after these and similar events had occurred, but not so long after that they had been forgotten. The Founding Fathers certainly shared no unanimity of religious belief or creed; a few years after the Constitution was drafted it has been estimated (by Dr. Ernest Trice Thompson, a Presbyterian seminary teacher, minister and religious historian of note) that not more than five or six Americans out of a hundred were members of the church. This sparing observance of church and organized religious procedures should not be interpreted to mean that early Americans were a bunch of atheists; the Constitution itself, especially including the Bill of Rights, is strong evidence that its framers were, more than they proclaimed, men of God. The First Amendment, however, clearly reflects the charity and the honesty of intelligent men who realized that religion can not be codified by some men for all men; that faith lives always on the edge of doubt; that the origin and ultimate allegiance of mankind can not be demonstrated by science, logic nor logarithms; and that, as Tennyson so aptly puts it (*In Memoriam*), faith is "Believing where we can not prove." Faith always has been and must be an individual matter, neither to be denied to others nor to be imposed upon them. All mankind of generations subsequent to Thomas the doubter must continue to live with both faith and doubt, and hope to come within the group of those prophetically described by Christ when He said:

"Blessed are those who have not seen and yet believe." *New Testament,* Book of John, Chapter 20, Verse 29.

In view of the bloody history of tyranny and ignorance which had so frequently followed the union of Cross and crown, the Founding Fathers were obviously interested in freedom *from* religion of state origin or sanction, as much as in freedom *of* religion of their own choice.

To discharge a teacher without warning because his answers to scientific and theological questions do not fit the notions of the local parents and teachers is a violation of the Establishment clause of the First Amendment. It is "an establishment of religion," the official approval of local orthodoxy, and a violation of the Constitution. Most people do not attend college. Many do not finish high school. To forbid discussions of scientific subjects like Darwin's theory of evolution on "religious" grounds is simply to postpone the education of those children until after they get out of school. If a teacher has to answer searching, honest questions only in terms of the lowest common denominator of the professed beliefs of those parents who complain the loudest, this means that the state through the public schools is impressing the particular religious orthodoxy of those parents upon the religious and scientific education of the children by force of law. The prohibition against the establishment of religion must not be thus distorted and thwarted. Epperson v. Arkansas, *supra.*

It is not called for, on this record, to speculate what restriction on honest inquiry might have been allowable *if* the school authorities had given clear advance notice to the teacher.

The plaintiff is entitled to relief. Counsel is requested to tender an appropriate judgment.

NOTES

1. See e.g., Sweezy v. New Hampshire by Wyman, 354 U.S. 234, 77 S.Ct. 1203, 1 L.Ed.2d 1311 (1957); Wieman v. Updegraff, 344 U.S. 183, 73 S.Ct. 215, 97 L.Ed. 216 (1952).
2. Keyishian v. Board of Regents, etc., 385 U.S. 589, 603, 87 S.Ct. 675, 683, 17 L.Ed.2d 629 (1967). Cf. Meyer v. Nebraska, 262 U.S. 390, 43 S.Ct. 625, 67 L.Ed. 1042 (1923).
3. Shelton v. Tucker, 364 U.S. 479, 485, 81 S.Ct. 247, 250, 5 L.Ed.2d 231 (1960).
4. 393 U.S. at 509, 89 S.Ct. at 738, quoting Burnside v. Byars, 363 F.2d 744, 749 (5th Cir. 1966).
5. 393 U.S. at 513, 89 S.Ct. at 740; see Pred v. Board of Public Instruction, etc., *supra,* 415 F.2d at 859.
6. NAACP v. Button, 371 U.S. 415, 432, 83 S.Ct. 328, 9 L.Ed.2d 405 (1963); Winters v. New York, 333 U.S. 507, 509-510, 68 S.Ct. 665, 92 L.Ed. 840 (1948); see Brooks v. Auburn University, 296 F.Supp. 188 (M.D.Ala.), aff'd, 412 F.2d 1171 (5th Cir. 1969).
7. Cf. Keyishian v. Board of Regents, etc., *supra,* 385 U.S. at 604, 87 S.Ct. 675.

A United States District Court in Florida decides against a high school biology teacher who had used his classroom as a "springboard for expounding his ideas concerning the superintendent, the school board and the school system" and who had told his tenth grade biology class of his personal dealings with prostitution in Japan and discussed masturbation "in a mixed class, to the extent that individual students were asked if they had ever masturbated and that if they said they hadn't, they were lying." Recognizing the teacher's right to speak on these matters outside the classroom, the court declared that "it is clear that this case does *not* concern First Amendment utterances or statements made by a teacher *outside* the classroom. It is imperative to note here that were that the case Mr. Moore in all probability would be entitled to relief." The tenth grade biology class students, said the Court, "have the right and freedom not to listen and as a captive audience should be able to expect protection from improper classroom activities. Plaintiff has the right to criticize his employers and the school administration but is limited in the exercise of that right to the extent that its exercise may not invade the classroom occupied by fifteen year olds and must be balanced against the need for meaningful school administration."

Moore v. *School Bd. of Gulf County, Florida*, 364 F.Supp. 355 (1973)

ORDER
PRELIMINARY STATEMENT OF ACTION

MIDDLEBROOKS, District Judge.

This action was commenced under Title 42, U.S.C.A. Section 1983 and the First and Fourteenth Amendments to the Constitution of the United States and jurisdiction is invoked pursuant to Title 28, U.S.C.A., Sections 1331 and 1343(3), (4). By order of this Court on August 19, 1972, an original party plaintiff in this action, the Florida Education Association, a non-profit Florida corporation, was dismissed as a party plaintiff for want of standing to sue. By further order of this Court on March 12, 1973, plaintiff Gwen Moore was added as a party plaintiff on motion to amend the complaint.

Plaintiff Melvin W. Moore seeks to permanently enjoin defendants' denial of continuing contract status as a teacher in the Gulf County School System, conditioning his continued employment on the offer of a fourth year annual contract upon a commitment to refrain from utterances and statements protected by the First Amendment to the Constitution of the United States and from imposing retributive sanctions

upon him or any other person employed by the school board as a result of the exercise of First Amendment protected rights.

Plaintiff Gwen Moore seeks an injunctive order requiring reinstatement to her previous employment with full benefits and seniority.

Both plaintiffs seek compensatory damages, costs and attorney's fees.

Plaintiffs' amended complaint alleges that on or about May 2, 1972, the defendants informed plaintiff Melvin Moore that he would not receive a continuing contract of employment and that a fourth year annual contract of employment was offered conditioned on his acceptance of that contract with a commitment to the school board that he would talk about nothing but Biology on school property; that the sole reason for denial of a continuing contract was based on statements and utterances made by plaintiff Melvin Moore which were within the protection and guarantees of the First Amendment and that said condition being imposed and continuing contract being denied were violative of his protective guarantees under the Fourteenth Amendment. Plaintiff Melvin Moore further alleged that the above mentioned actions of the defendant school board were designed and intended to penalize him for protected utterances and statements and to chill and inhibit the exercise by other teachers of their right to engage fully in constitutionally protected forms of speech.

Plaintiffs' amended complaint further alleges that on or about May 3, 1972, plaintiff Gwen Moore, wife of plaintiff Melvin W. Moore, was notified by defendant thet her employment as secretary to the principal of Port St. Joe High School was being terminated. Plaintiffs allege that this termination was based solely on plaintiff Melvin Moore's refusal to relinquish his First Amendment rights as guaranteed by the Constitution of the United States.

Having considered pleadings, exhibits, stipulations, evidence and argument of counsel before the Court in this cause, having considered the demeanor of the witnesses who have testified and having resolved as trier of fact the credibility choices to be made, this Court makes the following findings of fact and conclusions of law as may be required by Rule 52 (a), Federal Rules of Civil Procedure:

FINDINGS OF FACT

1. Plaintiff Melvin W. Moore is a citizen of the United States and was Biology teacher from September 1969 through the 1971-1972 school year at Port St. Joe High School, Gulf County, Florida.

2. Plaintiff Gwen Moore, wife of plaintiff Melvin W. Moore, is a citizen of the United States and was a secretary to the principal of Port St. Joe High School from December 1970 through the 1971-1972 school year.

3. The defendant Gulf County School Board is the governmental body charged with the organization and control of the public schools of Gulf County.

4. The defendants Gene Raffield, William Roemer, Waylon Graham, Kenneth Whitfield and Billy Joe Rich were the duly elected and acting members of the Gulf County School Board during the year 1972. On November 21, 1972, defendants Wallace Guillot and Herman Ard, newly elected members of the Gulf County School Board, replaced defendants Graham and Rich in their capacity as board members.

5. Up to and including April 11, 1972, plaintiff Melvin W. Moore received at least two evaluations from the principal of Port St. Joe High School, Zach Wuthrich and by letter dated April 26, 1972, plaintiff Melvin W. Moore was advised by Mr. Wuthrich that his reappointment as a teacher under a continuing contract was being recommended for the school year 1972-1973.

6. Testimony indicates that noninstructional personnel such as the plaintiff Gwen Moore are not entitled to tenure and are employed on a year to year basis.

EVENTS PRIOR TO MAY 2, 1972

7. Testimony disclosed that during the early part of April 1972, Mr. Wuthrich, then principal at Port St. Joe High School, was advised by the Superintendent of Public Instruction for Gulf County, Florida, that he would no longer continue in his capacity as principal of Port St. Joe High School after the 1971-1972 school year.

8. Further testimony disclosed that Mr. Wuthrich advised his secretary, plaintiff Gwen Moore, of his termination of duties as principal and advised that it would be announced publicly at a later date. Testimony also disclosed that plaintiff Gwen Moore informed her husband, plaintiff Melvin Moore of Mr. Wuthrich's situation.

9. Various members of the school board had received complaints regarding plaintiff Melvin W. Moore in his teaching capacity prior to the early part of April 1972, but the testimony produced evidenced that the bulk of complaints as to Mr. Moore's utterances and statements occurred after Mr. Wuthrich was advised that he would no longer serve as principal after the completion of the 1971-1972 school year.

10. During that period from early April through May 1, 1972, numerous complaints were made to defendants Graham, Rich and Raffield. These complaints were mainly from parents although a few were made by students and in one instance by a teacher. In essence, the complaints were directed toward plaintiff Melvin W. Moore's use of classroom time to discuss teacher salaries and his personal financial status, in addition to criticism of the Superintendent, the Gulf County School Board, High School policies and the allocation of funds to the High School Athletic Department. These complaints were relayed to Superintendent Craig by the board members and in at least one instance by a teacher/coach at the high school.

EVENTS OF MAY 2, 1972

11. On May 2, 1972, defendant school board summoned plaintiff Melvin W. Moore to appear at their regular meeting. After his arrival at said meeting, Mr. Moore was advised that he had not been recommended by the Superintendent for continuing contract status for the 1972-1973 school year based on reports received from parents and children of his improper use of classroom time.

12. In lieu of continuing contract status (which grants tenure to the holder) the Superintendent had recommended and the defendant school board offered Mr. Moore a fourth year annual contract that was probationary in nature, conditioned on Mr. Moore's agreeing that he would refrain from using substantial portions of his classroom time in discussions of sub-

jects unrelated to the subject of Biology. If Mr. Moore accepted this fourth year annual contract he was to advise the Superintendent the next day and sign his acceptance of said conditional contract.

EVENTS AFTER MAY 2, 1972

13. On May 3, 1972, plaintiff Melvin W. Moore advised the secretary to the Superintendent of Schools that he was declining the offer of the fourth year annual contract.

14. On May 3, 1972, plaintiff Gwen Moore was informed by Superintendent Craig that after the end of the school year on June 30, 1972, she would no longer be needed as secretary to the principal of Port St. Joe High School. By letter dated May 23, 1972, from Superintendent Craig, Mrs. Moore was formally advised of the termination of her employment due to the feeling of the Superintendent and the school board that the new principal should have the prerogative of recommending his secretary.

15. During the latter part of May or the early part of June, at a high school workshop with the desegregation center, plaintiff Gwen Moore met the new principal of Port St. Joe High School, a Mr. Kenneth D. Herring, at which time Mrs. Moore spoke with Mr. Herring about the possibility of employment as his secretary for the coming 1972-1973 school year.

16. The new principal Herring advised plaintiff Gwen Moore that he would consider her for the position. She was not hired by the new principal as secretary.

17. Part of the dissatisfaction of the board and the Superintendent with plaintiff Melvin W. Moore arose from information given by parents of students that Mr. Moore had not confined himself to criticisms of the educational system but had also dealt with his personal sexual experiences during classroom time. Of particular interest to the Court was the testimony of Benjamin Morris Gibson and his comments concerning plaintiff Melvin W. Moore's telling his Biology class of his personal dealings with prostitution houses in Japan. Gibson related that Mr. Moore had told the class about him and some other men buying some prostitutes and taking them to a hotel and that it was the first time for the one he had bought and that she was crying and upset and the other men with him wanted to trade but that he kept her. This testimony was substantiated by a number of other students.

18. At trial on July 31, 1973, this Court entered an order from the Bench directing the School Board of Gulf County, Florida, to convene a hearing for the purpose of taking testimony relating to whether Melvin W. Moore engaged in classroom utterances of a nature deemed sufficient by the Court to deny him reemployment pursuant to a continuing contract. This Court was concerned as to whether plaintiff Melvin W. Moore should be allowed inside any classroom at all, notwithstanding his right to a continuing contract should the Court rule that denial of said contract was a result of subordination of his First Amendment rights by the defendant school board.

19. On August 7 1973, plaintiffs through their counsel filed a motion requesting a vacation of the order of July 31, 1973, due to an article in the Port St. Joe weekly newspaper, The Star, indicating that plaintiff Melvin W. Moore was unfit to teach, had engaged in improper classroom behavior and relating further prejudicial comments concerning Mr. Moore.

20. On August 9, 1973, this Court entered an order granting plaintiffs' motion and vacating the July 31, 1973, order and further ordering that the trial would continue on August 14, 1973.

21. Testimony at trial on August 14, 1973, by at least four students substantiated the Japanese prostitute experience and related instances of Mr. Moore's discussing masturbation in a mixed class, to the extent that individual students were asked if they had ever masturbated and that if they said they hadn't, they were lying. Also revealed were instances of Mr. Moore telling his class about a confrontation with homosexuals and of a bizarre sounding treatment for gonorrhea.

22. Further substantiated by testimony at trial were classroom discussions during which the school board, Superintendent and high school athletic program and the athletic department were criticised by plaintiff Melvin W. Moore.

CONCLUSIONS OF LAW

1. This Court has jurisdiction over the subject matter of and the parties to this action. Title 28, U.S.C.A., Sections 1331 and 1345.

2. Florida law provides that a certified teacher who has completed three years of service in the same county and who has been reappointed for a fourth year of service must be recommended by the Superintendent for a continuing contract before the school board is authorized to issue same. Section 231.36(3) (a), Florida Statutes Annotated.

3. The Superintendent in making his recommendation may base his decision on successful performance of duty and the demonstrated professional competence of the teacher, Section 231.36(3) (a) (4), Florida Statutes Annotated.

4. The three year service requirement for a continuing contract may be extended to four years when prescribed by the school board and agreed to in writing by the employee. Section 231.36(3) (c), Florida Statutes Annotated.

5. The crux of the matter here for determination is

whether Mr. Moore's utterances and statements are those protected by the First Amendment and whether the denial of his continuing contract and offer of a fourth year annual contract subject to certain conditions and the termination of Mrs. Moore were violative of any property or procedural due process rights due plaintiffs by operation of the Fourteenth Amendment.

6. Regarding Mr. Moore's First Amendment claim, clearly a citizen, be he teacher or technician, may not be denied benefits in a manner that inhibits his freedom of enjoyment of constitutionally protected interests, particularly the enjoyment of the freedom to speak. To do otherwise would penalize and deter his enjoyment and use of those guaranteed freedoms. Perry v. Sindermann, 1972, 408 U.S. 593, 92 S.Ct. 2694, 33 L.Ed.2d 570, Cf. Shelton v. Tucker, 1960, 364 U.S. 479, 485-486, 81 S.Ct. 247, 5 L.Ed.2d 231; Keyishian v. Board of Regents, 1967, 385 U.S. 589, 605-606, 87 S.Ct. 675, 17 L.Ed.2d 629.

It is clear that this case does *not* concern First Amendment utterances or statements made by a teacher *outside* the classroom. It is imperative to note here that were that the case Mr. Moore in all probability would be entitled to relief.

7. There is overwhelming evidence in this case to the effect that plaintiff Melvin W. Moore utilized classroom time in criticizing the Superintendent, the school board and the school system. Not only was this brought out by testimony at trial and in depositions filed with the Court, but in the minutes of the school board's May 2, 1972, meeting. These were the motivating factors that led the Gulf County School Board to offer Mr. Moore a fourth year annual contract in lieu of a continuing contract and in this Court's opinion, at first blush and in the final analysis, the school board was well within its rights to do so.

8. Mr. Moore obviously used his classroom as a springboard for expounding his ideas concerning the Superintendent, the school board and the school system. No evidence appears of any activity of this nature outside the classroom.

Tenth Grade Biology students have the right and freedom not to listen and as a captive audience should be able to expect protection from improper classroom activities. Close v. Lederle, 424 F.2d 988 (1st Cir. 1972), cert. den. 400 U.S. 903, 91 S.Ct. 141, 27 L. Ed.2d 240.

9. Plaintiff has the right to criticize his employers and the school administration but is limited in the exercise of that right to the extent that its exercise may not invade the classroom occupied by fifteen year olds and must be balanced against the need for meaningful school administration. Pickering v. Board of Education of Lp. H. S. Dist. 205 Ill., 391 U.S. 563, 569, 88 S.Ct. 1731, 1735, 20 L.Ed.2d 811 (1968); Moore v. Winfield City Board of Education, 452 F.2d 726, 728 (5th

Cir. 1971). Whether Mr. Moore's criticism of the Superintendent, the school board and the school administration are protected by the First Amendment can only be decided by "a weighing of the asserted interests". Moore v. Winfield City Board of Education, *supra,* at 728; Fluker v. Alabama State Board of Education, 441 F.2d 201, 207 (5th Cir. 1971); Pred v. Board of Public Instruction of Dade County, Florida, 415 F.2d 851, 857 (5th Cir. 1969).

10. In weighing the interests in this case, that is, Mr. Moore's rights against Gulf County's need for meaningful school administration, this Court is quick to note again that there has been little indication of utterances or statements critical of the Superintendent, school board or school administration made outside the classroom[1]. This Court realizes that from time to time it may be necessary for a school teacher to delve into thought provoking discussions with students that may well concern areas of interest other than English, Biology, American History, or the like. Even then a teacher, above all, has a serious responsibility in that the teacher is guiding a student in the development of his mind and may well leave an immeasurable impact on that student's mind. It would appear to this Court that criticisms of a school board, Superintendent and school administration in the classroom could well lead students to hold these officials as well as some of their other teachers in various degrees of contempt. This is certainly no assistance to the educational processes existing in Gulf or any other county.

While the classroom may be "[t]he 'Marketplace of ideas' [with] [t]he nation's future depend[ing] upon leaders trained through wide exposure to that robust exchange of ideas which discovers truth 'out of a multitude of tongues, [rather] than through any kind of authoritative selection'"[2], straight criticism by a teacher of an educational system is quite a different matter than the presentation of ideas with commentary reflecting two sides of an issue, leaving a preference as to that issue left up to the individual student's discretion.

Here we have a high school Biology teacher utilizing as much as a full class period in criticism of the Superintendent, the school board and the school system, to include comments brought out at trial such as "You'd better tell your parents to get off their ass and elect a new school board" and "You can't call yourself a Christian if you vote for Mr. Craig (the Superintendent)". Comments such as these and lengthy discussions on the inadequacy of teacher salaries in general and in particular Mr. Moore's salary can in no beneficial way aid a teacher in preparing his high school students for an adult life or for further educational endeavors. Testimony of a Marine Biology student of Mr. Moore was to the effect that he advised the class that some students were telling their parents about his talking about the school board so he thought that he should desist from such comments in the future.

11. Even if Mr. Moore were due relief, this Court sitting as a court of equity could not and *would* not order the Gulf County School Superintendent and the school board to reinstate him as a teacher with continuing contract status and granting him in essence, a life-time contract, for Mr. Moore abused his authority and left legitimate areas of discussion when he began relating personal experiences with Japanese prostitutes who were "innocent", among other illegitimate topics.

12. As to plaintiff Melvin Moore's Fourteenth Amendment claim, it is the opinion of his Court that Mr. Moore's rights have not been violated at all. Mr. Moore was given two choices, one to accept a fourth year annual contract on the condition that he not discuss subjects other than Biology in the classroom and two, to seek employment elsewhere. Mr. Moore, rather than accepting the school board's offer and then begin litigating this matter, chose to seek other employment and found same in the Jefferson County, Florida, school system.

13. The only legitimate loss Mr. Moore would have suffered had he remained under an annual contract, was tenure. As to that tenure this is not a case of a warranted "expectancy" of employment or a case where Mr. Moore has some property interest at stake. Perry v. Sindermann, *supra;* see also Moore v. Knowles, 482 F.2d 1069, CA5, 1973, opinion on rehearing; and Zimmer v. Spencer etc. et al., 485 F.2d 176, CA5, 1973.

A teacher without any form of tenure or contract of employment is entitled to a hearing if a decision to not rehire him deprived him of any of his liberties and the decision was made absent any recognized standards of due process. Board of Regents v. Roth, 408 U.S. 564, 92 S.Ct. 2701, 33 L.Ed.2d 548 (1972); See also Moore v. Knowles et al., *supra.* Such is not the case here.

Mr. Moore's refusal to accept the offer of a fourth year annual contract was a rejection of a reasonable offer by the school board. Rather than act harshly and with finality on the multitude of adverse reports from parents, students and at least one teacher as to Mr. Moore's actions in the classroom, these reports coming in fast and furiously during a period of less than a month, the Superintendent and board offered Mr. Moore an annual contract, giving him an opportunity to reverse his aggressively destructive course.

14. Turning briefly to the plaintiff, Mrs. Moore, and her Fourteenth Amendment claim couched on a violation of her plaintiff husband Melvin W. Moore's First Amendment rights and guarantees, simply put, Mrs. Moore may prevail only if Mr. Moore prevails.

15. By her own testimony the job as secretary to the principal at Port St. Joe High School, as other non-instructional or supervisory positions, is on a year to year basis, without written contract. The Court, in retrospect, feels that a common sense approach to her status may have been taken. As the wife of a teacher who wants to teach, the likelihood of her remaining in Gulf County was no doubt minimal. The evidence shows that she and her husband were dissatisfied with the decision of the Superintendent not to continue Mr. Wuthrich as principal.

16. Mrs. Moore found other employment during the summer with higher pay and on her family's being relocated obtained further employment at an even greater rate of pay. Accordingly, it is

Ordered and Adjudged:

1. That plaintiff Melvin W. Moore's request for a permanent injunction enjoining the denial of his continuing contract status as a teacher in the Gulf County school system be and the same hereby is denied.

2. That plaintiff Gwen Moore's request for an injunctive order reinstating her to her previous employment with all benefits and seniority therein be and the same hereby is denied.

3. That the request of plaintiffs Melvin W. Moore and Gwen Moore seeking compensatory damages, costs and attorney's fees be and the same hereby is denied.

4. That each party to this action shall bear his own costs.

NOTES

1. At a meeting of the Gulf County Education Association later in May and at a special school board meeting shortly thereafter, some statements may have been made that were critical of Superintendent Craig, the school board or the administration. However, these statements would not have been a motivating factor in deciding not to grant Mr. Moore a continuing contract.
2. Keyishian v. Board of Regents, 385 U.S. 589, 603, 87 S.Ct. 675, 683, 17 L.Ed.2d 629, 640-641 (1967); quoted with approval in Tinker v. Des Moines Community School Dist., 393 U.S. 503, 512, 89 S.Ct. 733, 739, 21 L.Ed.2d 731, 741; Pred v. Bd. of Public Instruction of Dade County, Fla., *supra* at 856 of 415 F.2d.

THE United States Court of Appeals, Sixth Circuit, asserts at the outset of its opinion on the nonrenewal of a nontenured professor: "This appeal requires us to decide whether the First Amendment prevents a state university from discharging a teacher whose pedagogical style and philosophy do not conform to the pattern prescribed by the school administration." In deciding against the professor, the Court states: "Plaintiff would . . . have us convert the vague, inclusive term 'teaching methods' into a specific, protected form of speech that cannot be considered by a school administration in determining whether a nontenured teacher should be renewed. In effect, plaintiff would have us substitute the First Amendment for tenure, and would thereby succeed in elevating contract law to constitutional status. We do not accept plaintiff's assertion that the school administration abridged her First Amendment rights when it refused to rehire her because it considered her teaching philosophy to be incompatible with the pedagogical aims of the university."

Hetrick v. *Martin*, 480 F.2d 705 (1973)

McCREE, Circuit Judge.

This appeal requires us to decide whether the First Amendment prevents a state university from discharging a teacher whose pedagogical style and philosophy do not conform to the pattern prescribed by the school administration. The district court, sitting without a jury, held that the Constitution did not bar officials of Eastern Kentucky University from refusing to renew plaintiff's teaching contract on the ground of impermissible deviation from the teaching standards thought appropriate by her superiors. We affirm.

Plaintiff Phyllis Hetrick was employed as a nontenured assistant English professor at Eastern Kentucky for the 1969-70 school year, and during her first semester was assigned to teach two sections of freshman composition, one sophomore literature course, and an upper level modern drama course. Her troubles with the school administration apparently began when unnamed students as well as the parents of one student complained about certain of her in-class activities. Specifically, at one point, in an attempt to illustrate the "irony" and "connotative qualities" of the English language, she told her freshman students "I am an unwed mother." At the time, she was a divorced mother of two, but she did not reveal that fact to her class. Also, she apparently on occasion discussed the war in Vietnam and the military draft with one of her freshman classes. The district court found that even though the school administration was concerned about the appropriateness of these occurrences, "it does not appear that any of the faculty members felt that Dr.

Hetrick had on those particular occasions exceeded the bounds of her teaching prerogative." The student complaints during October and November 1969 allegedly centered on their inability to comprehend what she was attempting to teach them or what was expected of them, although no students were produced at trial to testify that he or she had complained about or was dissatisfied with plaintiff's teaching methods.

Other conflicts between Dr. Hetrick and her superiors developed. She did not obtain her PhD until late in her second semester, although she agreed that she would do so by the close of the first semester. She covered only 11 plays in her modern drama course, from a textbook that had been ordered by her predecessor, and the head of the English Department, Dr. Thurman, testified that plaintiff had been told that she was expected to cover between 20 and 25 plays and that he thought the work load she assigned was too light.

In February 1970, Dr. Thurman convened a "secret evaluating committee" of four other faculty members of the English Department to meet with him. The committee, according to Dr. Thurman, was to evaluate all the nontenured teachers. Dr. Thurman recommended to the committee that plaintiff not be rehired for the following year because: her freshman class assignments were inconclusive; she was inclined to discuss extraneous matter in class; she lacked "a sense of camaraderie" and did not seem to adjust to the other members of the English Department; and she had not fulfilled her PhD requirements as promised.

The committee voted to terminate Dr. Hetrick.

The district court found that these reasons asserted by Dr. Thurman were "supported by fact." However, the court finds from the tenor of the evidence, that the nonrenewal of Dr. Hetrick's contract was not based so much on those specific reasons, as it was on the feeling of Dr. Thurmond [sic] and the other faculty members of the English Department that Dr. Hetrick's teaching philosophy and the manner in which she implemented it were not adaptable to the achievement of the academic goals of the University.

The evidence to which the court referred consisted in part of plaintiff's testimony and that of her students, and the testimony of the defendants concerning what was expected of teachers at Eastern Kentucky. The school administration considered the students as generally unsophisticated and as having "somewhat restrictive backgrounds," and for this reason apparently expected the teachers to teach on a basic level, to stress fundamentals and to follow conventional teaching patterns—in a word, to "go by the book." Plaintiff's evidence, on the other hand, tended to show that her teaching emphasized student responsibility and freedom to organize class time and out-of-class assignments in terms of student interest, all in an effort, she claims, to teach them how to think rather than merely to accept and to parrot what they had heard.

After her termination by the University, plaintiff brought this action under 42 U.S.C. § 1983 for declaratory and injunctive relief against the president and regents of Eastern Kentucky University. She asserted that her First and Fourteenth Amendment rights had been violated by her termination without a hearing or written statement of reasons, on an arbitrary basis, for making in-class statements about the war and the draft, and because of her beliefs and ideas. The intervening decisions of the Supreme Court in Board of Regents of State College v. Roth, 408 U.S. 564, 92 S.Ct. 2701, 33 L.Ed.2d 548 (1972), and Perry v. Sindermann, 408 U.S. 593, 92 S.Ct. 2694, 33 L.Ed.2d 570 (1972), narrowed the issue in this case to whether plaintiff had been terminated for conduct on her part protected by the First Amendment. See Perry v. Sindermann, *supra*, 408 U.S. at 596-598, 92 S.Ct. 2694.

The district court concluded that the decision not to renew plaintiff's contract was the result of defendants' "concern for her teaching methods and ability," and was not prompted by her exercise of First Amendment rights. In discussing the scope of the protection afforded teachers by the First Amendment, the court stated:

The First Amendment guarantee of academic freedom provides a teacher with the right to encourage a vigorous exchange of ideas within the confines of the subject matter being taught, but it does not require a University or school to tolerate any manner of teaching method the teacher may choose to employ. A University has a right to require some conformity with whatever teaching methods are acceptable to it. In this case it simply appears that Dr. Hetrick's teaching techniques were not acceptable to the University. The court is not in a position to weigh the merits of Dr. Hetrick's educational philosophy—it may be that her methods of teaching were and are more desirable than those embraced by the other members of the English Department—but the fact that the University decided that they were not and chose not to renew her contract, does not mean that her constitutional rights to academic freedom and freedom of speech were impinged.

In a memorandum opinion filed with the court's findings of fact and conclusions of law, the court elaborated on its findings in this regard:

It is Dr. Hetrick's position that the non-renewal of her contract resulted from certain statements she made in her classes relating to the Vietnam War and the military draft. Were this contention adequately corroborated it may be that relief would be proper, however, the evidence produced at the hearing leads only to the conclusion that the University's determination not to rehire was based solely upon concern for her pedagogical attitudes. Although the court is inclined to believe that the classroom inadequacies that Dr. Hetrick was alleged to have displayed—inconclusive assignments, extraneous classroom discussions, and insufficient coverage of suggested materials—were largely superficial and thus easily correctable, it is not the duty of the court to evaluate the wisdom of the University's decision not to renew the contract. It simply seems that Dr. Hetrick's teaching methods were too progressive, or perhaps less orthodox than the other faculty members in her department felt were conducive to the achievement of the academic goals they espoused. The court must conclude that a State University has the authority to refuse to renew a non-tenured professor's contract for the reason that the teaching methods of that professor do not conform with those of the tenured faculty or with those approved of by the University.

On appeal, plaintiff has raised two issues: does it violate the First Amendment for a public university to terminate a teacher because her teaching methods and educational philosophy do not conform with those approved by the university; did the district court err in concluding that the decision to terminate was not based on or influenced by constitutionally protected statements she made in the classroom, *i.e.*, the "unwed mother" remark and statements about the Vietnam war and the draft?

With respect to the latter issue, assuming *arguendo* that the uttering of these in-class statements would be protected by the First Amendment,[1] we conclude upon examination of the record that the findings of the district court are fully supported by the evidence and that plaintiff was not discharged because of any statements she may have made.

Thus, we are squarely presented with the question whether the administration of a public school may, consistent with the First Amendment, fail to renew a nontenured teacher because of displeasure with her "pedagogical attitudes." We conclude, as did the district court, that it may.

This is not a case of dismissal of a teacher for exercising her right as a citizen to comment on matters of public concern, *see* Pickering v. Board of Education, 391 U.S. 563, 88 S.Ct. 1731, 20 L.Ed.2d 811 (1968); cf. Tinker v. Des Moines Independent Community School District, 393 U.S. 503, 89 S.Ct. 733, 21 L.Ed.2d 731 (1969), or a case of a state's attempting to regulate the fitness and competence of its teachers by investigating the teachers' out-of-class associations, *see* Keyishian v. Board of Regents, 385 U.S. 589, 87 S.Ct. 675, 17 L.Ed.2d 629 (1967); Shelton v. Tucker, 364 U.S. 479, 81 S.Ct. 247, 5 L.Ed.2d 231 (1960); Sweezy v. New Hampshire, 354 U.S. 234, 77 S.Ct. 1203, 1 L. Ed.2d 1311 (1957), or even a case of a state's effort to restrict in-class utterances or assignments in order to maintain curriculum control, *compare* Keefe v. Geanakos, 418 F.2d 359 (1st Cir. 1969); Mailloux v. Kiley, 323 F.Supp. 1387 (D.Mass.), aff'd, 448 F.2d 1242 (1st Cir. 1971); Parducci v. Rutland, 316 F.Supp. 352 (M.D.Ala.1970), *with* Clark v. Holmes, 474 F.2d 928 (7th Cir. 1972), cert. denied, 411 U.S. 972, 93 S.Ct. 2148, 36 L.Ed.2d 695 (1973); Parker v. Board of Education, 237 F.Supp. 222 (D.Md.), aff'd, 378 F.2d 464 (4th Cir. 1965), cert. denied, 382 U.S. 1030, 86 S.Ct. 653, 15 L.Ed.2d 543 (1966); *cf.* Epperson v. Arkansas, 393 U.S. 97, 89 S.Ct. 266, 21 L.Ed.2d 228 (1968); Meyer v. Nebraska, 262 U.S. 390, 43 S.Ct. 625, 67 L.Ed. 1042 (1923); *see generally* Developments in the Law—Academic Freedom, 81 Harv.L.Rev. 1045, 1051-54 (1968).

Instead, this is a case of the nonrenewal of a nontenured teacher, who was not even entitled to notice and hearing upon receipt of the university's decision not to renew her contract. Board of Regents of State College v. Roth, *supra*. Although her renewal could not have been denied on a basis that invaded a constitutionally protected interest such as her interest in freedom of speech, Perry v. Sindermann, *supra*, 408 U.S. at 597, 92 S.Ct. 2694, under the holding in Board of Regents of State College v. Roth, *supra*, she presumably could have been terminated for entirely arbit-

rary reasons that did not invade First Amendment rights. She seeks to escape the effect of this principle by claiming that what is at issue here is her constitutional right to "teach her students to think" and that the First Amendment protects her from termination for using teaching methods and adhering to a teaching philosophy that are "well-recognized within the profession" (although it does not appear that plaintiff introduced expert testimony on this question, *Compare* Mailloux v. Kiley, *supra*, 323 F.Supp. 1387). Plaintiff would thus have us convert the vague, inclusive term "teaching methods" into a specific, protected form of speech that cannot be considered by a school administration in determining whether a nontenured teacher should be renewed. In effect, plaintiff would have us substitute the First Amendment for tenure, and would thereby succeed in elevating contract law to constitutional status.

We do not accept plaintiff's assertion that the school administration abridged her First Amendment rights when it refused to rehire her because it considered her teaching philosophy to be incompatible with the pedagogical aims of the University. Whatever may be the ultimate scope of the amorphous "academic freedom" guaranteed to our Nation's teachers and students, Healy v. James, 408 U.S. 169, 180-181, 92 S.Ct. 2338, 33 L.Ed.2d 266 (1972), *see generally* Developments in the Law—Academic Freedom, *supra*, it does not encompass the right of a nontenured teacher to have her teaching style insulated from review by her superiors when they determine whether she has merited tenured status just because her methods and philosophy are considered acceptable somewhere within the teaching profession. A contrary holding would effectively emasculate the holding in Board of Regents of State College v. Roth, *supra*, by rendering every nonrenewal decision a likely candidate for a court suit, and we decline to accomplish the *sub silentio* overruling of that recent Supreme Court decision as well as our own in Orr v. Trinter, 444 F.2d 128 (6th Cir. 1971), cert. denied, 408 U.S. 943, 92 S.Ct. 2847, 33 L.Ed.2d 767 (1972).

For the foregoing reasons, and the reasons advanced by the district court, the judgment of the district court is affirmed.

NOTE

1. *Compare, e.g.,* Mailloux v. Kiley, 323 F.Supp. 1387 (D.Mass.), aff'd, 448 F.2d 1242 (1st Cir. 1971), *with* Clark v. Holmes, 474 F.2d 928 (7th Cir. 1972), cert. denied, 411 U.S. 972, 93 S.Ct. 2148, 36 L.Ed.2d 695 (1973).

A United States District Court in Michigan decides against a teacher and a physician who sought an injunction prohibiting enforcement of the Michigan statutes which prohibited "instruction, advice or information on the subject of birth control in the course of sex and health education classes in Michigan schools" and which provided that "any student upon the written request of parent or guardian shall be excused from attending classes in which the subject of sex education is under discussion and no penalties as to credits or graduation shall result therefrom." The Court argues that the physician does not have standing "to raise the rights of students or their parents." In deciding against the teacher, the Court declared: "Among other things, teachers are engaged to impart to the students the various bodies of knowledge and learning contained in and offered by the curriculum. There is nothing in the First Amendment that gives a person employed to teach the constitutional right to teach beyond the scope of the established curriculum. Nor are there any judicial decisions giving the teacher the right to teach beyond an established curriculum." The Court does say, however, that "there may be situations where application of the challenged statutes would raise constitutional questions. The instant case, however, involves an abstract challenge to the validity of the statute and not a challenge to the constitutional application of the statute. The court should wait until someone is alleged to have violated the statute and there are facts, as cold and hard as concrete instead of hypothetical, before attempting to write the outer limits of constitutional authority in this area."

Mercer v. *Michigan State Bd. of Education*, 379 F.Supp. 580 (1974)

JOINER, District Judge.

I. Background

This action was commenced on August 7, 1973 when the plaintiffs filed a complaint for declaratory and injunctive relief against the state education law which prohibits discussion of birth control in the public schools. Plaintiffs seek declaratory relief and preliminary and permanent injunctions prohibiting enforcement of Michigan Statutes Annotated, §§ 15.3782 and 15.3789(3), M.C.L.A. §§ 340.782 and 340.789c, which prohibit instruction, advice or information on the subject of birth contol in the course of sex and health education classes in the Michigan schools, and further involve parents withdrawing a student for no reason, other than the parents' own from classes on sex education, hygiene, or the symptoms of disease. The plaintiff Richard Goldfine is a

physician, and the plaintiff Alexander Mercer is a teacher in the Detroit school systems. Plaintiffs sought in their complaint (1) the convening of a three judge district court pursuant to 28 U.S.C. §§ 2281 and 2284; (2) preliminary and permanent injunctions against enforcement of Michigan Statutes Annotated §§ 15.3782 and 15.3789 (3)* and a declaratory judgment that said statutes violate the First and Fourteenth Amendments and are unconstitutional; and (3) an order taxing all reasonable costs against the defendants and granting plaintiffs other relief deemed necessary, just or proper. With their complaint the plaintiffs filed an application for a three judge court and a memorandum of law in support of the application for the three judge court.

In September the defendants filed a motion to dismiss the plaintiffs' complaint. It was the position of the defendants that:

1. Plaintiff Dr. Goldfine lacked standing to main-

tain this action both on his own behalf and in a representative capacity on behalf of third persons not parties to this cause and, further, plaintiff Mr. Mercer lacked standing to maintain this action in a representative capacity on behalf of third persons not parties to this cause.

2. The plaintiffs' complaint failed to state a claim upon which relief could be granted, for the reason that the statutory provisions attacked therein are constitutional in every respect.

3. The plaintiffs' complaint failed to allege any grounds upon which any injunctive relief could be granted against the defendants; and

4. The plaintiffs' complaint failed to state a claim upon which relief could be granted against the defendant individual members of the State Board of Education.

The defendants also filed a response in opposition to plaintiffs' application for a three judge court wherein they asserted the same objections.

The Northeast Mothers Alert filed an *Amicus* brief with the consent of all the parties in support of the defendants' position seeking a denial of the relief sought by the plaintiffs.

The motion to dismiss was argued before the court, Judge Joiner sitting alone, and denied. In the court's order it was indicated that a three judge court would be requested.

The plaintiffs filed a motion for preliminary injunction, a brief supporting the motion for preliminary injunction, with exhibits, and the defendants filed a brief supporting their original motion to dismiss and opposing the motion for preliminary injunction. *Amicus* briefs were also submitted by the American Civil Liberties Union, and the Michigan Education Association, supporting the plaintiffs' motion for a preliminary injunction. Certain persons filed a motion to intervene as defendants. This was opposed by the plaintiffs.

II. Standing

Dr. Goldfine does not have standing to maintain this action either on his own behalf or on behalf of any other persons. A litigant must show a demonstrable injury before he may be said to possess a sufficient interest in the action to entitle him to be heard on the merits. Barlow v. Collins, 397 U.S. 159, 90 S.Ct. 832, 25 L.Ed.2d 192 (1970).

In the present case Dr. Goldfine has failed to show any such injury. The statute under attack does not limit Dr. Goldfine's dissemination of birth control information anywhere except in a classroom, and Dr. Goldfine is not a certified teacher.

Courts are required " . . . to determine whether there is a logical nexus between the status asserted and the claim sought to be adjudicated." Flast v. Cohen, 392 U.S. 83, 102, 88 S.Ct. 1942, 1953, 20 L.Ed.2d 947 (1968). Such inquiry determines whether or not the plaintiff is the proper and appropriate party to invoke federal jurisdiction. We find no nexus exists between Dr. Goldfine's status and the statute sought to be set aside. The statute causes no injury to Dr. Goldfine, and this is due to the lack of connection between Dr. Goldfine and the activity controlled by the statute. Indeed even if the existence of a nexus is compelled by pointing to the prohibition against "any person" offering instruction, it becomes so attenuated by its lack of effect that it can no longer be said to be a logical nexus. Flast v. Cohen, *supra*.

Nor does it appear the plaintiffs are unaware of Dr. Goldfine's lack of standing. The plaintiffs have called the court's attention to Doe v. Bolton, 410 U.S. 179, 93 S.Ct. 739, 35 L.Ed.2d 201 (1973), to support an argument that standing need not be resolved if there are other plaintiffs remaining to raise or press the lawsuit's substantive issues. This interpretation of the Supreme Court's action is not justified. The Supreme Court declined to determine whether or not certain peripheral plaintiffs had standing when other plaintiffs remained to force the issues in the *Bolton* lawsuit. This result is far from a mandate to lower courts to refuse resolution of standing questions merely because at least one of the other plaintiffs, in a group of plaintiffs, appears to have the requisite degree of standing.

United States v. Richardson, ——U.S.——, 94 S. Ct. 2940, 41 L.Ed.2d 678 (1974), and Schlesinger v. Reservists Committee to Stop the War et al., ——U.S. ——, 94 S.Ct. 2925, 41 L.Ed.2d 706 (1974), both reinforce the Supreme Court's insistence that litigation be carried on only by those who have standing.

The defendants concede Mr. Mercer has standing to raise the substantive issues. The defendants do not concede Mr. Mercer has standing to raise the rights of students or their parents. The defendants' objections are well taken.

The plaintiffs place primary reliance on Eisenstadt v. Baird, 405 U.S. 438, 92 S.Ct. 1029, 31 L.Ed.2d 349 (1971). This reliance is misplaced in that in *Eisenstadt* the persons whose rights were being asserted had no way in which to raise their rights, *Eisenstadt*, p. 446, 92 S.Ct. 1029.

Similarly distinguishable is Griswold v. Connecticut, 381 U.S. 479, 85 S.Ct. 1678, 14 L.Ed.2d 510 (1965) wherein the court relied, at least in great part, on the confidential relationship between doctor and patient.

It has long been the rule that federal courts will find no standing when persons seek to assert the rights of third persons not before the court. Tileston v. Ullman, 318 U.S. 44, 63 S.Ct. 493, 87 L.Ed. 603 (1974). There are no doubt exceptions to the general rule, Eisenstadt and Griswold, *supra*, but the plaintiff has not placed himself within any of those exceptions.

Indeed, permitting Mr. Mercer to press the rights of students and teachers presents some rather peculiar problems not the least of which is how does the court determine whether or not any parents or students desire these laws to be changed. No student and no parent has come forth in this proceeding, or, to the court's knowledge, in any other proceeding, to seek an adjudication of their rights in their own behalf. In *Tileston* a doctor was not permitted to assert a third party's right to life. Here Mr. Mercer seeks to assert a third person's right to learn. The similarity is striking and this court is compelled to rule that Mr. Mercer has no standing to assert the rights of others which those others could easily assert themselves.

Mr. Mercer further purports to bring this action on behalf of all others similarly situated. No serious effort has been made by either side to determine whether or not the requirements of Rule 23 of the Federal Rules of Civil Procedure have been met. This proceeding is thus not certified as a class action. The court is cognizant, however, that Mr. Mercer is probably representative of a good many teachers and as such today's ruling may be felt by other than Mr. Mercer, for general principles of law are not enunciated for the individual. Rather, general principles of law encompass entire spectra of society, which, in this case, happens to be teachers.

III. The Constitutional Issues

Mercer's basic contention is that his First Amendment rights are being infringed by the statutory prohibition against teaching birth control. Mercer's contention is in essence a question of who controls the school's curriculum and to what extent.

The Supreme Court has answered the question in part by recognizing the undoubted right of the State to establish the curriculum. Epperson v. Arkansas, 393 U.S. 97, 107, 89 S.Ct. 266, 21 L.Ed.2d 228 (1968). The Supreme Court has also recognized that the right of the State is not absolute. Meyer v. Nebraska, 262 U.S. 390, 43 S.Ct. 625, 67 L.Ed. 1042 (1923), and Epperson v. Arkansas, *supra*. It is the duty of this court to sift the law and the facts and determine whether or not the State has overstepped its boundaries in prohibiting the teaching of birth control.

The State may establish its curriculum either by law or by delegation of its authority to the local school boards and communities. This is a long recognized system of operation within our Nation. *Epperson, supra,* 393 U.S. p. 104, 89 S.Ct. 266. This is in part a deference to local control which is a recognition of the varying wants and needs of the Nation's diverse and varied communities, each with its unique character, stan-

dards and sense of social importance of a variety of values.

The statutes under attack represent both forms of curriculum establishment. Michigan Statutes Annotated § 15.3782 forbids the teaching of birth control. Other statutes authorize the communities to establish a sex education program. The statute neither commands that such a program be established nor forbids its establishment. Thus the wants and needs of a tiny rural community wherein sex education might be vehemently opposed, and the wants and needs of the cosmopolitan university-oriented community that might be overwhelmingly in favor of sex education are both accommodated. The statute permits individual community members to be accommodated still further by permitting withdrawal of children from any sex education programs.

Among other things, teachers are engaged to impart to the students the various bodies of knowledge and learning contained in and offered by the curriculum. There is nothing in the First Amendment that gives a person employed to teach the Constitutional right to teach beyond the scope of the established curriculum. Nor are there any judicial decisions giving the teacher the right to teach beyond an established curriculum.

There are cases which touch on curriculum control. The Supreme Court struck down a law which " . . . sought to prevent . . . teachers from discussing the theory of evolution because it is contrary . . . " to the Book of Genesis. *Epperson, supra,* p. 107, 89 S.Ct. p. 272. The law was struck down on First Amendment Anti-establishment grounds.

Meyer v. Nebraska, 262 U.S. 390, 43 S.Ct. 625, 67 L.Ed. 1042 (1923), involved a teacher in a private school who was criminally prosecuted for teaching the German language. The statute there was struck down because it unconstitutionally interfered with the right of the individual guaranteed by the Due Process Clause to engage in any of the common occupations of life. The present case does not involve any of those three factors, to wit: a private school teacher, a statute including criminal sanctions or a common occupation of life.

On the other hand, courts have realized that certain limitations on what is to be taught are necessary. In Goldwasser v. Brown, 135 U.S.App.D.C. 222, 417 F.2d 1169 (1969), a teacher had been fired for what he had said in the classroom. The court sustained the firing despite protestations of suppression of First Amendment rights. The teacher had been hired to teach English and not to express his views on the Nation's Viet Nam policies and Anti-Semitism. There is a balancing test: the State's interest in heightening the level of the public services it offers by assuring the efficiency of its employees in the performance of their tasks on the one hand, and the teachers' free speech interest on the other hand. In *Goldwasser* the employer thought English was best taught by omitting controversial and politically explosive issues; here, the State apparently believes its educational goals are best accomplished by omitting any discussion of birth control.

The application of *Goldwasser* to the present case is not an inappropriate decision. The whole range of knowledge and ideas cannot be taught in the limited time available in public school. This is especially true as to any given year or to any given course. Additionally, it is important that a student's program fit together and it therefore becomes necessary to make certain choices. The authorities must choose which portions of the world's knowledge will be included in the curriculum's programs and courses, and which portions will be left for grasping from other sources, such as the family, peers, or other institutions.

Parents are not compelled to send their children to public schools. They are presented with a choice. They may opt to send their children to either public or private schools. This is a choice which is protected by the Constitution, Pierce v. Society of Sisters, 268 U.S. 510, 45 S.Ct. 571, 69 L.Ed. 1070 (1925). This gives the parents a degree of authority concomitant with the State and the local authorities in molding, shaping and selecting the type of education to which their children are exposed. Often the most obvious reason for choosing one over the other is a desire for sectarian or nonsectarian educations.

The parents who send their children to public schools accept the curriculum which is offered with certain limited exceptions. Parents may and often times do work at local and state levels in an effort to add to or delete from the curriculum certain material. Part of this state's curriculum is a further option for the parents; whether or not to permit their children to receive the benefits, if any, of a sex education program implemented by the local school boards. Other such options exist perhaps in choosing whether or not to take a certain course or courses. No teacher has the right to demand that his particular specialty be imparted to each and every student. The legislature has seen fit to insure a particularly sensitive subject be left to the wisdom of parents. *See* Goldwasser v. Brown, *supra.*

The statutes which have been presented for the court's scrutiny are not overly broad nor do they violate the First Amendment Anti-establishment Clause. The State has the power to establish the curriculum or to delegate some of its authority to local agencies for the final shaping of the curriculum. It also has the power to permit the parents to make the final decision as to exactly which courses the child should take. Implicit in such a state of the law is the observation that a teacher does not have a right, Constitutional or otherwise, to teach what he sees fit, or to overrule the

parents' decision as to which courses their children will take unless, of course, the State has in some manner delegated this responsibility to the teacher which is not the case here.

There is no question but that a Constitutional statute may be applied in an unconstitutional manner, but the plaintiffs' contention that the statute is vague or overbroad to the point of causing the plaintiffs to refrain from certain constitutionally protected conduct to avoid the possibility of penalty cannot be decided in this case.

There is no indication that there have been any threats or reprisals against any teacher for conduct or speech in connection with family planning courses. Problems of abuse of this sort cannot be solved in the abstract pronouncements found in declaratory judgments, but can be reached and solved only in connection with concrete problems presented after the facts have been fully defined. Solutions to this type of problem are best left until there is an ability to define specifically the acts and words that are asserted to offend, in other words, the acts and words that do not involve the teaching, advising, etc., on birth control but do fall within the overall concept of family planning or sex education.

The thrust of this suit is to obtain an abstract determination of the invalidity of the statute on its face at a time when there are no concrete problems before the court. No one is charged with violating the act. This is exactly the kind of case in which a declaration of invalidity of certain application would not be appropriate. The statute on its face is valid. The only question, if any, will come from its application. A plaintiff will not be heard to attack a Constitutional statute on the ground it might some day be applied to him in an unconstitutional manner. United States v. Raines, 362 U.S. 17, 21, 80 S.Ct. 519, 4 L.Ed.2d 524 (1959); Yazoo & Mississippi Valley R. Co. v. Jackson Vinegar Co., 226 U.S. 217, 219, 33 S.Ct. 40, 57 L.Ed. 193 (1912). There is no indication there have been efforts to apply improperly the statute or that its application is causing any problems in connection with attempting to teach matters directed and authorized by the state.

There may be situations where application of the challenged statutes would raise Constitutional questions. The instant case, however, involves an abstract challenge to the validity of the statute and not a challenge of the Constitutional application of the statute. The court should wait until someone is alleged to have violated the statute and there are facts, as cold and hard as concrete instead of hypothetical, before attempting to write the outer limits of Constitutional authority in this area.

The defendants' motion to dismiss as to both statutes is granted. The motion of the intervenor to intervene in this case is denied as moot.

So ordered.

ENGEL, Circuit Judge (concurring in dismissal).

This is a classic example of a cause in search of a controversy.

Examination of the complaint filed demonstrates that it fails to allege a case of actual controversy within the meaning of either the Declaratory Judgment Act, 28 U.S.C. § 2201 or Article III, Section 2 of the United States Constitution.

The federal Declaratory Judgment Act neither creates nor enlarges jurisdiction. It merely provides an additional remedy in cases wherein an actual controversy, and hence jurisdiction, already exists. Skelly Oil Co. v. Phillips Petroleum Co., 339 U.S. 667, 70 S.Ct. 876, 94 L.Ed. 1194 (1950). "Case or controversy" has been defined by the Supreme Court in Maryland Casualty Co. v. Pacific Coal and Oil Co., 312 U.S. 270, 273, 61 S.Ct. 510, 512, 85 L.Ed. 826 (1941):

> "The difference between an abstract question and a 'controversy' contemplated by the Declaratory Judgment Act is necessarily one of degree, and it would be difficult, if it would be possible, to fashion a precise test for determining in every case whether there is such a controversy. Basically, the question in each case is whether the facts alleged, under all the circumstances, show that there is a substantial controversy, between parties having adverse legal interests, of sufficient immediacy and reality to warrant the issuance of a declaratory judgment."

I would readily agree that governmental action which is claimed to have a chilling effect on First Amendment rights has historically been subject to the special scrutiny of the courts, but the constitutional requirement that there be a case or controversy to be adjudicated does not disappear in First Amendment cases.

> "The constitutional question, First Amendment or otherwise, must be presented in the context of a specific live grievance."

Golden v. Zwickler, 394 U.S. 103-110, 89 S.Ct. 956, 960, 22 L.Ed.2d 113 (1969).

In United Public Workers v. Mitchell, 330 U.S. 75, 67 S.Ct. 556, 91 L.Ed. 754 (1947), certain federal employees who desired to engage in some type of political conduct challenged the constitutionality of the Hatch Act, which they conceived would prohibit it. As to those employees who had not violated the Act, the court found there was no case or controversy:

> The power of courts, and ultimately of this Court, to pass upon the constitutionality of acts of Congress arises only when the interests of litigants require the use of this judicial authority for their protection against actual interference. A hypothetical threat is not enough. We can only speculate as to the kinds of political activity the appellants desire to engage in or as to the contents of their proposed

public statements or the circumstances of their publication. It would not accord with judicial responsibility to adjudge, in a matter involving constitutionality, between the freedom of the individual and the requirements of public order except when definite rights appear upon the one side and definite prejudicial interferences upon the other.

> The Constitution allots the nation's judicial power to the federal courts. Unless these courts respect the limits of that unique authority, they intrude upon powers vested in the legislative or executive branches. Judicial adherence to the doctrine of the separation of powers preserves the courts for the decision of issues, between litigants, capable of effective determination. Judicial exposition upon political proposals is permissible only when necessary to decide definite issues between litigants. When the courts act continually within these constitutionally imposed boundaries of their power, their ability to perform their function as a balance for the people's protection against abuse of power by other branches of government remains unimpaired. Should the courts seek to expand their power so as to bring under their jurisdiction ill-defined controversies over constitutional issues, they would become the organ of political theories. Such abuse of judicial power would properly meet rebuke and restriction from other branches. By these mutual checks and balances by and between the branches of government, democracy undertakes to preserve the liberties of the people from excessive concentrations of authority. No threat of interference by the Commission with rights of these appellants appears beyond that implied by the existence of the law and the regulations.

United Public Workers v. Mitchell, *supra*, 89-91, 67 S.Ct. 564-565.

Similarly, the plaintiffs here have alleged "no threat of interference by the [defendants] beyond that implied by the existence of the law . . ." Thus, while plaintiff Mercer alleges generally that he must "delete or omit curriculum material such as books, pamphlets," etc. "in his work with the development of curriculum materials," he neither claims that defendants have prevented him from using any particular source material, nor does he name a particular source that he wishes to use. We are left, as was the court in *Mitchell*, to speculate as to what he desires to use, and to presume that whatever he would ultimately choose would be prohibited by the defendants in obedience to the statute.

Likewise, Dr. Goldfine claims that he has "refrained from giving lectures because of the law in question." The complaint neither describes the content of the lectures he desired to give nor indicates that the defendants forbade him to give a suggested lecture, or even advised against it.

"Allegations of a subjective 'chill' are not an adequate substitute for a claim of specific present objective harm, or threat of specific future harm. . . . " Laird v. Tatum, 408 U.S. 1, 13, 92 S.Ct. 2318, 2326, 33 L.Ed.2d 154 (1971).

Unlike Susan Epperson, who was required by the school administration to employ a textbook teaching the Darwinian Theory in direct contravention of an Arkansas statute, Epperson v. Arkansas, 393 U.S. 97, 89 S.Ct. 266, 21 L.Ed.2d 228 (1968), or Richard Steffel who at least was twice threatened with arrest under a Georgia criminal trespass statute when he and others distributed handbills in a shopping center opposing the Vietnam War, Steffel v. Thompson, 415 U.S. 452, 94 S.Ct. 1209, 39 L.Ed.2d 505 (1974), plaintiffs give us nothing concrete against which to measure the effect, intent, or constitutionality of the statutes challenged here.

The Supreme Court in Steffel v. Thompson, supra, held that, where petitioner had been actually threatened with reprisal for his actions, "it is not necessary that petitioner first expose himself to actual arrest or prosecution to be entitled to challenge a statute that he claims deters the exercise of his constitutional rights". 415 U.S. at 459, 94 S.Ct. at 1216. So here, it may not be necessary that plaintiffs Mercer or Goldfine expose themselves to actual discharge from employment or other serious sanction, in order to arouse a justiciable controversy. Neither, however, is it necessary for this court to hypothesize one on their behalf.

Since there is no actual case or controversy to be adjudicated, this court has jurisdiction to do no more than dismiss the action. Thus I am unable to join in that portion of the majority opinion which addresses itself to the issue of constitutionality of the state statutes, as thoughtful and scholarly as it may be.

A regard for the principles of federalism suggests to me that we should refrain from expression on the constitutionality or unconstitutionality of these statutes until such time as it is necessary to a decision which this court has the power and duty to reach.

I would dismiss the complaint for lack of jurisdiction. F.R.Civ.P. 12(b) (1).

NOTE

* Those statutes read as follows:

§ 15.3782 "It shall be the duty of boards in all school districts having a population of more than 3,000 to engage competent instructors of physical education and to provide the necessary place and equipment for instruction and training in health and physical education; and other boards may make such provision: Provided, That nothing in this chapter shall be construed or operate to authorize compulsory physical examination or compulsory medical treatment of school children. The board of any school district may provide for the teaching of health and physical education and kindred subjects in the public schools of the said districts by qualified instructors in the field of physical education: Provided, That any program of instruction in sex hygiene be supervised by a registered physician, a registered nurse or a person holding a teacher's certificate, qualifying such person as supervisor in this field: Provided, however, That it is not the intention or purpose of this act to give the right of instruction in birth control and it is hereby expressly prohibited to any person to offer or give any instruction in said subject of birth control or offer any advice or information with respect to said subject: Provided further, That any child upon the written request of parent or guardian shall be excused from attending classes in which the subject of sex hygiene or the symptoms of disease is under discussion and no penalties as to credits or graduation shall result therefrom."

§ 15.3789 (3) "Any student upon the written request of parent or guardian shall be excused from attending classes in which the subject of sex education is under discussion and no penalties as to credits or graduation shall result therefrom."

THE United States Court of Appeals, Eighth Circuit, decides against a high school teacher who had brought action against the school board that had terminated his employment after the teacher, upon hearing that U.S. Army personnel would be speaking to the students, said, among other things to his algebra class, that the students were "4,000 strong" and could get the military off the campus. In deciding against the teacher, the Court of Appeals said: "The conduct of this probationary teacher in utilizing his algebra class as a forum from which to suggest, none too subtly, to young and immature minds, that they employ measures of violence as a demonstrative device, presented a grave situation, with respect to which the board was well authorized to exercise its implied authority."

Birdwell v. *Hazelwood School District*, 491 F.2d 490 (1974)

TALBOT SMITH, Senior District Judge.

The appellant, a former teacher employed by the Hazelwood School District, St. Louis County, Missouri, instituted this action against the Board of Education of the School District,[1] the members of the Board individually, and three administrative officers of the Hazelwood School District. Violations of 42 U.S.C. §§ 1981 and 1983 were alleged, with jurisdiction based on 28 U.S.C. § 1343(3) and (4). The complaint sought reinstatement, back pay, injunctive relief, and, in the alternative, money damages for loss of reputation and breach of contract in the amount of $100,000 for the alleged violations of appellant's constitutional rights of free speech and due process of law, and for violation of R.S.Mo. § 168.126 (1969), V.A. M.S., requiring a written statement of charges and ninety days' notice before termination. A trial to the court, Judge Wangelin, held for the appellees. Birdwell v. Hazelwood School District, 352 F.Supp. 613 (E.D.Mo.1972). We affirm.

The opinion in the District Court set forth the facts in detail. We here summarize only those relevant to the issues raised. The appellant was a probationary teacher. Prior to the incidents giving rise to the charges here made he had objected to the presence of the R.O.T.C. at the school, expressing the view that they had "no right to be on the campus." It was his position that the students and faculty should decide who should visit the campus, but his arguments were rejected by the principal, Mr. Fuqua, who informed appellant that he, the principal, was the agent of the Board of Education in the matter and that it was his responsibility, not the appellant's, to make such determinations. The appellant at this time was a probationary teacher and not in a policy-making position in the school hierarchy.

On May 19, 1971, it was announced over the public address system that United States Army personnel would be in the building and students were invited to speak with them. This announcement was made at the beginning of a class period during which appellant was conducting a class in Algebra II for students of all three years. A general class discussion of the visit by military personnel ensued. Appellant indicated that before such visitors were invited onto the campus there should be a consensus of faculty and students in favor of the visit. He became emotionally upset as he continued the discussion, although the trial court found that he "retained some control over his emotional state." One of the students testified that appellant observed to the class that the students at Hazelwood were "4000 strong," that they could get the military off the campus, and that at Washington University the students would not tolerate the military coming onto the campus. This reference was taken by student Stephens to pertain to an incident where "at this time last year Washington University had just burned down their R.O.T.C. building." There was no suggestion that the students actually remove the recruiters physically, but reference to the use of force against them was made. It happened to be on this date that a student organization distributed apples to the faculty members to show their appreciation of their work. Several students testified that appellant suggested that the students could throw their apples at the recruiters. "[H]e was serious, he meant it" testified one of the students. And, also, "to get them in a crowd, and push them and kick them, make them feel like they weren't wanted." This latter was accomplished in part during the recess period when many students were in the hall. Appellant approached Sergeant Smith, who, with his two companions, were standing near their table in their khaki uniforms. Appellant pointed his finger at the Sergeant and said in a loud voice "On behalf of myself and other faculty members and the students, we don't want you here. We are getting together a petition to have a restraining order having you restrained from the school." Sergeant Smith made no comment in reply, simply acknowledging the greeting. The servicemen were there with permission for the purpose of discussing with students a military career. They brought with them no firearms, but literature. "We were strictly in the hall with a table of literature, strictly providing information to those who requested it," testified the sergeant. We are constrained to observe at this juncture that the appellant's zealous advocacy in our court of his constitutional right of free speech contrasts sharply with his obvious intolerance of the exercise of such speech by others with whose views he disagrees.

The incident was reported to the Principal Fuqua by Mr. Henner, the assistant principal, who requested that appellant meet with him that day, but appellant did not respond. The next day, following a complaint from one of the parents, appellant was requested to, and did, meet with the school's administrative officials to discuss the incident. At this meeting, the District Court found, appellant admitted confronting the soldiers in the hall as well as making the statement to his class that the student body was some 4000 strong and that at Washington University the presence of the military visitors would not be tolerated by the students. Mr. Huss, Hazelwood Co-ordinator of Secondary Education, thereupon advised appellant that he was suspended from his classroom duties until the matter was resolved.

A report was made to Dr. McDonald, Superintendent of Education for the Hazelwood School District. It was the recommendation of Mr. Huss, according to the oral testimony of Dr. McDonald, that appellant should be dismissed because a) he was inciting the students to disruptive processes, and b) he was interrupting the educational process. Dr. McDonald confirmed the suspension, instructed Hess to notify appellant that the Board would meet that night, and to inform the appellant that he was invited to appear and speak. Huss so advised appellant of the Board meeting, that his dismissal would be recommended, and that he was invited to attend. Appellant did not do so, upon advice of counsel, and the Board, after consideration, unanimously voted to terminate his employment.

Before this court the appellant argues that he was dismissed for constitutionally impermissible reasons,

namely, "because he informed his students of his opposition to the campus visitation by military recruiters in violation of his right of free speech as guaranteed by the First and Fourteenth Amendments to the Constitution of the United States." The right of free speech, thus asserted, is not, of course, an absolute right. Schenk v. United States, 249 U.S. 47, 39 S.Ct. 247, 63 L.Ed. 470 (1919). We must weigh the interests asserted by the state officials against the infringement of the protected rights of the individual.[2] Particularly demanding is this process in the educational field where freedom of expression is peculiarly appropriate, since the classroom is peculiarly the "market place of ideas."[3] In the situation presented we must "arrive at a balance between the interests of the teacher, as a citizen, in commenting upon matters of public concern and the interests of the State, as an employer, in promoting the efficiency of the public service it performs through its employees."[4]

The controlling law in this area, as we noted in Gieringer v. Center School Dist. No. 58, 477 F.2d 1164 (8th Cir. 1973), is found in *Pickering, supra*, note 2. It was there held (1) that a teacher retains the right as a citizen to comment on matters of public concern; (2) that to the degree such commentary is substantially accurate, it provides no grounds for dismissal absent a showing of disruption of the teacher's classroom duties or the regular operation of the school, and (3) that, even if the commentary is inaccurate, a showing of disruption is still required unless it can be proved that the statements in question were knowingly or recklessly made.

The District Court found that the appellant's statements, both in class and in the hallway, interfered with the educational process. The statements were completely irrelevant to appellant's duties of teaching mathematics and diverted the time and attention of both students and teacher from the prescribed curriculum. They embodied, as well, an attempt to defeat a school policy by improper means. But, beyond matters of school policy and curriculum, it was found that appellant's statements were "infused with the spirit of violent action" to the degree that the school authorities found a situation of potential disruption.[5]

The findings thus made we do not disturb, absent such clear error as to leave us, on the entire evidence, with the definite and firm conviction that a mistake has been committed.[6] We note, as well, that this rule applies also to factual inferences from undisputed facts. Commissioner v. Duberstein, 363 U.S. 278, 80 S.Ct. 1190, 4 L.Ed.2d 1218 (1960); St. Louis Typographical Union No. 8 v. Herald Company, 402 F.2d 553, 557 (8th Cir. 1968). So examined, the conduct of the appellant comes squarely within the proscriptions of *Pickering, supra*, note 2.

But appellant urges to us that Tinker v. Des Moines

Independent Community School District, 393 U.S. 503, 89 S.Ct. 733, 21 L.Ed.2d 731 (1969), warrants his exculpation on the ground that there must be actual disruption before the authorities may act. It is argued that "there was no material or substantial disruption of the school" and that, in fact, the only tangible result of appellant's statements was the circulation of a petition by one of the students supporting appellant's views. *Tinker*, however, is inapposite. It involved only the silent wearing of armbands, a situation not analogous to a thinly veiled exhortation to violence. Moreover, *Tinker* itself distinguishes the conduct we here consider.[7] *See also* Esteban v. Central Missouri State College, 415 F.2d 1077 (8th Cir. 1969), cert. denied, 398 U.S. 965, 90 S.Ct. 2169, 26 L.Ed.2d 548 (1970).[8] In a situation of potential disruption there is no requirement in the law that the proper authorities must wait for the blow to fall before taking remedial measures.

Moreover, even should violence not have occurred, we do not take it that such is a *sine qua non* of disruptive conduct. The trial court found that the appellant's actions, both in the classroom and in the hallway, were "disruptions of the orderly and disciplined operation of the school in and of themselves." It is clear upon this record that appellant's termination did not result from the exercise of a constitutionally protected right of free speech.

Appellant also argues that he was denied due process as to the Board's hearing. He asserts that he must be given a reasonable opportunity to be heard and to be advised of the identity of witnesses against him, as well as other procedural rights. He complains that the hearing was held "behind closed doors" and that neither the Army personnel nor students were present to testify. We need not catalog the numerous offenses to due process claimed by appellant after the event. He is in no position before us to complain of these alleged deficiencies. He was aware of the time and the place of the Board meeting, that his continued employment was at stake, and that his dismissal was being recommended because of his statements in class and his actions towards the servicemen in the building. Nevertheless, with this knowledge, and after conferring with legal counsel, it was his decision not to attend the meeting.

The "standards of procedural due process are not wooden absolutes."[9] The sufficiency of the procedures must be judged in the light of the totality of the circumstances. The fundamental requirement of due process "is the opportunity to be heard, 'at a meaningful time and in a meaningful manner,' * * * This opportunity must be 'appropriate to the nature of the case.' * * * 'The very nature of due process negates any concept of inflexible procedures universally applicable to every imaginable situation.' "[10]

The opportunity thus demanded was here afforded but appellant deliberately chose not to avail himself of it and not to present to the Board the arguments made to us. He cannot now scour the record of the hearing he thus ignored for flaws in its conduct. We find a voluntary and knowing waiver. Johnson v. Zerbst, 304 U.S. 458, 58 S.C. 1019, 82 L.Ed. 1461 (1938).

It is also the urging of the appellant that, being a probationary teacher, his discharge was governed by the provisions of R.S.Mo. § 168.126, subd. 2 (1969), V.A.M.S.,[11] stating that a board of education "may terminate the employment of the probationary teacher" for incompetency. From this the appellant apparently argues that there is no further authority, express or implied, in the Board to dismiss for any other cause and thus, not having been discharged for incompetency, his discharge was in violation of his contractual rights. For this he seeks monetary damages. These claims, asserted under the statutes of the State of Missouri, arose from the same incident as did the federal claims heretofore considered. In view of the interrelation of the claims under the circumstances of this case the District Court properly concluded that it had pendent jurisdiction over such state claim. *See* United Mine Workers v. Gibbs, 383 U.S. 715, 86 S.Ct. 1130, 16 L.Ed.2d 218 (1966).

The District Court rejected the argument made, pointing out that such construction of the act would vest in a probationary teacher far greater security than that afforded a permanent teacher,[12] obviously not the intent of the act. In addition the court found, after exhaustive analysis of the applicable statutes of the State of Missouri, and the judicial interpretations thereof, ranging from McCutchen v. Windsor, 55 Mo. 149 (1874), Arnold v. School District, 78 Mo. 226 (1883), Magenheim v. Board of Education, 347 S.W.2d 409 (St. Louis C.A. 1961) to Williams v. Longtown School District No. 71, 468 S.W.2d 673 (St. Louis C.A. 1971), that, whatever the Missouri law may have been prior to the passage of the Teacher Tenure Act,[13] it is now clear from a comparison of the requirements of §168.116, subd. 1[14] relating to the termination of permanent teachers, with those of § 168.126, subd. 2, *supra*, note 12, relating to the termination of probationary teachers, that it was the legislative intent to grant the Board implied authority to act as it did in the circumstances here presented. We concur in the interpretation made. The conduct of this probationary teacher in utilizing his algebra class as a forum from which to suggest, none too subtly, to young and immature minds, that they employ measures of violence as a demonstrative device, presented a grave situation, with respect to which the Board was well authorized to exercise its implied authority.

We find no error in the proceedings below. The judgment is affirmed.

NOTES

1. By amendment the Hazelwood School District was substituted as a party defendant in place of the Board of Education.
2. Pickering v. Board of Education, 391 U.S. 563, 88 S.Ct. 1731, 20 L.Ed.2d 811 (1968).
3. Keyishian v. Board of Regents, 385 U.S. 589, 603, 87 S.Ct. 675, 17 L.Ed.2d 629 (1967). The cases are collected in Emerson, *The System of Freedom of Expression,* "Academic Freedom," 593, 598-611 (1970). *See also* Healy v. James, 408 U.S. 169, 92 S.Ct. 2338, 33 L.Ed.2d 266 (1972); "Developments in the Law, Academic Freedom," 81 Harv.L.Rev. 1045 (1968).
4. Pickering v. Board of Education, 391 U.S. at 568, 88 S.Ct. at 1734.
5. Mr. Huss, a teacher of some twenty years' experience, regarded the situation following the incident as grave. The school was the largest in the state, overcrowded, and had had past problems with a student organization (SDS) seeking to "disrupt the educational process." It was his testimony that because of the "quick action" taken there had been no disruption, that "we headed it off." Continuing he explained in these terms: "You asked me or somebody asked me a while ago about my opinion on dealing with this type of kids and I know the longer they get the chance to talk about it and the fact that no action is taken, there might be something happen, and I think in my best judgment the action we took may have prevented any demonstrations or any severe action."
6. Fed.R.Civ.P. 52; Barryhill v. United States, 300 F.2d 690 (8th Cir. 1962).
7. "As we have discussed, the record does not demonstrate any facts which might reasonably have led school authorities to forecast substantial disruption of or material interference with school activities, and no disturbances or disorders on the school premises in fact occurred." *Tinker,* 393 U.S. at 514, 89 S.Ct. at 740.
8. "That emphasis [in the majority opinion in *Tinker*] is on the absence of 'actually or potentially disruptive conduct' by the participants * * *." *Esteban,* 415 F.2d at 1087.
9. Ferguson v. Thomas, 430 F.2d 852, 856 (5th Cir. 1970).
10. Ahern v. Bd. of Education, 456 F.2d at 403.
11. "Probationary teachers, how terminated—reemployed, how.
    If in the opinion of the board of education any probationary teacher has been doing unsatisfactory work, the board of education through its authorized administrative representative, shall provide the teacher with a written statement definitely setting forth his alleged incompetency and specifying the nature thereof, in order to furnish the teacher an opportunity to correct his fault and overcome his incompetency. If improvement satisfactory to the board of education has not been made within ninety days of the receipt of the notification, the board of education may terminate the employment of the probationary teacher immediately or at the end of the school year."
12. R.S.Mo. § 168.106 (1969), V.A.M.S., provides: "Indefinite contract, what affects
    The contract between a school district and a permanent teacher shall be known as an indefinite contract and shall continue in effect for an indefinite period, subject only to:
    (1) Compulsory or optional retirement when the teacher reaches the age of retirement provided by law, or regulation established by the local board of education;
    (2) Modification by a succeeding indefinite contract or contracts in the manner hereinafter provided;
    (3) The death of the teacher;
    (4) Resignation of the teacher with the written consent of the school board;
    (5) Termination by the board of education after a hearing as hereinafter provided; and
    (6) The revocation of the teacher's certificate."

A United States District Court in Ohio decides against parents who claimed their First Amendment rights had been violated because teachers refused to distribute to students in class documents critical of school authorities, which had been provided by the parents for the students to take home. Responding to the argument that the school had created a public forum by permitting other printed information to be sent home via school-aged children, the Court declared: " . . . the distribution via students of information concerning coming theatrical events, home safety measures, and the like, is not indicative of the establishment of a forum for First Amendment purposes. Dissemination of such material is a logical and a proper extension of the educational function of schools in our society, and such dissemination does not of itself give rise to any right of access to student distribution by parents or other concerned citizens."

Buckel v. *Prentice*, 410 F.Suppl. 1243 (1976)

DUNCAN, District Judge.

This is a civil rights action brought for declaratory and injunctive relief against various public officials who administer the Columbus Public Schools, Columbus, Ohio. The cause of action arises under 42 U.S.C. §1983 and the First and Fourteenth Amendments to the United States Constitution. Jurisdiction lies here pursuant to 28 U.S.C. § 1343(3). This matter is before the Court upon plaintiffs' motion for summary judgment. The Court has before it a final pretrial order containing certain agreed facts, four depositions, an affidavit, and various exhibits.

The following are stipulated facts from the final pretrial order entered in this case:

1. That at all times relevant to plaintiffs' complaint, plaintiffs were residents of Columbus, Ohio, and their children attended and were students at Kingswood Elementary School.

2. That at all times relevant to plaintiffs' complaint, defendants were board members and administrators of the Columbus Public Schools as alleged in plaintiffs' complaint.

3. That in July of 1970, the State of Ohio, Department of Education, published a document entitled "Minimum Standards for Ohio Elementary Schools".

4. That on or about December 17, 1973, material written by plaintiff Buckel and other concerned parents was sent to parents of all of the children of Kingswood Elementary School via the children.

5. That on or about April 3, 1974, additional material was presented to defendant Dorothy Scrivener to be sent home by the school children of Kingswood

Elementary School, and that defendant Dorothy Scrivener refused to allow the children to take such material home to their parents.

6. That on or about April 13, 1974, plaintiffs appealed defendant Scrivener's decision to defendant Ellis who upheld defendant Scrivener's decision.

7. That on or about May 14, 1974, plaintiffs appealed defendant Ellis' decision to the Board of Education which upheld defendant Ellis' decision.

The plaintiffs in this case are parents of grade school children attending Kingswood Elementary School, which is in the Columbus school system. Plaintiff Buckel and certain other parents believe that parental and community involvement in the management and administration of the schools in a particular community is a worthy goal. To this end, they abhor large, centralized school districts and attendant bureaucratic controls. In December of 1973, plaintiff Buckel and three other Kingswood parents proposed that certain changes be made in the purpose and composition of the Kingswood Evaluation Committee. They prepared a two-page document entitled "Proposed Changes to the Kingswood Evaluation Committee to Form: The Kingswood Task Force on Educational Improvements," and prevailed upon defendant Dorothy Scrivener, Principal of Kingswood Elementary School, to send copies of the proposal home to parents with students attending Kingswood. This document is the "December 17, 1973 material" referred to in the fourth numbered stipulation set out hereinabove.

Thereafter, in April of 1974, plaintiff Buckel and other Kingswood parents asked Scrivener to send another circular home to parents via Kingswood students. This circular was the "April 3, 1974 additional material" referred to in the fifth numbered stipulation set out hereinabove. The material, styled "Progress Report to Kingswood Parents," expressly disclaimed any connection between its authors and any formal school function or a P.T.A. sponsored activity. This second circular was critical of the school administration's alleged lack of responsiveness to the changes proposed in the December 17, 1973 material. Defendant Scrivener refused to send this second circular home with Kingswood students. After plaintiffs unsuccessfully attempted to have the Superintendent of the Columbus Public Schools and the Columbus Board of Education alter Scrivener's decision, this lawsuit was filed.

Plaintiffs argue that the defendants have created a public forum by permitting a wide variety of printed information to be sent home to parents via school-aged children. Once such a forum exists, they assert, plaintiffs may not, in conformity with the First and Fourteenth Amendments, be denied access to the forum. See, *e.g., Lehman* v. *City of Shaker Heights*, 418 U.S. 298, 94 S.Ct. 2714, 41 L.Ed.2d 770 (1974). As relief, plaintiffs seek an injunctive order requiring defendants to establish objective standards to be used by them in the future for purposes of deciding whether particular materials will be sent home to parents via school children.

The Columbus Public Schools have a written policy governing the dissemination of commercial advertising to parents by sending it home with students; this policy is not at issue in this case. There is no written policy governing distribution of non-commercial materials. Defendant Dr. John Ellis, Superintendent of the Columbus Public Schools, testified as follows during his September 25, 1975 deposition, at pages 8–9:

Q. In this case, do you have an opinion or viewpoint with respect to whether or not that material [*i.e.,* the April 3, 1974 circular] promotes nonschool interests?

A. In this instance again, my general opinion would be that this request doesn't fall within that particular policy [*i.e.,* the written policy governing dissemination of commercial advertising], but it would definitely fall within the policy that the principal is responsible for the operation of the school on the very broad conditions that have been explicitly stated by the Columbus Board of Education, and that the principal was totally empowered to make a judgment in this case, a judgment that I did not feel was appropriate to overrule.

Q. Are there any general practices that developed over the years that you have observed since the time you have been with the board concerning what kind of material goes home with students to parents?

A. The general practice is that material that is sent home is done so with the permission or approval of the principal. Generally speaking, such information would have to be of educational value directly related to the students' interests or the safety of the children.

Q. What about material that is merely informative to parents with respect to items which somehow relate to the school?

A. That would be a matter for the principal to determine whether it was in the best interest of the pupils and the educational system.

Q. Do the principals have any guidelines for exercising that discretion which you understand?

A. There are no written guidelines but the topic is reviewed in the administrative cadet program and the statements that you have just made are generally discussed and understood by most of the principals.

Q. With respect to the cadet program and the way in which those statements are reviewed, are there any written guidelines that are suggested for principals to use in making those decisions?

A. No.

Q. Are there any materials utilized in the cadet program which put in writing the suggested outline?

A. No.

The Columbus schools have in the past sent home with students to parents pamphlets of an informational nature. These include materials about home fire safety, musical instrument rental plans, school lunch menus, summer recreation facilities and programs, and musical concerts and recitals. The schools have also used student distribution to disseminate leaflets promoting tax levies and a state income tax.

There is insufficient evidence of record to support a finding that the Columbus Public Schools have developed a practice of permitting parents to use student distribution to express opinions or disseminate information to other parents. There are, however, two instances of record in which defendant Scrivener permitted such material to be sent home with Kingswood students. The first was a circular from "Interested and concerned Kingswood Parents" urging parents to attend a January 24, 1973 presentation at Kingswood Elementary School. The speaker was "Mr. Bruce Barlow, of the Columbus Board of Education," and his topic was decentralization of public schools. The second such distribution was the December 17, 1973 publication sent by plaintiff Buckel and others.

When asked during her deposition why she had approved the December 1973 distribution but rejected the April 1974 distribution, defendant Scrivener replied as follows, at pages 37–38:

A. Well, I think perhaps I was in error in approving it in the beginning, and I wouldn't want to make two errors.

Q. Why do you think you were in error in approving it in the beginning?

A. Because it did not work in the best interests of the school. The committee that we had was already working and functioning, and why should we make a change?

Q. In other words, you felt that the proposed changes—the original proposed changes—were without merit?

A. As we moved along and I could look back on it; yes, I think I did not recognize that at the very beginning and I think perhaps that was an error in judgment for our school.

Mr. Justice Blackmun observed in the plurality opinion in *Lehman* v. *City of Shaker Heights,* 418 U.S. 298, 302–303, 94 S.Ct. 2714, 2717, 41 L.Ed.2d 770, 777 (1974), "Although American constitutional jurisprudence, in the light of the First Amendment, has been jealous to preserve access to public places for purposes of free speech, the nature of the forum and the conflicting interests involved have remained important in determining the degree of protection afforded by the Amendment to the speech in question." The "nature of the forum" which plaintiffs seek to establish in the present case is perhaps unique. Plaintiffs do not seek access here to a forum consisting of a school newspaper, or a soapbox in a public place, or the advertising placards of a public transit system. Rather, they have fixed their sights upon the student population of the Columbus Public Schools, and assert that these students, as a matter of federal constitutional law, must be made available to them for use, as Mr. Buckel puts it, as "child messengers."

By failing to promulgate objective standards governing the distribution via students of non-commercial materials, defendants invite litigation such as the present action. Permitting individual principals to decide, on a case-by-case basis and without clear guidelines, whether particular groups or individuals may send particular pamphlets home with students, could give rise, on a proper set of facts, to serious constitutional questions. Plainly, officials acting under color of state law may not on the one hand open an avenue of communication for persons entertaining certain views, and on the other hand deny the same forum to persons who wish to advocate differing opinions.

The question presented here, however, is not whether the policy adopted by defendants has the *potential* for creating a forum. The issues are (1) whether the evidence shows that a forum has been in fact created, and (2) if so, whether the evidence shows that plaintiffs have been denied access to the forum without just cause.

In my judgment, the distribution via students of information concerning coming theatrical events, home safety measures, and the like, is not indicative of the establishment of a forum for First Amendment purposes. Dissemination of such material is a logical and a proper extension of the educational function of schools in our society, and such dissemination does not of itself give rise to any right of access to student distribution by parents or other concerned citizens.

The remaining incidents of student distribution which are part of the record of this case are mentioned hereinabove. These are the pamphlets promoting tax levies, the circular urging parents to attend Mr. Barlow's presentation and the December 17, 1973 material from Mr. Buckel and others. The Court is of the opinion that the past student distribution of these materials is insufficient to support a finding that defendants have created a public forum for the expression of ideas or the dissemination of information. If plaintiffs were seeking to take issue with the content of the materials heretofore permitted to be distributed, a different case might be presented. Plaintiff's more sweeping contention, that the student distribution which has occurred to date requires defendants to permit everyone access to such channels, subject only to reasonable standards, is rejected.

The Court, then, while in agreement with plaintiffs that there is no genuine issue as to any material fact herein, does not agree that plaintiffs are entitled to judgment as a matter of law. On the contrary, the Court concludes that on the facts present the defendants are entitled to judgment. The fact that defendants have not filed a cross-motion for summary judgment does not preclude entry of such a judgment if they are otherwise entitled thereto, see, *e.g., Watkins Motor Lines, Inc.* v. *Zero Refrigerated Lines,* 381 F.Supp. 363, 367 (N.D.Ill.1974); *Petroleo Brasileiro, S.A., Petrobras* v. *Ameropan Oil Corporation,* 372 F.Supp. 503, 508 (E.D.N.Y.1974).

It is accordingly ORDERED that judgment be entered for defendants and against plaintiffs on the cause of action set out in the amended complaint.

In deciding for an Arkansas college teacher who had been denied reappointment because, among other things, he had announced to his classes in world civilization and American civilization that he was a Communist and a member of the Progressive Labor Party, a United States District Court in Arkansas concluded "that Cooper's membership in the PLP was constitutionally protected. *A fortiori* Cooper's right to state publicly that he was a Communist and member of the PLP was also protected by the First Amendment." The District Court also concluded "that Cooper's announcement of his personal political and philosophical beliefs in his classes was constitutionally protected. . . . It is evident that the bare announcement of Cooper's personal views did not materially or substantially disrupt his classes. In fact, it caused remarkably little concern until the matter was publicized by the media. The subsequent public reaction is not the kind of disruption that can be balanced against a teacher's right to free expression." In summary, said the Court, "Cooper's membership in the PLP and his public acknowledgement of his beliefs, both inside and outside the university classroom, were protected conduct under the First and Fourteenth Amendments. The court finds that this protected activity was a substantial or motivating factor in the university's decision not to reappoint Cooper. The university failed to prove by a preponderance of the evidence that the same non-reappointment decision would have been made absent Cooper's exercise of First Amendment rights."

Cooper v. *Ross*, 472 F.Supp. 802 (1979)

HEANEY, Circuit Judge, Sitting by Designation.

On November 11, 1974, in the United States District Court for the Eastern District of Arkansas, Grant Cooper filed this action, alleging that he was not reappointed to the faculty of the University of Arkansas at Little Rock in violation of his rights of freedom of speech and association guaranteed by the First and Fourteenth Amendments of the Constitution and by 42 U.S.C. § 1983 (1976). Jurisdiction is premised upon 28 U.S.C. § 1343(3) (1976). The cause was tried to the court in October 1978. Pursuant to rule 52(a) of the Federal Rules of Civil Procedure, the court makes the following findings of fact.

FINDINGS OF FACT

1. In September 1969, Little Rock University was merged into the University of Arkansas, an educational institution of the State of Arkansas. Defendant G. Robert Ross was appointed Chancellor of the University of Arkansas at Little Rock (UALR or University) in January 1973. Defendant C. Fred Williams was named head of the History Department at the University in May 1973. The remaining defendants are all members of the University of Arkansas Board of Trustees.[1] All defendants are sued only in their official capacities.

2. Grant Cooper was employed as an assistant professor of history at the University for the 1970-71 academic year. He was reappointed as assistant professor for the 1971-72, 1972-73 and 1973-74 academic years.

3. Cooper did not have tenure. The faculty handbook provided that:

A non-tenure appointment may be terminated effective at the end of an academic or fiscal year as the case may be at the option either of the individual or the University.

4. During the fourth year of teaching at the rank of assistant professor, a faculty member was normally considered for promotion to associate professor. Promotion would automatically confer tenure. Alternatively, the teacher could be retained at the rank of assistant professor without tenure, or he could be notified that he would not be reappointed. The faculty handbook provided that one who had been a faculty

member for two or more years was entitled to at least one year's written advance notice if he was not going to be recommended for reappointment.

5. Prior to the spring of 1973 there were no established procedures and no specific standards for faculty evaluation and promotion purposes, either University-wide or within the History Department. Beginning in the spring of 1973 the Ross administration instituted a policy of merit pay increases and required periodic faculty evaluations.

6. Cooper became a member of the Progressive Labor Party (PLP) in June or July 1973. In mid-July 1973, at the beginning of the second summer school session, Cooper informed his classes in world civilization and American civilization that he was a communist and a member of the PLP, and that he taught his courses from a Marxist point of view. Other History Department members and Chancellor Ross learned of the statements shortly thereafter.

7. At registration for the fall 1973 term, Williams questioned Cooper about his statements to his classes and suggested to Cooper that it was inappropriate for him to announce his personal point of view to his classes. Bedford Hadley, Dean of the Division of Social Science, similarly discussed the matter with Cooper. Cooper was, however, not directed to discontinue the practice.

8. On September 20, 1973, *Essence*, an "underground" student newspaper, carried an article about Cooper and his statements to his summer school classes. On September 26, 1973, substantially the same article appeared on the front page of the *Arkansas Gazette*, a newpaper with statewide circulation. The articles apparently reported that Cooper had been ordered by the university not to state his personal political views in the classroom. Thereafter, Cooper became the subject of considerable public controversy and for several weeks the case received daily newspaper and television coverage.

9. On October 8, 1973, twenty-three state legislators, as individuals, filed suit in state court against Cooper, Chancellor Ross, and the Trustees of the University, to enjoin Cooper's further employment at the University. The suit was predicated on Ark.Stat.Ann. §§ 41–4111 and 41–4113 (1964). Section 41–4113(c) provided,

> No person who is a member of a Nazi, Fascist or Communist society, or any organization affiliated with such societies, shall be eligible for employment by the State of Arkansas, or by any department, agency, institution, or municipality thereof.

10. On approximately October 2, October 9, and October 23, 1973, Cooper participated in public forums sponsored by Students for Action and the PLP regarding the use by another UALR faculty member of *The Unheavenly City* by Edward Banfield as a required textbook. Cooper publicly criticized the book as racist and unscientific and argued that the book should not be required course material and should be banned from the University campus.

11. On October 3, 1973, Cooper met with Chancellor Ross at the latter's request. They discussed the statements Cooper made to his classes, Cooper's political beliefs and how these affected his teaching of his courses. They also discussed Cooper's statements about the Banfield book.

A second meeting was held on October 29, 1973, and the same general issues were discussed. At the conclusion of the discussion Ross inquired whether, if instructed by the University, Cooper would teach his courses from an objective point of view and refrain from identifying his own beliefs to his classes. Cooper responded that he felt it would be intellectually dishonest if he did not state his own beliefs, that he could not be entirely objective toward other points of view, and that if he were ordered not to teach from a Marxist point of view he would feel compelled to resist the order. At no time in either meeting were any other factors relating to Cooper's performance as a teacher discussed.

12. On November 7, 1973, Cooper was notified by Williams that he was not recommending Cooper's reappointment and that Cooper's 1974-75 appointment would be a terminal appointment.

13. Cooper requested and was granted a conference at which Williams explained his decision not to recommend Cooper's further employment. Cooper then requested and received a written list of reasons for the non-reappointment recommendation. The reasons given were as follows:

1. A student evaluation of faculty, published by the Student Government Association during the 1971/72 academic year, gave your courses in History of Civilization next to the lowest evaluation of any faculty member in the department. A student survey in the fall semester of 1973, conducted by a student, reflected a concern for your academic competence.

2. An evaluation by the acting department chairman, dated April 30, 1973, gave you the lowest merit rating of any of the full time departmental faculty with terminal degrees.

3. Over a period of some three years, a variety of irregularities have been brought to your attention. These include:

a. Questionable grading procedures and problems involving evaluation of students.

b. Student complaints about meeting and conducting scheduled classes.

4. The Dean of the Division of Social Science, who was a former chairman of the History Department, has stated that during the past three years he has received

more student complaints about your teaching responsibilities than has been received on any other faculty member in the division.

5. Students have repeatedly indicated that your courses did not cover the subject area as described in the University catalog; that you failed to adhere to the required text materials in assignments, lectures or discussion and your attitude toward those materials discouraged their use.

6. Changing, in a unilateral [sic] manner, the content and scope of a course required by the general faculty for graduation.

7. Your attempts to restrict the academic freedom of others in the academic community which reflects a lack of restraint and does not show proper respect for the opinion of others in the academic setting. Specifically, your statements about banning a book on the UALR campus.

8. You have indicated either a lack of awareness or concern for a well known and respected statement of the American Association of University Professors in a "1940 Statement of Principles and Interpretive Comments" on academic freedom and tenure. Paragraph "C" of that document, in reference to the college or university teacher, includes the following statements:

"As a man of learning and an educational officer, he (the teacher) should remember that the public may judge his profession and his institution by his utterances."

9. These reasons have led me to conclude that your professional development in scholarly endeavors and classroom instruction have not been satisfactorily demonstrated and, therefore, your appointment as assistant professor should not be renewed. I feel confident that a more qualified person can be readily employed as an assistant professor.

14. Reason 1 was subsequently withdrawn by Williams after Cooper objected that the student surveys were unscientific and unvalidated and that University officials had previously indicated that the surveys would not be considered in faculty appointment decisions.

Reason 2 referred to an evaluation of Cooper by T. Harri Baker, the former head of the History Department, prepared in the spring of 1973 for the purpose of granting merit pay increases. Cooper received ratings of average or superior in every category evaluated and the comments indicated he had shown improvement in his teaching. Cooper was awarded a six percent pay increase whereas the average increase for members of the History Department was slightly above seven percent. Cooper was not advised at the time that his was the "lowest merit rating" although he was aware that some other members of the department received higher raises than he did.

Reason 3 referred to several different factors including, inter alia, complaints by some students that Cooper graded too hard, fluctuations in Cooper's grades from the lowest in the department to the second highest, and permitting too many students to take "incomplete" grades in his courses. Cooper corrected the last problem after it was brought to his attention.

Reasons 3a,3b, 4 and 5 referred to a variety of student complaints. No records were available of the persons who made the complaints, the dates, or nature and number of the complaints. At the time they were received, little effort was made to verify or investigate the complaints. Although on occasion faculty members had casually mentioned student complaints to Cooper, they had indicated that the complaints were not considered to be serious.

Reason 6 referred, in part, to a handout Cooper used in his World Civilization course in the fall semester of 1973. This handout stated the proposition: "The history of all hitherto existing society is the history of class struggles." The handout attributed the statement to Marx and Engels and indicated Cooper's agreement with it. Students were assigned to write a term paper on a subject of their choosing to test the proposition.

Reason 7 referred to Cooper's public comments about the Banfield book.

With the exception of reasons 6, 7, and 8, which were discussed to some extent in the conferences with Chancellor Ross, Cooper had never previously been informed that his teaching performance was unsatisfactory in these or any other respects.

15. Cooper requested reconsideration of the decision. By letter dated January 21, 1974, Williams informed Cooper that he had reevaluated him without considering the student surveys, but would not change his recommendation.

16. Cooper requested that his case be reviewed by the Senate Standing Committee on Academic Tenure, as provided in the UALR Faculty Handbook. There was, however, at that time no such committee in existence. Therefore, the UALR faculty assembly created an ad hoc committee to review Williams's recommendation not to reappoint Cooper. In May 1974 the committee conducted hearings at which Cooper and his attorneys were present and were allowed to question the University witnesses. Cooper was not permitted to present witnesses. Because this was the first such review in the history of UALR, there was considerable confusion regarding the purpose and function of the committee. The committee initially agreed that its purpose was not to consider the merits of the decision, but only to consider its procedural adequacy, i.e., whether the procedural requirements set out in the handbook regarding notice and hearings in non-

reappointment cases had been complied with. In fact, however, there was some discussion of the reasons for the non-reappointment decision.

In a cryptic report the committee concluded that the decision not to recommend Cooper's reappointment was "the result of adequate consideration in terms of the relevant standards of the institution."[2] However, the committee also reported that many of its members expressed "deep concern" about "the ambiguities in the eight stated reasons for non-reappointment, the quality of the evidence and documentation submitted by the History department, the timing of the non-reappointment announcement, and the generally unprofessional administration of this matter."

17. Cooper then requested and was granted interviews with Hadley and with James Fribourgh, Vice-Chancellor for Academic Affairs. By letter dated July 9, 1974, Hadley and Fribourgh informed Cooper that they concurred in the recommendation that he not be reappointed.

18. Prior to Cooper, no full-time faculty member had ever been non-reappointed or dismissed from UALR from the time it became a part of the state university system in 1969.

19. In the interim, the state lawsuit was tried in Pulaski County Chancery Court. The University joined with Cooper in contesting the suit on the ground that the Arkansas statutes were unconstitutional. On March 28, 1974, the court entered a decree upholding the statutes and enjoining further payment of Cooper's salary.

20. The University allowed Cooper to finish the spring term of 1974, but did not allow him to teach during the 1974–75 academic year, which was to have been his terminal appointment year, despite his offer to do so without pay.

21. Cooper and the University appealed the decision of the Chancery Court to the Arkansas Supreme Court and on April 7, 1975, the court declared Ark.Stat.Ann. § 41–4113(c) unconstitutional.

22. The fact that Cooper was a communist and a member of the PLP and publicly stated both in and out of the classroom that he was a communist and a member of the PLP were substantial or motivating factors in the decision not to renew his appointment.

23. Other factors also played some part in the decision not to renew Cooper's appointment, including evaluations of his teaching performance by the department chairman and other members of the History Department faculty, and the manner in which he expressed his criticism of the Banfield book.

24. However, the same non-reappointment decision would not have been made had it not been for the fact that Cooper was a communist and a member of the PLP and publicly acknowledged these facts. The factors relied on by the University, considered individual-

ly or collectively, would not alone have caused the nonrenewal of Cooper's contract.

25. The University, through the History Department, prescribed the general subject matter for each course in the department. For the World Civilization course, which was divided into multiple sections taught by different teachers, there was general agreement among the department faculty on the text to be used in the course and on the periods of history to be covered each semester. Beyond this, each instructor had considerable latitude in organizing and presenting the material. Specifically, there were no department standards or policies requiring that this course, or any other course, be taught from an objective or any other specific point of view. Different faculty members taught their courses from different points of view.

26. Cooper substantially covered the subject matter of his courses. The record does not support the University's position that the fact Cooper professed to teach his courses from the Marxist point of view necessarily limited his coverage of the prescribed subject matter. Similarly, the handout distributed to Cooper's World Civilization course in the fall term of 1973 is not alone sufficient to establish that the course deviated in content and scope from the prescribed curriculum. There is simply no evidence of what in fact was covered in his courses other than Cooper's testimony that he covered the prescribed course material.

27. Cooper did not use his classes to proselytize students for membership in the PLP. In fact, he encouraged students to challenge and dispute his views.

28. Although Cooper would have been reappointed had it not been for the fact that he openly stated he was a communist and member of the PLP, he would not necessarily or automatically have been promoted to associate professor and given tenure.

29. As a result of the nonrenewal of his appointment at UALR, Cooper has not been able ot obtain comparable teaching positions at other schools. Despite his diligent efforts to obtain such employment, Cooper has experienced periods of unemployment and underemployment in the years since he left UALR.

MEMORANDUM OPINION & CONCLUSIONS OF LAW

The Court is cognizant that "[j]udicial interposition in the operation of the public school system of the Nation raises problems requiring care and restraint" and that "[b]y and large, public education in our Nation is committed to the control of state and local authorities." *Epperson* v. *Arkansas*, 393 U.S. 97, 104, 89 S.Ct. 266, 270, 21 L.Ed.2d 228 (1968). *Accord, Board of Curators* v. *Horowitz*, 435 U.S. 78, 91, 98 S.Ct. 948, 55 L.Ed.2d 124 (1978). Consistent with fundamental constitutional safeguards, university officials have "comprehensive authority" to prescribe and control conduct in the schools. *Healy* v. *James*, 408 U.S. 169, 180, 92 S.Ct. 2338, 33 L.Ed.2d 266 (1972); *Tinker* v. *Des Moines Independent Community School District*, 393 U.S. 503, 507, 89 S.Ct. 733, 21 L.Ed.2d 731 (1969). Similarly, a state university has the undoubted right to prescribe its curriculum, to select its faculty and students and evaluate their performances, and to define and maintain its standards of academic accomplishment. *See Board of Curators* v. *Horowitz, supra; Epperson* v. *Arkansas, supra*, 393 U.S. at 107, 115, 89 S.Ct. 266; *Shelton* v. *Tucker*, 364 U.S. 479, 485, 81 S.Ct. 247, 5 L.Ed.2d 231 (1960).

On the other hand, "state colleges and universities are not enclaves immune from the sweep of the First Amendment. 'It can hardly be argued that either students or teachers shed their constitutional rights to freedom of speech or expression at the schoolhouse gate.'" *Healy* v. *James, supra*, 408 U.S. at 180, 92 S.Ct. at 2345, *quoting Tinker* v. *Des Moines Independent Community School District, supra*, 393 U.S. at 506, 89 S.Ct. 733. Thus, despite their reluctance to intrude into the academic community, courts have on occasion found this necessary to ensure "[t]he vigilant protection of constitutional freedoms [which] is nowhere more vital than in the community of American schools." *Shelton* v. *Tucker, supra*, 364 U.S. at 487, 81 S.Ct. at 251. *Accord, Healy* v. *James, supra*, 408 U.S. at 180, 92 S.Ct. 2338.

A non-tenured faculty member has no right to continued employment beyond the duration and terms of his contract. The university is free not to rehire him for good reasons or for poor reasons or even "for no reason whatever." *Mt. Healthy City School District Board of Education* v. *Doyle*, 429 U.S. 274, 283, 97 S.Ct. 568, 50 L.Ed.2d 471 (1977). The decision not to rehire may not, however, be predicated on the teacher's exercise of constitutionally protected rights, particularly the First and Fourteenth Amendment guarantees of freedom of speech and association.[3] *Mt. Healthy City School District Board of Education* v. *Doyle, supra*, 429 U.S. at 283–84, 97 S.Ct. 568; *Perry* v. *Sindermann*, 408 U.S. 593, 597–98, 92 S.Ct. 2694, 33 L.Ed.2d 570 (1972); *Keyishian* v. *Board of Regents*, 385 U.S. 589, 87 S.Ct. 675, 17 L.Ed.2d 629 (1967); *Shelton* v. *Tucker, supra*. When a non-tenured teacher alleges that he was not rehired in violation of his First Amendment rights, he bears the initial burden of establishing that his conduct was constitutionally protected and that this protected conduct was a "substantial factor" or a "motivating factor" in the school's decision not to reappoint him. *Mt. Healthy City School District Board of Education* v. *Doyle, supra*, 429 U.S. at 287, 97 S.Ct. 568. If this burden is sustained, the school then has the burden of showing by a preponderance of the evidence that it would have reached the same non-

reappointment decision even in the absence of the protected conduct. *Id.*

The Court emphasizes that its function in this type of case is very limited. The Court does not review the merits of the University's decision not to rehire Cooper. "[I]t is not our function to evaluate a professor's competence nor to determine whether he any longer fits the needs of a school that is expanding its programs and attempting to upgrade the quality of its faculty. We may not so far involve this court in the discretionary decisions made by state-controlled colleges." *Cook County College Teachers Union, Local 1600* v. *Byrd*, 456 F.2d 882, 889 (7th Cir.), *cert. denied*, 409 U.S. 848, 93 S.Ct. 56, 34 L.Ed.2d 90 (1972). *See Megill* v. *Board of Regents*, 541 F.2d 1073, 1077 (5th Cir. 1976). Rather, the Court's only function is to decide the merits of Cooper's constitutional claim, that is, to determine as a factual matter whether he was not reappointed because of his exercise of constitutionally protected rights.

"Our form of government is built on the premise that every citizen shall have the right to engage in political expression and association." *Sweezy* v. *New Hampshire*, 354 U.S. 234, 250, 77 S.Ct. 1203, 1212, 1 L.Ed.2d 1311 (1957). It is now beyond question that mere association with or membership in a communistic organization is protected activity for which a state may not impose civil disabilities such as exclusion from state employment. *Baird* v. *State Bar*, 401 U.S. 1, 91 S.Ct. 702, 27 L.Ed.2d 639 (1971); *United States* v. *Robel*, 389 U.S. 258, 88 S.Ct. 419, 19 L.Ed.2d 508 (1967); *Keyishian* v. *Board of Regents, supra; Sweezy* v. *New Hampshire, supra; Cummings* v. *Hampton*, 485 F.2d 1153 (9th Cir. 1973); *Boorda* v. *Subversive Activities Control Board*, 137 U.S.App.D.C. 207, 421 F.2d 1142 (1969), *cert. denied*, 397 U.S. 1042, 90 S.Ct. 1365, 25 L.Ed.2d 653 (1970). "Mere knowing membership without a specific intent to further the unlawful aims of an organization is not a constitutionally adequate basis for exclusion from such positions as those held by [teachers in state universities]." *Keyishian* v. *Board of Regents, supra*, 385 U.S. at 606, 87 S.Ct. at 685. At trial, the University did not attempt to justify its decision by trying to prove that Cooper possessed the requisite specific intent.[4] Accordingly, the Court concludes that Cooper's membership in the PLP was constitutionally protected. *A fortiori* Cooper's right to state publicly that he was a communist and member of the PLP was also protected by the First Amendment.

Similarly, the Court concludes that Cooper's announcement of his personal political and philosophical beliefs in his classes was constitutionally protected. In *Tinker* v. *Des Moines Independent Community School District, supra*, the Supreme Court made clear that some in-class expression of political beliefs by teachers and students alike is protected. The Court stated the test as follows:

In order for the State in the person of school officials to justify prohibition of a particular expression of opinion, it must be able to show that its action was caused by something more than a mere desire to avoid the discomfort and unpleasantness that always accompany an unpopular viewpoint. Certainly where there is no finding and no showing that engaging in the forbidden conduct would "materially and substantially interfere with the requirements of appropriate discipline in the operation of the school," the prohibition cannot be sustained.

Id., 393 U.S. at 509, 89 S.Ct. at 738 (citation omitted).

It is evident that the bare announcement of Cooper's personal views did not materially or substantially disrupt his classes. In fact, it caused remarkably little concern until the matter was publicized by the media. The subsequent public reaction is not the kind of disruption that can be balanced against a teacher's right to free expression. The Court does not imply that it was desirable or even appropriate for Cooper to have informed his classes of his personal beliefs, except to note that the college classroom is peculiarly suited to the "robust exchange of ideas." Keyishian v. Board of Regents, supra, 385 U.S. at 603, 87 S.Ct. 675. The Court concludes only that, at least in the context of a university classroom, Cooper had a constitutionally protected right simply to inform his students of his personal political and philosophical views.[5]

The Court is persuaded that this protected conduct was a substantial or motivating factor in the decision not to reappoint Cooper. Several factors point to this conclusion including the timing of the nonrenewal decision, the fact that during the three years prior to his joining the PLP Cooper was never informed that the University was seriously concerned about his performance as a teacher, the fact that Chancellor Ross's October 1973 meeting with Cooper focused almost exclusively on the matter of his beliefs, and the fact that prior to Cooper no full-time faculty member had ever been non-reappointed or dismissed from UALR.

More significant and more disturbing to the Court, however, is the political furor which followed the newspaper reports about Cooper, particularly the action filed by certain state legislators to remove Cooper from the University. The Supreme Court has emphasized the importance of maintaining our universities free of political intervention.

The essentiality of freedom in the community of American universities is almost self-evident. No one should underestimate the vital role in a democracy that is played by those who guide and train our youth. To impose any strait jacket upon the intellectual leaders in our colleges and universities would imperil the future of our Nation. No field of education is so thoroughly comprehended by man that new discoveries cannot yet be made. Particularly is that true in the social sciences, where few, if any, principles are accepted as absolutes. Scholarship cannot flourish in an atmosphere of suspicion and distrust. Teachers and students must always remain free to inquire, to study and to evaluate, to gain new maturity and understanding; otherwise our civilization will stagnate and die.

Sweezy v. New Hampshire, supra, 354 U.S. at 250, 77 S.Ct. at 1211–1212. Accord, Keyishian v. Board of Regents, supra, 385 U.S. at 603, 87 S.Ct. 675. Concurring in Sweezy, Justice Frankfurter stressed the "grave harm resulting from governmental intrusion into the intellectual life of a university" and concluded, "Political power must abstain from intrusion into this activity of freedom, pursued in the interest of wise government and the people's well-being, except for reasons that are exigent and obviously compelling." Sweezy v. New Hampshire, supra, 354 U.S. at 261–62, 77 S.Ct. at 1217.

Clearly, the University was under considerable public and political pressure to discharge Cooper. Although the University contested the state lawsuit and joined with Cooper in challenging the Arkansas statutes as unconstitutional, this does not compel the conclusion that it remained unswayed by external influences. Rather, for a variety of reasons it could well have determined that the prudent course was to publicly contest the suit while privately resolving the problem by non-reappointment.

Cooper having established that protected activity was a substantial or motivating factor in his non-reappointment, the burden shifted to the University to show that it would have reached the same decision even in the absence of the protected conduct. Mt. Healthy City School District Board of Education v. Doyle, supra, 429 U.S. at 287, 97 S.Ct. 568. The University attempted to prove that Cooper was not rehired because his performance as a teacher and scholar was unsatisfactory, as specified in the list of reasons given Cooper in explanation of the non-reappointment decision. The University demonstrated that there were weaknesses in Cooper's performance as a teacher. The Court is convinced, however, that these weaknesses would not have resulted in the non-reappointment decision had Cooper not joined the PLP and publicly acknowledged his communist beliefs. Again, the Court notes that prior to Cooper no faculty member had ever been dismissed or not rehired. Cooper was reappointed for three successive years. During these years, he was not advised of any serious dissatisfaction with his teaching. In fact, in the only previous faculty evaluation he was rated average or superior in every category. Significantly, this evaluation was prepared just two months before Cooper joined the PLP.

Moreover, as noted by the ad hoc faculty committee, the reasons originally given for the decision were ambiguous and poorly substantiated. Testimony about the various alleged student complaints was vague and undocumented. It is quite evident that at the time whatever complaints were made, they were not seriously investigated or considered by the department as reflecting adversely upon Cooper's performance. Similarly, although the University earlier had discounted student surveys and indicated they would not be used for faculty appointment decisions, such surveys were initially cited to support the University's decision.

The Court reiterates that in commenting on the paucity of the evidence to substantiate the University's reasons, it does not suggest that these would not have been legitimate or adequate reasons for non-reappointment. Nor does it imply that a university must be able to document and justify its personnel decisions. The Court recognizes that there may be "a very wide spectrum of reasons, some subtle and difficult to articulate and to demonstrate, for deciding not to retain a [teacher]." *Roth* v. *Board of Regents*, 310 F.Supp. 972, 978 (W.D.Wis. 1970), *aff'd*, 446 F.2d 806 (7th Cir. 1971), *rev'd*, 408 U.S. 564, 92 S.Ct. 2701, 33 L.Ed.2d 548 (1972). Such decisions are in the discretion of the university and the Court does not review their merits.

However, in a case such as this one, when there has been a substantial claim that the decision was in derogation of First Amendment rights, the paucity of supporting evidence implies that the reasons given by the University were hastily prepared, make-weight reasons which do not fully reflect its true motivation. The Court concludes, therefore, that the University failed to sustain its burden of proving by a preponderance of the evidence that Cooper would not have been reappointed absent his protected conduct.

Several of the University's contentions require more detailed consideration because they pose very difficult constitutional questions. The University argues that Cooper's political philosophy was relevant to its non-renewal decision because he interjected his beliefs into the classroom not only by merely announcing that he was a communist and a member of the PLP, but also by announcing that he intended to teach, and by actually teaching, from the Marxist point of view. The University contends that along with its right to determine the curriculum and subject matter to be taught, it is the University's prerogative to determine that material should be presented from an objective point of view or from any other particular point of view. The ultimate question thus posed is whether Cooper's decision to teach his courses from a Marxist point of view was constitutionally protected so that if in fact this motivated his non-reappointment, his rights were violated.

Although academic freedom is not one of the rights enumerated in the First Amendment, it is now clear that it is entitled to some measure of constitutional protection. *See Healy* v. *James, supra*, 408 U.S. at 180–81, 92 S.Ct. 2338.

Our Nation is deeply committed to safeguarding academic freedom, which is of transcendant value to all of us and not merely to the teachers concerned. That freedom is therefore a special concern of the First Amendment, which does not tolerate laws that cast a pall of orthodoxy over the classroom. . . . The classroom is peculiarly the "marketplace of ideas." The Nation's future depends upon leaders trained through wide exposure to that robust exchange of ideas which discovers truth "out of a multitude of tongues, [rather] than through any kind of authoritative selection." *United States* v. *Associated Press*, D.C., 52 F.Supp. 362, 372.

Keyishian v. *Board of Regents, supra*, 385 U.S. at 603, 87 S.Ct. at 683. Yet, while the freedom is well recognized, its parameters are not well defined. The present case is particularly difficult because it involves a fundamental tension between the academic freedom of the individual teacher to be free of restraints from the university administration, and the academic freedom of the university to be free of government, including judicial, interference.

Case law considering the extent to which the First Amendment and academic freedom protect a teacher's choice of teaching methodology is surprisingly sparse and the results are not entirely consistent. *Compare Keefe* v. *Geanakos*, 418 F.2d 359 (1st Cir. 1969); *Sterzing* v. *Fort Bend Independent School District*, 376 F.Supp. 657 (S.D.Tex.1972), *vacated and remanded*, 496 F.2d 92 (5th Cir. 1974); *Mailloux* v. *Kiley*, 323 F.Supp. 1387 (D.Mass), *aff'd*, 448 F.2d 1242 (1st Cir. 1971); and *Parducci* v. *Rutland*, 316 F.Supp. 352 (M.D.Ala.1970) *with Brubaker* v. *Board of Education*, 502 F.2d 973 (7th Cir. 1974), *cert. denied*, 421 U.S. 965, 95 S.Ct. 1953, 44 L.Ed.2d 451 (1975); *Hetrick* v. *Martin*, 480 F.2d 705 (6th Cir.), *cert. denied*, 414 U.S. 1075, 94 S.Ct. 592, 38 L.Ed.2d 482 (1973); *Clark* v. *Holmes*, 474 F.2d 928 (7th Cir. 1972), *cert. denied*, 411 U.S. 972, 93 S.Ct. 2148, 36 L.Ed.2d 695 (1973); *Ahern* v. *Board of Education*, 456 F.2d 399 (8th Cir. 1972); and *Parker* v. *Board of Education*, 237 F.Supp. 222 (D.Md.), *aff'd*, 348 F.2d 464 (4th Cir. 1965), *cert. denied*, 382 U.S. 1030, 86 S.Ct. 653, 15 L.Ed.2d 543 (1966). *See generally* Goldstein, *The Asserted Constitutional Right of Public School Teachers to Determine What They Teach*, 124 U.Pa.L.Rev. 1293 (1976); Miller, *Teacher's Freedom of Expression Within the Classroom: A Search for Standards*, 8 Ga.L.Rev. 837 (1974); *Developments in the Law—Academic Freedom*, 81 Harv.L.Rev. 1045 (1968).

The Court concludes, however, that this sensitive

and difficult issue need not be reached in this case. At the time Cooper was notified he would not be reappointed he was not informed that the fact that he taught his classes from a Marxist point of view was one reason for the decision. This suggests this reason was an afterthought and not in fact a motivating factor in the discharge. The only one of the written reasons given to Cooper which is arguably related is reason 6. At trial, the University attempted to prove that because Cooper taught from the Marxist point of view, he deviated from the prescribed subject matter. However, there was little or no evidence that Cooper did not substantially cover the material. Furthermore, it is clear that there were no established standards or policies requiring that World Civilization or any other course be taught from any particular point of view or by any particular method. Different faculty members taught their courses from different points of view. Other than his express announcement of his point of view to his classes in the summer of 1973, Cooper's approach to his courses was substantially the same as it had been during his three previous years at UALR without objection. It is clear that other members of the History Department were aware from the time he joined the department that Cooper personally shared the Marxist interpretation of history and economics. The Court thus concludes as a matter of fact that had Cooper not become a member of the PLP and announced his personal beliefs to his classes, he would have been rehired, notwithstanding his Marxist viewpoint toward the teaching of history.

Moreover, several courts have held that academic freedom protects a teacher's choice of teaching methodology at least when, as here, the school has failed to establish standards or otherwise to notify the teacher that his methods are unacceptable. *Keefe* v. *Geanakos, supra; Sterzing* v. *Fort Bend Independent School District, supra; Mailloux* v. *Kiley, supra; Parducci* v. *Rutland, supra.*

> [P]articularly where the school board has not formulated standards to guide him, academic freedom affords a teacher a certain latitude in judging whether material is suitable and relevant to his instruction. "First Amendment freedoms need breathing space to survive. . . ." *NAACP* v. *Button,* 371 U.S. 415, 433, 83 S.Ct. 328, 9 L.Ed.2d 405 (1963).

Brubaker v. *Board of Education, supra* at 991 (Fairchild, J., dissenting).

> This exclusively procedural protection is afforded to a teacher not because he is a state employee, or because he is a citizen, but because in his teaching capacity he is engaged in the exercise of what may plausibly be considered "vital First Amendment rights." *Keyishian* v. *Board of Regents,* [supra, 385 U.S. at 604, 87 S.Ct. 675, 684, 17 L.Ed.2d 629.] In his teaching capacity he is not required to "guess what

conduct or utterance may lose him [that] position." [Id.]

Mailloux v. *Kiley, supra* at 1392.

> When a teacher is forced to speculate as to what conduct is permissible and what conduct is proscribed, he is apt to be overly cautious and reserved in the classroom. Such a reluctance on the part of a teacher to investigate and experiment with new and different ideas is anathema to the entire concept of academic freedom.

Parducci v. *Rutland, supra* at 357.

If Cooper's nonrenewal had in fact been motivated by his teaching methods, the Court would be inclined to invoke this doctrine. However, in view of the conclusion that the decision was not so motivated, this need not be done. The Court also need not decide the more difficult question whether, should it so choose, a university may constitutionally prohibit teaching from a Marxist point of view.

Cooper's comments about the Banfield book raise other potentially sensitive questions about academic freedom on a university campus. The University contends that Cooper's criticisms of the book were unprofessional and that this was a legitimate consideration in the nonrenewal decision. It is clear that a teacher's out of class statements on matters of public concern are entitled to considerable constitutional protection. *Pickering* v. *Board of Education,* 391 U.S. 563, 88 S.Ct. 1731, 20 L.Ed.2d 811 (1968). Nevertheless, a teacher's rights are not absolute and must be balanced against the interests of the state as an employer. *Id.* at 568, 88 S.Ct. 1731. Thus, some cases have held that a university teacher's out of class statements are unprotected and may properly be the basis of a nonrenewal decision when the statements are such that they reflect adversely on the teacher's professional competence and judgment. *See, e.g., Megill* v. *Board of Regents,* 541 F.2d 1073 (5th Cir. 1976) (profane and factually false and misleading statements); *Duke* v. *North Texas State University,* 469 F.2d 829 (5th Cir.), *cert. denied,* 412 U.S. 932, 93 S.Ct. 2760, 37 L.Ed.2d 160 (1973) (profane and obscene language in public criticism of university policy). It is, however, the Court's opinion that had it not been for his other clearly protected conduct, Cooper would have been reappointed, regardless of what he said about the Banfield book. It is therefore unnecessary to decide whether his comments were unprofessional and properly subject to consideration by the University in making the non-reappointment decision.

In summary, the Court concludes that Cooper's membership in the PLP and his public acknowledgement of his beliefs, both inside and outside the University classroom, were protected conduct under the First and Fourteenth Amendments. The Court finds that this protected activity was a substantial or motivating factor in the University's decision not to reappoint Cooper. The University failed to prove by a preponderance of the evidence that the same non-reappointment decision would have been made absent Cooper's exercise of First Amendment rights.

Cooper did not establish that he would automatically have been promoted to associate professor and granted tenure. The trial testimony was conflicting and the Court finds Cooper failed to meet his burden of proof on this issue. Accordingly, the Court orders that Cooper be reinstated to the position of assistant professor without tenure. The University is permanently enjoined from terminating Cooper's employment because of activities protected by the First and Fourteenth Amendments.

The parties dispute the propriety of a backpay award for the 1974–75 academic year during which the state court injunction was in effect. The University's position is essentially that it did not cause any injury Cooper may have suffered during that period. The University points out that it had every intention of permitting Cooper to teach that year as demonstrated by its offer of a terminal contract. He was not permitted to do so only because the University was obligated to comply with the state court injunction. The University actively contested the injunction by appealing it. The University contends that it was not also required to defy the injunction and risk contempt proceedings.

Cooper contends that the University could have accepted his offer to teach without pay since the state court order expressly enjoined only further payment of his salary. The Court finds this to be an unrealistically restrictive interpretation of the injunction. The Court agrees that the University's decision not to permit Cooper to teach during the 1974–75 academic year was a reasonable attempt to comply with the injunction and that had it failed to do so, it would have risked being in contempt notwithstanding the fact that the statute was subsequently declared unconstitutional. *See Walker* v. *City of Birmingham,* 388 U.S. 307, 87 S.Ct. 1824, 18 L.Ed.2d 1210 (1967); *Howat* v. *Kansas,* 258 U.S. 181, 42 S.Ct. 277, 66 L.Ed. 550 (1922).[6] Under these circumstances, the Court declines to award backpay for the period during which the University was subject to the state injunction.

Cooper is awarded backpay running from April 7, 1975 to the date reinstatement is offered. Backpay shall be based on the difference between his actual earnings and what he would have earned had he remained at UALR as an assistant professor. The award shall include all salary-related benefits which would have accrued to Cooper had he remained in the University's employ. If the parties cannot agree on the backpay award, they shall within thirty days of this order submit to the Court their separate proposals for final determination by the Court.

Plaintiff's counsel are directed to submit affidavits within twenty days to enable the Court to award reasonable attorneys' fees and costs. Counsel for defendants may submit counteraffidavits within ten days thereafter.

The motion of defendant Williams that he be dismissed as a party to this action is granted.

After the backpay and attorneys' fees proposals and affidivits are submitted to the Court, the Court will enter a final judgment in accordance with this opinion.

NOTES

1. For convenience, the defendants are sometimes collectively referred to as the University.
2. This language is taken directly from the Faculty Handbook which provides that the function of the Standing Committee on Tenure is "[t]o determine whether the decision of the faculty body or individual recommending nonreappointment was the result of adequate consideration in terms of the relevant standards of the institution, with the understanding that the Tenure Committee should not substitute its judgment for that of the faculty body or individual."
3. While freedom of association is not explicitly set out in the First Amendment, it has been held to be implicit in the freedoms of speech, assembly and petition. *Healy* v. *James,* 408 U.S. 169, 181, 92 S.Ct., 2338, 33 L.Ed.2d 266 (1972).
   Rights guaranteed to citizens by the First Amendment are made applicable to the states by the Fourteenth Amendment. *Baird* v. *State Bar,* 401 U.S. 1, 5, 91 S.Ct. 702, 27 L.Ed.2d 639 (1971); *Esteban* v. *Central Missouri State College,* 415 F.2d 1077, 1085 (8th Cir. 1969), *cert. denied,* 398 U.S. 965, 90 S.Ct. 2169, 26 L.Ed.2d 548 (1970).
4. Indeed, based on Cooper's trial testimony, his "expressions tend to be an abstract kind of marxis[m] ... call[ing] for social revolution at some future time but ... nowhere call[ing] for the kind of immediate, violent action that might constitute a direct threat" to the school or to the Nation. *Starsky* v. *Williams,* 353 F.Supp. 900, 926 (D.Ariz.1972), *aff'd in part, rev'd and remanded in part,* 512 F.2d 109 (9th Cir. 1975).
5. The Court intimates no view as to whether the same expression by a teacher in a public grade school or high school classroom would also be constitutionally protected. The Court emphasizes that its holding is strictly limited to a teacher's right simply to inform his students of his views and does not imply that a teacher has the right to proselytize students or to devote so much class time to such matters that his coverage of the prescribed subject matter is impaired.
6. An injunction duly issuing out of a court of general jurisdiction with equity powers, upon pleadings properly invoking its action, and served upon persons made parties therein and within the jurisdiction, must be obeyed by them however erroneous the action of the court may be, even if the error be in the assumption of the validity of a seeming but void law going to the merits of the case. It is for the court of first instance to determine the question of the validity of the law, and until its decision is reversed for error by orderly review, either by itself or by

a higher court, its orders based on its decision are to be respected, and disobedience of them is contempt of its lawful authority, to be punished.

Howat v. *Kansas, supra,* 258 U.S. at 189–90, 42 S.Ct. at 280–281, *quoted in Walker* v. *City of Birmingham, supra,* 388 U.S. at 314, 87 S.Ct. 1824.

A United States District Court decides against an elementary school teacher who had his fifth grade students write letters to his fiancee to practice their cursive handwriting. The students later received from the fiancee letters containing statements such as: "I am a communist, in the Progressive Labor Party, just like Phil [Burns, the teacher] is. . . . My son Chris is learning to be a Communist too!" "The issue is squarely presented," said the Court. "Does the interest of the Board of Education in prohibiting sectarian or partisan instruction at the fifth grade level of its school system outweigh the plaintiff's interest in First Amendment protection?"

Burns v. *Rovaldi*, 477 F.Supp. 270 (1979)

BLUMENFELD, District Judge.

The plaintiff Philip Burns was a tenured fifth grade teacher in the Plainfield school system until December 17, 1975, when his employment contract was terminated by a vote of the Plainfield Board of Education (the Board). Prior to the action of the Board, he was given specifications of the charges on which the termination was to be considered and a full public hearing before a quorum of the Board. He was represented at that hearing by himself and by his brother as counsel. Instead of taking an appeal to the Court of Common Pleas for review of the Board's decision, as provided for by Conn. Gen. Stat. § 10–151(f), he brought this action for a declaratory judgment, preliminary and permanent injunction, compensatory and punitive damages, and other equitable relief.

Plaintiff Burns alleges that the Board's termination of his contract was impermissibly based on his exercise of his First Amendment rights, and also that the Board's decision violated both procedural and substantive rights of due process guaranteed him by the Fourteenth Amendment. Upon those allegations he invokes the Civil Rights Act, 42 U.S.C. § 1983, and its jurisdictional counterpart, 28 U.S.C. § 1343(3), as the basis for jurisdiction in this court. The individual defendants, allegedly acting under color of state law, are sued in their official, as well as individual, capacities. *See Dunham* v. *Crosby,* 435 F.2d 1177, 1181 n. 3 (1st Cir. 1970). Thus, since the defendants allegedly deprived the plaintiff of his constitutional rights, the "two elements that are necessary for recovery" in an action based on 42 U.S.C. § 1983 are present. *Adickes* v. *S. H. Kress & Co.,* 398 U.S. 144, 150, 90 S.Ct. 1598, 1604, 26 L.Ed.2d 142 (1970). The defendants, who are members of the school board, challenge jurisdiction over them on the ground that they were acting only as

a Board of Education. Building on that premise, they further contend that a school board is not a "person" amenable to suit under 42 U.S.C. § 1983. While that contention once had some support, *see Monroe* v. *Pape,* 365 U.S. 167, 81 S.Ct. 473, 5 L.Ed.2d 492 (1961), the Supreme Court has recently held that its reasoning is not applicable to school boards. *Monell* v. *Department of Social Services of the City of New York,* 436 U.S. 658, 98 S.Ct. 2018, 56 L.Ed.2d 611 (1978).

This case now comes before the court on cross-motions for summary judgment. A motion for a preliminary injunction, previously filed by the plaintiff, was denied after a hearing in January of 1976. A hearing on the motions for summary judgment was held on November 13, 1978. It is to those motions I now turn.

The First Amendment Issue

Although there were three separate charges lodged against the plaintiff in the termination hearing before the Board, the principal one was based on conduct in class which directly affected the students. The classroom conduct of the plaintiff which provoked the institution of charges against him first came to the attention of Albert Mizak, the Superintendent of Schools, through letters from parents of fifth graders in Burns' class who wanted Burns fired. This sudden flurry of correspondence to the school authorities from those parents was their response to what Mr. Burns had done as a teacher of their children.

A. *The Pen-Pal Incident*

In September of 1975, the plaintiff assigned to his then fifth grade class at the Memorial School a penmanship lesson. As part of that lesson, the students could either practice cursive penmanship by writing the alphabet or write a letter to the plaintiff's then fiancee. As a result of that assignment, each student who wrote to the plaintiff's then fiancee received from her a letter in return. These return letters were directly sent to the plaintiff who, in the classroom, distributed them to his students. Each letter was addressed to a specific student and was enclosed in a sealed envelope.

Among other things, the aforesaid letters, written by the plaintiff's then fiancee and distributed to various students in the plaintiff's fifth grade class contained the following, or similar statements:

"I am a communist, in the Progressive Labor Party, just like Phil [Burns] is.[1] We are both working hard for the day when you kids and the rest of us working people kick out all the rich rotten bosses and then we can all run everything ourselves. That is what communism really means. Then we can all cooperate and have a good and happy life. My son Chris is learning to be a Communist too!"

Pl.'s Exh. C, Hearing on Motion for Preliminary Injunction (letter dated October 6, 1975 addressed "Dear Sherry," which was part of the record of the contract termination hearing of Philip Burns as well as part of the record of the Hearing on Plaintiff's Motion for Preliminary Injunction). See also other letters marked as Pl.'s Exh. K–1, Hearing on Motion for Preliminary Injunction.

It is not surprising that parents of some of the fifth graders who got those letters promptly reacted by calling for the discharge of the plaintiff as a teacher in communications to the Superintendent.

On October 17, 1975, the Superintendent (Mizak) called Burns into his office. When Burns answered "No" to Mizak's inquiry if he knew why he was there, Mizak said, "Well, I think you do. It's because of the [pen-pal] letters." Tr. at 8, Hearing on Motion for Preliminary Injunction, Jan. 26, 1976. He offered to let Mr. Burns resign and gave him a few days to think it over, and also told Burns that he was going to recommend to the school board that his contract to teach be terminated. By letter of October 28, 1975, Mizak wrote to Burns:

"In response to your request for a statement of the reasons for the proposed termination of your contract of employment, this is to notify you that the reasons are the following:

(1) insubordination. More specifically, you have violated a directive issued to all personnel by the Superintendent of Schools, and dated June 12, 1975, which is entitled 'Interruption of School Programs or Duties' in that, on at least on[e] occasion, you visited the classroom of a fellow teacher to discuss your personal affairs, thereby, interfering with that teacher in the performance of his duties.

(2) You have evidenced incompetence in the performance of your assigned teaching duties by using your classroom and your access to students in your classroom as a vehicle for the dissemination of your political convictions."

Pl.'s Exh. F, Hearing on Motion for Preliminary Injunction.

Thereafter, on November 19, 1975, Mizak again wrote to Burns about the letter-writing charge to which (2) above refers:

"The following is submitted in response to your request for a more specific statement of the charges which form the basis for the recommendation that your teaching contract with the Plainfield School System be terminated.

"   .   .   .

"You have also been charged, as stated in the October 28, 1975 letter to you, with incompetence, 'in that you have used you[r] classroom as a vehicle for the dissemination of your political convictions.' More specifically, you are charged with having caused letters written by a personal friend to your fifth grade students. These letters were written in response to letters written by your students as part of an in-class assignment and delivered by your class to these students. The letters in question which can, at best, be described as politically dogmatic in nature, were distributed by you to your students even though you knew their political content. Their distribution by you is a violation of the spirit, if not the letter, of the by-laws of the Plainfield Board of Education which prohibits sectarian or partisan instruction. In addition, your distribution of these letters which indicate extreme bias on the part of the writer evidences, at the least, a lack of judgment on your part and a misunderstanding of your role as a teacher.

"Please be advised that pursuant to your request and that of your attorney, a date will be set for a hearing on the above matters before the Plainfield Board of Education no sooner than fifteen (15) days from your receipt of this more specific statement."

Pl.'s Exh. G, Hearing on Motion for Preliminary Injunction.

A third charge was added on December 1, 1975:

"The following constitutes an amendment to, and an addition to, the statements of charges dated November 19, 1975. You should be prepared to answer these charges, as well as previous charges, to which I will refer at the hearing to be held before the Plainfield Board of Education:

1. You are charged with insubordination based on the events of Wednesday, the 26th of November 1975, at Plainfield Memorial School when Mr. Bahner indicated that Ms. Kingsley was not to enter your room. Nevertheless, you allowed Ms. Kingsley

to do so. . . .

.   .   .   .   .

"In regard to the charges, reference should be made to the Board of Education By laws, Article 6, Section 606, and to an item in the daily bulletin from Mr. Bahner distributed to the entire staff on November 24, 1975 and again on December 1, 1975."

Pl.'s Exh. H, Hearing on Motion for Preliminary Injunction (letter from Mizak to Burns, dated Dec. 1, 1975).

Finally, on December 10, 1975, Mizak again wrote to Burns:

"With regard to the charge of incompetence which is stated in my letter to you dated October 28, 1975, it has come to my attention from statements that you have made in the media that there may be some confusion in your mind about the nature of that charge.

"The basic facts of that charge form the essence of my claim that you have acted improperly in your classroom. It is clear that your actions in the classroom also support a charge of insubordination. To the extent that your actions indicate incompetence, I do not wish you to be misled to the extent that you feel that the charge is based on insufficient knowledge of the subject areas you teach. The charge of incompetence concerns itself not with your knowledge of the subject areas, but with your apparent inability to restrict your actions in the classroom to the subject areas you are assigned to teach. To the extent your classroom activities indicate a willful refusal to avoid the promulgation of sectarian political views to your students it is my judgment that your actions constitute insubordination. In this regard please make reference to the by-laws of the Plainfield Board of Education, sec 305, sub paragraph d.

"Should you have any questions in regard to this letter, which should be viewed as a clarification of the original charge of incompetence and as an additional charge of insubordination based on your conduct in the classroom, please do not fail to contact me."

Pl.'s Exh. J, Hearing on Motion for Preliminary Injunction. As the letter points out, the foundation for the principal charges against Burns is in the by-laws of the Plainfield Board of Education, specifically section 305 (d):

"No sectarian or partisan instruction shall be allowed, and no book tract designed to advocate the tenets of any particular sect or party shall be permitted in any of the schools."

Pl.'s Exh. K–1, Hearing on Motion for Preliminary Injunction (also Administration Exh. 16, Termination Hearing of Philip Burns).

Through his counsel, the plaintiff admitted in open court at the hearing on this motion for summary judgment that he knew what the contents of the letters were before he handed them out to his students. Nor is it seriously argued that this "pen-pal" project should be regarded as an exercise in penmanship. (The letters of the children went to Burns' fiancee. Her answering letters did not concern penmanship.)

The Board found that the foregoing charges had been proved. Indeed, there is no dispute over any of the essential facts. The Board then concluded:

"It is the conclusion of the Board of Education of the Town of Plainfield that Mr. Philip Burns has been insubordinate and has evidenced incompetence in that he has violated the rules of the Board of Education pertinent to partisan instruction and the directives of the Superintendent of Schools with regard to interruption of school programs or duties. It is also the specific finding of the Board of Education that Mr. Burns defied its agents and his superiors, the Superintendent of Schools and the Principal of Plainfield Memorial School based upon the facts as listed above, notably the incidents of November 26, 1975, and that this defiance constitutes insubordination on his part."

Pl.'s Exh. M, Hearing on Motion for Preliminary Injunction.

The plaintiff does not seriously complain of any denial of procedural due process at any stage of the proceedings, nor is there any basis for such a claim.[2] Nor does he deny complete responsibility for the distribution of the letters to his students. He does not contend that the contents of the letter were not sectarian or partisan.[3]

The issue is squarely presented: does the interest of the Board of Education in prohibiting sectarian or partisan instruction at the fifth grade level of its school system outweigh the plaintiff's interest in first amendment protection. "Where there is tension between the two, accommodation must be sought in the balancing process which not infrequently characterizes the task of constitutional interpretation." *Goldwasser* v. *Brown,* 135 U.S.App.D.C. 222, 229, 417 F.2d 1169, 1176 (D.C.Cir. 1969), *cert. denied,* 397 U.S. 922, 90 S.Ct. 918, 25 L.Ed.2d 103 (1970). *See also Pickering* v. *Board of Education,* 391 U.S. 563, 568, 88 S.Ct. 1731, 1734–35, 20 L.Ed.2d 811 (1968):

"The problem in any case is to arrive at a balance between the interests of the teacher, as a citizen, in commenting upon matters of public concern and the interest of the State, as an employer, in promoting the efficiency of the public services it performs through its employees."

The First Amendment's prohibition of any law "abridging the freedom of speech" is first among the freedoms safeguarded to the people. But this principle, like all of those in the law, is not absolute, and cannot always be perfectly sustained.[4] The plaintiff argues that academic freedom is inherent in the First Amendment, and he defends his conduct as falling within the concept of academic freedom. On this ground, plaintiff moves for summary judgment on his behalf. The justification for this is that "To preserve the 'marketplace of ideas' so essential to our system of democracy, we must be willing to assume the risk or argument and lawful disagreement." *James* v. *Board of Education*, 461 F.2d 566, 573, (2d Cir.), *cert. denied*, 409 U.S. 1042, 93 S.Ct. 529, 34 L.Ed.2d 491 (1972). Carried to its extreme limits, "academic freedom" permits a school teacher "to have his say on any and every thing about which he has feelings, provided there is no significant likelihood of impairment of his efficiency." *Goldwasser* v. *Brown, supra*, 417 F.2d at 1176, 135 U.S.App.D.C. at 229.

The rights of free speech, "while fundamental in our democratic society, still do not mean that everyone with opinions or beliefs to express may address a group at any public place and at any time. . . ."*Cox* v. *Louisiana*, 379 U.S. 536, 554, 559, 574, 85 S.Ct. 453, 464, 13 L.Ed.2d 471 (1965). "The college classroom with its surrounding environs is peculiarly 'the marketplace of ideas.' "*Healy* v. *James*, 408 U.S. 169, 180, 92 S.Ct. 2338, 2346, 33 L.Ed.2d 266 (1972). There are some limitations on who may play the game of academic freedom. The view that "assumptions of the 'free market-place of ideas' on which freedom of speech rests do not apply to school-aged children, especially in the classroom where the teacher may carry great authority," *Developments in the Law—Academic Freedom*, 81 Harv.L.Rev. 1045, 1053 (1968), has not been accepted without qualification. The view that *all* "school-aged children" were excluded from the academic freedom forum was qualified in *James* v. *Board of Education, supra*, 461 F.2d at 574, so as not to apply to 16- to 17-year-old juniors in a high school English class. *See also East Hartford Education Association* v. *Board of Education*, 562 F.2d 838, 843 (2d Cir.) (Oakes, J., for panel majority), *vacated en banc*, 562 F.2d 856 (2d Cir. 1977). As those cases suggest, both age and the extent of education of the students must be considered in determining whether the students have attained that degree of maturity which would enable them to evaluate the merits of communism versus capitalism. Even a most expansive concept of "a market-place of ideas" would not be extended to include a class of fifth graders among those with whom to discuss what is wrong with the world and how it can be put right. *See Mailloux* v. *Kiley*, 436 F.2d 565, 566 (1st Cir. 1971) (per curiam).

Despite the guarantee of a free trade in ideas, it has been authoritatively stated that "a State may permissibly determine that, at least in some precisely delineated areas, a child—like someone in a captive audience—is not possessed of that full capacity for individual choice which is the presupposition of First Amendment guarantees." *Ginsberg* v. *New York*, 390 U.S. 629, 649–50, 88 S.Ct. 1274, 1285–86, 20 L.Ed.2d 195 (1968) (Stewart, J., concurring). The plaintiff's contention that the contents of the pen-pal letters from his fiancee to his fifth grade students was permissible as within an exercise of academic freedom is a travesty on the concept of a "free trade in ideas."[5]

It is equally absurd to contend that a fifth grade schoolroom is a public forum traditionally devoted to speech and assembly. *Cf. Greer* v. *Spock*, 424 U.S. 828, 96 S.Ct. 1211, 47 L.Ed.2d 505 (1976); *Grayned* v. *City of Rockford*, 408 U.S. 104, 119–21, 92 S.Ct. 2294, 33 L.Ed.2d 222 (1972). The *Pickering* balance must be struck without giving the plaintiff any benefit of a schoolroom locale or academic freedom label.

In striking the *Pickering* balance, the statements in the pen-pal letters distributed to the plaintiff's students have significance simply because of the character of their subject matter. The action of the Board was not taken on the basis that it had the power to regulate the content of materials distributed to the students because of its political, social, or philosophical message. The position taken by the Board, and expressed in its decision, is that Burns had introduced a controversial subject wholly unrelated to the subject matter being studied. "Mr. Philip Burns has been insubordinate and has evidenced incompetence in that he has violated the rules of the Board of Education pertinent to partisan instruction. . . ." Pl.'s Exh. M, Hearing on Motion for Preliminary Injunction (Conclusions of Board following Contract Termination Hearing). Burns was supposed to be teaching cursive penmanship by having the students practice writing the alphabet or writing letters. "It must be remembered that the primary function of the schools is the education of the community's children." *Connecticut State Federation of Teachers* v. *Board of Education Members*, 583 F.2d 471, 479 (2d Cir. 1976). It is the function of education in the primary grades to teach children first to know the tools of learning, and then how to use them. This is the first step to overcome illiteracy. By no stretch of the imagination could the pen-pal letters to the fifth graders from Phil's fiancee have any relevance to instruction in cursive penmanship. The by-law prohibiting sectarian or partisan instruction was aimed at maintaining the efficient use of time in school to teach subjects which were on the regular curriculum of the primary grades. As such, it was "reasonably related to the needs of the educational process" and not an impermissible infringement on a teacher's first amendment rights. *James* v. *Board of Education, supra*, 461 F.2d at 574. One court of appeals has noted, "we see no substitute for a case-by-case inquiry into whether the legitimate interests of the authorities are demonstrably sufficient to circumscribe a teacher's speech." *Mailloux* v. *Kiley, supra,* 448 F.2d at 1243. Considerably less vague, and surely more workable, is the standard of review set forth by the Second Circuit Court of Appeals in *James* v. *Board of Education, supra,* 461 F.2d at 574: "What we require, then, is only that rules formulated by school officials be reasonably related to the needs of the educational process and that any disciplinary action taken pursuant to those rules have a basis in fact."

Not only did the plaintiff not teach his students the subject he had been hired to teach in this pen-pal incident, he used the time which was provided for that purpose to do what was forbidden by submitting them to "sectarian or partisan instruction" contrary to the prohibition of the by-laws. *Cf. Janusaitis* v. *Middlebury Volunteer Fire Department,* 607 F.2d 17 at 25–26 (2d Cir. 1979) (applying *Pickering,* volunteer fireman's first amendment rights were not violated when he was fired for making statements in contravention of department regulations). The bald facts are that the plaintiff used the school time of the students to arbitrarily indoctrinate them in concepts having nothing whatever to do with skill or knowledge of penmanship. Only in bad faith can one refuse to recognize the difference between impartial and undogmatic *instruction* and *advocacy* of a partisan political doctrine together with the rejection of everything opposed to it. "[C]ertainly a teacher is not paid to go into school and teach subjects the State does not hire him to teach as part of its selected curriculum." *Tinker* v. *Des Moines Independent Community School District,* 393 U.S. 503, 522, 89 S.Ct. 733, 744–45, 21 L.Ed.2d 731 (1969) (Black, J., dissenting). Burns introduced a controversial subject wholly unrelated to penmanship. His employment world was organized, and the students and the school board had a right to have him instruct the children in penmanship. Requiring him to do that did not jeopardize his right to espouse his own views when he was not working as a teacher. But to say that he had personal freedom to impose his ideas upon the students during class time would grant the teacher control of curriculum and content. With that door open, any policies of a school board could be set aside at the will of a teacher. The First Amendment does not go so far. "When a teacher is only content if he persuades his students that his values and only his values ought to be their values, then it is not unreasonable to expect the state to protect impressionable children from such dogmatism." *James* v. *Board of Education, supra,* 461 F.2d at 573. His job demanded some surrender of personal freedom to impose his ideas on his students. Invocation of the phrases "academic freedom" or "market-place of ideas" does not put upon the defendants the burden of justification for its by-laws.[6] "The question is whether or not there is a real abridgement

of the rights of free speech." *Connecticut State Federation of Teachers* v. *Board of Education Members, supra,* 538 F.2d at 479.

The extent to which the plaintiff's rights were jeopardized does not outweigh the rights of the school board to require that he stick to his teaching responsibilities. The operation of public schools has been described as "perhaps the most important function of state and local governments." *Brown* v. *Board of Education,* 347 U.S. 483, 493, 74 S.Ct. 686, 691, 98 L.Ed. 873 (1954). "The very notion of public education implies substantial public control. Educational decisions must be made by someone; there is no reason to create a constitutional preference for the views of teachers over those of their employers." *East Hartford Education Association* v. *Board of Education, supra,* 562 F.2d at 859. Insisting that he do his job as a teacher did not deprive the plaintiff of any first amendment rights. *See Goldwasser* v. *Brown, supra,* 135 U.S. App.D.C. at 230, 417 F.2d at 1177. On the basis of what has been considered above, there is ample support for the Board's determination that Burns' first amendment interests are not entitled to prevail in a *Pickering* v. *Board of Education* balancing against the policies of the school board.

B. *Additional Grounds for Contract Termination*

In addition to the conclusion that Burns had violated section 305(d) of the by-laws, the Board concluded that Burns was guilty of the two other charges which were considered at the hearing. The Board found that Burns was guilty of having interrupted a fellow teacher to discuss matters personal to him during her performance of her school duties, contrary to a specific memo to all teachers prohibiting such conduct. There was ample proof that such an incident had occurred prior to the "pen-pal letters" incidents.

The Board also concluded that the plaintiff wilfully violated a directive of his immediate superior, the school principal, by insisting that his fiancee, the pen-pal of incident number one, and her minor son, be permitted to be present in his classroom during an instruction period. His insistence provoked a confrontation between Burns and the principal which was resolved only by calling the police to enforce the order against visitors during classroom activities.

Each of these conclusions was amply supported by evidence. It is immaterial what standard of judicial review is applied to test the validity of these conclusions—whether that of " ' 'arbitrary, capricious, an abuse of discretion, or otherwise not in accordance with law,' rather than the possible stricter standard of . . . 'unsupported by substantial evidence.' " *Cf. Automobile Club of New York, Inc.* v. *Cox,* 592 F.2d 658, 664 (2d Cir. 1979). It is clear that under either test, the conclusions of the Board are supportable. Thus, permissible grounds existed for the Board's firing of the plaintiff. On the basis of the foregoing, the plaintiff's motion for summary judgment is denied.

Other Protected Conduct

However, this does not mean that the *defendants'* motion for summary judgment must be granted, for the contention is made by Burns that his contract would not have been terminated on the basis of his violations of the rule against interference with a teacher and the order against allowing Ms. Kingsley into his fifth grade class if the Board had not also given weight to the "pen-pal" incident as a motivating factor in its decision. *See generally Davis* v. *Village Park II Realty Co.,* 578 F.2d 461, 464 (2d Cir. 1978). Burns argues that reliance on the pen-pal incident would be improper for two reasons. First, he argues that the pen-pal incident consisted of conduct constitutionally protected by the First Amendment. That reason is invalid, as I have held above. Secondly, he contends that even if his conduct in the pen-pal incident taken by itself as a basis for contract termination was not constitutionally protected, the decision to terminate the contract nevertheless was motivated by *other conduct of Burns prior* to the pen-pal incident, which was constitutionally protected. Therefore, the argument continues, the decision based upon the pen-pal incident was itself so tainted as to infect all other grounds for termination with impermissible motivating factors. If that premise were established, it would be incumbent on the Board, according to the rule in *Mt. Healthy City Board of Education* v. *Doyle,* 429 U.S. 274, 287, 97 S.Ct. 568, 50 L.Ed.2d 471 (1977), to show "by a preponderance of the evidence that it would have reached the same decision as to [Burns' discharge] even in the absence of the protected conduct." The "other conduct of Burns" is said to consist of Burns' openly avowed and activist membership in the Progressive Labor Party, the goals of which include the violent overthrow of the capitalist system, expressed in part in the rhetoric included in the "pen-pal" letters. *See also Turner* v. *Air Transport Lodge,* 590 F.2d 409, 413–14 & n. 2 (2d Cir. 1978) (Mulligan, J., concurring). Thus, Burns contends that the Board must establish that it would have made the same decision without regard to anything he may have done in the past.

Before these defendants can be called upon to make that kind of a *Mt. Healthy* "same decision anyway" determination, the burden is on Burns "to show [not only] that his conduct was constitutionally protected, [but also] that this conduct was a 'substantial factor'—or, to put it in other words, that it was a 'motivating factor' in the Board's decision not to rehire him." *Mt. Healthy, supra,* 429 U.S. at 287, 97 S. Ct. at

576; *see Givhan* v. *Western Line Consolidated School Dist.,* 439 U.S. 410, 99 S.Ct. 693, 58 L.Ed.2d 619 (1979); *Waterbury Community Antenna, Inc.,* v. *NLRB,* 587 F.2d 90, 99–100 (2d Cir. 1978); *Davis* v. *Village Park II Realty Co., supra,* 578 F.2d at 464. In effect, such a contention by Burns is in the nature of an affirmative defense. In *Mt. Healthy* it was clearly established that the school board considered constitutionally protected incidents not directly connected with Doyle's duties or role as a teacher—one of which was Doyle's telephone call to a radio station about a joint teacher-administration adoption of a dress code—which the board cited as a ground for not rehiring him. 429 U.S. at 282–83 & n.1, 97 S.Ct. 568.

In this case it is not clear whether the Board considered any conduct of Burns other than what was set forth in the formal charges against him. In the charges before the Board, Burns was only required to defend against the specified charges, not every particular action of his life. There is nothing in the record to show that there was any evidence before the Board concerning prior conduct or statements of Burns in connection with his political activities. Apart from the notice of charges against Burns, it does not appear on the record that anything done or said by Mizak, other than the formal charges,[7] came to the attention of the Board members who heard and voted on the charges against Burns.

The hurdle which the plaintiff must clear before the defendants are put to the necessity of proving that they would have reached the same decision anyway consists of proof that other constitutionally protected conduct was "a 'motivating factor' in the Board's decision" to relieve him. 429 U.S. at 298, 97 S.Ct. at 576. The claim that Burns' prior conduct was a motivating factor in the Board's decision was not pleaded, and, as indicated above, it was not made an issue in the proceedings before the Board. That issue crept into the case during the course of a hearing on the plaintiff's application for a preliminary injunction. Even though it may be a technical flaw not to raise that issue by an amendment to the pleadings, some evidentiary matter relating to the issue had been introduced during the course of the hearing on the motion for preliminary injunction. While rules of procedure are important for assuring the wise exercise of the deliberative process, they ought not be thoughtlessly applied so as to foreclose decision on the merits.

At this stage of the proceedings, where defendants' motion for summary judgment is being considered, the court is not called upon to determine whether plaintiff has proven that his outside activities were a "motivating" factor in the Board's termination decision. For purposes of a summary judgment motion, the court does not try issues of fact but only determines whether there are issues to be tried. *E.g., United States* v.

Bosurgi, 530 F.2d 1105, 1110 (2d Cir. 1976); *Heyman* v. *Commerce & Industry Ins. Co.,* 524 F.2d 1317, 1319–20 (2d Cir. 1975). Furthermore, the party opposing a motion for summary judgment is to be given the benefit of all favorable inferences to be drawn from the moving papers. *See, e.g., Adickes* v. *S. H. Kress & Co.,* 398 U.S. 144, 90 S.Ct. 1598, 26 L.Ed.2d 142 (1970); *United States* v. *Diebold, Inc.,* 369 U.S. 654, 82 S.Ct. 993, 8 L.Ed.2d 176 (1962).

The question to be decided here, therefore, is whether, drawing all reasonable inferences in favor of the plaintiff, the plaintiff has established the existence of a genuine factual dispute as to whether the prior conduct of the plaintiff was a motivating factor in the decision of the Board members to fire him. Plaintiff elicited testimony in a deposition of the Superintendent of the Plainfield Public Schools, Albert Mizak, in which Mizak acknowledged that plaintiff's outside political activities were considered a "problem" by Mizak and by people in the community at large. *See* Deposition of Albert Mizak at 25–26. Mizak indicated that, in his opinion, plaintiff's outside political activities would be less likely to be accepted in the area of Plainfield than in other more liberal areas. *See id.* at 27, 32. Statements such as these indicate the possibility that plaintiff's outside activities *may* have played a significant role in the attitude of members of the community, including the Board members, regarding whether the plaintiff should have been terminated as a teacher at the Plainfield Public Schools. Though Mizak himself was not a member of the Board of Education, and thus did not formally vote at the termination hearing, it is not impossible that like-minded members on the Board who had selected him as Superintendent of Schools might have been influenced in their termination decision by plaintiff's outside political activities. Since defendants concede that plaintiff's communist affiliation was "common knowledge," Memorandum in Support of Defendants' Motion for Summary Judgment at 13, for purposes of summary judgment it would not be totally farfetched to acknowledge that plaintiff might be able to establish at trial that members of the Board were influenced by this knowledge in deciding to terminate plaintiff from his position.

This in no way implies that plaintiff has carried his burden of proof, as required by *Mt. Healthy,* of establishing that his protected activities were a "motivating" factor in the Board's decision, but simply that plaintiff has succeeded in raising a genuine triable issue of fact as to the motivation of the board members at the time of the termination vote. The fact that those members of the Board who voted to terminate plaintiff's employment have submitted affidavits that their decision was based solely on the evidence adduced at the hearing, and not on prejudice or bias toward the plaintiff or his political beliefs or associations, is not sufficient to support the defendants' motion for summary judgment. As a general rule, summary judgment is to be used sparingly "where motive and intent play leading roles." *Poller* v. *Columbia Broadcasting System, Inc.,* 368 U.S. 464, 473, 82 S.Ct. 486, 491, 7 L.Ed.2d 458 (1962); *see* cases cited *infra.*

Under functionally similar circumstances, the District of Columbia Court of Appeals recently reversed a grant of summary judgment for the employer stating,

"[The employee's] termination was not an *overt* retaliation for engaging in protected activities, if it was a retaliation at all. . . . His only likely avenue of success lay in making credibility an issue, for resolution of the first amendment issue essentially required a determination of state of mind [of the employer]. When motivation is involved and credibility becomes of critical importance, or when essential facts are solely within the control of the moving party, summary judgment generally is inappropriate."

Mazaleski v. *Truesdell,* 562 F.2d 701, 717 (D.C.Cir. 1977) (emphasis in original).

In the instant case I am persuaded to follow this rule—that summary judgment is generally not appropriate where the motive or state of mind of the moving party is in issue—under the rationale developed in support of the rule in prior cases in this circuit. *See, e.g., Friedman* v. *Meyers,* 482 F.2d 435 (2d Cir. 1973); *Cali* v. *Eastern Airlines, Inc.,* 442 F.2d 65, 71 (2d Cir. 1971); *Union Insurance Soc. of Canton, Ltd.* v. *Wm. Gluckin & Co.,* 353 F.2d 946, 951 (2d Cir. 1965); *Cross* v. *United States,* 336 F.2d 431, 433 (2d Cir. 1964); *Subin* v. *Goldsmith,* 224 F.2d 753, 758–59 (2d Cir. 1955). In the last-cited case, uncontroverted affidavits of the movants were considered insufficient to support summary judgment on the ground that the credibility of the affiants raised a triable issue since the facts in issue were particularly within the knowledge of the movants. *See also Glomac Plastics, Inc.* v. *NLRB,* 592 F.2d 94, 99 (2d Cir. 1979) (finder of fact permitted not only to find witness' testimony false but that "the truth is the opposite of his story").

I am not unmindful that the principle applied by this decision may leave the courts open to time-consuming and often fruitless attempts to impeach the integrity of decision makers, *see Withrow* v. *Larkin,* 421 U.S. 35, 47, 95 S.Ct. 1456, 1464, 43 L.Ed.2d 712 (1975) (there is a "presumption of honesty and integrity in those serving as adjudicators"), but judicial economy must take a subordinate role in cases where state officials are alleged to have retaliated against employees for their exercise of first amendment rights. In such cases, the courts have shown a zealous regard for the protection of the constitutional right to freedom of speech. Thus the opportunity to prove the denial of this constitutional right should not be narrowly restricted by the policy underlying the summary judgment rule. It follows that the defendants' motion for summary judgment must also be denied.

For all of the foregoing reasons, both the plaintiff's and the defendants' motions for summary judgment are denied.

So ordered.

ON THE MERITS

This is the final stage in the case of Philip Burns, a tenured fifth-grade teacher in the Plainfield, Connecticut school system whose employment contract was terminated by a vote of the defendant Plainfield Board of Education (the Board) in December of 1975. Shortly after the contract termination, plaintiff Burns brought an action in this court alleging that the Board's action violated his rights under the First and Fourteenth Amendments to the United States Constitution.

A hearing on plaintiff's motion for a preliminary injunction was held on January 26 and 27, 1976. That motion was denied for lack of a showing of irreparable injury. *See* Ruling on Motion for Preliminary Injunction, filed March 3, 1976. Thereafter the parties filed cross-motions for summary judgment on the basis of accompanying affidavits and on the basis of the evidence presented at the hearing on the preliminary injunction. In ruling on the cross motions, this court found that permissible reasons existed for the Board's decision to dismiss plaintiff from employment as a teacher. Ruling on Cross-Motions for Summary Judgment, 477 F.Supp. 270 (D.Conn. 1979). Since all of the facts up until the time the Board voted to terminate the plaintiff's employment are stated in that ruling, and what slight additional or repetitive evidence relating to them introduced at the trial did not modify them in any significant way, the facts set forth in that opinion are incorporated herein by reference. *See* Fed.R.Civ.P. 65(a)(2).

The only issue left unresolved by that opinion was the *"Mt. Healthy* issue": whether conduct of Burns outside of the classroom, which was constitutionally protected, was a motivating factor in the Board's decision to discharge him. *See* Ruling on Cross-Motions for Summary Judgment. This issue was left unresolved because there existed a genuine issue of fact as to what factors motivated the Board's decision. To resolve this issue, a trial on the merits of plaintiff's complaint was held on June 26, 1979.

Discussion

Under the rule of *Mt. Healthy City Board of Education* v. *Doyle,* 429 U.S. 274, 97 S.Ct. 568, 50 L.Ed.2d 471 (1977), in order to establish a violation of first

amendment rights, the initial burden of proof is on the discharged employee "to show [not only] that his conduct was constitutionally protected, [but also] that this conduct was a 'substantial factor'—or, to put it in other words, that it was a 'motivating factor' in the Board's decision. . . ." *Id.* at 287, 97 S.Ct. at 576. Plaintiff has failed to meet this initial burden of proof.

The decision of the Board to discharge plaintiff, which plaintiff challenges in this action, was made by a unanimous vote of six members of the Board. Plaintiff called as witnesses five of those six: Board members Dumaine, Yonta, Tetreault, Nicholson, and Krecidlo. Plaintiff elicited no testimony from any of these witnesses indicating that any of plaintiff's out-of-classroom political activities—such as his membership in the Progressive Labor Party or his participation in leafletting activities—were a motivating factor in their decision to terminate plaintiff's employment contract.

Plaintiff argues, however, that the "minutes" of the December 1975 Board meeting, which followed the public hearing on the charges brought against the plaintiff, reveal that his protected first amendment conduct did play an important role in the Board's decision. The minutes of that meeting state that plaintiff was found guilty by the Board members on four counts:

"1st count: Violation of administrative directive (insubordination) Vote was unanimous.
"2nd count: Classroom used to disseminate political views (incompetence) Vote was unanimous.
"3rd count: Ms. Kingsley's visit to Memorial School (insubordination) Vote was unanimous.
"4th count: Passing out of leaflets to students and other [sic] (incompetence and insubordination). Vote was unanimous."

Plaintiff's Trial Exh. 1. Plaintiff argues that the "fourth count" listed in the minutes involved protected first amendment conduct, and that this was a substantial factor in the Board's decision to discharge him.

The evidence does not support plaintiff's argument. The Board's formal "Findings of Fact and Conclusions" make no mention of plaintiff's leafletting activities. *See* Plaintiff's Trial Exh. 6. The Board's formal findings and conclusions only make reference to the pen-pal incident, plaintiff's interruption of another teacher's classroom, and plaintiff's disregard of a directive of the school principal, *see id.,*—conduct which I have previously held to be a permissible basis for plaintiff's discharge. *See* Ruling on Cross-Motions for Summary Judgment. In light of the testimony presented at the trial on June 26, 1979, the most reasonable explanation for the absence of any mention of plaintiff's leafletting activities in the "Findings of

Fact and Conclusions" of the Board is that these activities played no significant role in the Board's decision. All five of the Board members who were called as witnesses testified that, to the best of their recollection, they did not base their decision to discharge plaintiff on plaintiff's leafletting activities. To the extent that the Board members could remember their reasons for voting to discharge plaintiff, they testified that the reasons were the pen-pal incident and plaintiff's disregard for the authority of the school principal.

Plaintiff asks this court not only to disbelieve the testimony of all of these witnesses but to believe the opposite, that plaintiff's outside political activities were a major factor in the Board members' decision to discharge plaintiff. Nothing in the demeanor of these witnesses on the witness stand, and nothing elicited during plaintiff's examination of these witnesses, leads this court to discredit any of the witnesses' testimony. Thus I find that plaintiff has not proven by a preponderance of the evidence, as is his burden, that a "substantial" or "motivating" factor in the Board's decision to discharge him was his protected first amendment conduct.[7] Accordingly, judgment shall enter for the defendants on the complaint.

The foregoing shall constitute the court's findings of fact and conclusions of law. *See* Fed.R.Civ.P. 52.

So ordered.

NOTES

1. Even without identifying herself and Phil as communists, the rest of the letter was a simplified but explicit exposition of Marxist communism. It implied the abolition of private property, the abolition of classes, and with the end of "classes" the abolition of conflicts of interests and the establishment of the unity of society. This entirely conforms to the Marxist doctrine which assumes that all the important social conflicts are rooted in class divisions, and it is the sectarian view of a number of persons united in opinion and interest.

2. The plaintiff had full and timely notice of the charges against him and the proposed action of the Board. He also had the opportunity to attend a public hearing, to be represented by counsel, and to be heard. *See Wood* v.

Goodman, 381 F.Supp. 413, 420 (D.Mass.1974), *aff'd,* 516 F.2d 894 (1st Cir. 1975).

3. At the hearing before the members of the Board of Education, Mr. Burns stated not only that he knew of the general contents of the letters, but that he would have distributed them to his students in class even if he had known of the exact language used in them. Tr. at 190, Contract Termination Hearing of Philip Burns, Dec. 16, 1975 (introduced as Pl.'s Exh. K, Hearing on Motion for Preliminary Injunction) .

4. "It is a *non sequitur* to say that First Amendment rights may not be regulated because they hold a preferred position in the hierarchy of the constitutional guarantees of the incidents of freedom." *Poulos* v. *New Hampshire,* 345 U.S. 395, 405, 73 S.Ct. 760, 766, 97 L.Ed. 1105 (1953).

5. From the dissenting opinion of Mr. Justice Holmes in *Abrams* v. *United States,* 250 U.S. 616, 630, 40 S.Ct. 17, 63 L.Ed. 1173 (1919).

6. "[S]chool boards must meet a burden of justification if they are to enforce a regulation which infringes on teachers' First Amendment rights. But the mere invocation of the words 'speech' and 'association' in a complaint does not put the boards to this test. Rather, before CFT can put the defendant school boards to this burden of justification, CFT must show that its members' First Amendment rights have in fact been infringed by the school boards' policies. The question is whether or not there is a real abridgement of the rights of free speech. *Kovacs* v. *Cooper,* 336 U.S. 77, 85, 69 S.Ct. 448, 93 L.Ed. 513 (1949) (plurality opinion). First Amendment claims must always be adjudicated in light of the special characteristics of the environment involved in the particular case. *Tinker, supra,* 393 U.S. at 506, 89 S.Ct. 733; *Healy* v. *James, supra,* 408 U.S. at 180, 92 S.Ct. 2338."
Connecticut State Federation of Teachers v. *Board of Educ. Members, supra,* 528 F.2d at 479.

7. The Superintendent, Mizak, who prepared the charges against Burns was aware for years that Burns was a member of the Progressive Labor Party, and that he had been active in passing out posters and literature of the party. Despite that knowledge of Burns' beliefs and activities, which consisted of his political pronouncements in circulars and pamphlets that he sent around the community, Mizak had previously recommended Burns for tenure. Mizak had often told Burns that what he did out of school was his business, and within his rights as an individual. Tr. at 119-20, Hearing on Motion for Preliminary Injunction.

$\mathbf{T}$HE United States Court of Appeals, Seventh Circuit, decides for a teacher who sued the Board of Education and several school officials because, she claimed, she had been involuntarily transferred to another school in retaliation for certain constitutionally protected speech. The Court observed that the school officials had not shown that the teacher's statements regarding collective bargaining and her disagreements with the principal interfered with the regular operation of the school or impeded her classroom duties. The Court held "that such retaliation [transferring the teacher to another school] can take the form of a retaliatory transfer as well as a retaliatory discharge. It is no answer to say that she had a right to engage in the constitutionally protected speech after her transfer, since even a discharged teacher has the right to continue to speak out. The test is whether the adverse action taken by the defendants is likely to chill the exercise of constitutionally protected speech. . . . This chilling effect can be accomplished through an unwanted transfer as well as through outright discharge. . . . There was testimony that plaintiff was not making the other teachers upset, that she was highly qualified, and that there were no complaints about the way she conducted her class. Therefore, there was substantial evidence for the jury to conclude that the plaintiff would not have been transferred but for her protected conduct."

McGill v. *Bd. of Ed. of Pekin Elementary Sch.*, 602 F.2d 774 (1979)

Before CUMMINGS and SPRECHER, Circuit Judges, and BONSAL, Senior District Judge.*

CUMMINGS, Circuit Judge.

Pursuant to the Civil Rights Act (42 U.S.C. § 1983), plaintiff school teacher sued her employer, the Board of Education, its seven members, a school superintendent and the principal of Broadmoor School in Pekin, Illinois. The gravamen of her complaint was that she was involuntarily transferred to another school in retaliation for certain constitutionally protected speech.

Plaintiff alleged that in March 1977, the Broadmoor School principal informed her that she would be transferred to a different school for the 1977–78 school term because "she had complained about school procedures on a number of occasions, and that she was 'stirring up trouble' in the teachers' lounge." Plaintiff charged that during the 1976–77 school term, she had engaged in discussions with other faculty in the teachers' lounge stating that she favored a master collective bargaining contract and also that she had privately disagreed with some of her principal's decisions and had brought these disagreements to his attention. She further alleged that in April and May 1977 the school superintendent informed her she was being transferred because of "comments that she had made at open meetings of the Defendant Board of Education* *" and also because "she had made references concerning the master [collective bargaining] contract in the teachers' lounge." In August 1977, the Board of Education approved her transfer to a different school. Plaintiff charged that this transfer amounted to a denial of her rights of free speech and association.

In response, the defendants stated that the student population of the Broadmoor School had changed so that it was necessary to reassign plaintiff to another elementary school. Defendants also asserted that the court did not have jurisdiction over the case because no federal statutory or constitutional right was alleged to have been abridged.

In a pretrial ruling, the district court noted that plaintiff had alleged "that the basis for the transfer was comments that she had made at open meetings * * *, and also the fact that she had made remarks concerning the master contract in the teachers' lounge." Judge Morgan held that if plaintiff was transferred "in retaliation for her peaceful expression of opinions outside the classroom," plaintiff would have a cause of action under *Perry* v. *Sindermann,* 408 U.S. 593, 92 S.Ct. 2694, 33 L.Ed.2d 723, and therefore the case was held for a jury trial. Subsequently the jury returned a verdict in favor of plaintiff, and the district court entered judgment for plaintiff reinstating her to her teaching position at the Broadmoor School and awarding plaintiff costs.[1] We affirm.

The Jury Properly Found That Plaintiff Was Transferred For Protected Conduct

Defendants first argue that plaintiff did not prove that her communications were entitled to First Amendment protection in view of *Pickering* v. *Board of Education,* 391 U.S. 563, 88 S.Ct. 1731, 20 L.Ed.2d 811, and *Clark* v. *Holmes,* 474 F.2d 928 (7th Cir. 1972), certiorari denied, 411 U.S. 972, 93 S.Ct. 2148, 36 L.Ed.2d 695. *Pickering* held that school teachers may not constitutionally be compelled to relinquish their First Amendment rights "to comment on matters of public interest in connection with the operation of the public schools * * *." 391 U.S. 568, 88 S.Ct. at 1734. The Court applied the First Amendment to the teacher's statements critical of his employer "which are neither shown nor can be presumed to have in any way either impeded the teacher's proper performance of his daily duties in the classroom or to have interfered with the regular operation of the schools generally" (footnote omitted). 391 U.S. at 572, 573, 88 S.Ct. at 1737. Thus *Pickering* can be read as establishing that two limits on a teacher's right to speak out may be permissible. First, speech that is so disruptive as to impede the teacher's performance or to interfere with the operation of the school may be proper grounds for discipline. Second, if the speech does not involve matters of public interest it may not be entitled to constitutional protection.

In the present case defendants have not shown that plaintiff's statements impeded her classroom duties or interfered with the regular operation of the schools generally. Although defendants adduced some evidence tending to show that plaintiff was a source of friction and lack of cooperation among the teachers, plaintiff rebutted that evidence with testimony from the relevant teachers that such tension did not exist and that plaintiff was a respected and valued colleague.[2] The jury was instructed that the teacher's criticism would not be protected if "the teacher's actions materially and substantially interfere with the operation of the education process in the classroom" (Tr. 209).[3] Clearly the jury made a credibility determination in this regard, and we cannot disturb it. Consequently, because plaintiff has established that her speech was not unduly disruptive, *Pickering* does not support defendants' position.

Clark v. *Holmes, supra,* does not require reversal either, because there the disruptive nature of the

plaintiff's speech was plainly established. Teacher Clark's statements consisted of "uncontrolled expression at variance with established curricular contents and internally destructive of the proper functioning of the [university] institution" (474 F.2d at 931).[4] Instead this case is controlled by *Donahue* v. *Staunton,* 471 F.2d 475, 480 (7th Cir. 1972), certiorari denied, 410 U.S. 955, 93 S.Ct. 1419, 35 L.Ed.2d 687. There we observed that public employees do have a right to criticize their employers because dismissal from their employment for making critical statements would "inhibit the propensity of a citizen to exercise his right to freedom of speech and association."[5] In *Donahue* we held that defendants could not dismiss a hospital chaplain even though his accusations were extensive, critical, vociferous and exaggerated and even false. Judge Hastings' majority opinion supported this result because the defendants did not show that plaintiff's accusations impeded the performance of his duties or interfered with the functioning of the hospital.

Defendants also urge plaintiff's statements were not protected by the First Amendment because they involved only matters of private concern.[6] However, her complaint alleges that the reason for her transfer was advocacy of a collective bargaining agreement in the teachers' lounge and in an open meeting of the school board. Judge Morgan evidently concluded that this speech involved a matter of public concern, and we agree. The jury was instructed as follows (court's Instruction No. 7; defendants' Instruction No. 23):

"Plaintiff has the burden of proving the following propositions as to each defendant:

"First, that plaintiff has made remarks at open meetings and in the teachers' lounge concerning the teachers' master contract.

"Second, the transfer to another school was made as a result of the aforementioned comments.

"If you find that both of the aforementioned propositions have been proven, then your verdict should be for the plaintiff; but if, on the other hand, you find that either of the propositions has not been proved, then your verdict should be for the defendants." (Tr.204.)

Plaintiff had unsuccessfully objected to this instruction of defendants because it was limited to plaintiff's remarks concerning the teachers' master contract (Tr. 213-214). Consequently, it is apparent that the district judge agreed with defendants that the only comments by plaintiff which were protected by the First Amendment were her remarks in the teachers' lounge and at the open meeting in favor of a master collective bargaining contract. Such a subject is, of course, of public concern, so that defendants may not complain that the jury was permitted to decide in plaintiff's favor with respect to any of her comments on private issues. The jury instruction quoted above precluded any such decision.

Finally, *Givhan* v. *Western Line Consolidated School District*, 439 U.S. 410, 99 S.Ct. 693, 58 L.Ed.2d 619, punctures defendants' insistence that plaintiff's speech was not protected by the First Amendment to the extent that some otherwise protected comments were made privately. In *Givhan*, the plaintiff teacher's comments to her school principal consisted of insulting, hostile, loud and arrogant, petty and unreasonable demands, according to the defending school district. Her complaints involved employment policies and practices at the school which she conceived to be racially discriminatory in purpose or effect. However, the Supreme Court considered her private comments and expressions of opinions to the principal to be protected under the First Amendment. It reiterated its *Pickering* view that the content of the teacher's statements would be protected if, as here, they did not impede the proper performance of his daily duties in the classroom or interfere with the regular operation of the schools generally (439 U.S. 415 n.4, 99 S.Ct. 696), but the case was remanded so that the district court could decide whether Givhan would have been rehired but for her criticism.

We therefore conclude that plaintiff's advocacy of a collective bargaining contract was protected by the First Amendment and that the jury's consideration was properly limited to this constitutionally protected speech.

Instruction No. 20 Was Not Erroneous

The court's Instruction No. 20 (derived from plaintiff's Instruction No. 3) provided as follows:

"A government entity, such as a school district, does not have a right to transfer an employee because the employee has engaged in speech which has no bearing on proper performance of the employee's assigned duties. This is because to permit such could have a chilling effect upon exercise of the employee's right to freedom of speech as guaranteed by the Constitution of the United States.

"This does not mean, however, that any person who speaks critically of the employer or supervisor is, thereafter, insulated against transfer. The test must be whether the protected speech was, or was not, the motivating factor in making an otherwise completely legitimate transfer.

"That is the question for you to decide in this case—whether Barbara McGill was transferred because of her speech or for other legitimate reason. Would she have been the one transferred if she had not spoken as she did." (Tr. 210.)

Defendants' only objection to this instruction was to the final sentence. They objected on the ground that it "tends to emphasize the plaintiff's theory of the case" (Tr. 214–215). Apparently defendants' position is that

pursuant to this instruction the jury could have found for the plaintiff on the basis of purely private, unprotected complaints which were also in evidence. However, Instruction No. 20 was proper because the protected speech was already defined in the court's Instruction No. 7 (which was defendants' Instruction No. 23 and is reproduced *supra*) as consisting of plaintiff's remarks in the teachers' lounge and at open meetings concerning the teachers' master collective bargaining contract (Tr. 204). As seen, Judge Morgan also told the jury that the teacher's right to criticize is lost when the teacher's actions materially and substantially interfere with the educational process in the classroom (Tr. 209) and that protected speech must have "no bearing on proper performance of the employee's assigned duties" (Tr. 210). Furthermore, the jury was told that "the defendants * * * had every right to transfer her for a legitimate reason" (Tr. 207).[7] Defendants did not tender an instruction requiring the jury specifically to balance the teacher's interest in commenting on matters of public concern with the interests of the defendants in promoting the efficiency of the educational services they render. Construing the instructions as a whole, the jury could not decide for plaintiff unless it found that her constitutionally protected speech was the motivating factor in defendants' decision to transfer her.

This test has consistently been applied by the Supreme Court. *Pickering* v. *Board of Education, supra*, 391 U.S. at 574, 88 S.Ct. 1731 (protected speech may not "furnish the basis" for dismissal); *Mt. Healthy* v. *Doyle*, 492 U.S. 274, 285–287, 97 S.Ct. 568, 50 L.Ed.2d 471 (question is whether the discharge would have occurred even in the absence of the protected conduct). In its most recent relevant opinion, *Givhan* v. *Western Line Consolidated School District, supra*, the Supreme Court also held that for the dismissed teacher to be reinstated the protected speech must be the motivating factor in discharging her. The instruction here that plaintiff could only recover if she showed that her protected speech was the motivating factor in the transfer is equivalent to the *Givhan* test that the teacher could only recover if the jury found that she would have been left in the former position "but for the criticism."[8]

Since whether protected speech was the "motivating factor" for the adverse action is a correct standard, and since the jury was correctly instructed as to what constituted protected speech, defendants' objections to Instruction No. 20 must fail.

A Retaliatory Transfer Can Trigger First Amendment Rights

Defendants contend that the principles developed in *Pickering* and *Givhan*, both *supra*, do not apply here because plaintiff was not discharged but merely transferred to another school within the district with no loss of pay, seniority or other rights. Furthermore, according to defendants, "[f]rom a practical standpoint her right to comment on a master contract is preserved" (Br. 19). However, plaintiff specifically alleged that her involuntary transfer was discriminatory and in retaliation for her constitutionally protected speech. The question is not, as in a procedural due process case, whether plaintiff had a protected property interest in her position at any particular school. Clearly she did not. Rather, the question is whether the defendants unconstitutionally retaliated against the plaintiff on account of her protected speech.

We hold that such retaliation can take the form of a retaliatory transfer as well as a retaliatory discharge.[9] It is no answer to say that she had a right to engage in the constitutionally protected speech after her transfer, since even a discharged teacher has the right to continue to speak out.[10] The test is whether the adverse action taken by the defendants is likely to chill the exercise of constitutionally protected speech. *Pickering* v. *Board of Education, supra,* 391 U.S. at 574, 88 S.Ct. 1731. This chilling effect can be accomplished through an unwanted transfer as well as through outright discharge.

In this case the school from which plaintiff was transferred was brand-new and the only school in the district operating on an "open classroom" plan. It is unclear whether plaintiff's objections to the transfer stemmed from her perceptions of the professional advantages at the Broadmoor School or from more personal concerns. It seems clear, however, that the threat of transfer—whether it be to a school with a less desirable reputation or one perceived as dangerous or one that is difficult to get to—could be an effective means of chilling constitutionally protected speech.

The Jury Verdict Was Supported By A Preponderance Of The Evidence

In its opening statement to the jury, the district court charged that the plaintiff must prove her contention by a preponderance of the evidence in order to recover. Here the crucial evidence is whether plaintiff's comments concerning the master collective bargaining contract were the motivating factor in her transfer. The evidence shows that plaintiff discussed the need for a master contract in the teachers' lounge and that at a later board meeting she said how important it was to have such matters reduced to writing. She was told by the principal and the superintendent that this advocacy was the reason for her transfer. One of the board members, Jenny McDonald, testified that when the transfer of plaintiff came up at a board meeting, defendant Principal Hamra complained to the board that plaintiff had talked in the teachers' lounge. Likewise, there was testimony that plaintiff was not making the other teachers upset, that she was highly

qualified, and that there were no complaints about the way she conducted her class. Therefore, there was substantial evidence for the jury to conclude that the plaintiff would not have been transferred but for her protected conduct.

Judgment affirmed.

NOTES

* The Honorable Dudley B. Bonsal, Senior District Judge of the Southern District of New York, is sitting by designation.

1. The record does not reveal that plaintiff recovered attorneys' fees, as requested in her complaint. Since the district court's judgment granted her "the relief prayed for in the complaint" (R. 16), perhaps the fixing of attorneys' fees was awaiting the outcome of this appeal.

2. Defendants also sought to establish that friction between Principal Hamra and plaintiff affected the operation of the school. In this regard they sought to demonstrate such tension by relying upon the fact that in May 1977 plaintiff requested of Superintendent Caringello that someone other than Mr. Hamra should complete her end-of-year evaluation. This request came after Mr. Hamra had told plaintiff he was recommending that she be involuntarily transferred and his reasons for requesting the transfer, and after plaintiff had made clear her intention to resist the transfer. The jury was certainly entitled to conclude that this request did not demonstrate that serious personal friction between plaintiff and Mr. Hamra had motivated the transfer decision.

3. The jury was also instructed that "the burden is on the plaintiff to establish that the transfer is based on the exercise of protected Constitutional rights" (Tr. 204).

4. In addition, defendants relied on *Roseman* v. *Indiana University of Pennsylvania,* 520 F.2d 1364 (3rd Cir. 1975). In *Roseman,* the plaintiff professor erroneously complained to the college dean about the foreign language department's acting chairman, alleging that he wrongfully suppressed a colleague's application for the chairmanship of the department. Since Roseman's attack on the acting chairman interfered with the harmonious relationship with her superiors and coworkers, her statements were deemed to be outside the First Amendment protection. In contrast, McGill's statements were not shown to have had such a disruptive impact. The *Roseman* court also held that the statements were not protected because they were made privately rather than publicly. That aspect of the case has been overruled by *Givhan* v. *Western Line Consolidated School District,* 439 U.S. 410, 99 S.Ct. 693, 58 L.Ed.2d 619, discussed *infra.*

5. This quotation in *Donahue* was taken from *Kiiskila* v. *Nicholls,* 433 F.2d 745, 749 (7th Cir. 1970).

6. In this regard defendants rely on *Schmidt* v. *Fremont County School District,* 558 F.2d 982 (10th Cir. 1977). However, in *Schmidt,* the trial court found that the reason for the non-renewal of the plaintiff's contract was not retaliation for protected speech, but failure to improve the attendance record and other inadequacies in his performance. The Tenth Circuit, affirming, added that in any event the speech at issue did not involve questions of public concern, but only differences of opinion between the principal and the school board over how the school should be run. In the present case, the relevant speech does not involve policy differences

between plaintiff and her superiors, but advocacy of a collective bargaining agreement, which is clearly a matter of public concern.

7. The district court quoted at length from the Illinois statutes vesting authority to employ and transfer teachers in the school board and the superintendent.

8. At oral argument, counsel for defendants conceded that plaintiff's speech was a factor involved in her transfer.

9. *Simpson* v. *Weeks,* 570 F.2d 240 (8th Cir. 1978), certiorari denied,——U.S.——, 99 S.Ct. 3101, 61 L.Ed.2d 876, supports this conclusion. In *Simpson* a policeman who suffered a discriminatory reassignment and nega-tive evaluations in retaliation for constitutionally protected speech recovered under 42 U.S.C. § 1983.

10. It is true that because plaintiff would continue to have a stake in the school system and daily contact with other teachers, her forum for engaging in the protected speech at issue would be somewhat less impaired than is usually the case when a public employee is discharged. However, the key question is whether the retaliatory action is likely to dissuade this and other employees from speaking out on public issues, not whether they continue to have a theoretically available forum for doing so.

IN deciding against a probationary kindergarten teacher who, because of her religious beliefs, refused to teach subjects dealing with love of country, the flag, and other patriotic matters, the United States Court of Appeals, Seventh Circuit, declares at the outset of its opinion: "Plaintiff states the issue to be whether or not a public school teacher in her classes has the right to refuse to participate in the Pledge of Allegiance, the singing of patriotic songs, and the celebration of certain national holidays when to do so is claimed to violate her religious principles. The issue is more correctly stated to be whether or not a public school teacher is free to disregard the prescribed curriculum concerning patriotic matters when to conform to the curriculum she claims would conflict with her religious principles." The Court observes that "because of her religious beliefs, plaintiff would deprive her students of an elementary knowledge and appreciation of our national heritage. She considers it to be promoting idolatry, it was explained during oral argument, to teach, for instance, about President Lincoln and why we observe his birthday.... Plaintiff's right to her own religious views and practices remains unfettered, but she has no constitutional right to require others to submit to her views and to forego a portion of their education they would otherwise be entitled to enjoy."

Palmer v. *Board of Ed. of City of Chicago*, 603 F.2d 1271 (1979)

Harlington WOOD, Jr., Circuit Judge.

Plaintiff states the issue to be whether or not a public school teacher in her classes has the right to refuse to participate in the Pledge of Allegiance, the singing of patriotic songs, and the celebration of certain national holidays when to do so is claimed to violate her religious principles. The issue is more correctly stated to be whether or not a public school teacher is free to disregard the prescribed curriculum concerning patriotic matters when to conform to the curriculum she claims would conflict with her religious principles. Plaintiff also claims her ultimate discharge denied her due process of law.

Plaintiff, a member of the Jehovah's Witnesses religion, was a probationary kindergarten teacher in the Chicago public schools. After her appointment, but prior to the commencement of classes, plaintiff informed her principal that because of her religion she would be unable to teach any subjects having to do with love of country, the flag or other patriotic matters in the prescribed curriculum. Extraordinary efforts were made to accommodate plaintiff's religious beliefs at her particular school and elsewhere in the system, but it could not reasonably be accomplished.[1]

The trial court allowed defendants' motion for summary judgment. As there is no substantive factual dis-

pute, additional recitation of the factual details is not required. Plaintiff argues that the offended curriculum is so broad and vague as to be incomprehensible.

In *Epperson* v. *Arkansas*, 393 U.S. 97, 107, 89 S.Ct. 266, 21 L.Ed.2d 228 (1968), the Court held invalid as offending the First Amendment an Arkansas statute prohibiting the teaching of a particular doctrine of evolution considered contrary to the religious views of most citizens. The Court recognized, however, that the states possess an undoubted right so long as not restrictive of constitutional guarantees to prescribe the curriculum for their public schools. Plaintiff would have us fashion for her an exception to that general curriculum rule. The issue is narrow.

Our decision in *Clark* v. *Holmes*, 474 F.2d 928 (7th Cir. 1972), *cert. denied*, 411 U.S. 972, 93 S.Ct. 2148, 36 L.Ed.2d 695 (1973), is of some guidance. In that case the complaint about a university teacher was that he ignored the prescribed course content and engaged in unauthorized student counseling. We held that the First Amendment was not a teacher license for uncontrolled expression at variance with established curricular content. The individual teacher was found to have no constitutional prerogative to override the judgment of superiors as to the proper content for the course to be taught. In *Ahern* v. *Board of Education*,

456 F.2d 399 (8th Cir. 1972), the court upheld a teacher dismissal for insubordination on the basis that the Constitution bestowed no right on the teacher to disregard the valid dictates of her superiors by teaching politics in a course on economics. In *Adams* v. *Campbell County School District,* 511 F.2d 1242 (10th Cir. 1975), the court stated that the Board and the principal had a right to insist that a more orthodox teaching approach be used by a teacher who was found to have no unlimited authority as to the structure and content of courses.

Plaintiff relies on a cross-section of First Amendment cases, but they are of little assistance with the specific issue in this case. Plaintiff argues that the defendants are trying to determine and limit the extent of her religious freedoms. The facts do not justify that legal perspective. The issue in this case is not analogous to a case:

(a) where plaintiff is forced by statute to display on his automobile license plate a patriotic ideological motto repugnant to a follower of the Jehovah's Witnesses faith, *Wooley* v. *Maynard,* 430 U.S. 705, 97 S.Ct. 1428, 51 L.Ed.2d 752 (1977); or,

(b) where the state attempts to prohibit the issuance of a professional license because of the applicant's beliefs, *Baird* v. *State Bar of Arizona,* 401 U.S. 1, 91 S.Ct. 702, 27 L.Ed.2d 639 (1971); or,

(c) where First Amendment rights may be chilled by a governmental investigative and data gathering activity causing actual or threatened injury, *Laird* v. *Tatum,* 408 U.S. 1, 92 S.Ct. 2318, 33 L.Ed.2d 154 (1972); or,

(d) where a person's right to the free exercise of his religion is conditioned on the surrender of his right to office, *McDaniel* v. *Paty,* 435 U.S. 618, 98 S.Ct. 1322, 55 L.Ed.2d 593 (1978); or,

(e) where a religious sect is forced to send its children to a public school contrary to the sect's religious beliefs, *Wisconsin* v. *Yoder,* 406 U.S. 205, 92 S.Ct. 1526, 32 L.Ed.2d 15 (1972); or,

(f) where students are being required to participate in a patriotic pledge contrary to their beliefs, *West Virginia State Board of Education* v. *Barnette,* 319 U.S. 624, 63 S.Ct. 1178, 87 L.Ed. 1628 (1943); or,

(g) where the wearing of armbands by students in a Vietnam protest could not be prohibited where it did not interfere with school activities or impinge upon the rights of others, *Tinker* v. *Des Moines Independent Community School District,* 393 U.S. 503, 89 S.Ct. 733, 21 L.Ed.2d 731 (1969).

Plaintiff also cites *Russo* v. *Central School District No. 1,* 469 F.2d 623 (2d Cir. 1972), *cert. denied,* 411 U.S. 932, 93 S.Ct. 1899, 36 L.Ed.2d 391 (1973), as squarely considering the present issue, but it does not. The court held that a high school art teacher could not be dismissed for her silent refusal to participate in her school's daily flag ceremonies. She would only stand silently and respectfully at attention while the senior instructor led the program. Her job was not to teach patriotic matters to children, but to teach art. The court carefully indicated that through its holding it did not mean to limit the traditionally broad discretion that has always rested with local school authorities to prescribe curriculum.

The curriculum which plaintiff complains about is not spelled out in specific detail, but can be found in the Board of Education policy and the directives of plaintiff's principal and superiors. There is after all nothing innovative or unique in this phase of the curriculum. It is traditional. There was no misunderstanding about what was expected to be taught.

Plaintiff in seeking to conduct herself in accordance with her religious beliefs neglects to consider the impact on her students who are not members of her faith. Because of her religious beliefs, plaintiff would deprive her students of an elementary knowledge and appreciation of our national heritage. She considers it to be promoting idolatry, it was explained during oral argument, to teach, for instance, about President Lincoln and why we observe his birthday. However, it would apparently not offend her religious views to teach about some of our past leaders less proudly regarded. There would only be provided a distorted and unbalanced view of our country's history. Parents have a vital interest in what their children are taught. Their representatives have in general prescribed a curriculum. There is a compelling state interest in the choice and adherence to a suitable curriculum for the benefit of our young citizens and society. It cannot be left to individual teachers to teach what they please. Plaintiff's right to her own religious views and practices remains unfettered, but she has no constitutional right to require others to submit to her views and to forego a portion of their education they would otherwise be entitled to enjoy. In this unsettled world, although we hope it will not come to pass, some of the students may be called upon in some way to defend and protect our democratic system and Constitutional rights, including plaintiff's religious freedom. That will demand a bit of patriotism.

There remains the plaintiff's claim that plaintiff's right to due process was violated by her discharge. It is conceded that as an untenured teacher plaintiff had no property interest in the teaching position. It is plaintiff's claim that her right to freedom of religion is a liberty interest which can only be extinguished by due process. Due process, it is argued, required that plaintiff be afforded an adversary hearing prior to dismissal. The statement of this issue is likewise contorted. Plaintiff's religious freedom is not being extinguished. The Fourteenth Amendment does not create a protected interest, but if one is found to exist by reason of some independent source, the Fourteenth Amendment protects it. No state statute or other rule or policy creates a protected interest for an untenured teacher in those circumstances. There is no claim that plaintiff has suffered a stigma by reason of her discharge. She should not and she has not. *Board of Regents* v. *Roth,* 408 U.S. 564, 92 S.Ct. 2701, 33 L.Ed.2d 548 (1972); *Colaizzi* v. *Walker,* 542 F.2d 969 (7th Cir. 1976), *cert. denied,* 430 U.S. 960, 97 S.Ct. 1610, 51 L.Ed.2d 811 (1977).

We affirm the grant of summary judgment by the district court.

Affirmed.

NOTE

1. Numerous faults with plaintiff's teaching were claimed by defendants, but on appeal they are not urged as justification for plaintiff's discharge.

THE United States Court of Appeals, Fifth Circuit, decides for a high school history teacher whose contract was not renewed as a result, according to the district court, of her use of a role playing teaching technique known as "Sunshine simulation" which had brought some parental complaints. The Court of Appeals declares that the school district's "argument that the Sunshine project was unprotected by the First Amendment because it was a private expression must fail in light of *Givhan* . . . , which holds that private expression by a public employee is protected speech. We thus join the First and Sixth Circuits in holding that classroom discussion is protected activity. . . . It follows that Cooper's discharge for discussions conducted in the classroom cannot be upheld unless the discussions 'clearly . . . over-balance [her] usefulness as an instructor. . . . ' The district court found that such a condition was not present, and the District does not contest this finding. Thus, the district court's finding that Cooper sustained her prima facie burden of showing a violation of her constitutional rights must be upheld."

Kingsville Independent School Dist. v. *Cooper*, 611 F.2d 1109 (1980)

GODBOLD, Circuit Judge:

Beginning in 1967, Janet Cooper was employed by the Kingsville [Texas] Independent School District as a high school teacher under a series of annual contracts and without tenure. In the spring of 1972 the District decided not to renew her contract for the 1972–73 academic year. The District initiated this suit, seeking a declaratory judgment that it had not violated Cooper's rights. Cooper counterclaimed for equitable relief, including reinstatement with back pay, alleging violation of her First and Fourteenth Amendment rights and basing her action on 42 U.S.C. § 1983 and on the Constitution.

In August 1973, after a trial, the district court found for Cooper and awarded her $15,000, described as "the damages for all the injuries of any kind suffered by her as a result of the controversy," plus attorneys' fees of $4,500. Presumably the "damages" were intended to be approximately the amount of her salary for the 1972–73 and 1973–74 school years.[1]

The Board appealed and Cooper cross-appealed raising as one of her issues the failure of the district court to order that she be reinstated. By an unpublished opinion this court vacated the judgment and remanded for full consideration in light of several intervening Supreme Court decisions. We stated our intention that the remand "open all issues to all parties," with right to amend all pleadings.

On remand the district court entered a pre-trial order in which it noted that Cooper's claim for reinstatement was before the court and that, if she prevailed, she would be entitled to reinstatement. The district court, in 1977, held § 1983 inapplicable but inferred a direct cause of action under the Constitution with jurisdiction grounded on 28 U.S.C. § 1331. The court again found for Cooper and again awarded $15,000 damages and attorneys' fees of $4,500. It also ordered that she be reinstated.

The District again appealed and Cooper cross-appealed. At the request of the District the trial court stayed Cooper's reinstatement pending appeal.

I. The facts

Cooper was hired as an American history teacher in 1967. The District has no formal system of tenure, and all teachers are employed under annual teaching contracts. Renewal decisions are made each spring for the following academic year. Despite the fact that some complaints were received about Cooper's teaching, her contract was renewed each year until 1972. The number of complaints received was about average for a Kingsville teacher, and most were neither investigated nor discussed with Cooper.

In the fall of 1971, Cooper employed a technique known as "Sunshine simulation" to teach American history of the post-Civil War Reconstruction period. The technique involved role-playing by students in order to recreate the period of history. It evoked strong student feelings on racial issues. Parental complaints about Cooper increased significantly as a result of the Sunshine project. Cooper was twice called before the principal to discuss the project. The District's personnel director was present at the second meeting, and he told Cooper "not to discuss Blacks in American history" and that "nothing controversial should be discussed in the classroom." However, no District official ever prohibited her from completing the project, and she did complete it.

Despite the controversy engendered by the Sunshine project, both the principal and the superintendent recommended that Cooper's contract be renewed for the 1972–73 academic year. The Board of Trustees disagreed, however, and declined to renew her contract. Board members testified at trial and by deposition that they disapproved of the Sunshine project and that the volume of complaints received diminished Cooper's effectiveness as a teacher. Although vague references were made to other complaints, Board members, when pressed, could remember few complaints other than those about the Sunshine project. The district court found that the nonrenewal was "precipitated" by Cooper's use of the Sunshine technique and that other complaints were "minimal in effect."

The District raises three grounds on appeal: that no cause of action existed under either § 1983 or the Constitution; that no violation of Cooper's constitutional rights occurred; and that the court had no power to award attorneys' fees. In her cross-appeal Cooper contends that the $15,000 "damages," awarded in 1973 and re-awarded in 1977, plus the order to reinstate her (entered in 1977 and still stayed), were an insufficient remedy, and that the re-award of $4,500 attorneys' fees was insufficient because it included no fees for the first appeal or for proceedings on remand.

II. The cause of action

The District contends that an independent school district does not come within the purview of *Monell* v. *Department of Social Services,* 436 U.S. 658, 98 S.Ct. 2018, 56 L.Ed.2d 611 (1978), which overruled *Monroe* v. *Pape,* 365 U.S. 167, 81 S.Ct. 473, 5 L.Ed.2d 492 (1961), and held "local governing bodies" amenable to suit under § 1983. This court has already held *Monell* applicable to a Texas junior college, *Goss* v. *San Jacinto Junior College,* 588 F.2d 96, 98 (5th Cir.), *modified on other grounds,* 595 F.2d 1119 (5th Cir. 1979), which "enjoy[s] the same legal and constitutional status as 'independent school districts'" under Texas law. *Hander* v. *San Jacinto Junior*

College, 519 F.2d 273, 279 n. 3 (5th Cir. 1975). *See also Moore* v. *Tangipahoa Parish School Board,* 594 F.2d 489 (5th Cir. 1979) (*Monell* applicable to parish school board); *White* v. *Dallas Independent School District,* 581 F.2d 556 (5th Cir. 1978) (en banc) (§ 1983 action remanded for reconsideration in light of *Monell,* strongly suggesting that Texas independent school district is within scope of *Monell*). The District's argument is therefore unpersuasive. Moreover, prior to *Monell* this court held a Texas independent school district subject to suit under § 1983 for equitable relief, including back pay, notwithstanding *Monroe* v. *Pape's* interdiction of damage suits against municipalities. *Harkless* v. *Sweeny Independent School District,* 427 F.2d 319 (5th Cir. 1970), *cert. denied,* 400 U.S. 991, 91 S.Ct. 451, 27 L.Ed.2d 439 (1971). Thus, Cooper's action was maintainable at the time it was before the district court, and it remains so now.

The District also contends that *Monell* itself bars this action by forbidding suits based on decisions that are not "officially adopted and promulgated" by a governing body. 436 U.S. at 690, 98 S.Ct. 2018, 56 L.Ed.2d at 635. In essence, the District argues that liability here is based solely on the doctrine of respondeat superior and is therefore explicitly precluded by *Monell.* This argument is patently without merit. School district personnel decisions by the body entrusted with such decisions are "officially adopted and promulgated." *Moore* v. *Tangipahoa Parish School Board, supra,* 594 F.2d at 493. The District is liable for the actions of the Board of Trustees not on the basis of respondeat superior but because the only way the District can act, practically as well as legally, is by and through its Board of Trustees. *See Stoddard* v. *School District No. 1,* 590 F.2d 829, 835 (10th Cir. 1979).

Finally, the District contends that even if it is subject to suit under § 1983, it is entitled to qualified immunity—and thus to a good faith defense—on the basis of *Wood* v. *Strickland,* 420 U.S. 308, 95 S.Ct. 992, 43 L.Ed.2d 214 (1975). This court has already held that *Wood* does not apply to awards against a school district but only to awards against individual members of the Board.[2] *Hander* v. *San Jacinto Junior College, supra,* 519 F.2d at 277 n. 1. The District's argument is therefore without merit, and there is no bar to Cooper's § 1983 action.[3]

III. Constitutional violations

The District makes three separate arguments to support its contention that no violation of Cooper's constitutional rights occurred. The District asserts, first, that the district court's finding that the Sunshine project precipitated the nonrenewal is clearly erroneous; second, that Cooper's conduct was unprotected activity; and third, that the district court refused to determine, as it was required to do under *Mt. Healthy City School District* v. *Doyle,* 429 U.S. 274, 97 S.Ct. 568, 50 L.Ed.2d 471 (1977), whether the Board would have made the same decision without considering the Sunshine project.

The district court's finding on a factual issue will not be disturbed unless it is clearly erroneous, that is, unless this court is "left with the definite and firm conviction that a mistake has been committed." *U.S.* v. *U.S. Gypsum Co.,* 333 U.S. 364, 395, 68 S.Ct. 525, 542, 92 L.Ed. 746, 766 (1948).

The findings that the Sunshine project precipitated the nonrenewal and that other complaints about Cooper were minimal in effect are not clearly erroneous. We reach this conclusion on the basis of the evidence considered by the district court. Both the principal and the superintendent, to whom Cooper was directly responsible, and who were best able to observe her performance, recommended that her contract be renewed. In his final evaluation of her the principal rated her as "outstanding" or as "thoroughly satisfactory" on each category of her teaching performance. Until the Sunshine controversy arose most complaints about Cooper were neither investigated nor discussed with her, and the Board voted to renew her contract despite these complaints. Several Board members stated in depositions that they thought the Sunshine technique and subject matter inappropriate for a high school history class. Board members who testified that the volume and not the substance of complaints influenced their decisions placed primary emphasis on the Sunshine complaints. One Board member testified that complaints about the Sunshine project were the sole reason for her vote. Finally, the difference between the handling of earlier complaints and the handling of complaints about Sunshine—the latter included two conferences with the principal and several reports to the Board—suggest that all concerned considered the earlier complaints routine and insignificant when compared with the Sunshine project.

The District's argument that the Sunshine project was unprotected by the First Amendment because it was private expression must fail in light of *Givhan* v. *Western Line Consolidated School District,* 439 U.S. 410, 99 S.Ct. 693, 696, 58 L.Ed.2d 619, 623 (1979), which holds that private expression by a public employee is protected speech. We thus join the First and Sixth Circuits in holding that classroom discussion is protected activity. *Minarcini* v. *Strongsville City School District,* 541 F.2d 577 (6th Cir. 1976); *Keefe* v. *Geanakos,* 418 F.2d 359 (1st Cir. 1969).

It follows that Cooper's discharge for discussions conducted in the classroom cannot be upheld unless the discussions "clearly . . . over-balance [her] usefulness as an instructor. . . ." *Kaprelian* v. *Texas Wo-*

man's University, 509 F.2d 133, 139 (5th Cir. 1975); *see also Lindsey* v. *Board of Regents,* 607 F.2d 672 (5th Cir. 1979). The district court found that such a condition was not present, and the District does not contest this finding.[4] Thus, the district court's finding that Cooper sustained her prima facie burden of showing a violation of her constitutional rights must be upheld.

The District also argues, however, that it should have been given, and was denied, a chance to rebut this finding by demonstrating that it would have made the decision to discharge Janet Cooper even had it not considered the Sunshine project, citing *Mt. Healthy City School District* v. *Doyle,* 429 U.S. 274, 287, 97 S.Ct. 568, 576, 50 L.Ed.2d 471, 484 (1977). The district court's findings that the Sunshine project precipitated the nonrenewal and that other complaints were minimal in effect together satisfy the requirement of *Mt. Healthy* and *Givhan* v. *Western Line Consolidated School District,* 439 U.S. 410, 417, 99 S.Ct. 693, 697, 58 L.Ed.2d 619, 625 (1979). The district court did not explicitly find that Cooper would have been rehired but for the Sunshine project. However, that court's findings of fact adequately support such an inference. This case is therefore unlike that before the Supreme Court in *Mt. Healthy,* where the district court found only that the protected activity played a "substantial part" in the discharge, or in *Givhan,* where the factual determination of causation "could not, on [the] record, be resolved by the Court of Appeals." 439 U.S. at 417, 99 S.Ct. at 697, 58 L.Ed.2d at 626.

IV. Damages

As already pointed out, the initial award of $15,000, made in August 1973, approximated Cooper's salary for the 1972–73 year, already completed, and the 1973–74 year, just commencing. Damages were not at that time available because *Monroe* v. *Pape,* 365 U.S. 167, 81 S.Ct. 473, 5 L.Ed.2d 492 (1961), had not been overruled. The equitable remedy of back pay was, however, available. *Harkless* v. *Sweeny Independent School District, supra.* On remand, when the district court again awarded damages it made no new and independent assessment of the amount of the award but merely reinstated the earlier $15,000 award and added a provision for Cooper's reinstatement to her teaching position. The district court did not indicate whether it intended the right to reinstatement to be effective as of the entry of its judgment in 1977 or as of some earlier date.

The usual award of back pay covers the period from wrongful termination to effective reinstatement. *See, e.g., Lee* v. *Selma City School System,* 552 F.2d 1084 (5th Cir. 1977); *Ward* v. *Kelly,* 515 F.2d 908 (5th Cir. 1975); *Cole* v. *Choctaw County Board of Education,* 471 F.2d 777 (5th Cir.), *cert. denied,* 411 U.S. 948, 93

S.Ct. 1926, 36 L.Ed.2d 410 (1973). Nothing in this case supports awarding Cooper any less when the court entered its judgment on remand in August 1977. Since reinstatement was then stayed at the request of the Board, Cooper is entitled to judgment for back pay beginning with the 1972–73 year and continuing until effective reinstatement, subject to principles of mitigation. In order that a fresh judgment can be entered making such award, the award of $15,000 is vacated.

V. Attorneys' fees

The district court had authority to award attorneys' fees under 42 U.S.C. § 1988, as that statute applies to all cases pending at the time of its enactment. *Crowe* v. *Lucas*, 595 F.2d 985 (5th Cir. 1979); *Miller* v. *Carson*, 563 F.2d 741 (5th Cir. 1977); *Gore* v. *Turner*, 563 F.2d 159 (5th Cir. 1977); *Hodge* v. *Seiler*, 558 F.2d 284 (5th Cir. 1977); *Rainey* v. *Jackson State College*, 551 F.2d 672 (5th Cir. 1977).

The district court erred, however, in not awarding attorneys' fees for the initial appeal and remand. *Harkless* v. *Sweeny Independent School District*, 608 F.2d 594, 597 (5th Cir. 1979); *Johnson* v. *Mississippi*, 606 F.2d 635 (5th Cir. 1979); *Iranian Students Ass'n* v. *Edwards*, 604 F.2d 352 (5th Cir. 1979). We vacate the award of $4,500 attorneys' fees in order that the court can enter a fresh award that takes into consideration the new judgment entered for back pay, and the services on initial appeal and remand and on this appeal and remand therefrom.

Affirmed in part, *vacated* in part and *remanded.*

NOTES

1. For the 1971–72 year her salary had been $7,020. She would have received an increase of approximately $400 for the 1972–73 year and an additional increase for the 1973–74 year.
2. There is a conflict among the circuits on this question. *Compare Bertot* v. *School District No. 1*, 613 F.2d 245 (10th Cir. 1979) (en banc) *with Paxman* v. *Campbell*, 612 F.2d 848 (4th Cir. 1980) (en banc) *and Owen* v. *City of Independence*, 589 F.2d 335 (8th Cir. 1978). The Supreme Court has granted certiorari in *Owen,*——U.S.——, 100 S.Ct. 42, 62 L.Ed.2d 28 (1979).
3. Because we hold that Cooper's action is maintainable under § 1983, we need not decide whether there is also an implied cause of action under the Constitution.
4. This district argues instead that the district court applied the wrong standard and that any substantial disruption of academic discipline justifies discharge for exercise of First Amendment rights. *Kaprelian* makes clear that the test is not whether substantial disruption occurs but whether such disruption overbalances the teacher's usefulness as an instructor.

$\mathbf{T}$HE Supreme Court of Washington State decides against two high school teachers who had claimed their First Amendment rights had been abridged because they were not allowed to team-teach a "Global Studies" course as an alternative to the more conventional history course. In deciding against the teachers, the Court stated that "case law recognizes the right of a teacher to select teaching methods and materials. On the other hand, the school board asserts that a teacher has no right to select or use teaching methods or course materials contrary to administrative instructions." The Court argued: "It is clear Global Studies differs from the more conventional course of study in more than teaching method—it differs in coverage and content as well. Since significant course content differences exist and course content is manifestly a matter within the board's discretion, petitioners' claims of academic freedom are not well taken.

Millikan v. *Board of Directors of Everett*, 611 P.2d 414 (1980)

WRIGHT, Justice.

This is an action by two high school teachers who claim their First Amendment rights have been abridged because they are not allowed to team-teach a course according to their own plan. Defendant-respondent school board prevailed on summary judgment. The Court of Appeals dismissed the appeal for lack of an adequate record. *Millikan* v. *Board of Directors,* 20 Wash.App. 157, 579 P.2d 384 (1978). We reversed the Court of Appeals, remanded the matter to the trial court for supplementation of the record and retained the case for a decision on the merits. *Millikan* v. *Board of Directors,* 92 Wash.2d 213, 595 P.2d 533 (1979).

Petitioners Gordon Millikan and Robert Petersen developed a method of teaching history known as "Global Studies," in which the class is divided into small groups to work with two teachers. Individual study, research and writing projects for each student are stressed.[1]

In 1973 a group of teachers, including petitioners, requested that a pilot program be instituted for the teaching of Global Studies as an alternative to a more conventional history course. The school district approved and implemented the pilot program. Subsequently, however, students were given a choice between conventional history and Global Studies. A vast majority chose the more conventional course, which resulted in fewer Global Studies classes. During the 1976 spring semester, Millikan was assigned to teach one traditional history class and four Global Studies classes. As a consequence of the student-preference registration the Global Studies program for the 1976 fall semester was reduced to one class. Millikan was required to teach his other four history classes in the conventional manner.

In the spring of 1976, Robert Petersen was transferred from his team-teaching assignment with Millikan to the science laboratory. Petersen alleges the new assignment was intended to destroy Global Studies and to retaliate against him for joining Millikan in the filing of a grievance regarding the student registration procedure.

Following adverse decisions at all levels of the grievance process, Millikan and Petersen appealed to the superior court pursuant to RCW 28A.88.010 and RCW 28A.88.015, which provide for de novo review of school board decisions, and RCW 28A.58.460–28A.58.480. In granting summary judgment for the school board, the trial court concluded it was being asked to review administrative matters. It held the decision to offer particular courses and to allow student preference in the selection of courses was the prerogative of the school board. The court also found there had been no First Amendment violation.

Millikan and Petersen contend the trial court erred by granting the summary judgment, asserting the school district is not entitled to judgment as a matter of law and that there is a genuine issue of material fact. This issue raises three questions: (1) Do the restrictions imposed on petitioners' teaching violate their right to academic freedom? (2) Does the reassignment of Petersen abridge his First Amendment rights as a retaliation for filing a grievance? (3) Does the school district violate petitioners' right to equal protection by subjecting their course to student preference registration?

ACADEMIC FREEDOM

Petitioners argue the restrictions imposed upon their team-teaching methods and the requirement that they teach in the conventional manner violate their right to academic freedom. They assert that case law recognizes the right of a teacher to select teaching methods and materials. On the other hand, the school board asserts that a teacher has no right to select or use teaching methods or course materials contrary to administrative instructions.

The Supreme Court has long recognized that academic freedom at the college level is protected under the First Amendment. It only recently extended that protection to the noncollegiate level, however. In *Tinker* v. *Des Moines Independent Community School Dist.*, 393 U.S. 503 89 S.Ct. 733, 21 L.Ed.2d 731 (1969), the Court found unconstitutional a ban on student black armbands worn to protest the Vietnam war. The Court stated:

First Amendment rights, applied in light of the special characteristics of the school environment, are available to teachers and students. It can hardly be argued that either students or teachers shed their constitutional rights to freedom of speech or expression at the schoolhouse gate.

393 U.S. at 506, 89 S.Ct. at 736.

Millikan and Petersen rely on a number of cases purportedly recognizing a teacher's substantive right to select teaching methods and materials. *Sterzing* v. *Fort Bend Independent School Dist.*, 376 F.Supp. 657 (S.D.Tex.1972), *remanded for reconsideration of relief granted*, 496 F.2d 92 (5th Cir. 1974); *Mailloux* v. *Kiley*, 323 F.Supp. 1387 (D.Mass.1971), *aff'd* 448 F.2d 1242 (1st Cir. 1971); *Parducci* v. *Rutland*, 316 F.Supp. 352 (M.D.Ala.1970); *Keefe* v. *Geanakos*, 418 F.2d 359 (1st Cir. 1969). All of these cases involve discharge or suspension stemming from a high school teacher either having provided materials with a controversial content or making allegedly profane or objectionable remarks to students. In each case, the court was attempting to protect both the right of the teacher, as speaker, and the right of the student to receive the communication. These cases are not in point, however. Here the students have expressly indicated they do not wish to participate in the Global Studies course. Petitioners' case is undercut because the right they assert is independent from the students' rights.

Furthermore, in each of the above-cited cases the court found a due process violation because the teaching method had not been proscribed before the non-retention or firing. Since these factors are not present in the instant case the value of those cases is questionable as precedent for a teacher's right to choose materials and methods. *See, e.g., Mailloux* v. *Kiley*, 323 F.Supp. 1387, 1393 (suspension may be in order where

teacher with notice uses a disapproved method not appropriate to teaching the subject).

As noted above, controversial statements and methods of conveying a point underlie the cases cited by petitioners. In the case at bar, however, the content of specific communications is not actually involved. At most, the effect of the student preference registration system is to force Millikan to teach courses in a more conventional manner. He acknowledges that neither his specific course material nor his technique have been disapproved. Instead, only a broad methodology and course approach has, in effect, been forbidden. Arguably, judicial nonintervention is called for. This conflict does not "directly and sharply implicate basic constitutional values." *Epperson* v. *Arkansas*, 393 U.S. 97, 104, 89 S.Ct. 266, 270, 21 L.Ed2d 228 (1968). But because of the novelty and importance of the question, we will directly confront the academic freedom issue.

The applicable cases take the position that a school district has authority to prescribe both course content and teaching methods. *Adams* v. *Campbell County School District, Campbell County, Wyoming*, 511 F.2d 1242 (10th Cir. 1975); *Saunders* v. *Reorganized School District No. 2 of Osage County*, 520 S.W.2d 29 (Mo. 1975); *Hetrick* v. *Martin*, 480 F.2d 705 (6th Cir. 1973), *cert. denied*, 414 U.S. 1075, 94 S.Ct. 592, 38 L.Ed.2d 482 (1973); *Clark* v. *Holmes*, 474 F.2d 928 (7th Cir. 1972), *cert. denied*, 411 U.S. 972, 93 S.Ct. 2148, 36 L.Ed.2d 695 (1973).

In *Hetrick*, a First Amendment challenge to contract nonrenewal, the school administration expected teachers to teach on a basic level, stressing fundamentals and following conventional teaching patterns. Plaintiff's teaching, however, emphasized student responsibility, as well as freedom to organize class time and assignments in terms of student interest. In an unpublished memorandum opinion, the Federal District Court for the Eastern District of Kentucky reasoned that while the First Amendment guarantee of academic freedom gives a teacher the right to encourage a vigorous exchange of ideas within the confines of the subject matter being taught,

it does not require a University or school to tolerate any manner of teaching method the teacher may choose to employ. A University has a right to require some conformity with whatever teaching methods are acceptable to it.

480 F.2d at 707.

On appeal, the teacher claimed a constitutional right to "teach her students to think" and argued the First Amendment protected her from termination for using teaching methods and adhering to a teaching philosophy that are "well-recognized in the profession." The Sixth Circuit Court of Appeals concluded plaintiff's rights had not been abridged by the refusal to rehire her because of her teaching philosophy. The court held academic freedom

> does not encompass the right of a nontenured teacher to have her teaching style insulated from review by her superiors ... just because her methods and philosophy are considered acceptable somewhere within the teaching profession.

480 F.2d at 709.

Like the plaintiff in *Hetrick*, Millikan and Petersen have utilized unconventional but professionally recognized methods designed to teach the student to think. Notwithstanding this worthy objective, *Hetrick* indicates an educational institution may require some conformity in teaching methods. Under the reasoning in *Hetrick*, the respondent-defendant board's requirement that petitioners teach history classes in a conventional manner contrary to their own preferred teaching philosophy is not violative of their rights.

In a similar vein, see *Adams* v. *Campbell County School District, Campbell County, Wyoming, supra,* in which nontenured high school teachers sued the school district following nonrenewal of their employment contracts. That court concluded that even though the teachers' methods may have had educational value, plaintiffs did not have an absolute constitutional right to use those methods in preference to more orthodox ones. *See also, Clark* v. *Holmes, supra,* and *Saunders* v. *Reorganized School District No. 2 of Osage County, supra,* which held the school board need not tolerate a significant deviation from prescribed course content or the course calendar.

Accordingly, if Global Studies detracts from the scope of a conventional history course—because it emphasizes small groups, independent reading and writing, and inquiry—discovery techniques—petitioners may be compelled to abandon their own preferred techniques and to teach history in a more conventional manner. While teachers should have some measure of freedom in teaching techniques employed, they may not ignore or omit essential course material or disregard the course calendar.

Millikan and Petersen characterize this controversy as one involving the right to choose a teaching method. Yet, Petersen's own affidavit stresses that unless the school district is enjoined "there will be a tremendous loss of *coverage and content.*" (Italics ours.) Paul G. Treckeme, supervisor of secondary social studies, states in his affidavit that Global Studies is "significantly different both in *subject matter content and teaching methodology*" from the traditional survey course. (Italics ours.) Further, a University of Washington professor familiar with Global Studies characterizes it as differing from the conventional history course as much as "new math" differs from traditional math. Consequently, it is clear Global Studies differs from the more conventional course of study in more than teaching method—it differs in coverage and content as well.

Since significant course content differences exist and course content is manifestly a matter within the board's discretion,[2] petitioners' claims of academic freedom are not well taken.[3]

Millikan and Petersen also assert the school board's actions violate their contractual right to academic freedom guaranteed by article III, § 3 of the Everett School District 1975–76 Handbook. It reads:

General Statement
Education can best be carried out in an atmosphere in which academic freedom for staff is encouraged and guaranteed with due consideration to the rights of the students and community in connection therewith.
Suggested Procedures for Handling Complaints
The right of community involvement in matters or issues relating to academic freedom is herein recognized. It is recommended that citizen complaints relevant to academic freedom follow this procedure:

In support of their secondary position petitioners cite *In re Department of Education, State of Hawaii and Hawaii State Teachers Ass'n,* 66 L.A. 1221 (1976), a case based primarily on the need to foster and preserve the students' right to hear and learn even controversial subjects and issues. The Hawaii decision is inapposite, however. Here, students' right to hear and learn are not directly involved. The contract provision in question—which clearly contemplates complaints over books and other controversial materials—does not support the teachers' position that being assigned to teach conventional history courses violates their right to academic freedom.

PETERSEN'S REASSIGNMENT

Petitioners next contend Petersen's reassignment violates his First Amendment rights of free speech and academic freedom. They argue the reassignment cannot stand if it was employed to meet his grievance, retaliate for his grievance, or to infringe on the exercise of his right to academic freedom.

First, as indicated previously, Petersen has no right to teach Global Studies. The contention a school administration is required to perpetuate a program of "team-teaching" is not well taken. The allegation Petersen was reassigned as punishment for filing a grievance merits closer examination, however.[4] The Cascade High School principal said the reassignment was "not related to the [student preference] procedures recommended by Mr. Treckeme." Petersen claims the principal would not explain the reassignment. Petersen's affidavit states:

There were other certified staff that could have been assigned to that science lab without any problem, and also a teacher's aid was available to cover the science lab assignment. On checking the schedule I found at least two other periods where certified staff were not assigned to cover periods in the science lab. During this period only two or three students at most would come into the learning center . . . I also checked with the science department supervisor . . . and was informed that the change in assignment which I requested could have been made with no disruption of any program.

On the other hand, Petersen, a forestry teacher, does not perform a teaching function at the one-period lab so the assignment is not incompatible with his educational background. Further, since each teacher ordinarily receives a one-period nonacademic assignment, it is not unreasonable for the administration to require Petersen to supervise students in the laboratory.

In ruling on a motion for summary judgment, the court must consider the material evidence and all reasonable inferences therefrom in favor of the nonmoving party. If reasonable persons might reach different conclusions the motion should be denied. *Novenson* v. *Spokane Culvert and Fabricating Co.,* 91 Wash.2d 550, 552, 588 P.2d 1174 (1979); *Balise* v. *Underwood,* 62 Wash.2d 195, 199, 381 P.2d 966 (1963). We do not believe a person would conclude the reassignment resulted from the filing of the grievance. Summary judgment on this issue was proper.

EQUAL PROTECTION

Finally, Millikan and Petersen argue the school district violates their rights to equal protection by subjecting their Global Studies program to student preference registration while not subjecting other courses to the same procedure. They urge there is no difference between Global Studies and the traditional course justifying the different treatment. As we have stated previously, differences—in content, coverage and teaching approach—justify the disparate treatment.

The notice of appeal and complaint by which petitioners initiated this action allege Global Studies involves a "particular teaching methodology and subject matter content." Further, the fact petitioners requested a pilot course shows Global Studies is considered significantly different from a conventional history course. The request states the purpose is to enable teachers to arrange "team-teaching . . . and teaching techniques new to them." The course utilizes techniques of inquiry-discovery and small groups. Study-writing exercises for two-week periods are common.

In short, the record refutes Millikan's contention that the differences are no more significant than the differences in style, methods and content used in conventional history courses taught by other teachers. Substantial differences clearly exist between Global Studies and conventional history courses. Consequently, a summary judgment in favor of the school board was warranted.

The judgment of the trial court dismissing petitioners' action is affirmed.[5]

UTTER, C.J., and ROSELLINI, STAFFORD, HOROWITZ, BRACHTENBACH, DOLLIVER, HICKS and WILLIAMS, JJ., concur.

NOTES

1. Students enrolled in Global Studies courses receive credit for the state curriculum requirements for world history or American history and government.
    Global Studies is described on pages 417 and 418, *infra.* For a description of the "team-teaching" technique, see *Francisco* v. *Board of Directors of the Bellevue Public Schools, District No. 405,* 85 Wash.2d 575, 537 P.2d 789 (1975).

2. RCW 28A.58.758(1) gives each common school district board of directors final responsibility for setting policies "ensuring quality in the content and extent of its educational program." Paragraphs (a) and (e), subsection (2) of RCW 28A.58.758 charge the board, acting through its administrative staff, with establishment of "performance criteria and an evaluation process . . . for all programs constituting a part of such district's curriculum" and establishment of "final curriculum standards" consistent with statutes and regulations of the State Board of Education.
    RCW 28A.58.760(2)(a) provides it is the responsibility of the certified teaching and administrative staff to implement the district's prescribed curriculum. Failure to do so constitutes cause for discharge.
    RCW 28A.59.180(5) empowers the boards of directors of first-class districts to prescribe a course of study consistent with that prepared by the State Board of Education. *And see,* RCW 28A.58.090 (school boards accountable for education offered to district students) and RCW 28A.58.754(1)(e) (school districts have sole authority to designate portion of high school curriculum).

3. The logical extension of petitioners' argument was well stated by the board's counsel in oral argument:
    "If the plaintiff-appellants are correct in their analysis . . . [i]f the district wanted to have new math they would not be able to do it because the teacher who wanted to teach traditional math would have [the right] to do it . . . [I]f you accept plaintiff's theory, a district would be completely unable at any time to direct teaching methods . . . it would be completely unable to keep control of its curriculum."

4. It is doubtful Petersen seriously relies upon this argument. Petersen's affidavit states the reassignment was "possibly" to retaliate for filing the grievance. Petitioners' counsel said in oral argument Petersen was reassigned "for the *sole* reason of scuttling these courses and making it more difficult to teach them." (Italics

ours.) When asked whether Petersen was abandoning the retaliation claim, however, petitioners' counsel assured the court his client was not dropping the argument.

5. We do not express an opinion on the desirability of the Global Studies teaching method. The record shows much to recommend the system and we certainly do not condemn it. The court, however, may not substitute its judgment about the merits of courses for that of the school authorities.

T HE Court of Appeals of Ohio, Hamilton County, decides against a high school Spanish teacher who had been issued a written reprimand from the principal because of her use of classroom time to denounce the local police department which she contended had not handled correctly an automobile accident she had been involved in. Deciding for the school board, the Court said: "We believe appellees acted lawfully, and did not violate any constitutionally protected right of appellant in issuing her a written reprimand for expending classroom instruction time in a Spanish class to discuss in some detail personal experiences and feelings unrelated to the subject for which the class was scheduled. We recognize that the power of local school boards to discipline is subject to constitutional limitations and may not be exercised in an unconstitutionally arbitrary or discriminatory manner. So also is there the rule of law that a teacher may be disciplined or discharged for failure to comply with reasonable regulations which are adopted for the proper administration of the schools . . . . There was no dismissal here, no forfeiture of wages or the like, and the reprimand seems to us to be couched in reasonable and moderate language."

Petrie v. *Forest Hills School Dist. Bd. of Ed.*, 449 N.E.2d 786 (1982)

KEEFE, Presiding Judge.

Plaintiff-appellant, Marilou Petrie, is presently a Turpin High School Spanish teacher under continuing contract with the Forest Hills School District of Hamilton County, and has been for a number of years. On the morning of January 31, 1980, while driving to school, she was involved in an automobile accident at an intersection in the village of Newtown, Hamilton County. Representatives of the Newtown Police Department handled the investigation of the accident. Marilou Petrie was not pleased with the accident investigation by the Newtown Police Department, and she allegedly made known her feelings of displeasure to students in one of her Spanish classes. As indicated, the targets of her denunciation apparently were Newtown officialdom and the police department. Her allegedly derogatory remarks during a class session soon prompted a number of complaints about Miss Petrie's criticism. The complaints came to Gerald Chance, an employee of the Forest Hills School District Board of Education serving in the capacity of principal of Turpin High School. Principal Chance investigated, and after talking with many persons, including Miss Petrie and over twenty students, ultimately issued a written reprimand to her, on or about February 25, 1980. Plaintiff filed suit against the board of education and Chance on March 5, 1980, with an amended complaint later, seeking principally money and, somewhat indirectly, removal of the reprimand from her personal file. Defendants submitted a motion for summary judgment on July 2, 1981 which the court of common pleas granted. The plaintiff then filed her notice of appeal.

Significant portions of the reprimand from Principal Chance to Miss Petrie follow:

"I reviewed with Miss Petrie what had transpired during the past 48 hours * * *.

"At that point in the conversation Miss Petrie interrupted saying that she made the statement in class, that the police chief of Newtown was corrupt—and I could fire her if I wanted to. I explained to Miss Petrie that firing her was not the purpose of this conference—but I was trying to review what had happened during the last 48 hours and hear her side of the story.

"It was at this point that I asked Miss Petrie if she referred to the police in Newtown as 'Pigs.' Her reply was 'I probably used that term.' Miss Petrie wanted to relate why she made these statements—because of her automobile accident. I explained to Miss Petrie that the events surrounding the accident were not germane to our discussion. She insisted that the accident was germane to the classroom incident and discussed some of its events.

"At this point in the conversation, I explained to Miss Petrie that regardless of her feeling about the Newtown Police as to how they handled her accident that statements made in class about the police or the village of Newtown, depicting them in a derogatory manner, was [sic] inexcusable.

"After a review of this incident in Miss Petrie's classroom, it is my feeling that Miss Petrie used poor judgment and acted in a manner unbecoming to the teaching profession; specifically, making derogatory statements about the Chief of Police and his department, and the Village of Newtown. These statements are personal opinions derived at as a result of an accident in the village of Newtown and have nothing to do with the instruction of Spanish.

"Incidents of this type must not happen in the future at Turpin High School. Relate personal feelings of this nature to the individuals involved through the proper channels—not in the classroom. The incident is serious enough to warrant [sic] this written reprimand."

Appellees rate this litigation as absurd and frivolous, contending that "this case concerns nothing more than notifying a teacher that she should not use Spanish class time to discuss automobile accidents and police handling of automobile accidents." However, appellant advances two assignments of error: first, the trial court erred generally in granting summary judgment in favor of the appellees, and second, the court below erred specifically in granting summary judgment to the appellees "considering the legitimate First Amendment issue present here." We dispose of the two assignments in reverse order. Assignment two is overruled. We believe appellees acted lawfully, and did not violate any constitutionally protected right of appellant in issuing her a written reprimand for expending classroom instruction time in a Spanish class to discuss in some detail personal experiences and feelings unrelated to the subject for which the class was scheduled. We recognize that the power of local school boards to discipline is subject to constitutional limitations and may not be exercised in an unconstitutionally arbitrary or discriminatory manner. So also is there the rule of law that a teacher may be disciplined or discharged for failure to comply with reasonable regulations which are adopted for the proper administration of the schools. 68 American Jurisprudence 2d Schools 499, Section 166 (1973). There was no dismissal here, no forfeiture of wages or the like, and the reprimand seems to us to be couched in reasonable and moderate language. Therefore we overrule assignment two.

We next review assignment one in which appellant generally attacks the summary judgment for appellees. Following the reprimand, Miss Petrie requested that an investigation of the contents of her personal information file be made. This she was authorized to do pursuant to R.C. 1347.09. (The section of R.C. Chapter 1347 which apply to the instant appeal are those which became effective in 1977. Counsel agree that the statutory changes made January 23, 1981, do not apply here.) An investigation was conducted, one in which Miss Petrie fully participated, following which the appellee school board through its agents decided that the reprimand, supra, should remain in the teacher's file. She then prepared a lengthy rebuttal statement as to the information in her file which she disputed, and this rebuttal statement was placed in her file together with a copy of a polygraph report which she asked be included. We conclude that R.C. Chapter 1347, commonly called the Ohio Privacy Act, has been complied with in all respects by the defendants-appellees with respect to appellant and thus there is no genuine issue as to any material fact. The moving parties were entitled to judgment as a matter of law. We note with particularity the correctness of the summary judgment with respect to R.C. 1347.10, pertinent sections of which provide as follows:

"(A) A person harmed by the use of personal information system may recover damages in a civil action from any person who directly and proximately caused such harm * * *. (Emphasis added.)

"* * *

"(B) Any person or state or local agency that violates or proposes to violate any provision of Chapter 1347 of the Revised Code may be enjoined by any court of competent jurisdiction. * * *"

On the state of the record, reasonable minds can come only to the conclusion that appellant had not been harmed. It is positively undisputed that Miss Petrie at the present time has a continuing contract with the Forest Hills School District and she does not allege that her salary has in any way been reduced or jeopardized to date. This is made clear in Miss Petrie's deposition of May 15, 1980. With respect to section (B), we emphasize that as a matter of law R.C. Chapter 1347 was not violated by either appellee.

We elect to comment upon the following language in appellees' brief:

"The Act [Ohio Privacy Act] could not be more clear with respect to the remedy for an individual who believes material in his or her personnel [sic] file is not accurate. The remedy provided in the Act is the right to have rebuttal statements and information placed in the individual's personnel [sic] file. For obviously good reason, the courts are entirely kept out of this remedial procedure. If the courts are overworked and court dockets overcrowded now, they would be absolutely ground to a halt if the courts were open to every public employee who has a gripe about something which has been placed in his or her personnel [sic] file."

It is manifest from the provisions of R.C. 1347.10, some of which appear above, that the courts are *not* "entirely kept out of this remedial procedure." We do believe, however, that R.C. 1347.10 provides the principal grounds for recourse to the courts so far as the Ohio Privacy Act is concerned. Regardless, whatever may be the full scope of permissible judicial review under the said Act—a determination not necessary to this decision—we judge that the General Assembly did not provide for court review of a situation in which an agency in good faith maintains that such and such occurred or was said, and its employee, also in good faith, disputes it, in the absence of mistake, fraud,

collusion or arbitrariness on the part of the agency. Cf. *State, ex rel. Ohio High School Athletic Assn.,* v. *Judges* (1962), 173 Ohio St. 239, 181 N.E.2d 261 [19 O.O.2d 52]. If and when the sole controversy between the agency and employee is a difference in versions of the contention, as here, seemingly the Act provides to the employee merely the right to a fair investigation and to include in his or her file an explanation or protest pursuant to R.C. 1347.09.

The error assignments are overruled. We affirm.

Judgment affirmed.

DOAN and KLUSMEIER, JJ., concur.

A United States District Court in Michigan decides against a school board which had suspended a junior high school biology teacher after a few parents alleged that he was "behaving improperly and teaching 'sex education' in an extremely insensitive manner." The District Court, however, decides against the teacher in his claim that the parent complaining to the school board about his teaching constituted a conspiracy with the school board to infringe on his academic freedom and First Amendment rights. In deciding against the school board, Judge James Harvey wrote: "The school board defendants claim that no evidence was presented which would permit a conclusion that Stachura's First Amendment freedoms were infringed. The court believes that its instructions on Stachura's First Amendment claim were a correct exposition of the standards which should guide the jury in evaluating this claim. Specifically, the jury was instructed that the plaintiff's 'academic freedom' is limited by the right of the school board to inculcate community values through control of the substantive content of the curriculum. However, the jury was also instructed that an instructor's teaching methods are entitled to First Amendment protection as long as the substantive values the school board seeks to inculcate are not subverted by those methods."

As for the complaining parent, a private citizen, Judge Harvey said: "In the instant case, it is clear that defendant Truszkowski was petitioning the government for a redress of grievances. Moreover, even viewing the evidence in the light most favorable to the plaintiff, there is no evidence that Truszkowski was abusing the legislative process."

Stachura v. *Memphis Community Sch. Dist.*, Civ. no. 79-3002 (E.D.Mich., Ap. 11, 1983)

HARVEY, Judge.

Plaintiff's brought this action pursuant to 42 USC 1983. Plaintiff Stachura was a junior high school biology teacher in the Memphis Community School District. In April of 1979, a few parents in the Memphis School District alleged that Stachura was behaving improperly in the classroom and teaching "sex education" in an extremely insensitive manner. These allegations were made public at a school board meeting held on April 23, 1979. As a result of the meeting, Stachura was suspended with pay. This suspension had the effect of removing Stachura from the classroom for the remainder of the academic year. Both the allegations of impropriety and the subsequent suspension received widespread publicity. Plaintiff James MacDonald was a student in one of Stachura's classes during the 1979 academic year.

The defendants in this case include the school board members who held office in April of 1979. Certain school administrators were also named as defendants, along with two parents who were alleged to have conspired with the school board.

Plaintiff Stachura maintained that the actions of the defendants had deprived him of his right to "academic freedom." In addition, Stachura claimed that the actions of the defendants had deprived him of liberty and property without due process of law. Plaintiff MacDonald claimed that he also had an interest in "academic freedom," which the defendants had infringed.

At the close of trial, the jury returned a verdict in the form of answers to ten interrogatories. The jury found in favor of plaintiff Stachura, but against plaintiff MacDonald. The jury awarded Stachura $275,000 in compensatory damages, and $46,000 in punitive damages. However, the jury did not find that all the defendants were liable to Stachura, and different damage amounts were assigned to those who were found liable.

This matter is before the Court on the following motions:

1.) Defendants Memphis Community School District, Board of Education of the Memphis Community Schools, Herbert Kubisch, Genevieve Walters, Margaret Guoin, Timothy Kelly, Lawrence Delekta, Ernest Beaudrie, Beatrice Dolan and Donald C. Russell's (hereinafter, the school board defendants) motion for judgment notwithstanding the verdict;

2.) The school board defendants' motion in the alternative for a new trial or remittitur;

3.) Defendant Truszkowski's motion for judgment notwithstanding the verdict;

4.) Defendant Truszkowski's motion in the alternative for a new trial or remittitur.

The Court will address these motions in the order listed above.

I. *The School Board Defendants' Motion for a Judgment Notwithstanding the Verdict.*

Judgment notwithstanding the verdict (JNOV) is proper only if the evidence is such that there can be but one reasonable conclusion as to the proper verdict. If there is sufficient evidence which would permit a reasonable jury to find for plaintiff, then a motion for JNOV should not be granted. *Greer* v. *United States,* 408 F.2d 631 (CA6, 1969). In deciding a motion for JNOV, the Court must view the evidence in the light most favorable to the party against whom the motion is made, while also giving that party the advantage of every reasonable inference the evidence can justify. *National Plymer Products* v. *Borg Warner Corp.,* 660 F.2d 171, (CA6, 1981). The school board defendants argue that a JNOV is warranted because of the plaintiff's failure of proof in the following areas:

A.) Plaintiff Stachura's first amendment claim;
B.) Plaintiff Stachura's property interest claim;
C.) Plaintiff Stachura's liberty interest claim;
D.) The defense of good faith immunity;
E.) The award of punitive damages.

The Court will analyze each of these issues in the order listed above, looking for sufficient evidence to raise a question of fact for the jury. If there is sufficient evidence to permit a reasonable jury to find for plaintiff, then the Court must deny the motion for JNOV.

A.) *Plaintiff Stachura's First Amendment Claim*

The school board defendants claim that no evidence was presented which would permit a conclusion that Stachura's First Amendment freedoms were infringed. The Court believes that its instructions on Stachura's First Amendment claim were a correct exposition of the standards which should guide the jury in evaluating this claim. Specifically, the jury was instructed that the plaintiff's "academic freedom" is limited by the right of the school board to inculcate community values through control of the substantive content of the curriculum. However, the jury was also instructed that an instructor's teaching methods are entitled to First Amendment protection as long as the substantive values the school board seeks to inculcate are not subverted by those methods. *McGill* v. *Board of Ed. of Pekin Elementary School,* 602 F.2d 774 (CA7, 1979); *East Hartford Ed. Ass'n.* v. *Board of Ed. of the Town of East Hartford,* 562 F.2d 838 (CA2, 1977).

Evidence was presented that the biology text used by Stachura was approved by the board of education, as was the film used to supplement the text discussion of reproduction. Stachura testified concerning the instruction techniques he used in teaching reproduction. This testimony was at odds with the allegations of the parents and the claims of the defendants. Moreover, plaintiff was suspended only after a vehement protest by certain parents; evidence which certainly raises the inference that Stachura was suspended in retaliation for his allegedly improper teaching methods. This evidence would permit a reasonable jury to find for plaintiff Stachura. Thus, questions of credibility and issues of fact arose which were properly submitted to the jury. JNOV will not lie under this theory.

B.) *Plaintiff Stachura's Property Interest Claim*

The school board defendants do not challenge the Court's instructions in this area. Rather, they claim that no evidence was presented which established a property interest entitled to protection. And, in the alternative, if there were such an interest, defendants claim that an adequate hearing was given. The Court instructed the jury that, under the facts of this case, a property interest could arise in either of two ways. First, the Michigan Teacher Tenure Act gives rise to a property interest if the teacher is "discharged" or "demoted". MCLA 38.101. Second, Stachura's contract of employment gives rise to a property interest if a teacher is disciplined, reprimanded, reduced in rank or compensation, or deprived of any professional advantage.

As is fully detailed in plaintiff's brief in opposition to the motion for JNOV, the record contained testimony which gave rise to inferences that Stachura was terminated and that he was deprived of professional advantages. Stachura himself testified that he believed he had been dismissed. Indeed, the testimony of defendant Russell gave rise to an inference that Stachura was dismissed. This testimony would permit the jury to find that plaintiff had a property interest under the Tenure Act, and the employment contract. If such a property interest were found, the record also contained evidence which raised issues as to whether an adequate hearing was held. Accordingly, the school board defendants' motion for JNOV will not succeed on this ground.

C.) *Plaintiff Stachura's Liberty Interest Claim*

Under this claim, the school board defendants contend that the evidence presented did not permit a finding that plaintiff's liberty interests were infringed. In addition, the defendants claim that a suspension with pay cannot constitute an infringement of a liberty interest. Finally, the school board defendants argue that even if the plaintiff's liberty interests were infringed, then a sufficient due process hearing was afforded.

Turning first to the question of whether plaintiff's liberty interests were infringed, the Court instructed the jury that a liberty interest is infringed if the actions of the school board defendants imposed a stigma on Stachura, and foreclosed a definite range of employment opportunities that the plaintiff would otherwise have had available to him. *Board of Regents* v. *Roth*, 408 US 564 (1972); *Perry* v. *Sindermann*, 408 US 593 (1972). The plaintiff presented an extensive amount of evidence which detailed the stigma resulting from the various actions by the school board defendants. Furthermore, testimony by Professor Grinstead detailed how plaintiff's employment possibilities would be foreclosed. Thus, a reasonable jury could find for plaintiff on this ground, and JNOV is thus inappropriate.

In discussing whether plaintiff's liberty interests were infringed, the defendants also argue that a suspension with pay was not sufficient to trigger a liberty interest. This argument flows from the decision in *Paul* v. *Davis*, 424 US 693 (1976), which held that defamation by a state defendant is not enough to establish that a liberty interest has been infringed. Rather, the defamation must occur in the context of a termination of the employee, or the infringement of an employment interest protected by state law. The school board defendants assert that the question of whether a suspension with pay and subsequent transfer meet the requirements of *Paul* was answered in *Sullivan* v. *Brown*, 544 F.2d 279 (CA6, 1979). In *Sullivan*, the Court of Appeals held that "A transfer *under the circumstances of this case* does not give rise to a due process right." *Sullivan* v. *Brown*, *id* at 283 (emphasis added). The Court believes the circumstances of the instant case give rise to a due process right. Stachura was removed from the classroom under circumstances which invited stigmatization. Given the humiliating nature of the publicity surrounding the removal, Stachura had a right to a forum which would permit an opportunity for swift public vindication. Plaintiff's liberty interest claim was properly submitted to the jury.

Finally, the school board defendants argue that the plaintiff was afforded a sufficient hearing and defendants are thus entitled to JNOV. The Court instructed the jury that, at a minumum, due process requires that the plaintiff must be given adequate notice of the reasons for the action against him, and a hearing.

Board of Regents v. *Roth, supra.* Stachura presented evidence which raised the inference that he was never given adequate notice concerning the basis for the actions against him, or any opportunity to present his position in a fair way. Thus, the school board defendants are not entitled to JNOV on this basis.

D.) *Defendants' Claim of Good Faith Immunity*

The school board defendants claim that the evidence in the record permits only the conclusion that they acted in good faith. The Court's instruction on the defense of good faith immunity was in accord with *Wood* v. *Strickland*, 420 US 308 (1975). The Court's instruction also comports with more recent expositions of the standards governing good faith immunity, where the Supreme Court has stated that government officials "are shielded from liability for civil damages insofar as their conduct does not violate clearly established statutory and constitutional rights of which a reasonable person would have known." *Harlow* v. *Fitzgerald,*—— US ——, 102 S.Ct. 2727, 73 L.Ed.2d 396, 410, (1982). From the statements of various board members, inferences were clearly raised that defendants knew they were violating Stachura's statutory and constitutional rights. This evidence, along with the actions of defendants, would permit a juror to conclude that the defendants were violating clearly established constitutional and statutory rights, of which a reasonable person would have known.

The defendants also complain that the Court's instructions on good faith immunity improperly shifted the burden of persuasion to the defendants. The Court believes that the burden was properly placed on the defendants asserting the immunity. In discussing good faith immunity, the Supreme Court stated that " . . . if the official pleading the defense . . . *can prove* that he neither knew nor should have known of the relevant legal standard, the defense should be sustained." *Harlow* v. *Fitzgerald, id* at 411 (emphasis added). This language implies that the burden was on the defendants, and the Court will not grant a motion for JNOV on the basis that the burden of proof was incorrectly shifted.

E.) *Punitive Damages*

The school board defendants argue that the punitive damage awards in this case were completely unsupported by the evidence. The jury was instructed that they could, in their discretion, award punitive damages if they found an individual defendant had acted maliciously, wantonly or oppressively. *Morrow* v. *Igleburger*, 384 F.2d 787 (CA6, 1978). As delineated in plaintiff's brief, various statements and actions on the part of defendants indicate that they acted maliciously or wantonly. In the context of this case, the inaction of the defendants can often be construed as being maliciously motivated. Thus, sufficient evidence existed to permit the awarding of punitive damages.

In summary, for the reasons stated above, the school board defendants' motion for a judgment notwithstanding the verdict is hereby DENIED.

II. *The School Board Defendants' Motion for a New Trial or in Lieu Thereof, a Remittitur*

The school board defendants claim that a new trial is warranted because of an excessive damage award, a purported error in instructing on the monetary value of a deprivation of constitutional rights, and a flaw in the special interrogatories submitted to the jury. The power of a trial court to order a new trial in a jury case is a limitation on the jury's power to render a verdict, and is designed to prevent gross injustice. *Montgomery Ward & Co.* v. *Duncan*, 311 US 243 (1940). The improper admission of evidence is a ground for a new trial, as is the giving of an erroneous instruction or in the failure to give a proper requested instruction, but only if such errors are prejudicial. 6A *Moore's Federal Practice and Procedure*, Section 59.08 (2) at 59-82, 96. On a new trial motion, unlike on a motion for JNOV, the trial court may weigh the evidence. The decision to grant or deny a new trial is one confided to the sound discretion of the trial court. *TCP Indus, Inc.* v. *Uniroyal, Inc.*, 661 F.2d 542 (CA6, 1981).

Defendants' first contention is that the damage award is excessive. The Court will not substitute its judgment for that of the jury, unless the verdict is either shocking to the conscience or is the result of prejudice, passion, or other improper influences. Because this verdict does not shock the conscience, and because there is no showing of improper influence, the Court will not award a new trial based on an excessive damage award. Since there is not an excessive verdict which warrants a new trial, remittitur is also inappropriate. See generally, 11 Wright and Miller, *Federal Practice and Procedure*, Section 2815 at p. 99.

Defendants' next argument is that the instruction concerning damage relief for the deprivation of constitutional rights is flawed. The Court would agree that such damages are difficult to measure, but nevertheless, they should be available in a case like the present one. *Corritz* v. *Naranjo*, 667 F.2d 892 (CA10, 1981); *Herrara* v. *Valentine* 653 F.2d 1220 (CA10, 1981). Although the instant case does not involve a physical injury like *Herrara*, the mental anguish, destruction of reputation, and personal humiliation which arguably flowed from the defendants' actions justify the Court's instruction on damage relief for constitutional deprivations.

Finally, defendants argue that it was error for the Court to submit interrogatories to the jury which failed to distinguish between damages that resulted from a deprivation of a liberty interest and damages that resulted from a deprivation of a property interest.

The defendants did not object to this aspect of the interrogatory form at trial. Thus, the issue is not properly before the Court, and will not support a motion for a new trial. FR Civ P 51.

Accordingly, for the reasons stated above, the school board defendants motion for a new trial or remittitur is hereby DENIED.

III. *Defendant Truszkowski's Motion for a Judgment Notwithstanding the Verdict*

In April of 1979, defendant Truszkowski was not a school board member. Her role during that time was a private citizen complaining about Stachura to the school board. Plaintiff alleged that Truszkowski conspired with the school board to infringe on his rights. Defendant Truszkowski proceeded *in propria persona* at trial. The thrust of her defense was that she was merely petitioning the government for a redress of grievances. In the postjudgment phase of trial, defendant Truszkowski is being assisted by counsel for the school board defendants. Once again, the thrust of Truszkowski's argument is that her actions were privileged because she was petitioning the government pursuant to the First Amendment.

When a private citizen petitions his government for redress of grievances, that citizen's actions are absolutely privileged unless the citizen is abusing the legislative or administrative processes. *Gorman Towers, Inc.* v. *Bogoslavsky*, 626 F.2d 607 (CA8, 1980); *Weiss* v. *Willow Tree Civic Association*, 467 F. Supp. 803 (S.D. NY, 1979). A petitioner abuses the legislative process if, by a pattern of conduct, the petitioner effectively closes to the other parties the "machinery of the agencies and the courts." *Willow Tree Civic Association, id*, at 818 (quoting *California Motor Transport Co.* v. *Trucking Unlimited*, 404 US 508 (1972).

In the instant case, it is clear that defendant Truszkowski was petitioning the government for redress of grievances. Moreover, even viewing the evidence in the light most favorable to the plaintiff, there is no evidence that Truszkowski was abusing the legislative process. Accordingly, defendant Truszkowski's motion for a judgment notwithstanding the verdict is hereby GRANTED. An appropriate judgment will be entered.

IV. *Defendant Truszkowski's Motion for a New Trial or Remittitur*

Although the Court has granted defendant Truszkowski's motion for JNOV, FR Civ P 50 (c) provides that the Court must conditionally rule on Truszkowski's motion for a new trial. Truszkowski claims that a new trial is warranted because of an error in jury

instructions, an error in the form of the special interrogatories, and an excessive damage award. Truszkowski's arguments in support of these grounds for
new trial mirror the arguments advanced by the school
board defendants. For the reasons stated when addressing the school board defendants' motion for a new
trial, the Court CONDITIONALLY DENIES defendant Truszkowski motion for a new trial.

V. *Conclusion*

Accordingly, for the reasons stated, the Court hereby rules as follows:

1.) Defendants Memphis Community School District, Board of Education of the Memphis Community
Schools, Herbert Kubisch, Genevieve Walters, Margaret Guoin, Timothy Kelly, Lawrence Delekta, Ernest Beaudrie, Beatrice Doland, and Donald C.
Russell's motion for judgment notwithstanding the
verdict is DENIED;

2.) Defendants Memphis Community School District, Board of Education of Memphis Community
Schools, Herbert Kubisch, Genevieve Walters, Margaret Guoin, Timothy Kelly, Lawrence Delekta, Ernest Beaudrie, Beatrice Doland, and Donald C.
Russell's motion for a new trial or remittitur is
DENIED;

3.) Defendant Truszkowski's motion for judgment
notwithstanding the verdict is GRANTED;

4. Defendant Truszkowski's motion for a new trial
or remittitur is CONDITIONALLY DENIED.

It is so ordered.

THE United States Court of Appeals, Sixth Circuit, in upholding Judge James Harvey's *Stachura* decision, states: "Judge Harvey wrote a lengthy opinion dealing with the two appeals which have been taken in this case. We have reviewed that opinion and adopt and rely upon it. Additionally, however, we make the following comments about the two appeals. Appellee Truszkowski was responsible for starting the sequence of events which transpired in these two cases. She organized and transmitted complaints to the school board concerning Stachura's teaching of a life science class alleging improper teaching methods. . . . While Ms. Truszkowski's role in these events is not a pretty one, we agree with the district judge that it was a petition addressed to the proper authority and as a consequence, her actions were immunized from this suit by her First Amendment rights. . . .

As to Stachura's suit against the school board and other defendants, we again find ourselves in agreement with the district judge. . . . There is evidence in the record that in relation to various aspects of teaching human reproduction, Stachura had consulted with and secured the approval of his teaching methods and instructions from the principal who was his superior officer in the school system. It appears, however, that when public protest arose neither the administrative officials of the school nor the school board itself saw fit to defend the embattled teacher, or publicly to assume responsibility for their own decisions. . . . The facts recited above also indicate clearly that Stachura was never given a fair opportunity to present his defense to the school board nor do we believe that the board's action can be held as a matter of law to have been taken in good faith."

Stachura v. *Truszkowski*, 763 F.2d 211 (1985)

GEORGE CLIFTON EDWARDS, Jr., Circuit Judge.

Plaintiffs Edward Stachura and James MacDonald brought this action under 42 U.S.C. § 1983. They alleged violations of plaintiff Edward Stachura's rights under the Fourteenth Amendment guarantees of liberty and property against the Memphis Community School Board, the Memphis Community School District, individual members of the School Board, Donald Russell, School Superintendent, during the period involved, Robert Phillips, school superintendent who succeeded Donald Russell, Charles Becker, Principal of the Memphis Middle School and two private citizens, Delores Truszkowksi and Marilyn Moore. As to all of the individuals, plaintiffs alleged a conspiracy to violate their First Amendment rights as a teacher in the instance of Stachura and as a student in the instance of MacDonald. After a lengthy jury trial, the jury found in favor of plaintiff Stachura against most of the defendants (including Trusz-

kowski) and against plaintiff MacDonald in all of his claims.

Two motions for judgment n.o.v. were filed. Truszkowski filed one such motion relying on the First Amendment. The School Board, its members and the named school officials also filed a motion for judgment n.o.v.

Judge Harvey granted judgment notwithstanding the verdict to defendant Truszkowski and plaintiff Stachura appeals. The jury had found $18,250 damages, $10,000 of which were punitive, against Truszkowsi. Judge Harvey set these judgments aside. He held that Truszkowski was entitled to immunity on the basis of the right to petition contained in the First Amendment to the Constituion of the United States.

As to the second appeal named above, *Stachura* v. *Memphis Community School Board, et al.,* the Board and other named defendants-appellants, appeal from a jury award of $321,000 punitive and compensatory damages.

Judge Harvey wrote a lengthy opinion dealing with the two appeals which have been taken in this case. We have reviewed that opinion and adopt and rely upon it. Additionally, however, we make the following comments about the two appeals.

Stachura v. Truszkowski

Appellee Truszkowski was responsible for starting the sequence of events which transpired in these two cases. She organized and transmitted complaints to the School Board concerning Stachura's teaching of a Life Science class alleging improper teaching methods. Various other parents in the community joined her subsequently in vehement and continuing protests, based on unfounded rumors, leading directly to Stachura's removal. Although Truszkowski's role was pivotal in initiating these protests, it was made to the public body having charge of the educational system in the community concerned. As such, it was protected, as the District Judge held, by the right to petition encompassed in the First Amendment to the Constitution of the United States. In applicable part the First Amendment says: "Congress shall make no law . . . abridging . . . the right of the people . . . to petition the government for a redress of grievances." While Ms. Truszkowski's role in these events is not a pretty one, we agree with the District Judge that it was a petition addressed to the proper authority and as a consequence, her actions were immunized from this suit by her First Amendment rights. *Gorman Towers* v. *Bogoslavsky*, 626 F.2d 607, 614–15 (8th Cir. 1980); *see California Motor Transport Co.* v. *Trucking Unlimited*, 404 U.S. 508, 92 S.Ct. 609, 30 L.Ed.2d 642 (1972); *Eastern Railroad Presidents Conference* v. *Noerr Motor Freight*, 365 U.S. 127, 81 S.Ct. 523, 5 L.Ed.2d 464 (1961).

For these reasons, we affirm the judgment of the District Court in entering judgment notwithstanding the verdict thus setting aside the jury's verdict against defendant Truszkowski.

Stachura v. Memphis Community School District, et al.

As to Stachura's suit against the School Board and other defendants, we again find ourselves in agreement with the District Judge. The record in this case, when the motion for judgment notwithstanding the verdict is considered, must be viewed in the light most favorable to the party against whom the motion is made while giving that party the advantage of any reasonable inference the evidence can justify. The District Judge rejected defendants' position on plaintiff Stachura's First Amendment claim, his property interest claim, his liberty interest claim, the defense of good faith immunity and the question of punitive damages. As the District Judge pointed out, the text he used in teaching the Life Science class was approved by the School Board itself. The Life Science text included the following outline of Chapter 12 entitled "Reproduction."

CHAPTER 12 REPRODUCTION   205
The Nature of the Process 205
Cells can reproduce themselves • Cells can grow • Cells can specialize • Lesson Review

Asexual and Sexual Reproduction 209
Asexual reproduction is simple and fast • Sexual reproduction is more complicated • Sexual reproduction is the more common method • Genes enter the picture • Sexual reproduction is a safety mechanism • Lesson Review

Laboratory Activity
How Fast Does Yeast Reproduce Asexually?   212
The Human Reproductive Process 215
Human beings reproduce only sexually • The male system produces sperm • The female system has three functions • The ovaries produce eggs and estrogen • Other organs aid the reproductive process • The female has a menstrual cycle • Lesson Review

Growth, Birth, and Early Development   220
The embryo stage lasts two months • The fetus develops into a baby • Labor causes birth • What are the needs of a newborn baby? • Lesson Review
Applying What You Have Learned   225
W. Smallwood, *Challenges to Science: Life Science*, McGraw-Hill, at ix (1978).

The films subsequently complained about had been shown for a number of years previous to the 78–79 school year. There is evidence in the record that in relation to various aspects of teaching human reproduction, Stachura had consulted with and secured the approval of his teaching methods and instructions from the Principal who was his superior officer in the school system. It appears, however, that when public protest arose neither the administrative officials of the school nor the School Board itself saw fit to defend the embattled teacher, or publicly to assume responsibility for their own decisions.

The meeting of the School Board on April 23, 1979 occurred after Stachura showed two films in his Life Science class. These films had been provided by the County Health Department and were shown pursuant to the direction of the School Principal. They were entitled "From Boy to Man" and "From Girl to Woman." They were shown separately to boys and girls and parental permission slips were required for viewing the films. They had been shown before to other seventh grade classes. Subsequent, however, to this showing, community discussion and protest pro-liferated leading the School Superintendent to warn Stachura that he was in "a heck of a lot of trouble" and to advise him to stay away from the scheduled April 23, 1979 School Board meeting to avoid the "angry hotheads." After Ms. Truszkowski read a statement to the Board, there were calls to tar and feather Stachura. A member of the board described the meeting as follows:

"At this time, the public was in total uproar and completely out of control. Two board members asked Mr. Kubisch to close meeting [sic], but did not to the best of my knowledge. One of the members of the public asked Mr. Kubisch what would you do if your child was in that class and he replied I wouldn't let my child go to that class. That put the meeting over the edge. People were hollering and shouting and the statement was made from the public that if Mr. Stachura was allowed to return to school in the morning, they would be there and picket the school. At this point of total panic, Mr. Russell stated in order to maintain peace in our school district, we would suspend Mr. Stachura with full pay and get this mess straightened out." (App. 586–87).

On April 24, 1979, Stachura was suspended by Superintendent Russell from the classroom and told that he would "never see the inside of a Memphis classroom again." Stachura's suspension pending "administration evaluation" was confirmed by the Board on May 21, 1979. Stachura engaged counsel who, on May 22, 1979, made representations to the Board regarding the allegations and his suspension. Stachura's counsel objected to the appointment of a committee of parents to investigate their own complaints, to the lack of any actual investigation or opportunity to respond to the allegations, to the lack of notice or guidelines regarding teaching methods which the Board alleged were improper and to the lack of any notice or hearing on the allegations prior to his summary suspension. The Board did not respond to the May 22, 1979 letter. On May 29, 1979, Superintendent Russell handed Stachura a "letter of reprimand," dated April 20, 1979, which was based on Truszkowski's unsubstantiated allegations. Stachura's counsel responded with a second letter dated May 31, 1979 reiterating Stachura's position and his request for immediate reinstatement to the classroom and removal of the "reprimand letter" from his personnel file. On June 4, 1979, the Board's attorneys responded by letter referring Stachura's attorney to an article in the Detroit Free Press for a statement of the Board's position on the matter. The Board subsequently informed Stachura that his rights under the contract would not be restored unless he accepted the "letter of reprimand."

We believe that Judge Harvey properly submitted to the jury the issues which were occasioned by the public attacks upon this teacher and by the letter of reprimand. We also hold that there was ample proof of actual injury to plaintiff Stachura both in his effective discharge by the Memphis Community School District and by the damage to his reputation and to his professional career as a teacher. Contrary to the situation in *Carey* v. *Piphus,* 435 U.S. 247, 89 S.Ct 1042, 55 L.Ed.2d 252 (1978), relied on by appellant School District, there was proof from which the jury could have found, as it did, actual and important damages.

Turning directly to the appellate issues in Stachura's suit against the School District defendants, we hold, as indicated above, that plaintiff Stachura's First Amendment rights were infringed and that his exercise of "academic freedom" had followed rather than violated his superior's instructions. *See Mailloux* v. *Kiley,* 448 F.2d 1242, 1243 (1st Cir.1971) and *Fern* v. *Thorp Public School,* 532 F.2d 1120 (7th Cir.1976). We also agree with the District Judge and the jury that Stachura's property interests were invaded by his being effectively discharged. We likewise agree that the actions of the School Board "imposed a stigma on Stachura and foreclosed a definite range of employment opportunities" which plaintiff would otherwise have available. *See Board of Regents* v. *Roth,* 408 U.S. 564, 92 S.Ct. 2701, 33 L.Ed.2d 548 (1972); *Perry* v. *Sindermann,* 408 U.S. 593, 92 S.Ct. 2694, 33 L.Ed.2d 570 (1972). Defendants' claims based on *Parratt* v. *Taylor,* 451 U.S. 527, 101 S.Ct. 1908, 68 L.Ed.2d 420 (1981) and *Vicory* v. *Walton,* 721 F.2d 1062 (6th Cir.1983) are similarly without force. The holding in *Parratt* that the provision of post-deprivation remedies by state courts will, in some cases, suffice to provide all of the process due in property deprivation claims applies only where, as in *Parratt,* 451 U.S. at 540–542, 101 S.Ct. at 1915–1916, a pre-deprivation hearing was "impracticable" or "impossible." Here a pretermination due process hearing was both practical and feasible. *Loudermill* v. *Cleveland Board of Education,* 721 F.2d 550, 562 (6th Cir.1983), aff'd, ——— U.S.———, 105 S.Ct. 1487, 84 L.Ed.2d 494 (1985). The facts recited above also indicate clearly that Stachura was never given a fair opportunity to present his defense to the School Board nor do we believe that the Board's action can be held as a matter of law to have been taken in good faith.

From the point of view of this appellate court, our most substantial concern has been whether we should exercise the limited authority appellate courts have to enter a remittitur of the substantial damages awarded by this jury. Stachura suffered the embarrassment of extensive publicity in the local media which repeated the allegations against him, which included that he was a "sex maniac." Media coverage went around the world as the story was picked up by Stars and Stripes.

Esquire magazine noted the event in its Dubious Achievement Awards. He and his family suffered the harassment of crank phone calls and refuse left on their porch, which continued up through the time of the trial three years after the events. He testified that the tension and pressure resulted in nightmares and sleepless nights and forced him to sleep on the living room floor so as not to disturb his wife. He became very withdrawn from friends and neighbors. Substantial as are the jury awards, it is clear to us that the damages that Stachura suffered will affect his professional career for his entire lifetime. While some may accept his vindication in court, there may still be many doors closed to him in his future which otherwise would have been open.

For these reasons and others spelled out in the Memorandum Opinion and Order of District Judge James Harvey, dated April 11, 1983, the judgments appealed from are hereby affirmed.

The Supreme Judicial Court of Maine decides against a teacher, student and speaker who had claimed their constitutional rights had been violated when the school board cancelled a proposed "Tolerance Day" at the high school because the scheduling of a homosexual speaker as part of the "Tolerance Day" program led to threats of picketing and to bomb and sabotage threats against the school. The Court states that it "cannot fault the decision of the board in the face of likely bomb threats, a threatened sabotage of the school's heating plant in the middle of the Maine winter, and the numerous parents expected to keep their children at home or to picket the school on Tolerance Day." The Court also indicated what this case did *not* involve: "The board did not attempt to discipline Solmitz [the teacher] for proposing and organizing the Tolerance Day symposium. It did not tell Solmitz how he was to teach his history course. It did not restrict Solmitz in any way in freely expressing his views on any subject within or without the school. Similarly, the board did not prohibit any other discussions of tolerance or of prejudice against homosexuals, whether in Solmitz's classes or otherwise within Madison High School. When the board cancelled a proposed forum disruptive to the education of its students, it exercised its responsibility for directing the course of instruction of the school. That action did not infringe on the rights of teacher Solomitz and did not impermissibly restrict the free marketplace of ideas at Madison High School."

Solmitz v. *Maine Sch. Administrative Dist.*, 495 A.2d 812 (1985)

McKUSICK, Chief Justice.

Plaintiffs David O. Solmitz, Sonja Roach, and Dale McCormick appeal an order of the Superior Court (Kennebec County) denying injunctive relief that would have permitted a "Tolerance Day" program to be held at Madison High School in School Administrative District No. 59 (S.A.D. 59). Plaintiffs argue that the cancellation of the proposed program by the Board of Directors of S.A.D. 59 (the Board) violated the rights of each of the plaintiffs to freedom of speech under the First Amendment of the United States Constitution and under article I, § 4 of the Maine Constitution. Plaintiffs also contend that the action of the Board violated homosexuals' right to equal protection of the laws. After full consideration of all of these contentions, we find no reversible error in the judgment of the Superior Court.

In the fall of 1984, David Solmitz, a teacher at Madison High School, began planning an all-day "Symposium on Tolerance" in reaction to the tragic drowning of a Bangor homosexual by three Bangor high school students. Tolerance Day, as the program became known, was designed to bring to the school representatives of some dozen different groups who

have experienced prejudice in society. The program, to begin with a school-wide assembly, would replace scheduled classes throughout the school day on Friday, January 25, 1985.

On January 14, Solmitz met with the school's principal, Anthony Krapf, to discuss the proposed symposium. At that meeting, Krapf instructed Solmitz that he should not invite a homosexual to speak at Tolerance Day. The next day the two men met with Robert Woodbury, superintendent of S.A.D. 59, who also advised Solmitz that he should not include a homosexual in the program. On Friday, January 18, Solmitz and Woodbury reached a compromise whereby Dale McCormick, a lesbian who had agreed to speak at Tolerance Day, would participate in the symposium. As modified, the program would begin with a mandatory assembly of all students at which a speaker would discuss the issue of tolerance in general and the representatives of the various groups would be introduced. Those representatives would then disperse to different classrooms, and each would speak separately for two class periods. The students would have the option of attending such sessions as they might choose or of attending a study hall.

While he was negotiating with school administrators from January 15 through 18, Solmitz obtained counsel who scheduled a court date for a hearing seeking injunctive relief. News of the proposed symposium appeared in the local papers on Saturday morning, January 19, and during the weekend school administrators and school board members received fifty or more telephone calls and visits from people critical of McCormick's scheduled appearance. Some callers suggested that picketing might occur on the day of the program, and some parents threatened to keep their children out of school, or to attend school themselves to monitor the symposium. A few of the phone calls warned the Board to expect bomb threats against the school and sabotaging of the school furnace if the program were held.

As a result of those calls, the Board of S.A.D. 59 decided to discuss the Tolerance Day program at its regular meeting set for Monday evening, January 21. At the outset of the meeting Superintendent Woodbury summarized the events of the preceding several days and reported on the threats of disruption at the school. The Board members then went into executive session to discuss the issue; and when they resumed the open meeting, they voted unanimously to cancel Tolerance Day because of concerns they had about the effect the program would have on the "safety, order, and security" at Madison High School.

On the next day, January 22, Solmitz, McCormick, and Sonja Roach, a freshman student in Solmitz's history class, filed the present suit against S.A.D. 59, as well as against all members of the Board, Woodbury, and Krapf, personally and in their official capacities. The complaint, brought both under 42 U.S.C. § 1983 (1981) and M.R. Civ. P. 80B, alleged that defendants had violated plaintiffs' constitutional rights by cancelling the Tolerance Day symposium, and sought preliminary and permanent relief allowing the full program to proceed on the scheduled date of January 25. The Superior Court heard the motion for a temporary restraining order on January 23 and denied the motion the following day. A full hearing took place on February 8 and 11, and the trial justice promptly issued his judgment denying injunctive relief on February 14. On appeal we limit our inquiry to the narrow issue of whether the Board[1] acted impermissibly in cancelling Tolerance Day. We hold that the Board did not violate any constitutional rights[2] by its actions, and we deny plaintiffs' appeal.[3] We also deny all parties' motions for attorney's fees.

I. *Freedom of Speech*

When the Board of Directors of S.A.D. 59 cancelled the proposed Tolerance Day symposium, it acted within its broad power to manage the curriculum of the Madison schools. Although we wholeheartedly endorse the statement of the United States Supreme Court that "[i]t can hardly be argued that either students or teachers shed their constitutional rights to freedom of speech or expression at the schoolhouse gate," *Tinker* v. *Des Moines Independent Community School District,* 393 U.S. 503, 506, 89 S.Ct. 733, 736, 21 L.Ed.2d 731 (1969),[4] that principle does not require a court to overturn the decision of the Board in this case.

It is beyond question that "local school boards have broad discretion in the management of school affairs." *Board of Education, Island Trees Union Free School District No. 26* v. *Pico,* 457 U.S. 853, 863, 102 S.Ct. 2799, 2806, 73 L.Ed.2d 435 (1982) (herinafter *Pico*). In Maine local control over education is established by article VIII, § 1 of our constitution, providing that "the legislature are authorized, and it shall be their duty to require, the several towns to make suitable provision, at their own expense, for the support and maintenance of public schools. . . . " Moreover, 20—A M.R.S.A. § 2 (2) (1983) provides:

It is the intent of the Legislature that the control and management of the public schools shall be vested in the legislative and governing bodies of local school administrative units, as long as those units are in compliance with appropriate state statutes.

Additionally, 20—A M.R.S.A. § 1001(6) (1983) requires that the school board "shall direct the general course of instruction." In the case at bar, plaintiffs could make no realistic claim that the Tolerance Day program was anything other than a proposed addition to the course of instruction at Madison High School. Even the compromise Tolerance Day program would have required all students to attend a morning assembly and would have displaced the school's regular classes for part of the day. We must address the arguments of the teacher Solmitz, the student Roach, and the speaker McCormick, in the context of the broad discretion granted school boards in discharging their responsibilities for the curriculum of public schools.

A. *David O. Solmitz*

Plaintiff Solmitz argues that the Board's rejection of his plans for a school-wide Tolerance Day program violated his rights to academic freedom under the First Amendment. *See Keyishian* v. *Board of Regents of the University of the State of New York,* 385 U.S. 589, 603, 87 S.Ct. 675, 683, 17 L.Ed.2d 629 (1967) ("[academic] freedom is . . . a special concern of the First Amendment"). Solmitz, however, does not, nor could he, contend that the Board's veto infringed in any way upon his right to teach his assigned courses as he deemed appropriate, or to express himself freely on tolerance, prejudice against homosexuals, or any other subject. However broad the protections of academic freedom may be, they do not permit a teacher to insist upon a given curriculum for the whole school where he teaches. The facts as found by the Superior Court demonstrate beyond any doubt that Tolerance Day was designed by Solmitz to add to the school-wide curriculum of Madison High School. No right of Solmitz to speak freely was violated by the Board's decision to veto his curriculum proposal, and in cancelling the symposium the Board acted well within the permissible range of its discretion in S.A.D. 59.

We stress that in this case there is no indication that the Board was attempting to "cast a pall of orthodoxy over the classroom," *Keyishian* v. *Board of Regents*, 385 U.S. at 603, 87 S.Ct. at 683, or to restrict impermissibly the marketplace of ideas within the high school. *See Pico*, 457 U.S. at 871, 102 S.Ct. at 2810. The Superior Court justice found as a fact that "concerns about disruptions [by those opposed to having a homosexual speak] and the fact that such disruptions might make Tolerance Day 'a lost day educationally' . . . were the *decisive factors* in the decision to vote to cancel." (Emphasis added.) The justice further found that "concerns about disruption of educational activities, *not desire to suppress ideas,*" motivated the Board to cancel the proposed Tolerance Day program; "concerns directed at potential disruption . . . were the *actual* factors leading to the cancellation." (Emphasis added.) There is no reason to disturb those findings. Factual determinations by a trial justice will not be reversed on appeal unless they are clearly erroneous; that is, unless there is *no* competent evidence in the record to support those findings. *Harmon* v. *Emerson*, 425 A.2d 978, 981–82 (Me. 1981). In this case there was a great deal of testimony to support the trial justice's factual determinations. Six of the nine members of the Board testified at the hearing that they voted to cancel the program because they feared that holding the symposium would result in a serious disruption of the educational process at Madison High School.[5]

Despite the Superior Court's unequivocal factfinding as to the actual motive of the Board, plaintiffs urge that we overrule the trial court and find on our own that the true motive that prompted the Board to cancel Tolerance Day was that of the townfolk who were opposed to having a homosexual appear at the school. We decline to take the novel step of declaring that a permissible decision of elected officials is infected with the invidious motives of their constituents. Plaintiffs have cited no authority from this, or any other jurisdiction, to support their demand that we delve into the minds of citizens who lobbied their elected officials. Indeed, courts are generally hesitant to require even the decisionmakers themselves to explain in court testimony the motivation of their official actions. *See Citizens to Preserve Overton Park, Inc.* v. *Volpe*, 401

U.S. 402, 420, 91 S.Ct. 814, 825, 28 L.Ed.2d 136 (1971); *Frye* v. *Town of Cumberland*, 464 A.2d 195, 200 (Me. 1983). It was entirely appropriate for the Superior Court to refuse to substitute the motives of the complaining citizens for those of the Board.

The Board of S.A.D. 59 responded reasonably when faced with the prospect that the educational processes at Madison High School would be seriously disrupted if the Tolerance Day program was held. The Board has wide latitude in managing the curriculum of its schools, and its most basic obligation is to maintain order in the schools and to create a stable environment for the education of its students. Even in cases where First Amendment rights are *directly implicated,* a school board may act to restrict protected speech or conduct that "materially disrupts classwork or involves substantial disorder." *Tinker* v. *Des Moines*, 393 U.S. at 513, 89 S.Ct. at 740. Surely then, in the present case the Board could permissibly veto a teacher's proposed addition to the curriculum that threatened to force the entire school to suffer "a lost day educationally." This court cannot fault the decision of the Board in the face of likely bomb threats,[6] a threatened sabotage of the school's heating plant in the middle of the Maine winter, and the numerous parents expected to keep their children at home or to picket the school on Tolerance Day.

In announcing our decision in the case at bar, we stress what this case does *not* involve. The Board did not attempt to discipline Solmitz for proposing and organizing the Tolerance Day symposium. It did not tell Solmitz how he was to teach his history course. It did not restrict Solmitz in any way in freely expressing his views on any subject within or without the school. Similarly, the Board did not prohibit any other discussions of tolerance or of prejudice against homosexuals, whether in Solmitz's classes or otherwise within Madison High School. When the Board cancelled a proposed forum disruptive to the education of its students, it exercised its responsibility for directing the course of instruction of the school. That action did not infringe on the rights of teacher Solmitz and did not impermissibly restrict the free marketplace of ideas at Madison High School.

B. *Sonja Roach*

The free speech rights of Sonja Roach, a student of Solmitz, similarly were not violated by the action of the Board.[7] Students have no right to demand a curriculum of their own choice. In the *Pico* case, 457 U.S. 853, 102 S.Ct. 2799, the various opinions of the justices demonstrate that at least five members of the United States Supreme Court believe that the right to receive information as a component of the First Amendment does not allow students to insist upon a given curriculum.[8] *See Seyfried* v. *Walton,* 668 F.2d 214 (3d Cir. 1981) (production of the musical "Pippin" was part of the curriculum and could be cancelled over students' objections). We follow their analysis in interpreting article I, § 4 of the Maine Constitution.

Again, we stress that the findings of the Superior Court that we have ruled to be beyond reversal on appeal demonstrate that Tolerance Day was cancelled for safety, order, and security reasons, and not in an attempt to cast a "pall of orthodoxy" over the school. Sonja Roach has no right to impose upon the Board her ideas for the curriculum at Madison High School, and none of her freedoms under article I, § 4 of the Maine Constitution or the First Amendment was in any way infringed by the action of the Board.

C. *Dale McCormick*

Plaintiff Dale McCormick has no right to speak at Madison High School arising from the invitation she received from Solmitz, and she could demand successfully to address the student body only if the school had become a public forum. *See Perry Education Association* v. *Perry Local Educators' Association,* 460 U.S. 37, 103 S.Ct. 948, 74 L.Ed.2d 794 (1983). We hold that Madison High School is not a public forum, and deny this plaintiff's appeal.

In *Perry* the Supreme Court described the circumstances under which government property becomes a public forum. After discussing traditional public forums such as streets and parks, the Court stated:

> A second category consists of public property which the State has opened for use by the public as a place for expressive activity. The Constitution forbids a State to enforce certain exclusions from a forum generally open to the public even if it was not required to create the forum in the first place. Although a State is not required to indefinitely retain the open character of the facility, as long as it does so it is bound by the same standards as apply in a traditional public forum.
>
> Public property which is not by tradition or designation a forum for public communication is governed by different standards. We have recognized that the "First Amendment does not guarantee access to property simply because it is owned or controlled by the government." In addition to time, place, and manner regulations, the State may reserve the forum for its intended purposes, communicative or otherwise, as long as the regulation on speech is reasonable and not an effort to suppress expression merely because public officials oppose the speaker's view.

Id. at 45–46, 103 S.Ct. at 955 (citations omitted).

Plaintiffs assert that Madison High School was a limited public forum where McCormick had a right to speak and that, even if the property was not open to the public, the action of the school board was an attempt to suppress the lesbian speaker's view. Neither of these arguments successfully impugns the ruling of the Superior Court that the Board did not violate McCormick's fundamental freedoms when it cancelled Tolerance Day.

In arguing that the high school was a limited public forum, plaintiffs contend that school policy encouraged the use of outside speakers, that Solmitz had invited a number of speakers to the school in the past, and that the Board had allowed the prior programs without comment.[9] These assertions do not demonstrate that the school, as opposed to an individual classroom, was open to all speakers invited by a faculty member. The school policy statement introduced into evidence by plaintiffs does state that "controversial questions shall have a legitimate place in the work of the public schools," but the same statement is explicit that "no individual or group may claim the right to present arguments directly to students." Solmitz had invited a score or more speakers to the school during his 16 years of teaching,[10] and those individuals had spoken without prior approval of the Board. An average of one or two speakers per nine-month school year, with almost none addressing more than a single class, does not make the high school a "public property that the state has opened for use by the public as a place for expressive activity." Similarly, the lack of involvement by the Board in the past presentations does not mean that the school was not "reserved for its intended purpose." It is clear that the S.A.D. 59 Board only became concerned with Solmitz's program when public reaction to the proposed speakers threatened to disrupt the educational process. The purpose of Madison High School is to educate the youth of the community. The use in the past of an occasional outside speaker to accomplish that end does not create an independent right in any speaker who wishes thereafter to address the students in their classrooms.

In addition, based on the findings of the Superior Court, we are unable to hold that the Board acted to suppress a point of view to which its members were opposed. The Board cancelled the *entire* program in the face of threats of disruptive activity by some members of the community. As discussed fully above, the action of the Board of S.A.D. 59 was not taken to forbid the discussion of any issue or point of view at Madison High School. The Board's cancellation of Tolerance Day did not violate the free speech rights of Dale McCormick.

II. *Equal Protection*

Plaintiff McCormick also argues that, contrary to the ruling of the court below, homosexuals constitute a specially protected class and that the cancellation of Tolerance Day violated their right of equal protection of the laws. Whether the attack is grounded in article I, section 6—A of the Maine Constitution or in the counterpart provision of the federal constitution, we affirm the Superior Court in rejecting her contention of invidious discrimination. Even if she were a member of a specially protected class, McCormick suffered no discrimination. She was not the only Tolerance Day speaker prevented from speaking. Nor did the Board members act out of a desire to suppress McCormick's ideas. On the contrary, they were concerned with protecting the education of the Madison students from disruption, and cancelled the entire Tolerance Day program solely to further that end.

III. *Attorney's Fees*

The Superior Court justice declined to rule on the parties' cross motions for attorney's fees "pending resolution of the appeal which is certain in this case." As a matter of general policy, we disapprove of such piecemeal disposition of any case. After deciding the merits of a section 1983 case, Superior Court judges should allow or deny attorney's fees when requested. It does not promote judicial economy to have cases come to the Law Court in bits and pieces. The Superior Court should avoid any practice that encourages appeal of some, but not all, of the issues in a lawsuit. *Cf. Cole* v. *Peterson Realty, Inc.,* 432 A.2d 752 (Me. 1981) (dismissal of appeal because of improvident grant of M.R.Civ.P. 54(b) certificate).

Given our ruling on appeal, however, we find no need to remand this case to the Superior Court for disposition of the motions for fees. We deny plaintiffs' request for attorney's fees under 42 U.S.C. § 1988 (1981).[11] That section provides for the award of attorney's fees to "the prevailing party" in suits seeking to vindicate a party's rights under the federal civil rights laws. The plaintiffs have prevailed on none of their claims in this lawsuit, and thus the award of attorney's fees to them would be improper.

In their answer to plaintiffs' complaint, defendants sought a like award of attorney's fees. We similarly rule on the defendants' request, deferred also by the Superior Court, and deny it as well. Although the defendants were the "prevailing parties" in this lawsuit, they are not entitled to an award of fees under section 1988. "[T]he standard for deciding a defendant's motion for attorney's fees is different from that used when a plaintiff has made the motion. For a defendant to succeed, he must show that plaintiff's claim 'was frivolous, unreasonable, or groundless, or that plaintiff continued to litigate after it clearly became so'." *Lotz Realty Co., Inc.* v. *United States Department of Housing and Urban Development,* 717

F.2d 929, 931 (4th Cir. 1983) (citation omitted). *See Christianburg Garment Co.* v. *Equal Employment Opportunity Commission,* 434 U.S. 412, 98 S.Ct. 694, 54 L.Ed.2d 648 (1978) (employing same standard under another similarly worded section of the civil rights laws). Plaintiffs' arguments in this lawsuit were not wholly without merit and they litigated their case fully, in a manner that was helpful to the courts. Accordingly, defendants are not entitled to an award of attorney's fees.

The entry is:

Judgment affirmed.

Remanded for entry of order denying the cross motions for attorney's fees.

All concurring.

NOTES

1. We need not consider the actions of the school administrators named as defendants. Superintendent Woodbury and Principal Krapf agreed to let McCormick speak at the compromise program, and in any event, any decision they made was overruled and superseded by the decision of the Board.
2. Although much of the following discussion is phrased in terms of the First Amendment to the United States Constitution, the Maine Constitution, art. I, § 4, "Every citizen may freely speak," is equally applicable. *See State* v. *John W.,* 418 A.2d 1097, 1101 (Me. 1980) (Maine Constitution no less restrictive than the Federal Constitution).
3. Plaintiffs assert a variety of other errors by the trial court. Careful consideration does not reveal any merit in those contentions.
4. *See also National Gay Task Force* v. *Board of Educ. of Oklahoma City,* 729 F.2d 1270 (10th Cir. 1984) *aff'd mem.,* ——U.S. ——, 105 S.Ct. 1858, 84 L.Ed.2d 776 (1985) (striking down as overbroad a statute limiting teacher's right to advocate, encourage, or promote homosexual activity).
5. The parties stipulated that the three Board members who did not testify at the hearing would have testified to the same effect as did the six who did testify.
6. The Superior Court received testimony that it was standard practice, upon receiving a bomb threat, to evacuate the school for one hour to permit a search of the building.
7. It is beyond question that if Solmitz or McCormick has a right to speak at the school, Roach has a right to hear them. We focus our analysis on the question whether a student asserting her own rights can compel the presentation of a Tolerance Day program.
8. In *Pico* only three justices in the plurality explicitly found that "the right to receive ideas follows ineluctably from the *sender's* First Amendment rights to send them. . . . [And that] the right to receive ideas is a necessary predicate to the *recipient's* meaningful exercise of his own rights of speech. . . ." 457 U.S. at 867, 102 S.Ct. 2808 (emphasis in original). The four-judge dissent wrote that a student should not be able to force a school "to be the conduit for [any] particular information." *Id.* at 889, 102 S.Ct. at 2819 (Burger, C.J., dissenting). And Justice Blackmun, while concurring with

the plurality, wrote: "I do not suggest that the State has any affirmative obligation to provide students with information or ideas, something that may well be associated with a 'right to receive'." *Id.* at 878, 102 S.Ct. at 2814 (Blackmun, J., concurring). Justice White also concurred separately in the judgment affirming the court of appeals' reversal of the grant of summary judgment by the district court, but he did not discuss the First Amendment question. *Id.* at 883, 102 S.Ct. at 2816 (White, J., concurring). *Pico* was limited to the removal of library books from the school, and even the plurality opinion recognized the broad power of school boards in controlling curriculum. *See id.* at 862, 869, 102 S.Ct. at 2805, 2809.

9. Plaintiffs also assert that the program was part of an ongoing humanities program funded by the State. There is no evidence in the record to support this contention.

10. Only one past program, however, was designed to displace the normal curriculum of the whole high school to the extent of Tolerance Day. Most of the speakers appeared only before Solmitz's classes.

11. 42 U.S.C. § 1988 states in pertinent part:
In any action or proceeding to enforce a provision of sections 1981, 1982, 1983, 1985, and 1986 of this title, title IX of Public Law 92—318, or title VI of the Civil Rights Act of 1964, the court, in its discretion, may allow the prevailing party, other than the United States, a reasonable attorney's fee as part of the costs.

T HE dismissal of a tenured Fairbanks, Alaska, high school teacher is upheld by the Alaska Supreme Court because, among other reasons, the teacher had continued to use in his "American Minorities" class a book titled *The Front Runner* which dealt with homosexuality, after being warned by the school principal not to use the book. In deciding against the teacher, the Court supported its position by relying on previous cases "vesting control of the selection of educational materials in the school administration and school board, rather than the teacher" and declining to follow those cases "suggesting that in the event of conflict, secondary school teachers rather than their supervisors or school boards have a right protected by the First Amendment to determine what instructional materials to use." The court asserted the school board's authority was not "entirely unfettered by the Constitution. A board may not design a curriculum to favor a particular religion. . . . Similarly, any effort by a board to force racial bias or partisan political preference into the classroom would be constitutionally suspect. . . . Further, in cases of doubt as to what may and what may not be distributed or taught to students, advance notice may be required before punishment can be imposed." However, said the Court, this case "involves none of the above limitations."

Fisher v. *Fairbanks North Star Borough Sch.*, 704 P.2d 213 (1985)

MATTHEWS, Justice.

Rex Fisher, a tenured teacher at Lathrop High School in Fairbanks, was not rehired for the 1978–79 school year. Three reasons were given by the School Board for his non-retention: (1) violation of sick leave regulations by claiming he was sick on two days when he was actually on a trip to San Francisco; (2) violation of the District's policy against using books in class that had not been approved; and (3) violation of the School District's requirement that lesson plans be submitted after having been requested in writing numerous times to do so. Fisher sought and received a trial *de novo* before the superior court, which concluded that his non-retention was justified on each of the stated grounds.[1]

Under AS 14.20.175(b)(3) a tenured teacher may be non-retained for "substantial noncompliance with the . . . regulations or bylaws of the department, the bylaws of the district, or the written rules of the superintendent. . . ." The superior court found that Fisher was in substantial noncompliance with the regulations and bylaws of the district in each respect charged. These findings will not be disturbed on appeal unless they are clearly erroneous. Civil Rule 52 (a). The evidence amply supports each of the court's findings and they therefore must stand.

Fisher's challenge to the superior court's finding concerning his unauthorized use of the book *The Front Runner* raises a number of additional issues. Fisher used *The Front Runner* in the homosexual rights unit of his American Minorities class. Fisher acknowledges that he did not have approval for use of the book, but argues that there was no applicable school district regulation or by-law requiring advance approval.

A school district rule, denominated Policy 6160.1a, provided as follows:

For all courses in which textbooks are to be used, the textbooks shall meet in style, organization, and content the basic requirements of the course for which they are intended. The term "textbook" shall refer to books which are used as the basic source of information in any class, and may include literary works, collections of literary works and literary selections, collections of musical selections designed for instructional purposes, and laboratory manuals.

The Superintendent of Schools is responsible for presenting a list of recommended textbooks to the Board of Education for formal adoption.

Supplementary printed materials are used to enrich the curriculum in the classroom. The term "supplementary printed materials" shall refer to those books not intended for use as textbooks which cover part or all of the course affected, drill and exercise books, pamphlets, newspapers, periodicals, etc.

The Superintendent of Schools is responsible for approving selection of supplementary printed materials for enrichment purposes, subject to budget limitations.

Fisher argues that *The Front Runner* was "supplementary printed materials" rather than a "text book" under the terms of the rule. Although both types of materials require prior approval, there is evidence that the rule had not been enforced with respect to supplementary materials, suggesting that if the book fell within the supplementary materials category, the school district may have waived its right to enforce the rule against Fisher.

Fisher, however, was given clear prior written notice that the rule would be enforced with respect to any materials that he proposed to use in teaching the homosexual rights unit. The school principal, William Brannian, wrote a memorandum to Fisher dated October 14, 1977, stating in relevant part:

At our meeting of October 6, 1977, you mentioned that you planned or had already ordered classroom sets of books on "gay civil rights" or about "gays." May I point out, that according to School Board Policy 6160.1a, the Superintendent of Schools is responsible for presenting a list of recommended textbooks to the Board of Education for formal adoption. I would also like to point out that according to this same policy the Superintendent of Schools is responsible for approving selections of supplementary printed material for enrichment purposes, subject to budget limitations.

Since the books that you have ordered have not been approved, I am instructing you not to use them in your class until they have been authorized.

And, on January 13, 1978, Brannian wrote another memo to Fisher:

I have been advised that you are using a classroom set of books, in your American Minorities class, that have not been approved as per School Board Policy #6160.1a.

I am instructing you not to use these books until they are approved and to submit a copy of the book to me for approval.

Failure to do so as requested would be in violation of School Board Policy #6160.1a and my memorandum to you dated October 14, 1977.

I would consider your failure to do so insubordination and report same to the superintendent.

On January 16th, Fisher responded in a memo to Brannian stating in part: "What is the name of the book you are talking about? Certainly the book has a title and an author. How am I to respond unless you communicate with me more clearly?" On January 18th, Brannian entered Fisher's class and observed the class using *The Front Runner*. Despite the posture taken by Fisher in his memo of January 16th, it is clear that no approval of *The Front Runner* had been conveyed to Fisher.

Where the requirement of a rule or condition has been waived, the requirement may be reinstated by giving notice to the other party.[2] The notice reflected by Brannian's memos of October 14th and January 13th suffices to render enforceable the rule requiring prior approval of supplementary materials.

Fisher also contends that the prior approval rule violates the principle of freedom of speech under the First Amendment to the United States Constitution.[3] He argues that *The Front Runner* was appropriate to the subject taught as it illustrates how society discriminates against homosexuals, and that he therefore had the right to use the book. We have no occasion to doubt the truth of his assertion that the book was appropriate, nor did the trial court. The question, however, is not whether the use of a particular book in a course is appropriate but whether the teacher or the administrator is to decide appropriateness in cases of conflict.

State law resolves this question against the teacher. *Kenai Peninsula Borough School District* v. *Kenai Peninsula Education Association*, 572 P.2d 416, 422–23 (Alaska 1977). In *Kenai Peninsula*, we held that school boards have the sole authority to determine matters of educational policy and may not negotiate with teacher's unions concerning them. The selection of instructional materials was held to be a nonbargainable element of educational policy, committed to the discretion of school boards. This holding did not, however, consider the constitutional question raised by Fisher.

There are cases suggesting that in the event of conflict, secondary school teachers rather than their supervisors or school boards have a right protected by the First Amendment to determine what instructional materials to use. *Keefe* v. *Geanakos*, 418 F.2d 359, 362 (1st Cir. 1969); *Parducci* v. *Rutland*, 316 F.Supp. 352 (M.D.Ala.1970); *Dean* v. *Timpson Independent School District*, 486 F.Supp. 302 (E.D.Tex. 1979). There are also cases, however, vesting control of the selection of educational materials in the school administration and school board, rather than the teacher. *Pratt* v. *Independent School District*, 670 F.2d 771, 775 (8th Cir. 1982); *Zykan* v. *Warsaw Community School Corp.*, 631 F.2d 1300, 1305 (7th Cir. 1980); *Cary* v. *Board of Education*, 598 F.2d 535 (10th Cir. 1979); *Palmer* v. *Board of Education*, 603 F.2d 1271, 1274 (7th Cir. 1979), *cert. denied*, 444 U.S. 1206, 100 S.Ct. 689, 62 L.Ed.2d 659 (1980); *Brubaker* v. *Board of Education*, 502 F.2d 973, 984–85 (7th Cir. 1974), *cert. denied*, 421 U.S. 965, 95 S.Ct. 1953, 44 L.Ed.2d 451 (1975); *Parker* v. *Board of Education*, 237 F.Supp.

222, 229 (D.Md.1965). The issue has received much scholarly attention.[4]

Dicta in *Board of Education, Island Trees Union Free School District No. 26* v. *Pico,* 457 U.S. 853, 102 S.Ct. 2799, 73 L.Ed.2d 435 (1982), suggests that the constitutional issue should be decided in favor of the school boards. The principal question in *Pico* was whether a school board had violated the First Amendment by removing certain books from school libraries. The district court had granted summary judgment in favor of the board, but the court of appeals reversed, finding an issue of fact as to the board's motivation for removing the books. The Supreme Court upheld the court of appeals' decision, finding that the First Amendment imposes limits on the discretion of school boards to remove library books. The Court held that issues of fact existed as to whether the board's motive in ordering the books removed was to deny students access to ideas with which the board disagreed, and thus was constitutionally impermissible or, whether the books were removed because they were "pervasively vulgar" or educationally unsuitable, permissible motives under the Constitution. 457 U.S. at 871, 102 S.Ct. at 2810, 73 L.Ed.2d at 449–50. In so holding, the Court distinguished library control from curriculum control, suggesting that school boards have great authority as to the latter.

Petitioners [the board] might well defend their claim of absolute discretion in matters of *curriculum* by reliance upon their duty to inculcate community values. But we think that petitioners' reliance upon that duty is misplaced where, as here, they attempt to extend their claim of absolute discretion beyond the compulsory environment of the classroom, into the school library and the regime of voluntary inquiry that there holds sway. 457 U.S. at 869, 102 S.Ct. at 2809, 73 L.Ed.2d at 448.

The Court also stated:

We are . . . in full agreement with petitioners that local school boards must be permitted to "establish and apply their curriculum in such a way as to transmit community values," and that "there is a legitimate and substantial community interest in promoting respect for authority and traditional values be they social, moral, or political." 457 U.S. at 864, 102 S.Ct. at 2806, 73 L.Ed.2d at 445.

The Court's emphasis on the school board's right to control curriculum in order to inculcate community values seems distinctly inconsistent with those decisions which suggest that teachers have the final say with respect to instructional materials. We therefore decline to follow those cases and instead regard those cases which place control over instructional material in school boards as more accurately reflective of federal constitutional law.

We add that while those authorities which we accept hold that the school board's authority over the classroom materials is very broad, it is not entirely unfettered by the Constitution. A board may not design a curriculum to favor a particular religion. *Cary* v. *Board of Education,* 598 F.2d at 544; *Epperson* v. *Arkansas,* 393 U.S. 97, 89 S.Ct. 266, 21 L.Ed.2d 228 (1968). Similarly, any effort by a board to force racial bias or partisan political preference into the classroom would be constitutionally suspect, *Board of Education* v. *Pico,* 457 U.S. at 870–71, 102 S.Ct. at 2810, 73 L.Ed.2d at 449, as would an attempt to exclude discussions of "an entire system of respected human thought." *Epperson* v. *Arkansas,* 393 U.S. at 116, 89 S.Ct. at 276, 21 L.Ed.2d at 241 (Stewart, J. concurring); *Cary* v. *Board of Education,* 598 F.2d at 543. Further, in cases of doubt as to what may and what may not be distributed or taught to students, advance notice may be required before punishment can be imposed. *Epperson* v. *Arkansas,* 393 U.S. at 112, 89 S.Ct. at 274, 21 L.Ed.2d at 239 (Black, J. concurring); *Cary* v. *Board of Education,* 598 F.2d at 541.

This case, however, involves none of the above limitations.[5] To sustain Fisher's position we would have to hold that the advance approval rule is unconstitutional on its face. Such a holding would go far to eliminate a school board's right to control curriculum, a result clearly not required by the First Amendment.

Fisher raises various other contentions which we find to be without merit.[6]

The judgment is *Affirmed.*

COMPTON, J., dissents.
RABINOWITZ, C.J., not participating.
COMPTON, Justice, dissenting in part.

Although I agree with the court's disposition of matters alluded to in n. 6, I cannot agree with its treatment of the principal issue in the case, i.e., whether Fisher's First Amendment rights were violated by the manner in which his use of *The Front Runner* was treated.[1]

Analysis of this issue is made no easier by the fact that neither Brannian, nor anyone else as far as this record discloses, knew just what materials were meant to be encompassed by Policy 6160.1a, how that policy was to be implemented, or by whom. His October memorandum to Fisher merely paraphrases the policy, and admonishes Fisher not to use the book until it has been approved. His January memorandum only refers to Policy 6160.1a, a requirement that the book be approved, and that Fisher is to "submit a copy of the book to me [Brannian] for approval." Since the text of Policy 6160.1a does not require a teacher to do anything, the correspondence leaves one wondering whether it is the school board, the superintendent or Brannian, the principal, from whom approval must be obtained. Further, Brannian cannot unequivocally characterize the material as a textbook or as supplementary printed material, or either, if such a distinction is material to this case. Brannian's unfamiliarity with the terrain may be best understood in light of the total absence in the record of any evidence that anyone was ever required to submit supplementary printed material to anyone for their approval.

James R. Ranney, social studies department head at Lathrop High School and Fisher's supervisor, knew that *The Front Runner* had not been approved, since it had not been submitted to a newly created district wide social studies department curriculum committee for approval. However, Fisher had submitted the book to Ranney for purchase by the school and Ranney had leafed through it. Brannian had declined to purchase it for budgetary reasons. There is no evidence that any books Fisher requested to be purchased were submitted by Ranney to anyone for substantive approval. Furthermore, the policy makes no reference to any departmental curriculum committee.

If the issue before the court was simply whether school boards possess broad authority over curriculum in a secondary education setting, I would have little hesitancy in joining the court's opinion. Certainly as far as the federal Constitution is concerned, *Pico*'s[2] plurality, concurring and dissenting opinions almost conclusively so indicate. This indication is dicta, but strong enough to leave little room for doubt as to the outcome.

However, broad authority over curriculum does not mean that the First Amendment places no restrictions on school board conduct, a point acknowledged by the court. While the court identifies some areas of activity by teachers and students protected by the First Amendment, it neglects to identify those predicates that must exist before a school board may properly override otherwise protected conduct. It is here that the analysis fails.

In this case there is a prior restraint on Fisher's constitutionally protected right. While prior restraints are not unconstitutional *per se*, their invalidity is heavily presumed. *Bantam Books, Inc.* v. *Sullivan*, 372 U.S. 58, 70, 83 S.Ct. 631, 639, 9 L.Ed.2d 584, 593 (1963); *Wilson* v. *Chancellor*, 418 F.Supp. 1358, 1364 (D.Ore. 1976). The school board has established no criteria for determining what texts it will or will not approve, nor any criteria to guide superintendents (or principals or curriculum committees) in the exercise of their responsibility regarding supplementary materials. *Wilson* at 1364. Indeed, the policy is so vague that Brannian cannot even tell us whether *The Front Runner* is a text (and hence required to be approved by the school board) or supplementary printed material (and hence required to be approved by the superintendent).

The policy, such as it is, suffers from yet another defect, that being its failure to provide any review mechanism when a teacher's request for approval of textual or supplementary materials has been denied. Worse, there is no procedure whatsoever for obtaining substantive approval of such materials. Brannian's memorandum to Fisher simply tells him to quit what he is doing. Brannian offers no guidance whatsoever. No written school board policy does, either.

If Policy 6160.1a is not unconstitutional on its face, a point I would not concede, it is unconstitutional as applied to Fisher in this case. None of the predicates for prior restraint of First Amendment rights have been established.

NOTES

1. The trial *de novo* was held pursuant to AS 14.20.205, which provides:

   If a school board reaches a decision unfavorable to a teacher, the teacher is entitled to a de novo trial in the superior court. However, a teacher who has not attained tenure rights is not entitled to judicial review according to this section.

2. *See* Restatement (Second) of Contracts § 84, at 220 (1979); 5 Williston on Contracts § 689, at 309 (3d ed. 1961); *Stephens* v. *State*, 501 P.2d 759, 761 (Alaska 1972); *Fehl-Haber* v. *Nordhagen*, 59 Wash.2d 7, 365 P.2d 607 (1961); *Cottonwood Plaza Associates* v. *Nordale*, 132 Ariz. 228, 644 P.2d 1314, 1319 (Ariz.App.1982); *Bell* v. *Yale Dev. Co.*, 102 Ill.App.3d 108, 57 Ill.Dec. 777, 429 N.E.2d 894 (1981).

3. Fisher does not mention, nor does he place any reliance on the free speech provision of the Alaska Constitution, art. I, sec. 5. Accordingly, we do not address his claim under that provision.

4. *See, eg.,* Developments in the Law—Academic Freedom, 81 Harv.L.Rev. 1045 (1968); Van Alystyne, The Constitutional Rights of Teachers and Professors, 1970 Duke L.J. 841 (1970); Goldstein, The Asserted Constitutional Right of Public School Teachers to Determine What They Teach, 124 U.Pa.L.R. 1293 (1976); Hunter, Curriculum, Pedagogy, and the Constitutional Rights of Teachers in Secondary Schools, 25 Wm & Mary L.Rev. 1 (1983); Diamond, The First Amendment and Public Schools: The Case Against Judicial Intervention, 59 Tex.L.Rev. 477 (1981).

5. The worst that could be said about the school district's refusal to approve *The Front Runner* was that it was motivated by a desire not to accord what was felt to be undue emphasis to a controversial subject. Fisher's supervisor, to whom the book had been presented, testified that he felt the topic should be covered with current materials, periodicals, and newspapers and only a short time should be spent covering it. Fisher's supervisor, and another teacher, also formally reviewed the book and concluded that it was unsuitable because of its explicit descriptions of homosexual acts, objectionable language, and glorification of homosexuality. However, these formal reviews were only conducted after the principal had discovered on January 18th that Fisher was

using the book and thus cannot be regarded as the reasons in fact that the book was not approved.

6. They are that Fisher proved that he was the victim of discrimination because of his teacher's union activities, and that he was not accorded full discovery. The first point is a factual one whose resolution against Fisher is not clearly erroneous. On the second point we find no abuse of discretion.

DISSENTING OPINION NOTES

1. I expressly disassociate myself from the court's venture into fact finding presented in n. 5. What the "worst" is, I suppose, lies like beauty in the eyes of the beholder. One could find from this record that Fisher enjoyed a good reputation with administrators until he became active in union affairs. He was then suspended, but voluntarily reinstated during a superior court trial *de novo*, which the school district lost anyway. Its appeal was dismissed for lack of progress. He was later again suspended for activities arising out of union affairs, but again reinstated.

When Fisher decided to include "gay rights" in his class, Brannian ordered Fisher not to teach it, but recanted on advice of counsel. Right about the time Brannian notified Fisher he was recommending non-retention, Fisher contacted the Fire Marshall about apparently impermissibly chained doors. This upset Brannian, who complained to custodians that he would "get the son-of-a-bitch yet." He did.

The "worst" may thus be that Brannian and other administrators, displeased with Fisher and frightened by the spectre of notoriety arising from teaching too much about "gay rights," used Policy 6160.1a to score a double victory. However, what is "worst" ought not concern us. What the Constitution requires should.

2. *Board of Education, Island Trees Union Free School District No. 26* v. *Pico,* 457 U.S. 853, 102 S.Ct. 2799, 73 L.Ed.2d 435 (1982).

In deciding against a Texas college teacher who had used profanity and epithets in the classroom, the United States Court of Appeals, Fifth Circuit, concluded that the teacher's language was unprotected because it "constituted a deliberate, superfluous attack on a 'captive audience' with no academic purpose or justification." Relying heavily on the United States Supreme Court's *Fraser* decision [the high court deciding against a high school student who has used sexual puns and innuendoes during a speech delivered at a high school assembly], the court of appeals declared: "To the extent that Martin's profanity was considered by the college administration to inhibit his effectiveness as a teacher, it need not be tolerated by the college any more than Fraser's indecent speech to the Bethel School assembly."

Judge Robert Madden Hill, while concurring, rejected the Court's reliance on *Fraser* and argued that the high school setting is significantly different from the college: "The fact that the maturity level of college students is higher than high school students is one factor to consider. In addition, it is worthy to note that attending college is voluntary while attending high school is mandatory. Young adults attend college expecting to be exposed to new views and ideas, including ones that do not mesh with their existing beliefs. In the case at hand, it appears that the students in Martin's economics class voluntarily chose to take the class, and may have voluntarily selected him as their teacher as well."

Martin v. *Parrish*, 805 F.2d 583 (1986)

EDITH HOLLAN JONES, Circuit Judge:

Whether a publicly employed college teacher is constitutionally protected in the abusive use of profanity in the classroom is the most significant issue presented by this appeal. We hold that the Constitution does not shield him and therefore AFFIRM the judgment of the district court.

I. BACKGROUND

Appellant Martin was an economics instructor at Midland College in Midland, Texas. Appellees are the president, vice president, dean and trustees of the college. The dean and vice president originally disciplined Martin in 1983, following a formal student complaint regarding Martin's inveterate use of profane language, including "hell," "damn," and "bullshit", in class. Martin was warned orally and in writing that should his use of profanity in the classroom continue, disciplinary action requiring suspension, termination or both would be recommended. Heedless of the administrators' concerns, Martin continued to curse in class, using words including "bullshit," "hell," "damn," "God damn," and "sucks." Two students filed written complaints concerning Martin's speech in the classroom on June 19, 1984, which included the following statements: "the attitude of the class sucks," "[the attitude] is a bunch of bullshit," "you may think economics is a bunch of bullshit," and "if you don't like the way I teach this God damn course there is the door." Following notice of this outburst, the dean initiated actions to terminate Martin, which culminated, following several administrative steps, in approval by the college's board of trustees.

Martin's subsequent § 1983 lawsuit alleged deprivation of his first amendment right of free speech, abridgement of an alleged right of academic freedom, and denials of due process and equal protection. The jury found in Martin's favor on issues pertaining to free speech[1] and equal protection and awarded damages, but denied his due process claim. The district court granted judgment n.o.v. to the defendants, finding no evidentiary support for the equal protection allegations and concluding that Martin's profanity was not constitutionally protected. Martin appeals all but the due process claim.

II. ANALYSIS

Appellant asserts his language was not obscene, *Roth* v. *United States,* 354 U.S. 476, 77 S.Ct. 1304, 1 L.Ed.2d 1498 (1957), but only profane and as such enjoys constitutional protection unless it caused disruption.[2] *Chaplinsky* v. *New Hampshire,* 315 U.S. 568, 62 S.Ct. 766, 86 L.Ed. 1031 (1942). We find this argument an incomplete and erroneous expression of pertinent First Amendment jurisprudence.

The Constitution protects not simply words but communication, which presupposes a speaker and a listener, and circumscribes this protection for purposes which enhance the functioning of our republican form of government. The "rights" of the speaker are thus always tempered by a consideration of the rights of the audience and the public purpose served, or disserved, by his speech. Appellant's argument, by ignoring his audience and the lack of any public purpose in his offensive epithets, founders on several fronts.

Connick v. *Myers,* 461 U.S. 138, 103 S.Ct. 1684, 75 L.Ed.2d 708 (1983), recently explained the limits of first amendment protection of speech afforded public employees like Martin. The Supreme Court reiterated that the goal of such protection is to prevent suppression of such employees' participation in public affairs and "chilling" of their freedom of political association. 461 U.S. at 145–46, 103 S.Ct. at 1689. It is limited to speech on matters of "public concern," otherwise, government would be hobbled in its regulation of employment conditions, and public employees would enjoy an immunity from the consequences of their speech not shared by anyone in the private sector. If the offending speech does not bear upon a matter of public concern, "it is unnecessary for us to scrutinize the reasons for [the] discharge." *Connick,* 461 U.S. at 147, 103 S.Ct. at 1690. Moreover, "whether an employee's speech addresses a matter of public concern must be determined by the content, form, and context of a given statement. . . . " *Id.*[3]

There is no doubt that Martin's epithets did not address a matter of public concern. One student described Martin's June 19, 1984, castigation of the class as an explosion, an unprovoked, extremely offensive, downgrading of the entire class. In highly derogatory and indecent terms, Martin implied that the students were inferior because they were accustomed to taking courses from inferior, part-time instructors at Midland College. The profanity described Martin's attitude toward his students, hardly a matter that, but for this lawsuit, would occasion public discussion. Appellant has not argued that his profanity was for any purpose other than cussing out his students as an expression of frustration with their progress—to "motivate" them—and has thereby impliedly conceded his case under *Connick.*

Ignoring that his audience consisted of students also led to Martin's undoing. Indecent language and profanity may be regulated in the schools, *Bethel School District No. 403* v. *Fraser,* ——U.S.——, 106 S.Ct. 3159, 92 L.Ed.2d 549 (1986), and over the public airwaves. *FCC* v. *Pacifica Foundation,* 438 U.S. 726, 98 S.Ct. 3026, 57 L.Ed.2d 1073 (1978). The policies leading to affirmation of some speech restrictions in these circumstances support the college's termination of Martin. In *Bethel,* the Supreme Court affirmed disciplinary action against a high school senior who, against the advice of teachers and in violation of school rules, gave a sexually explicit and vulgar speech to a student assembly. As the majority opinion states,

> "Surely it is a highly appropriate function of public school education to prohibit the use of vulgar and offensive terms in public discourse. Indeed, the 'fundamental values necessary to the maintenance of a democratic political system' disfavors the use of terms of debate highly offensive or highly threatening to others. Nothing in the Constitution prohibits the states from insisting that certain modes of expression are inappropriate and subject to sanction."

Bethel, 106 S.Ct. at 3165 (citations omitted).

Moreover, the First Amendment does not prevent schools from determining "that the essential terms of civil, mature conduct cannot be conveyed in a school that tolerates lewd, indecent or offensive speech and conduct." *Id.*

Bethel admittedly involved a high school audience and it may be suggested that its justification for speech restraints rests largely on this fact. Nevertheless, we view the role of higher education as no less pivotal to our national interest. It carries on the process of instilling in our citizens necessary democratic virtues, among which are civility and moderation. It is necessary to the nurture of knowledge and resourcefulness that undergird our economic and political system. Repeated failure by a member of the educational staff of Midland College to exhibit professionalism degrades his important mission and detracts from the subjects he is trying to teach. The school officials uniformly made this point at trial, testifying that use of profanity in the classroom is unprofessional and hinders instruction. Parrish, the college president, emphasized that it is vital for the teacher to have respect for the students, especially when he is in an authority role. Parrish further observed that a teacher's conduct can strongly influence the students, even at the college level. Indirectly confirming these views, one student described Martin's outpouring as unprofessional and stated that he had lost interest in economics as a result of Martin's belittling comments. Another student expressed his reticence to asking questions in class for fear of Martin's ridicule. To the extent that Martin's profanity was considered by the college administration to inhibit his effectiveness as a teacher, it need not be tolerated by the college any more than Fraser's indecent speech to the Bethel school assembly.[4]

Martin's termination also draws support from *FCC* v. *Pacifica Foundation, supra,* in which the Supreme Court upheld an FCC order disapproving radio broadcast of a vulgar and indecent George Carlin monologue. A principal ground for the Court's conclusion was the fact that, going into private homes over the airwaves, the broadcast was thrusting patently offensive speech upon an unwilling, "captive" audience, likely including minors. 438 U.S. at 749–51, 98 S.Ct. at 3039–3040. It is true that vulgarity in Central Park may be tolerated and protected by the First Amendment because its unwilling viewer or listener has the right to turn away. *Cohen* v. *California,* 403 U.S. 15, 22–23, 91 S.Ct. 1780, 1787, 29 L.Ed.2d 284 (1971); *see also Erznoznik* v. *Jacksonville,* 422 U.S. 205, 95 S.Ct. 2268, 45 L.Ed.2d 125 (1975). However, we hold that the students in Martin's classroom, who paid to be taught and not vilified in indecent terms, are subject to the holding of *Pacifica,* which, like *Cohen,* recognizes that surroundings and context are essential, case-by-case determinants of the constitutional protection accorded to indecent language. Martin's language is unprotected under the reasoning of these cases because, taken in context, it constituted a deliberate, superfluous attack on a "captive audience" with no academic purpose or justification.

Were Martin an assistant district attorney who repeatedly used profanity in the courtroom, we have no doubt that he could be terminated for unprofessional behavior. Were he a member of Congress, such language could result in censure. *Bethel,* 106 S.Ct. at 3164. For the foregoing reasons, we conclude his status as a college teacher is no less sensitive to the use of such language than that of a courtroom lawyer or member of Congress.

Martin also challenges the district court's judgment n.o.v. on the issue of equal protection. We have reviewed the record and find that Martin failed to introduce evidence that he had been treated differently from other similarly situated persons, or even that there were others similarly situated. The district court correctly held for the defendants on this point.

The judgment of the district court is AFFIRMED.

ROBERT MADDEN HILL, Circuit Judge, concurring in the judgment.

I concur in the judgment because I believe that *Connick* v. *Myers,* 461 U.S. 138, 103 S.Ct. 1684, 75 L. Ed.2d 708 (1983), controls this case. I write separately, however, because I cannot agree with the majority's unnecessary dicta extending the rationale of *Pacifica, Bethel,* and *Pico* to a university setting.

Connick states that "when a public employee speaks not as a citizen upon matters of public concern, but instead as an employee upon matters only of personal interest, absent the most unusual circumstances, a federal court is not the appropriate forum in which to review the wisdom of a personnel decision taken by a public agency allegedly in reaction to the employee's behavior." *Connick,* 461 U.S. at 147, 103 S.Ct. at 1690. Whether an employee's speech addresses a matter of public concern must be determined "by the content, form and context of a given statement, as revealed by the whole record." *Id.* at 147–48, 103 S.Ct. at 1690.

The majority indicates that the profane nature of Martin's words precludes a finding that a matter of public concern is involved. The use of profane words by themselves, in my opinion, does not preclude a finding that an employee's speech addresses a matter of public concern. Instead, as *Connick* indicates, the record *as a whole* must be examined. Looking at Martin's comments as a whole, I agree with the majority's conclusion that they do not address a matter of public concern. While some of Martin's comments in isolation could be construed as challenging the attitude of the class in its approach to economics, the derogatory nature of the comments overall convinces me that no matter of public concern is involved. For the same reason, I agree with the majority that the question of Martin's first amendment right to "academic freedom" does not need to be reached in this case. While some of the comments arguably bear on economics and could be viewed as relevant to Martin's role as a teacher in motivating the interest of his students, his remarks *as a whole* are unrelated to economics and devoid of any educational function. Thus, I agree with the majority that Martin's discharge did not violate his first amendment rights.

Although I would end the analysis at this point, the majority proceeds to focus on the audience that Martin was addressing, and, citing three Supreme Court cases involving high schools and young children, concludes that the rationale of those cases is equally applicable to a college or university setting. I do not feel it is necessary to reach this issue; furthermore, an examination of the three cases involved raises questions about the majority's conclusion.

The majority first cites *Bethel School District No. 403* v. *Fraser,* 478 U.S.——, 106 S.Ct. 3159, 92 L.Ed.2d 549 (1986), as support for the proposition that "indecent language and profanity may be regulated in the schools." *Ante* at 585. Although the majority concedes that *Bethel* involved a high school audience, it extends the rationale of *Bethel* to colleges—without any case support—because it "view[s] the role of higher education as no less pivotal to our national interest." *Id.* at 585. While I agree with the majority's view as to the importance of higher education, my reading of *Bethel* indicates that the Court specifically limited the reach of its holding to high school students. In *Bethel,* the Court noted that the speech in question "could well be seriously damaging to its less mature audience, many of whom were only 14 years old and on the threshold of awareness of human sexuality." 478 U.S. at ——-——, 106 S.Ct. at 3164-65, 92 L.Ed.2d at 558-59. The Court went on to note that "[a] *high school* assembly or classroom is no place for a sexually explicit monologue directed towards an unsuspecting audience of *teenage students."* Id. 478 U.S. at ——, 106 S.Ct. at 3166, 92 L.Ed.2d at 560 (emphasis added). Justice Brennan's concurring opinion is also replete with references which indicate that the rationale of *Bethel* is limited to a high school setting. *See* 478 U.S. ——-——, 106 S.Ct. 3167-68, 92 L.Ed.2d 561-63 (Brennan, J., concurring).

The majority also cites *FCC* v. *Pacifica Foundation,* 438 U.S. 726, 98 S.Ct. 3026, 57 L.Ed.2d 1073 (1978), as support for its conclusion that Martin's first amendment rights were not infringed. In the majority's view, *Pacifica* is relevant because Martin's college students, like the radio audience in *Pacifica,* are a "captive" audience. The majority asserts that Martin's words "constituted a deliberate, superfluous attack on a 'captive audience' with no academic purpose or justification." *Id.* at 586. In addition to the fact that I think some of Martin's words have a possible "academic purpose," the majority again, in my view, reads the holding of that case too broadly. The *Bethel* court stated that *Pacifica* was a case where the Court "recognized an interest in protecting *minors* from exposure to vulgar and offensive spoken language." *Bethel,* 478 U.S. at ——, 106 S.Ct. at 3165, 92 L.Ed.2d at 559 (emphasis added). The opinion in *Pacifica* emphasized the fact that children were undoubtedly in the audience at the time of the broadcast containing indecent language. *See Pacifica,* 438 U.S. at 748 & n. 28, 98 S.Ct. at 3040 & n. 28, 57 L.Ed.2d at 1093-94 & n. 28. In addition, the language at issue in *Pacifica* was more profane than the language which Martin used before his students. The language which Martin used is no worse than that which a person walking down the streets of most American cities today would hear. Consequently, I do not believe that *Pacifica* is as broad as the majority suggests.

Finally, the majority relies on *Board of Education* v. *Pico,* 457 U.S. 853, 102 S.Ct. 2799, 73 L.Ed.2d 435 (1982), as support for its position that courts should defer to the judgment of the other faculty members at Midland College. I think the majority's interpretation of *Pico* is, at least, overbroad and, at worst, unsup-

ported by the language in the opinion. First, as in the other cases the majority relies on, *Pico* involved the question of whether the First Amendment limits the discretion of school board officials as it relates to *junior high* and *high school* students, not college students as are involved here. Second, I certainly do not disagree with the majority's statement that local school officials, and not the courts, should run the nation's public school systems. Even at the high school level, however, the Supreme Court has recognized that school officials do not have unlimited discretion. "It can hardly be argued that either students or teachers shed their constitutional rights to freedom of speech or expression at the schoolhouse gate." *Tinker* v. *Des Moines School District,* 393 U.S. 503, 506, 89 S.Ct. 733, 736, 21 L.Ed.2d 731 (1969).

Ultimately, as the majority implicitly concedes earlier in its opinion, *ante* n. 1, it is up to the courts and not the Midland College faculty to determine whether the first amendment rights of Martin have been infringed. The majority's approach, however, would appear to preclude a court from reviewing the judgment of an administrator that the use of profanity by a faculty member in the course of his teaching was undesirable because it would lower the "esteem" of the institution. The majority indicates that we must defer to school officials in "all but the most sensitive constitutional areas." *Ante* at n. 4. I fail to see a more sensitive constitutional area, however, than an individual's first amendment rights. The majority's citations from various Supreme Court cases do not convince me that their position is correct.

The largest problem in my view with the majority's extension of cases like *Bethel* and *Pico* is that the majority does not give sufficient weight to the differences between the high school instructional setting involved in the cases it cites, and the college instructional setting involved in this case. The purpose of education through high school is to instill basic knowledge, to lay the foundations to enable a student to learn greater knowledge, and to teach basic social, moral, and political values. A college education, on the other hand, deals more with challenging a student's ideas and concepts on a given subject matter. The college atmosphere enables students to rethink their views on various issues in an intellectual atmosphere which forces students to analyze their basic beliefs. Thus, high school is necessarily more structured than college, where a more free-wheeling experience is both contemplated and needed. What might be instructionally unacceptable in high school might be fully acceptable in college.

Consequently, the standard for examining statements in a high school setting such as that involved in *Bethel* should not necessarily be the same as in a college setting such as Midland. The fact that the maturity level of college students is higher than high school students is one factor to consider. In addition, it is worthy to note that attending college is voluntary while attending high school is mandatory. Young adults attend college expecting to be exposed to new views and ideas, including ones that do not mesh with their existing beliefs. In the case at hand, it appears that the students in Martin's economics class voluntarily chose to take his class, and may have voluntarily selected him as their teacher as well. It is possible, for example, that the students could have changed teachers or classes if they were dissatisfied with Martin's performance. *Cf. Pacifica,* 438 U.S. at 748 n. 27, 98 S.Ct. at 3040 n. 27, 57 L.Ed.2d at 1093 n. 27 ("Outside the home, the balance between the offensive speaker and the unwilling audience may sometimes tip in favor of the speaker, requiring the offended listener to turn away.")

I do not decide the scope of *Bethel, Pacifica* and *Pico.* Unlike the majority, however, I do not think that these cases as written are applicable to a university setting. Furthermore, I believe that this case can be properly disposed of on the basis of *Connick.*

NOTES

1. Some of the jury interrogatories regarding the free speech issue asked for a balancing of Martin's language between its usefulness to his instruction and its disruptive tendency. Such balancing involves a question of law

for the court. *Connick* v. *Myers,* 461 U.S. 138, 199 n. 7, 103 S.Ct. 1684, 1690 n. 7, 75 L.Ed.2d 708 (1983).

2. Appellant also argues vigorously that he has a first amendment right to "academic freedom" that permits use of the language in question. It is, however, undisputed that such language was not germane to the subject matter in his class and had no educational function. Thus, as in *Kelleher* v. *Flawn,* 761 F.2d 1079, 1085 (5th Cir. 1985), we find it unnecessary to reach this issue.

3. Only if the speech passes this first test of protection does the court "balance" the employee's rights against any disruptive effect on the employer's mission. *Connick,* 461 U.S. at 151–55, 103 S.Ct. at 1692–94.

4. Our conclusion that a public college teacher's classroom use of profanity is unprofessional and may be prohibited by the school relies on the judgment of the Midland College administrators who testified at trial. As the Supreme Court held in *Board of Education* v. *Pico,* 457 U.S. 853, 864–65, 102 S.Ct. 2799, 2806, 73 L.Ed.2d 435 (1982), federal courts should ordinarily decline to intervene in the affairs of the public schools, where the "comprehensive authority of States and of school officials . . . to prescribe and control conduct has historically been acknowledged". This rule has been enforced in all but the most sensitive constitutional areas. Several Midland College administrators testified on the basis of strong educational credentials and years of experience in their vocation and in the local community. On their shoulders rest the college's educational standards and its utility as a publicly-supported institution. The federal courts thus appropriately respect the professional conclusion of those whose past and future careers depend upon the esteem due to Midland College. "The determination of what manner of speech in the classroom . . . is inappropriate properly rests with the school board." *Bethel,* 106 S.Ct. at 3165.

T HE United States Supreme Court, in a 7–2 decision, declares unconstitutional Louisiana's "Creation Science" act which forbids the teaching of the theory of evolution in public elementary and secondary schools unless accompanied by instruction in the theory of "Creation Science." Delivering the opinion of the Court, Justice Brennan asserts: "Even if 'academic freedom' is read to mean 'teaching all of the evidence' with respect to the origin of human beings, the act does not further this purpose. The goal of providing a more comprehensive science curriculum is not furthered either by outlawing the teaching of evolution or by requiring the teaching of creation science. . . . It is clear that requiring schools to teach creation science with evolution does not advance academic freedom. The act does not grant teachers a flexibility that they did not already possess to supplant the present science curriculum with the presentation of theories, besides evolution, about the origin of life."

Edwards v. *Aguillard*, 107 S.Ct. 2573 (1987)

Justice BRENNAN delivered the opinion of the Court.

The question for decision is whether Louisiana's "Balanced Treatment for Creation-Science and Evolution-Science in Public School Instruction" Act (Creationism Act), La. Rev. Stat. Ann. §§ 17:286.1–17:286.7 (West 1982), is facially invalid as violative of the Establishment Clause of the First Amendment.

I

The Creationism Act forbids the teaching of the theory of evolution in public schools unless accompanied by instruction in "creation science." § 17:286.4A. No school is required to teach evolution or creation science. If either is taught, however, the other must also be taught. *Ibid.* The theories of evolution and creation science are statutorily defined as "the scientific evidences for [creation or evolution] and inferences from those scientific evidences." §§ 17.286.3 (2) and (3).

Appellees, who include parents of children attending Louisiana public schools, Louisiana teachers, and religious leaders, challenged the constitutionality of the Act in District Court, seeking an injunction and declaratory relief.[1] Appellants, Louisiana officials charged with implementing the Act, defended on the ground that the purpose of the Act is to protect a legitimate secular interest, namely, academic freedom.[2] Appellees attacked the Act as facially invalid because it violated the Establishment Clause and made a motion for summary judgment. The District Court granted the motion. *Aguillard* v. *Treen*, 634 F.Supp. 426 (ED La. 1985). The court held that there

can be no valid secular reason for prohibiting the teaching of evolution, a theory historically opposed by some religious denominations. The court further concluded that "the teaching of 'creation-science' and 'creationism,' as contemplated by the statute, involves teaching 'tailored to the principles' of a particular religious sect or group of sects." *Id.*, at 427 (citing *Epperson* v. *Arkansas,* 393 U.S. 97, 106 (1968)). The District Court therefore held that the Creationism Act violated the Establishment Clause either because it prohibited the teaching of evolution or because it required the teaching of creation science with the purpose of advancing a particular religious doctrine.

The Court of Appeals affirmed. 765 F.2d 1251 (CA5 1985). The court observed that the statute's avowed purpose of protecting academic freedom was inconsistent with requiring, upon risk of sanction, the teaching of creation science whenever evolution is taught. *Id.,* at 1257. The court found that the Louisiana legislature's actual intent was "to discredit evolution by counterbalancing its teaching at every turn with the teaching of creationism, a religious belief." *Ibid.* Because the Creationism Act was thus a law furthering a particular religious belief, the Court of Appeals held that the Act violated the Establishment Clause. A suggestion for rehearing en banc was denied over a dissent. 778 F.2d 225 (CA5 1985). We noted probable jurisdiction, 476 U.S.——(1986), and now affirm.

II

The Establishment Clause forbids the enactment of any law "respecting an establishment of religion."[3]

The Court has applied a three-pronged test to determine whether legislation comports with the Establishment Clause. First, the legislature must have adopted the law with a secular purpose. Second, the statute's principal or primary effect must be one that neither advances nor inhibits religion. Third, the statute must not result in an excessive entanglement of government with religion. *Lemon* v. *Kurtzman,* 403 U.S. 602, 612–613 (1971).[4] State action violates the Establishment Clause if it fails to satisfy any of these prongs.

In this case, the Court must determine whether the Establishment Clause was violated in the special context of the public elementary and secondary school system. States and local school boards are generally afforded considerable discretion in operating public schools. See *Bethel School District No. 403* v. *Fraser,* 478 U.S.——, —— (1986); *id.,* at ——(BRENNAN, J., concurring in judgment); *Tinker* v. *Des Moines Independent Community School Dist.,* 393 U.S. 503, 507 (1969). "At the same time . . . we have necessarily recognized that the discretion of the States and local school boards in matters of education must be exercised in a manner that comports with the transcendent imperatives of the First Amendment." *Board of Education* v. *Pico,* 457 U.S. 853, 864 (1982).

The Court has been particularly vigilant in monitoring compliance with the Establishment Clause in elementary and secondary schools. Families entrust public schools with the education of their children, but condition their trust on the understanding that the classroom will not purposely be used to advance religious views that may conflict with the private beliefs of the student and his or her family. Students in such institutions are impressionable and their attendance is involuntary. See, *e.g., Grand Rapids School Dist.* v. *Ball,* 473 U.S. 373, 383 (1985); *Wallace* v. *Jaffree,* 472 U.S. 38, 60, n. 51 (1985); *Meek* v. *Pittenger,* 421 U.S. 349, 369 (1975); *Abington School Dist.* v. *Schempp,* 374 U.S. 203, 252–253 (1963) (BRENNAN, J., concurring). The State exerts great authority and coercive power through mandatory attendance requirements, and because of the students' emulation of teachers as role models and the children's susceptibility to peer pressure.[5] See *Bethel School Dist. No. 403* v. *Fraser, supra,* at ——; *Wallace* v. *Jaffree, supra,* at 81 (O'CONNOR, J., concurring in judgment). Furthermore,

"[t]the public school is at once the symbol of our democracy and the most pervasive means for promoting our common destiny. In no activity of the State is it more vital to keep out divisive forces than in its schools. . . . " *Illinois ex rel. McCollum* v. *Board of Education,* 333 U.S. 203, 231 (1948) (opinion of Frankfurter, J.).

Consequently, the Court has been required often to invalidate statutes which advance religion in public elementary and secondary schools. See, *e.g., Grand Rapids School Dist.* v. *Ball, supra* (school district's use of religious school teachers in public schools); *Wallace* v. *Jaffree, supra* (Alabama statute authorizing moment of silence for school prayer); *Stone* v. *Graham,* 449 U.S. 39 (1980) (posting copy of Ten Commandments on public classroom wall); *Epperson* v. *Arkansas,* 393 U.S. 97 (1968) (statute forbidding teaching of evolution); *Abington School District* v. *Schempp, supra* (daily reading of Bible); *Engel* v. *Vitale,* 370 U.S. 421, 430 (1962) (recitation of "denominationally neutral" prayer).

Therefore, in employing the three-pronged *Lemon* test, we must do so mindful of the particular concerns that arise in the context of public elementary and secondary schools. We now turn to the evaluation of the Act under the *Lemon* test.

III

Lemon's first prong focuses on the purpose that animated adoption of the Act. "The purpose prong of the *Lemon* test asks whether government's actual purpose is to endorse or disapprove of religion." *Lynch* v. *Donnelly,* 465 U.S. 668, 690 (1984) (O'CONNOR, J., concurring). A governmental intention to promote religion is clear when the State enacts a law to serve a religious purpose. This intention may be evidenced by promotion of religion in general, see *Wallace* v. *Jaffree, supra,* at 52–53 (Establishment Clause protects individual freedom of conscience "to select any religious faith or none at all"), or by advancement of a particular religious belief, *e.g., Stone* v. *Graham, supra,* at 41 (invalidating requirement to post Ten Commandments, which are "undeniably a sacred text in the Jewish and Christian faiths") (footnote omitted); *Epperson* v. *Arkansas, supra,* at 106 (holding that banning the teaching of evolution in public schools violates the First Amendment since "teaching and learning" must not "be tailored to the principles or prohibitions of any religious sect or dogma"). If the law was enacted for the purpose of endorsing religion, "no consideration of the second or third criteria [of *Lemon*] is necessary." *Wallace* v. *Jaffree, supra,* at 56. In this case, the petitioners have identified no clear secular purpose for the Louisiana Act.

True, the Act's stated purpose is to protect academic freedom. La. Rev. Stat. Ann. § 17:286.2 (West 1982). This phrase might, in common parlance, be understood as referring to enhancing the freedom of teachers to teach what they will. The Court of Appeals, however, correctly concluded that the Act was not designed to further that goal.[6] We find no merit in the State's argument that the "legislature may not [have] use[d] the terms 'academic freedom' in the correct legal sense. They might have [had] in mind, instead, a basic concept of fairness; teaching all of the evidence." Tr. of Oral Arg. 60. Even if "academic freedom" is read to mean "teaching all of the evidence" with respect to the origin of human beings, the Act does not further this purpose. The goal of providing a more comprehensive science curriculum is not furthered either by outlawing the teaching of evolution or by requiring the teaching of creation science.

A

While the Court is normally deferential to a State's articulation of a secular purpose, it is required that the statement of such purpose be sincere and not a sham. See *Wallace* v. *Jaffree*, 472 U.S., at 64 (POWELL, J., concurring); *id.*, at 75 (O'CONNOR, J., concurring in judgment); *Stone* v. *Graham, supra,* at 41; *Abington School District* v. *Schempp*, 374 U.S., at 223–224. As JUSTICE O'CONNOR stated in *Wallace*: "It is not a trivial matter, however, to require that the legislature manifest a secular purpose and omit all sectarian endorsements from its laws. That requirement is precisely tailored to the Establishment Clause's purpose of assuring that Government not intentionally endorse religion or a religious practice." 472 U.S., at 75 (concurring in judgment).

It is clear from the legislative history that the purpose of the legislative sponsor, Senator Bill Keith, was to narrow the science curriculum. During the legislative hearings, Senator Keith stated: "My preference would be that neither [creationism nor evolution] be taught." 2 App. E621. Such a ban on teaching does not promote—indeed, it undermines—the provision of a comprehensive scientific education.

It is equally clear that requiring schools to teach creation science with evolution does not advance academic freedom. The Act does not grant teachers a flexibility that they did not already possess to supplant the present science curriculum with the presentation of theories, besides evolution, about the origin of life. Indeed, the Court of Appeals found that no law prohibited Louisiana public schoolteachers from teaching any scientific theory. 765 F.2d, at 1257. As the president of the Louisiana Science Teachers Association testified, "[a]ny scientific concept that's based on established fact can be included in our curriculum already, and no legislation allowing this is necessary." 2 App. E616. The Act provides Louisiana schoolteachers with no new authority. Thus the stated purpose is not furthered by it.

The Alabama statute held unconstitutional in *Wallace* v. *Jaffree, supra,* is analogous. In *Wallace,* the State characterized its new law as one designed to provide a one-minute period for meditation. We rejected that stated purpose as insufficient, because a previously adopted Alabama law already provided for such a one-minute period. Thus, in this case, as in

Wallace, "[a]ppellants have not identified any secular purpose that was not fully served by [existing state law] before the enactment of [the statute in question]." 472 U.S., at 59.

Furthermore, the goal of basic "fairness" is hardly furthered by the Act's discriminatory preference for the teaching of creation science and against the teaching of evolution.[7] While requiring that curriculum guides be developed for creation science, the Act says nothing of comparable guides for evolution. La. Rev. Stat. Ann. § 17:286.7A (West 1982). Similarly, research services are supplied for creation science but not for evolution. § 17:286.7B. Only "creation scientists" can serve on the panel that supplies the resource services. *Ibid.* The Act forbids school boards to discriminate against anyone who "chooses to be a creation-scientist" or to teach "creationism," but fails to protect those who choose to teach evolution or any other non-creation science theory, or who refuse to teach creation science. § 17:286.4C.

If the Louisiana legislature's purpose was solely to maximize the comprehensiveness and effectiveness of science instruction, it would have encouraged the teaching of all scientific theories about the origins of humankind.[8] But under the Act's requirements, teachers who were once free to teach any and all facets of this subject are now unable to do so. Moreover, the Act fails even to ensure that creation science will be taught, but instead requires the teaching of this theory only when the theory of evolution is taught. Thus we agree with the Court of Appeals' conclusion that the Act does not serve to protect academic freedom, but has the distinctly different purpose of discrediting "evolution by counterbalancing its teaching at every turn with the teaching of creation science. . . . " 765 F.2d, at 1257.

B

Stone v. *Graham,* invalidated the State's requirement that the Ten Commandments be posted in public classrooms. "The Ten Commandments are undeniably a sacred text in the Jewish and Christian faiths, and no legislative recitation of a supposed secular purpose can blind us to that fact." 449 U.S., at 41 (footnote omitted). As a result, the contention that the law was designed to provide instruction on a "fundamental legal code" was "not sufficient to avoid conflict with the First Amendment." *Ibid.* Similarly *Abington School District* v. *Schempp* held unconstitutional a statute "requiring the selection and reading at the opening of the school day of verses from the Holy Bible and the recitation of the Lord's Prayer by the students in unison," despite the proffer of such secular purposes as the "promotion of moral values, the contradiction to the materialistic trends of our times, the perpetuation of our institutions and the teaching of literature." 374 U.S., at 223.

As in *Stone* v. *Abington,* we need not be blind in this case to the legislature's preeminent religious purpose in enacting this statute. There is a historic and contemporaneous link between the teachings of certain religious denominations and the teaching of evolution.[9] It was this link that concerned the Court in *Epperson* v. *Arkansas,* 393 U.S. 97 (1968), which also involved a facial challenge to a statute regulating the teaching of evolution. In that case, the Court reviewed an Arkansas statute that made it unlawful for an instructor to teach evolution or to use a textbook that referred to this scientific theory. Although the Arkansas anti-evolution law did not explicitly state its predominate religious purpose, the Court could not ignore that "[t]the statute was a product of the upsurge of 'fundamentalist' religious fervor" that has long viewed this particular scientific theory as contradicting the literal interpretation of the Bible. *Id.,* at 98, 106–107.[10] After reviewing the history of anti-evolution statutes, the Court determined that "there can be no doubt that the motivation for the [Arkansas] law was the same [as other anti-evolution statutes]: to suppress the teaching of a theory which, it was thought, 'denied' the divine creation of man." *Id.,* at 109. The Court found that there can be no legitimate state interest in protecting particular religions from scientific views "distasteful to them," *id.,* at 107 (citation omitted), and concluded "that the First Amendment does not permit the State to require that teaching and learning must be tailored to the principles or prohibitions of any religious sect or dogma," *id.,* at 106.

These same historic and contemporaneous antagonisms between the teachings of certain religious denominations and the teaching of evolution are present in this case. The preeminent purpose of the Louisiana legislature was clearly to advance the religious viewpoint that a supernatural being created humankind.[11] The term "creation science" was defined as embracing this particular religious doctrine by those responsible for the passage of the Creationism Act. Senator Keith's leading expert on creation science, Edward Boudreaux, testified at the legislative hearings that the theory of creation science included belief in the existence of a supernatural creator. See 1 App. E421–422 (noting that "creation scientists" point to high probability that life was "created by an intelligent mind").[12] Senator Keith also cited testimony from other experts to support the creation-science view that "a creator [was] responsible for the universe and everything in it."[13] 2 App. E497. The legislative history therefore reveals that the term "creation science," as contemplated by the legislature that adopted this Act, embodies the religious belief that a super-

natural creator was responsible for the creation of humankind.

Furthermore, it is not happenstance that the legislature required the teaching of a theory that coincided with this religious view. The legislative history documents that the Act's primary purpose was to change the science curriculum of public schools in order to provide persuasive advantage to a particular religious doctrine that rejects the factual basis of evolution in its entirety. The sponsor of the Creationism Act, Senator Keith, explained during the legislative hearings that his disdain for the theory of evolution resulted from the support that evolution supplied to views contrary to his own religious beliefs. According to Senator Keith, the theory of evolution was consonant with the "cardinal principle[s] of religious humanism, secular humanism, theological liberalism, aetheistism [*sic*]." 1 App. E312–313; see also 2 App. E499–500. The state senator repeatedly stated that scientific evidence supporting his religious views should be included in the public school curriculum to redress the fact that the theory of evolution incidentally coincided with what he characterized as religious beliefs antithetical to his own.[14] The legislation therefore sought to alter the science curriculum to reflect endorsement of a religious view that is antagonistic to the theory of evolution.

In this case, the purpose of the Creationism Act was to restructure the science curriculum to conform with a particular religious viewpoint. Out of many possible science subjects taught in the public schools, the legislature chose to affect the teaching of the one scientific theory that historically has been opposed by certain religious sects. As in *Epperson,* the legislature passed the Act to give preference to those religious groups which have as one of their tenets the creation of humankind by a divine creator. The "overriding fact" that confronted the Court in *Epperson* was "that Arkansas' law selects from the body of knowledge a particular segment which it proscribes for the sole reason that it is deemed to conflict with . . . a particular interpretation of the Book of Genesis by a particular religious group." 393 U.S., at 103. Similarly, the Creationism Act is designed *either* to promote the theory of creation science which embodies a particular religious tenet by requiring that creation science be taught whenever evolution is taught *or* to prohibit the teaching of a scientific theory disfavored by certain religious sects by forbidding the teaching of evolution when creation science is not also taught. The Establishment Clause, however, "forbids *alike* the preference of a religious doctrine *or* the prohibition of theory which is deemed antagonistic to a particular dogma." *Id.,* at 106–107 (emphasis added). Because the primary purpose of the Creationism Act is to advance a particular religious belief, the Act endorses religion in violation of the First Amendment.

We do not imply that a legislature could never require that scientific critiques of prevailing scientific theories be taught. Indeed, the Court acknowledged in *Stone* that its decision forbidding the posting of the Ten Commandments did not mean that no use could ever be made of the Ten Commandments, or that the Ten Commandments played an exclusively religious role in the history of Western Civilization. 449 U.S., at 42. In a similar way, teaching a variety of scientific theories about the origins of humankind to school-children might be validly done with the clear secular intent of enhancing the effectiveness of science instruction. But because the primary purpose of the Creationism Act is to endorse a particular religious doctrine, the Act furthers religion in violation of the Establishment Clause.[15]

IV

Appellants contend that genuine issues of material fact remain in dispute, and therefore the District Court erred in granting summary judgment. Federal Rule of Civil Procedure 56(c) provides that summary judgment "shall be rendered forthwith if the pleadings, depositions, answers to interrogatories, and admisions on file, together with the affidavits, if any, show that there is no genuine issue as to any material fact and that the moving party is entitled to a judgment as a matter of law." A court's finding of improper purpose behind a statute is appropriately determined by the statute on its face, its legislative history, or its interpretation by a responsible administrative agency. See *e.g., Wallace* v. *Jaffree,* 472 U.S., at 56–61; *Stone* v. *Graham,* 449 U.S., at 41–42; *Epperson* v. *Arkansas,* 393 U.S., at 103–109. The plain meaning of the statute's words, enlightened by their context and the contemporaneous legislative history, can control the determination of legislative purpose. *See Wallace* v. *Jaffree, supra,* at 74 (O'CONNOR, J., concurring in judgment); *Richards* v. *United States,* 369 U.S. 1, 9 (1962); *Jay* v. *Boyd,* 351 U.S. 345, 357 (1956). Moreover, in determining the legislative purpose of a statute, the Court has also considered the historical context of the statute, *e.g., Epperson* v. *Arkansas, supra,* and the specific sequence of events leading to passage of the statute, *e.g., Arlington Heights,* v. *Metropolitan Housing Corp.,* 429 U.S. 252 (1977).

In this case, appellees' motion for summary judgment rested on the plain language of the Creationism Act, the legislative history and historical context of the Act, the specific sequence of events leading to the passage of the Act, the State Board's report on a survey of school superintendents, and the correspondence between the Act's legislative sponsor and its key witnesses. Appellants contend that affidavits made by two scientists, two theologians, and an education administrator raise a genuine issue of material fact and that summary judgment was therefore barred. The affidavits define creation science as "origin through abrupt appearance in complex form" and allege that such a viewpoint constitutes a true scientific theory. See App. to Brief for Appellants A–7 to A–40.

We agree with the lower courts that these affidavits do not raise a genuine issue of material fact. The existence of "uncontroverted affidavits" does not bar summary judgment.[16] Moreover, the postenactment testimony of outside experts is of little use in determining the Louisiana legislature's purpose in enacting this statute. The Louisiana legislature did hear and rely on scientific experts in passing the bill,[17] but none of the persons making the affidavits produced by the appellants participated in or contributed to the enactment of the law or its implementation.[18] The District Court, in its discretion, properly concluded that a Monday-morning "battle of the experts" over possible technical meanings of terms in the statute would not illuminate the contemporaneous purpose of the Louisiana legislature when it made the law.[19] We therefore conclude that the District Court did not err in finding that appellants failed to raise a genuine issue of material fact, and in granting summary judgment.[20]

V

The Louisiana Creationism Act advances a religious doctrine by requiring either the banishment of the theory of evolution from public school classrooms or the presentation of a religious viewpoint that rejects evolution in its entirety. The Act violates the Establishment Clause of the First Amendment because it seeks to employ the symbolic and financial support of government to achieve a religious purpose. The judgment of the Court of Appeals therefore is

Affirmed.

NOTES

1. Appellants, the Louisiana Governor, the Attorney General, the State Superintendent, the State Department of Education and the St. Tammany Parish School Board, agreed not to implement the Creationism Act pending the final outcome of this litigation. The Louisiana Board of Elementary and Secondary Education, and the Orleans Parish School Board were among the original defendants in the suit but both later realigned as plaintiffs.
2. The District Court initially stayed the action pending the resolution of a separate lawsuit brought by the Act's legislative sponsor and others for declaratory and injunctive relief. After the separate suit was dismissed on

jurisdictional grounds, *Keith* v. *Louisiana Department of Education,* 553 F.Supp. 295 (MD La. 1982), the District Court lifted its stay in this case and held that the Creationism Act violated the Louisiana Constitution. The court ruled that the State Constitution grants authority over the public school system to the Board of Elementary and Secondary Education rather that the state legislature. On appeal, the Court of Appeals certified the question to the Louisiana Supreme Court, which found the Creationism Act did not violate the State Constitution, *Aguillard* v. *Treen,* 440 So.2d 704 (La. 1983). The Court of Appeals then remanded the case to the District Court to determine whether the Creationism Act violates the Federal Constitution. *Aguillard* v. *Treen,* 720 F.2d 676 (CA5 1983).

3. The First Amendment states: "Congress shall make no law respecting an establishment of religion. . . . " Under the Fourteenth Amendment, this "fundamental concept of liberty" applies to the States. *Cantwell* v. *Connecticut,* 310 U.S. 296, 303 (1940).

4. The *Lemon* test has been applied in all cases since its adoption in 1971, except in *Marsh* v. *Chambers,* 463 U.S. 783 (1983), where the Court held that the Nebraska legislature's practice of opening a session with a prayer by a chaplain paid by the State did not violate the Establishment Clause. The Court based its conclusion in that case on the historical acceptance of the practice. Such a historical approach is not useful in determining the proper roles of church and state in public schools, since free public education was virtually nonexistent at the time the Constitution was adopted. See *Wallace* v. *Jaffree,* 472 U.S. 38, 80 (1985) (O'CONNOR, J., concurring in judgment) (citing *Abington School Dist.* v. *Schempp,* 374 U.S. 203, 238, and n. 7 (1963) (BRENNAN, J., concurring).

5. The potential for undue influence is far less significant with regard to college students who voluntarily enroll in courses. "This distinction warrants a difference in constitutional results." *Abington School Dist.* v. *Schempp, supra,* at 253 (BRENNAN, J., concurring). Thus, for instance, the Court has not questioned the authority of state colleges and universities to offer courses on religion or theology. See *Widmar* v. *Vincent,* 454 U.S. 263, 271 (1981) (POWELL, J.); *id.,* at 281 (STEVENS, J., concurring in judgment).

6. The Court of Appeals stated that: "[a]cademic freedom embodies the principle that individual instructors are at liberty to teach that which they deem to be appropriate in the exercise of their professional judgment." 765 F.2d at 1257. But, in the State of Louisiana, courses in public schools are prescribed by the State Board of Education and teachers are not free, absent permission, to teach courses different from what is required. Tr. of Oral Arg. 44–46. "Academic freedom," at least as it is commonly understood, is not a relevant concept in this context. Moreover, as the Court of Appeals explained, the Act "requires, presumably upon risk of *sanction* or *dismissal* for failure to comply, the teaching of creation-science whenever evolution is taught. Although states may prescribe public school curriculum concerning science instruction under ordinary circumstances, the compulsion inherent in the Balanced Treatment Act is, on its face, inconsistent with the idea of academic freedom as it is universally understood." 765 F.2d at 1257 (emphasis in original). The Act actually serves to diminish academic freedom by removing the flexibility to teach evolution without

also teaching creation science, even if teachers determine that such curriculum results in less effective and comprehensive science instruction.

7. The Creationism Act's provisions appear among other provisions prescribing the courses of study in Louisiana's public schools. These other provisions, similar to those in other states, prescribe courses of study in such topics as driver training, civics, the Constitution, and free enterprise. None of these other provisions, apart from those associated with the Creationism Act, nominally mandates "equal time" for opposing opinions within a specific area of learning. See, *e.g.,* La. Rev. Stat. Ann. §§ 17:261–17:281 (West 1982 and Supp. 1987).

8. The dissent concludes that the Act's purpose was to protect the academic freedom of students, and not that of teachers. *Post,* at 19. Such a view is not at odds with our conclusion that if the Act's purpose was to provide comprehensive scientific education (a concern shared by students and teachers, as well as parents), that purpose was not advanced by the statute's provisions. *Supra,* at 7–8.

Moreover, it is astonishing that the dissent, to prove its assertion, relies on a section of the legislation, which was eventually deleted by the legislature. Compare §3702 in App. E292 (text of section prior to amendment) with La. Rev. Stat. Ann. § 17:286.2 (West 1982). The dissent contends that this deleted section—which was explicitly rejected by the Louisiana legislature—reveals the legislature's "obviously intended meaning of the statutory terms 'academic freedom.'". *Post,* at 19. Quite to the contrary, Boudreaux, the main expert relied on by the sponsor of the Act, cautioned the legislature that the words "academic freedom" meant "freedom to teach science." App. E429. His testimony was given at the time the legislature was deciding whether to delete this section of the Act.

9. See *McLean* v. *Arkansas Bd. of Ed.,* 529 F.Supp. 1255, 1258–1264 (ED Ark. 1982) (reviewing historical and contemporary antagonisms between the theory of evolution and religious movements).

10. The Court evaluated the statute in light of a series of anti-evolution statutes adopted by state legislatures dating back to the Tennessee statute that was the focus of the celebrated *Scopes* trial in 1927. *Epperson* v. *Arkansas,* 393 U.S., at 98, 101, n. 8 and 109. The Court found the Arkansas statute comparable to this Tennessee "monkey law," since both gave preference to "'religious establishments which have as one of their tenets or dogmas the instantaneous creation of man.'" *Id.,* at 103, n. 11 (quoting *Scopes* v. *State,* 154 Tenn. 105, 126, 289 S.W. 363, 369 (1927) (CHAMBLISS, J., concurring)).

11. While the belief in the instantaneous creation of humankind by a supernatural creator may require the rejection of every aspect of the theory of evolution, an individual instead may choose to accept some or all of this scientific theory as compatible with his or her spiritual outlook. See Tr. of Oral Arg. 23–29.

12. Boudreaux repeatedly defined creation science in terms of a theory that supports the existence of a supernatural creator. See *e.g.,* 2 App. E501–502 (equating creation science with a theory pointing "to conditions of a creator"); 1 App. E153–154 ("Creation . . . requires the direct involvement of a supernatural intelligence"). The lead witness at the hearings introducing the original bill, Luther Sunderland, described creation sci-

ence as postulating "that everything was created by some intelligence or power external to the universe." *Id.*, at E9–10.

13. Senator Keith believed that creation science embodied this view: "One concept is that a creator however you define a creator was responsible for everything that is in this world. The other concept is that it just evolved." *Id.*, at E280. Besides Senator Keith, several of the most vocal legislators also revealed their religious motives for supporting the bill in the official legislative history. See *e.g., id.,* at E441, E443 (Sen. Saunders noting that bill was amended so that teachers could refer to the Bible and other religious texts to support the creation-science theory); 2 App. E561–E562, E610 (Rep. Jenkins contending that the existence of God was a scientific fact).

14. See, *e.g.,* 1 App. E74–E75 (noting that evolution is contrary to his family's religious beliefs); *id.,* at E313 (contending that evolution advances religions contrary to his own); *id.,* at E357 (stating that evolution is "almost a religion" to science teachers); *id.,* at E418 (arguing that evolution is cornerstone of some religions contrary to his own); 2 App. E763–764 (author of model bill, from which Act is derived, sent copy of the model bill to Senator Keith and advised that "I view this whole battle as one between God and anti-God forces. . . . if evolution is permitted to continue . . . it will continue to be made to appear that a Supreme Being is unnecessary . . . ").

15. Neither the District Court nor the Court of Appeals found a clear secular purpose, while both agreed that the Creationism Act's primary purpose was to advance religion. "When both courts below are unable to discern an arguably valid secular purpose, this Court normally should hesitate to find one." *Wallace* v. *Jaffree,* 472 U.S., at 66 (POWELL, J., concurring).

16. There is "no express or implied requirement in Rule 56 that the moving party support its motion with affidavits or other similar materials *negating* the opponent's claim." *Celotex Corp.* v. *Catrett,* 477 U.S.——, —— (1986) (emphasis in original).

17. The experts, who were relied upon by the sponsor of the bill and the legislation's other supporters, testified that creation science embodies the religious view that there is a supernatural creator of the universe. See *supra,* at ——.

18. Appellants contend that the affidavits are relevant because the term "creation science" is a technical term similar to that found in statutes that regulate certain scientific or technological developments. Even assuming *arguendo* that "creation science" is a term of art as represented by Appellants, the definition provided by the relevant agency provides a better insight than the affidavits submitted by appellants in this case. In a 1981 survey conducted by the Louisiana Department of Education, the school superintendents in charge of implementing the provisions of the Creationism Act were asked to interpret the meaning of "creation science" as used in the statute. About 75 percent of Louisiana's superintendents stated that they understood "creation science" to be a religious doctrine. 2 App. E798–799. Of this group, the largest proportion of superintendents interpreted creation science, as defined by the Act, to mean the literal interpretation of the Book of Genesis. The remaining superintendents believed that the Act required teaching the view that "the universe was made by a creator." *Id.,* at E799.

19. The Court has previously found the postenactment elucidation of the meaning of a statute to be of little relevance in determining the intent of the legislature contemporaneous to the passage of the statute. See *Wallace* v. *Jaffree,* 472 U.S., at 57, n. 45; *id.,* at 75 (O'CONNOR, J., concurring in judgment).

Index